W9-BKC-657

Advance Praise for *How We Win*

"Farah Pandith draws on her wide-ranging experience as a diplomat and communicator to lay out a comprehensive strategy against violent extremism. A timely book for government and civil society leaders."

—Michael Chertoff, former U.S. Secretary of Homeland Security and Cofounder and Executive Chairman of the Chertoff Group

"The private sector has a vital role to play in stopping violent extremism. Farah Pandith's revelatory *How We Win* is the playbook we've been waiting for. Read it and join in. Farah has much to tell us. The world will benefit from her insights."

—Shelly Lazarus, Chairman Emeritus, Ogilvy & Mather

"Farah has written a vitally important book on an incredibly important topic that for too long has received short shrift. Every policy maker involved in national security and foreign affairs needs to focus on how we still face a generational ideological challenge."

—Michael Leiter, former Director of the U.S. National Counterterrorism Center

"Farah Pandith offers a much-needed critique of nearly two decades of failed American efforts to counter violent extremist ideology. More important, she charts a thoughtful alternative course that demands the attention of policy makers and practitioners in the United States and around the world."

—William J. Burns, President of the Carnegie Endowment for International Peace, former U.S. Deputy Secretary of State, and former U.S. Ambassador to Russia and Jordan

"One of the most critical tools in the fight to keep our country and world safe is the effort to combat the ideology that underlies extremist activity. Farah Pandith offers a comprehensive look at the war of ideas and provides concrete solutions to this vexing problem. Her book is essential for anyone who cares about security and the resilience of democratic values."

—Leon E. Panetta, former U.S. Secretary of Defense and former CIA Director

"As former Supreme Allied Commander of NATO, I was on the front lines of the war against violent extremists, searching for strategies to thwart deadly attacks by eradicating recruitment of future terrorists and increasing the power of those who could be our best allies in the fight. *How We Win* is a much-needed corrective to those who argue primarily for military 'hard-power' solutions. Farah Pandith is a big thinker with a compelling global vision on what is truly a global problem. A smart, powerful thinker who discerns the hidden links underlying the phenomenon of extremism, she is uniquely qualified to write *How We Win*. I wish I'd had Farah Pandith's groundbreaking book then, and I hope that everyone concerned with stopping extremist violence and destruction will read it now."

—Admiral James Stavridis, U.S. Navy (Ret.), former Supreme Allied Commander of NATO

"When the threat of terrorism triggers our instincts to lock ourselves down or shout each other down, Ms. Pandith tells us to suit up and open up. Having survived from the frontlines of bureaucratic infighting, she optimistically calls us to be outgoing."

—Matthew Barzun, former U.S. Ambassador to the United Kingdom and Sweden and former Chief Strategy Officer at CNET Networks

"As the former Commander of the NATO International Security Assistance Force (ISAF) and U.S. Forces in Afghanistan, and later as President Obama's Special Presidential Envoy to the Global Coalition to Counter the Islamic State, I know how crucial it is that we win the war of ideas . . . ideological war. No one knows more about the appeal of ideology on Muslim youth than Farah Pandith. She's served multiple presidents—Democrat and Republican—traveled to almost one hundred countries, and consulted the highest ranks of the military and our diplomats in her search to reverse the catastrophic course we seem to be following. I wish I'd had *How We Win* as a resource during my critical leadership efforts against Al Qaeda, the Taliban, and the Islamic State."

—General John R. Allen, U.S. Marine Corps (Ret.), former Commander of the NATO International Security Assistance Force and U.S. Forces in Afghanistan (2011–2013) and Special Presidential Envoy to the Global Coalition to Counter the Islamic State

"*How We Win* offers sharp, incisive wisdom from someone who had a front-row seat at one of modern history's great inflection points. An expert and an experienced practitioner, Pandith brilliantly captures how to think differently about extremism and how to draw on the wisdom of great leaders to confront the extremist threat. *How We Win* should be required reading for anyone interested in harnessing new ideas to tackle some of the world's toughest international security challenges."

—Jared Cohen, Founder and CEO of Jigsaw

"For decades, policy makers, academics, and community leaders have struggled with the question *How do people of good faith stop extremism in their midst?* Pandith doesn't just ask the question but provides—for the first time—a concrete, detailed, and engaging answer: the solution lies with all of us. From the private sector to family members, Pandith tells us how to mobilize for action. She engages us rather than terrifies us. With sympathy and also hard-nosed realism, Pandith's *How We Win* is ultimately inspiring. If this is a war of ideas, Pandith is now our intellectual general."

—Juliette Kayyem, former Assistant Secretary at the Department of Homeland Security and Faculty Chair of the Homeland Security Project at the Harvard Kennedy School of Government

"In the all-out effort to defeat Al Qaeda and other terrorist groups, we have struggled to win the war of ideas. Pandith, who has served on the front lines of this ideological conflict, is uniquely qualified to confront the enduring system that gives rise to the extremist threat. In this indispensable book, Pandith sets forth a detailed and comprehensive approach to countering violent extremism that serves as a call to arms for governments, businesses, and communities alike."

—Matthew G. Olsen, former Director of the National Counterterrorism Center

"In *How We Win,* Farah Pandith offers fresh thinking, both profound and practical, on one of our most vexing challenges—combating violent extremism. She unearths ground truths, challenges assumptions, and questions orthodoxies in eye-opening ways. Drawing upon her extensive, firsthand experience, Pandith gets to the root causes of the problem and, as important, offers a clear, feasible path forward to solve it."

—Eric J. McNulty, Associate Director of the National Preparedness Leadership Initiative (a joint program of the Harvard T.H. Chan School of Public Health's Division of Policy Translation and Leadership Development and the Harvard Kennedy School's Center for Public Leadership)

"For more than a decade, Farah Pandith has been on the front lines of the battle against extremist ideologies across the world. She's provided her expertise to religious and political leaders, to diplomats and global leaders, and to two U.S. presidents. Now that expertise is available in this remarkable and timely book. This is the new paradigm in the fight against global extremism."

—Reza Aslan, author of *God: A Human History* and *Zealot: The Life and Times of Jesus of Nazareth*

"It is hard to think of anyone more knowledgeable than Farah Pandith when it comes to countering violent extremism. After traveling the world serving two presidents, she brings enormous experience and common sense to the task. This book is full of wisdom about how to deal with one of our great challenges."

—Joseph S. Nye Jr., University Distinguished Service Professor Emeritus at Harvard University and author of *The Future of Power*

"*How We Win* is a smart, original, and timely look at the ground reality of extremism in the Muslim world and, more important, how an unlikely alliance of entrepreneurs and technologists could provide the antidote. This is a must-read for policy makers and scholars alike, and all those interested in the future of the Muslim world."

—Vali Nasr, Dean of Johns Hopkins School of Advanced International Studies and author of *The Dispensable Nation: American Foreign Policy in Retreat*

"*How We Win* is surely the best book about how the U.S. government and others need to think about how best to counter violent extremism and also how to act to curb the spread of extremist ideologies. It is also a lively and well-written memoir of Farah Pandith's many years working for the State Department combating extremism around the world."

—Peter Bergen, author of *United States of Jihad: Who Are America's Homegrown Terrorists, and How Do We Stop Them?*

"Farah Pandith was a pioneer for Presidents George W. Bush and Barack Obama and was appointed America's first emissary to the Moslem World. Now a Harvard Senior Fellow, she illuminates in this indispensable book how America and her friends and allies can defeat the extremist threat and build a new and more positive relationship with the one-fourth of humanity who are Muslims."

—Nicholas Burns, Professor at the John F. Kennedy School of Government at Harvard University, former Under Secretary of State for Political Affairs, and former U.S. Ambassador to NATO and Greece

"I witnessed Farah Pandith innovate and shape the U.S. government and private sector's approach since 9/11 to confront the generational and global problem of violent extremism in its most virulent forms, while helping define a new form of power and diplomacy. Her travel to every corner of the world as America's first-ever Special Representative to Muslim Communities to understand and affect the manifestations of this ideological threat became a groundbreaking part of America's counterterrorism work and is richly described in this book with revealing glimpses of how the world has viewed the United States after 9/11 and how we tried to wage the 'battle of ideas.' There is no more important voice on how we should recognize and confront these morphing ideological threats; how we can enlist social, corporate, and economic power—including millennials and new technologies—to confront the underpinnings of terror globally; and ultimately how we win through the power of our ideas. For anyone who wants to understand how the field of countering violent extremism was born and what we must do in the face of continued threats, this is your book and Pandith is your guide."

—Juan Zarate, Chairman of Financial Integrity Network and former Deputy Assistant to the President and Deputy National Security Advisor for Combating Terrorism for President George W. Bush

"Farah is a well-respected expert with extensive government experience in this field. Her insights and firsthand perspective offer a unique vantage point on the cultural, ideological, and political forces that effect Muslim youth worldwide. Her book is much more than a provocative analysis of why we have yet to defeat the appeal of extremist ideology that is the backbone of terrorist organizations like Al Qaeda and ISIS. *How We Win* shows us exactly what we need to do, and *can* do, to turn the tide."

—The Honorable Stephen J. Hadley, Assistant to the President for National Security Affairs and Board Chair at the U.S. Institute of Peace

HOW WE WIN

HOW WE WIN

How Cutting-Edge Entrepreneurs, Political Visionaries, Enlightened Business Leaders, and Social Media Mavens Can Defeat the Extremist Threat

FARAH PANDITH

ch.
CUSTOM HOUSE

HarperCollins books may be purchased for educational, business, or sales promotional use. For information, please e-mail the Special Markets Department at SPsalesharpercollins.com.

FIRST EDITION

Designed by William Ruoto

Map by Nick Springer/Springer Cartographics, LLC.

Infographics by Nafisa Nandini Crishna

Library of Congress Cataloging-in-Publication Data has been applied for.

ISBN 978-0-06-247115-4

19 20 21 22 23 LSC 10 9 8 7 6 5 4 3 2 1

For my incredible mother,
who embodies the true meaning of love, faith, sacrifice,
and compassion

With heartfelt gratitude to
Barbara Pierce Bush and Hillary Rodham Clinton

CONTENTS

Arctic Ocean
Canada
Seattle
Ottawa
North Pacific Ocean
Chicago
New York
United States
Los Angeles
Washington, D.C.
North Atlantic Ocean
Houston
Miami
Mexico
Trinidad
Port of Spain
Guyana
Paramaribo
Suriname
EQUATOR
Brazil
Peru
South Pacific Ocean
Foz do Iguaçu
Chile
Buenos Aires
Argentina
Auckland
New Zealand
Southern Ocean

Russia
Helsinki
Oslo
Copenhagen
Moscow
Berlin
Brussels
Paris
Sarajevo
Prishtina
Istanbul
Turkey
Kosovo
Rome
Azerbaijan
Astana
Kazakhstan
Almaty
Mongolia
Tajikistan
Dushanbe
Afghanistan
Kabul
Islamabad
Beijing
Japan
Tokyo
China
Shanghai
Lebanon
Beirut
Israel
Iraq
Amman
Iran
Tunisia
Cairo
Jordan
Egypt
Algeria
Libya
Pakistan
New Delhi
Kunming
North Pacific Ocean
Muscat
India
Saudi Arabia
Oman
Bangladesh
Hong Kong
Jeddah
Mumbai
Burma
Thailand
Manila
Philippines
Mali
Khartoum
Sudan
Yemen
Bangkok
Phnom Penh
Timbuktu
Kano
Nigeria
Sri Lanka
Cambodia
Lagos
Somalia
Uganda
Maldives
Kuala Lumpur
Malaysia
Nairobi
Kenya
Malé
EQUATOR
Dem. Rep. of Congo
Dar es Salaam
Indonesia
Tanzania
Zanzibar
Jakarta
South Atlantic Ocean
Angola
Indian Ocean
Madagascar
Australia
South Africa
Cape Town
Sydney
Melbourne
Southern Ocean
Antarctica
Map by Nick Springer. Copyright © 2018 Springer Cartographics

INTRODUCTION

"So," she said, gesturing at me and smiling. "Tell me why you're here."

I smiled politely back. "Thank you, Madam Secretary. I'd like to talk about the importance of Muslims in Europe, and why we should focus on extremist ideology."

It was January 2009. The person gesturing at me was Hillary Clinton, the Obama administration's new secretary of state. A small group of us from the State Department's Bureau of European and Eurasian Affairs sat around the wood table in Secretary Clinton's large personal conference room, while key members of her team—Jake Sullivan, Cheryl Mills, Huma Abedin, and Anne-Marie Slaughter—sat nearby in seats ringing the walls. During her first week on the job, Secretary Clinton had been convening regional bureaus to brief her on their activities. I had worked in the European and Eurasian affairs bureau for the past two years, serving as the United States' chief official responsible for engaging with Muslim communities across Europe. It was a unique position, created by the bureau's assistant secretary, Ambassador Dan Fried, as part of a new initiative inside the State Department to change the way our country fought back against extremism.

Only months earlier, in August 2008, I had gone with two colleagues to Zanzibar, an island in the Indian Ocean just off the coast of Tanzania, to scout out "credible voices" within Muslim youth communities as part of a new approach I had helped develop to fight the war of ideas.* The U.S. government had previously sought to influence young Muslims directly through cultural interchange—music concerts, art exhibits, athletic events, student and professional exchanges, brochures, public statements, diplomatic gatherings, and so on. Our new model was to let young Muslims *themselves* do the talking and leading. Operating under a unique directive from then secretary of state Condoleezza Rice, we had $50,000 to use as seed money for projects that helped young local Muslims mobilize peers, influencers, and other partners across their communities against extremism.†

Our logic was simple: kids listen more readily to their peers than they do to some authority figure telling them what to do—especially when these kids are Muslim, and that authority figure is the U.S. government. These credible voices were out there—we just needed to find them, help them organize, and lend our support. Rather than tangling ourselves in the usual Washington bureaucracy, we would work directly with embassies and ambassadors that were willing to take reputational risks and innovate—and specifically, that would divert time, money, and staff that had been earmarked for public diplomacy programs.

Eager to test this paradigm in a region outside of Europe, we were traveling to places like Sri Lanka, India, Senegal, Mali, and Bangladesh, hoping to create new partnerships with individuals and groups. We had chosen to visit Zanzibar because the U.S. embassy

* To ensure the safety and privacy of everyone mentioned in this text, I have disguised certain details and identifying information.

† As undersecretary of public affairs and public diplomacy, Ambassador James Glassman spearheaded this effort at the State Department building on work piloted in the department's Bureau of European and Eurasian Affairs.

in Dar es Salaam had informed us that conservative ideology and sympathy for groups like Al Qaeda was intensifying, and the local community's small size might make the east African island a favorable location in which to test our approach. In advance of our two-day trip, our embassy liaison—called a "control officer"—had sent us a draft itinerary. At a glance, much of it looked promising. The embassy was arranging for us to visit schools and community centers, where we would listen to both youth and religious leaders. We would also visit sites related to Islam's rich ancient heritage in the country. That was important, since we wanted to figure out ways to stop extremist teachings from displacing local traditions (a trend described in chapter 3).

One part of the itinerary didn't look so good. The embassy had blocked off a substantial chunk of one day—almost half of our trip—to go diving for pearls. What was *that* about? We emailed our control officer in Dar es Salaam, telling her we had no intention of participating in such a frivolous outing. She informed us that the U.S. Agency for International Development (USAID) had provided funds to support the local trade of pearl diving. "It's a great program," she said, "you should really go see it." We protested that we weren't coming to see USAID programs—we were focusing on countering extremism. We pushed back hard, raising the issue with the control officer's boss. By the time we left for Africa, pearl diving had been taken off the agenda.

When we arrived in Zanzibar's Stone Town, we saw an updated agenda. Pearl diving was back on. Our control officer was annoyed with our protests. "No, no," she explained, "this pearl diving program helps with extremism. If our USAID dollars support traditional professions, we're sending the message to locals that we're doing good things to keep their economy going. By helping to create jobs, we'll help stop radicalization in this country."

We understood that rationale—we had heard it hundreds of times. Having worked at USAID twice during my career, I knew how important its traditional humanitarian and aid work was. But I also knew that the USAID program would do little to help counter extremism. Kids weren't falling prey to groups like Al Qaeda just because they lacked economic opportunity or perceived the United States as unfriendly. They were doing so because they were experiencing an identity crisis, one that might relate to economics and political frustrations, but that extended far beyond them. Funding the local pearl diving industry might have helped our image in the country, and it would have contributed an eco-friendly source of income,* but it wouldn't hit hard at the core problem.

We again made it clear—there was no way we would spend seven precious hours in Zanzibar going pearl diving. Instead, we would use that time to talk with youth, evaluate how to support ancient mosques, meet religious leaders, and learn from local influencers. Our control officer said she understood and would adjust the schedule.

The next morning, we met the control officer in front of the Tembo Hotel to kick off our day. She met us carrying a bag filled with what appeared to be beach paraphernalia. Uh-oh. Showing us to a waiting white van, she explained that we were heading off on the pearl diving expedition, and that she had invited representatives of a couple of local USAID partner organizations to join us. We "had" to go. Otherwise, we would make the embassy "look bad."

We flipped out, again refusing to go, protesting that the trip had little to do with our mission. In all my interactions with embassies around the world, I had come away deeply impressed by the sophistication, intelligence, and thoughtfulness of the embassy staff I'd encountered. I'd never met anyone like this control officer, who was both stubborn and seemingly unwilling to grasp what countering

* I certainly don't wish to disparage pearl farming and USAID's support for it in Zanzibar. Though not a traditional practice among local communities, the introduction of pearl farming has been beneficial, thanks in part to USAID programming. Pearl farming gives local women a sustainable source of income that they might otherwise lack. For more, please see the "Pearl Oyster Information Bulletin," *Secretariat of the Pacific Community* 18 (2008): 18.

extremism really meant. She had been briefed in advance of our visit, but she didn't seem to care.

Indicating that she was done arguing with us, she got in the van and drove off. We stood there in the middle of Stone Town, speechless, jetlagged, disoriented, and alone. Adnan Kifayat and Jared Cohen, my colleagues,* burst out laughing. I did, too. Was this really happening?

We still wanted to talk with that imam and see the old mosque. But how? None of us spoke Swahili. Or so I thought. For months, Jared had told us that he was fluent in Swahili, and we hadn't believed him. Now, as Adnan and I emailed the embassy trying to reconfigure our day's itinerary without an embassy staff member there to help us, Jared flagged down a local taxi. He waved us over. It was true—he was speaking Swahili with the taxi driver, laughing and pointing to an old, modest car with mismatched door panels and questionable tires. What! Seriously, Jared?

With Jared in the front seat, we drove to the other side of the island, passing by lush vegetation and through villages so small they barely deserved the name. Eventually we reached our destination on the island's southern tip, a twelfth-century mosque made of earth and wood, decorated with seashells and stones, and built at the edge of the sea, near a fishing village. This mosque was a cultural treasure, reflecting a mix of Swahili and Persian influences. It had fallen into disrepair, and we were visiting it to demonstrate our interest in preserving its unique heritage, and to affirm the existence of an older, local version of Islam that extremist narratives tried to displace. The elderly imam welcomed us warmly. Over the next hour, he described how kids in his country and elsewhere were falling under Saudi influence and losing sight of local traditions. These kids desperately

---

* At the time, Jared was serving on the secretary of state's Policy Planning Staff. He is now, as of this writing, president and founder of Jigsaw (formerly known as Google Ideas). Adnan was serving as a senior advisor to the undersecretary of state for public affairs and public diplomacy. As of this writing, he serves as head of global security ventures for the Gen Next Foundation.

needed to understand what "authentic" Islam was. His observations confirmed others that we'd heard recently, and emboldened us to focus on countering the homogenization of Islam by Wahhabism.

All these years later, this small episode epitomizes for me everything that was wrong then—and is *still* wrong—with the U.S. government's approach to fighting the war of ideas. One department or agency will write a report restating basic approaches, telling us we should "use technology" or "increase Islamic education." Another department will write another report recommending a different set of basic tactics, like "creating new opportunities through jobs," or "working with local police to identify radical elements." How does it all fit together? All too often, despite the best of intentions, it doesn't. A particular embassy might have hosted a "hackathon" to generate program ideas for fighting back against extremism messaging, and another country might have created a program to improve youth's critical awareness about extremist imams online, and a third embassy might have developed training programs for imams, but these efforts never synched up with one another, nor were they replicated subsequently in additional embassies. Their collective impact was minimal. Imagine if in a "hot" war the Army, Navy, and Marines all pursued their own strategies, with no coordination. What would happen? We'd lose! Yet this is exactly what was happening, and what continues to happen to this day.

But it gets worse. Consistently, U.S. government actions have lacked grounding in real-world experience. Senior officials in specific departments or agencies might possess expertise in adjacent areas, but they often haven't possessed expertise in relevant fields like behavioral psychology, anthropology, history, youth activism, identity studies, and so on. Many of these officials have never built grassroots programs, talked to global Muslim youth, explored the contextual changes on the ground, or had any clue about the vast and complex histories of Muslims throughout the world. How can they possibly make progress? They can't. Without the discipline of a strategy and a deep knowledge base, the efforts of these officials have amounted to tiny, uncoordinated, and often ineffectual attempts to push back the extremist tides. All too often, these efforts have backfired, alienating the young Muslims they were hoping to influence.*

Even when government efforts haven't turned Muslims off, they have almost always failed to attack the core problem. Determined initially to "win hearts and minds," the U.S. government has unveiled programs and initiatives designed to show Muslims abroad that America really does understand and care about them, that our policies aren't as bad as they seem, that we're prepared to invest in Muslim communities worldwide, and that our own Muslim populations are vibrant and happy. They've invited Islamic scholars to visit America, sent American imams abroad to showcase Islam in the United States, funded art exhibits depicting U.S. mosques, sent American Muslim musicians to perform oversees, and created brochures featuring images of "diverse" people. The U.S. government has also held glitzy media events designed to demonstrate to Muslims and the American public that we are taking extremism seriously, and doing so without disrespecting Islam.

It's obviously important to cultivate positive and accurate impressions of America among Muslims. And these programs and initiatives might prove valuable for any number of other diplomatic reasons. But they don't add up to a plan to defeat violent ideology's appeal. In recent years, the United States government has begun to counter the legitimacy of groups like so-called Islamic State more aggressively in order to stop recruitment. But the government has scarcely begun to understand and engage with Muslim youth across the globe in a connected way. It talks about engaging with Muslim youth, and talks, and talks some more, but it hasn't acted decisively to address the vast cultural and ideological system that supports

* In addition, government agencies and programs often hire contractors to help curb extremism. Such individuals and groups work on a one-off basis, affording little continuity.

the identity crisis among Muslim youth. It hasn't understood extremism for what it is—both a generational and a connected global problem—nor has it mustered an appropriate response, listening to youth around the world, identifying broad shifts in their mind-set and behavior, and responding to their needs around identity creatively and in real time.

In levying this critique, I'm not singling out any particular official or organ within the U.S. government, nor would I claim that every initiative ever attempted has ended in failure. On the contrary, many dozens of excellent, small-scale programs have fostered new dialogue between Muslims in other countries and non-Muslim Americans, allowing the former to see other sides of America and indeed of American Muslims. Broadly speaking, though, our approach to fighting the ideological war has been flawed. How could we muster a sustained and consistent effort when the officials responsible for designing and implementing programs lacked basic knowledge about Muslims or Islam? How could we fight extremism effectively if we rewarded officials for "checking the box" on this issue and moving on, as if they had many other important assignments that required their attention? How could we make headway when we lacked a single official in charge—someone with a master plan and long-term vision? We've needed high-level leadership on this issue from Washington, we've needed it to cut across the usual department and interagency silos. Otherwise, our government would fail to connect with Muslim communities around the world. Indeed, it has failed. No surprise that our enemies have enjoyed the upper hand.

There are other, even more fundamental reasons why the U.S. government's campaigns with millennials have not worked well. Focused narrowly on counterterrorism, the government's campaigns have drawn on virtually *no* understanding of Muslim millennials as real, live people. They've reflected none of the sophisticated demographic and ethnographic insight that corporations, for instance, have used for years to sell soap or bubble gum to the younger generation.

Terry Young is the founder and CEO of the consultancy sparks & honey, which provides consumer insight to companies like Procter & Gamble, PepsiCo, and Samsung. As he told me, brands and others seeking to influence young people must listen to them, paying close attention to "those little things [about their lives] that are changing every day." But since "the nuance of change," as Young puts it, "isn't just about the things we always think it is," we need to have a system in place—what we might call "social listening"—to help us "understand when something begins to change."* The U.S. government has no system in place—zero, none. Embassies around the world have collected insights about culture, but we have had no budget or protocol for compiling this "data," stitching it together, and analyzing it so that we can spot trends within a country or a region, and then use those trends to inform or shape our programs. Critically, we've had none of the ethnographic, sociological, psychological, technological, and cultural expertise assembled and directed to the task of interpreting the experience of Muslim youth.

Extremism's appeal isn't about anger at a specific U.S. policy. It doesn't derive from a particular misconception about the United States. Extremists succeed with recruiting because youth crave answers to the problem of who they are or are supposed to be, how to live as Muslims, and how to belong to a community. They feel disconnected from traditional authorities and the answers they

---

* Terry Young further explains that cultural change affecting the lives of youth is diffuse, interconnected, and rapid: "Sometimes it could be about families. Sometimes it could be about religion. Sometimes it could be about food and pop culture and influencers and all those other things that are adjacent. How do we know when those shifts begin to happen and how do we know how to lean into those shifts when they happen?" Social listening identifies relevant cultural shifts, measuring them 'at that level of culture.'" Terry Young, founder and CEO of sparks & honey, interview with the author, New York City, December 16, 2016.

offer. Challenged to find their own answers, they buy blindly into homogeneous notions of "correct" or "authentic" religion that they encounter and that are frequently embedded or expressed in their consumer activities. All of this leaves youth vulnerable to extremists and their narratives. These malevolent actors understand what youth are experiencing, and they patiently and proactively offer answers in an attempt to ensnare them. *That's* the real problem we need to address.

As vast as this problem is, the U.S. government can still win against extremist groups over the long term, dramatically reducing the threat posed by "lone-wolf" attacks in our homeland and beyond. In addition to unmatched financial resources, we possess cadres of talented, dedicated patriots throughout our civil and foreign services. What we must do is leverage all of our assets to finally go "all in" against extremist ideology. Setting aside half-measures and photo ops, the U.S. must prioritize stopping the appeal of the extremists' ideology as much as it does defeating the physical armies. It must consider the entire cultural, demographic, technological, ideological, economic, and emotional system underlying extremism, attacking on multiple fronts at once. I'm talking about a range of focused and concerted actions that government can take *at scale* to help change how young Muslims think about themselves and their identities. But even that's not enough. To put in place the necessary actions, we must change how we frame and execute policy on this issue, reorganizing the U.S. government's response internally so that it is more responsible, efficient, informed, dynamic, nimble, entrepreneurial, and creative. In particular, we must develop entirely new capacities related to sophisticated cultural analysis and social listening.

As smart and well-intentioned as most government officials are, they all too often seem stymied by government's own complexity and bureaucratic formality as they battle extremist groups. Bold statements of resolve by politicians haven't translated into actual momentum. And government officials have remained disconnected from the experiences and worldviews of youth in communities around the world. That's the crisis we face. If we can transform our efforts in a comprehensive, systemic way, we will have much more power than we might think to push Muslim youth out of extremism's sway. Before too long, and with a relatively modest financial investment on government's part, we'll cut off what extremists want and need most: a steady supply of fresh recruits.

My sweeping critique of our government's response, and my recounting of a visit to Zanzibar that took place way back in 2008, might seem puzzling to some people. Only in recent years have Americans become conscious of the fight against extremist ideology—around 2015 or later. It might surprise them to know that some people within government were aware of it as a threat more than a decade earlier, and that a new approach called CVE—countering violent extremism—had emerged to fight it. In the wake of Al Qaeda's high-profile and catastrophic attack on America, the Bush administration had unleashed America's vast military power against terrorist groups and their supporters, and it had put in place new systems to help fight the War on Terror. The president and his team then began to attack the problem of terrorism more broadly and think about how to stop recruitment. Initially they focused on Al Qaeda and how we might work with our partners in the Middle East to impede its growth. The release of the United Nations' Arab Development Report in 2002[1] provoked considerable discussion within the White House and the National Security Council about education, economics, and general prosperity, leading some officials to wonder how we might intensify our partnerships with Muslim-majority states in these areas. The next year, in a speech to the National Endowment for Democracy, President George W. Bush laid out what some came to call his "freedom agenda." Buttressing civil society in places like the Middle East, we would spread respect for values such as freedom and democracy, in addition to limiting the appeal of extremist ideology coming from groups like Al Qaeda.

Discussions began among a small group, including Dan Fried,* Deputy National Security Advisor Elliott Abrams, Director for European and Eurasian Affairs Kurt Volker, and Director for European and Eurasian Affairs Matt Bryza about how exactly we might wage a war of ideas against extremist groups. As we all recognized, extremism was a highly complex problem, and our small group alone did not have the full answer. We also acknowledged that our diplomatic corps were under great pressure, addressing many competing national security challenges, with limited resources on which to draw.

Bryza went on to draft a concept note (a paper within the bureaucracy that formalized a proposed new solution to a problem, so that others can understand and discuss it) that suggested mechanisms for pushing back against violent extremist ideology, emphasizing the concepts of openness and freedom. With officials at the National Security Council deliberating how exactly to structure government action on the issue, others in the State Department and the interagency (shorthand for departments or agencies, not all within State, coordinated by the National Security Council, that are charged with addressing a given policy issue)† resisted for reasons I'll discuss in the chapters ahead. Still, the president's team approved the focus on violent extremist ideology, and in 2004 initiated a formal mechanism for building up civil society in the Middle East—the Broader Middle

---

* At the time, Ambassador Fried was special assistant to the president and senior director for European and Eurasian affairs serving at the National Security Council.

† When policy makers at different agencies begin work on an issue, they often hold different positions and apply different perspectives. The National Security Council coordinates the various ideas, perspectives, and recommendations among agencies, navigating manifold personal and bureaucratic complexities. Through a deliberative process, policy positions and recommendations ascend the cross-agency bureaucratic hierarchy, becoming more coherent and consensual until they eventually reach the president's desk.

East and North Africa Initiative (BMENA).* BMENA would seek to advance reform efforts throughout the region by encouraging co-operation between civil society, the G-8, and Arab governments. It had seven pillars from which specific initiatives and programs were built, including democracy, entrepreneurship, education, financial networks, microfinance, investment, and literacy.

In late 2004, I arrived at the National Security Council to work on BMENA and our response to the appeal of groups like Al Qaeda. President Bush and his team were thinking even more deeply about why young Muslims were becoming more sympathetic to groups like Al Qaeda. A small brain trust of officials gathered to work on the issue, and to imagine a possible long-term national security strategy against extremist ideas. A year later, this effort gained momentum with the arrival of Juan Zarate as deputy assistant to the president and deputy national security advisor for combatting terrorism (previously Zarate was at the U.S. Department of the Treasury).† Zarate pushed hard for NSC colleagues and officials at relevant departments across the government to support such a strategy. Following the eruption of the Danish cartoon crisis in 2006, a new urgency arose around countering violent extremist ideology not just in the Middle East, but in Europe. Senior officials including Secretary of Defense Robert Gates and General David Petraeus agreed that we

---

* In an interview with me on March 7, 2016, Kurt Volker outlined the history of the BMENA initiative. He recalled that after hearing President George W. Bush welcome Philippines president Arroyo on the South Lawn in May of 2003, he approached his direct boss, Dan Fried, with the insight that more attention ought to be given to soft power. As he recalled Dan remarked, "The problem is not the speech, it is the idea. The idea now is to go kill the terrorists. You have got to have a better idea." Dan asked Kurt to talk with Elliott Abrams. Kurt relates that in that conversation, Elliott said, "You are absolutely right, we have to do that." They talked about a better solution than just hard power. As Kurt related, they were not saying "don't fight the terrorists" but rather "we can do both [soft and hard power]." In the period that followed, they both collaborated with others in the NSC and State to create the BMENA initiative. President Bush enthusiastically endorsed it ("he just latched on to it in a heartbeat"), making it a focal point of his 2003 NED speech, and his subsequent remarks at London's Royal Bank.

† Zarate was the first assistant secretary of the Treasury for terrorist financing and financial crimes.

needed to explore nonmilitary solutions to extremist recruiting.* Yet again, bureaucratic obstacles scuttled such thinking.

After taking an initial trip to Europe together, Dan Fried and I recognized how important it was for the U.S. government to understand what was happening on the ground in Europe's large Muslim communities. In early 2007, with the backing of Secretary of State Condoleezza Rice and National Security Advisor Stephen Hadley, Dan brought me to the State Department to spearhead our new efforts to counter violent extremist ideology in Europe. I spent the next two years asking questions, listening, learning, observing, and forging additional partnerships. Through such interactions, I also "talent scouted" in local communities, getting to know citizens who were speaking out against extremism and were the credible voices essential to our efforts. I developed and launched experimental networks and programs to promote these voices in partnership with local civil society organizations and our embassies.

While I was still at the National Security Council,† we debated for months what to call this approach. We entertained options like "Countering Radical Islamic Ideology" and "Countering Violent Islamic Extremism." But we realized that if we included words like "Islam," "Islamic," "Jihad," or "radical," we might inadvertently alienate Muslims in local communities whose help we needed to stop recruitment. Also, if we used a term with clear religious overtones, we would be excluding from our fight other kinds of violent ideologies, such as neo-Nazism. We wanted to make sure that we were accurately describing the war of ideas and what we could do to wage it

---

* Robert Gates, "Secretary of Defense Speech," U.S. Department of Defense, June 2, 2007, http://archive.defense.gov/Speeches/Speech.aspx?SpeechID=1160. As Gates says, "As was true in the Cold War, overcoming violent extremists will require a long, sustained effort measured in decades rather than years. . . . It is fundamentally an ideological struggle, where the appeal of principle and the power of example provided by secure, prosperous, and tolerant societies will become the decisive edge."

† By this time, some officials at regional bureaus of the State Department and at the National Counterterrorism Center began to appreciate our nascent efforts.

against Al Qaeda. We wound up dubbing the new discipline "Combatting Violent Extremism," or CVE, subsequently changing to "Countering Violent Extremism" because colleagues within the interagency thought "combatting" smacked too much of hard power. Avoiding overt references to Islam, the name could be applied as needed to any kind of violent ideology. "CVE" took hold, and to this day it remains a general term describing our evolving efforts in the war of ideas. That said, definitions of CVE have varied, and at times the term's precise meaning has seemed elusive. In relation to terrorist groups pursuing their nefarious goals in the name of Islam, I regard CVE as denoting efforts to destroy the appeal of the ideology of the terrorists and thwart their ability to attract new recruits. Whether you define CVE broadly or narrowly, the discipline focuses on strengthening the fabric of local communities to resist extremist ideas, exposing youth to alternative ideas about identity and belonging, and putting a social, mental, and cultural system in place to support these efforts. What the discipline *doesn't* include is taking police or military action to stop radicalized individuals from committing terrorist acts.[2]

Traditionally, U.S. embassies would seek to engage local populations, building relationships and framing U.S. foreign policy for foreign audiences. An important objective was to "get them to like or understand us." CVE was different. We weren't just aiming for increased one-way interaction with local Muslims. Rather, we were trying to listen to them in new ways. Venturing beyond the big cities into small villages and towns, we visited homes, community centers, mosques, speaking with a wide range of Muslims, including quieter voices that had previously been drowned out. We focused less on communicating our point of view, and instead sought to understand the texture of Muslims' lived experience, so that we could push back more effectively against extremist ideologies.

In Germany, for instance, Muslims told me that the tax paid by Germans to support religious institutions didn't support the construction of Muslim cemeteries. I also learned that Muslims had few opportunities to learn about coreligionists who had succeeded in the West. Such information, compiled across localities and nations, helped us to uncover new access points into Muslim communities, at a time when European governments themselves were keeping their distance. And because I had gone deeper into communities than our embassies normally did, I knew local activists interested in pushing back against extremism, and was in a position to connect them with one another across Europe. I could build networks of "credible voices" who might not have liked America or its foreign policy, but who were nonetheless dedicated to protecting their youth from radicalization. Helping to construct a grassroots movement against extremism within Muslim communities: that was CVE.*

If we could do CVE right, we could play offense rather than acting against extremism only once a crisis has broken out. We could actually *prevent extremist groups from forming* rather than trying to contain them once they had been established. No European country was mobilizing civil society in Europe as we were. Despite proclamations of proactive engagement and acceptance, they kept Muslim communities at arm's length, at best. If we could demonstrate early success, we might encourage other governments to experiment, and we might replicate the approach across the State Department's other regional bureaus as well.

Again, the history I'm recounting here took place prior to the election of Barack Obama as president in 2008. In January 2009, as I sat face-to-face with Secretary Clinton, I described how shocked I had been during my travels. Meeting with hundreds of youth and

* Put differently, I defined CVE as the collection of proactive methods focused on civil society that punctured the appeal and spread of violent ideologies, preventing radicalization in local communities by inoculating them from within, and by developing internal, self-motivating groups that could serve as "first responders" if individuals began developing an interest in violent ideology.

community leaders, I found that extremist ideas were making inroads among Muslims at an alarming rate, and especially among younger Muslims, members of the millennial generation, born between 1981 and 1997.[3] Although commentators today often explain extremism's pull by citing the role of poverty or lack of education or conflict within Islam, or by focusing primarily on a Muslim's frustrations or grievances against the United States, I came to a much different and more comprehensive conclusion: youth were latching on to extremist ideas because of a collective and unprecedented crisis of identity. Since 9/11, young Muslims were feeling the world's attention on them, and they were posing new kinds of questions about who they were and what they were supposed to be. How should they live as Muslims in European societies? What did it mean to be modern and Muslim? What was the difference between culture and religion? Although older Muslims tended to feel more secure in their identities, extremists knew that youth were struggling with these questions, and to win new adherents they adroitly put themselves forward as the answer. The West, they argued, was at war with Islam. Muslim youth would never find acceptance in European countries. The extremists' brand of supposedly "authentic" or "real" Islam was the only path to a strong, vibrant, and purposeful Muslim life.

The vast majority of Muslim youth rejected this message, but a few found it compelling. Just as worrisome, the broader cultural environment was changing. Local and federal laws were marginalizing Muslims, making them feel like "the other." Anger and a sense of alienation were mounting within local communities, and more and more people sympathized with extremist arguments, although not necessarily with the use of violence. If our allies didn't wake up and begin to counter violent extremist ideology, these ideas would spread unchecked, threatening European security and causing incalculable economic damage. Before too long, the ideology might even spread to the United States, which at the time had not yet experienced attacks perpetrated by "homegrown" extremists.* As I related to Secretary Clinton, the United States had to do everything possible to help our partners across the Atlantic. We would be making a huge mistake if we did not continue the work we had started there under the Bush administration.

When I finished my short briefing, Secretary Clinton asked a number of thoughtful questions. If European governments were aware of issues around "multiculturalism" and integration, why hadn't they done more to focus on identity? Did European governments have programs in place that were stopping the appeal of violent extremist ideology? Did I sense that European Muslims were getting the support they needed to fight back? Did they trust the U.S. effort to work with them, and if so, why?

I was pleasantly surprised by her reaction. Although key members of President Bush's staff supported our efforts to counter extremist ideology in Europe, the issue was not high on the agenda of many State Department officials. In general, government doesn't reward more speculative, long-term thinking. Who wants to spend his or her budget on a threat that may or may not materialize? Conscious of their careers, most government officials wouldn't take the risk—better to work on a high-profile issue already deemed "important" by the president and other high-ranking officials. At the time, the Department of Defense, State Department, and others were managing colossal operations in Afghanistan and Iraq. America was hunting Osama bin Laden and following terrorist money. It was working furiously on the "freedom agenda," promoting human rights and the rule of law in Middle Eastern countries. And of course, it was performing the normal business of diplomacy. In comparison with these priorities, CVE amounted to a pesky little gnat in most officials' minds—practically nonexistent. With other policy issues like

* In fact, European nations and members of Muslim communities were asking the U.S. government about the "secret" for making Muslims from various immigrant groups feel so included.

Russia, the rise of China, and NATO on the table, and with the extremist threat a fraction of what it is today, I hadn't anticipated that Secretary Clinton would have wanted to spend more than a minute or two talking about Muslim engagement. She would be busy enough getting up to speed on these other issues.

I proceeded to tell her that we could indeed push back against violent extremist ideology—in fact, we had to. And we needed to do something unprecedented: influence how Muslims thought about and formed their identities. Abrams, Zarate, Fried, and others in their circle were right in thinking that traditional public diplomacy tools were not shifting how skeptical Muslims perceived the United States. But there was an even more basic problem. Traditional public diplomacy techniques like artistic and sporting events, student exchanges, people-to-people interactions, and the dissemination of educational materials were designed to foster knowledge about and affection for the United States, but they couldn't address the underlying phenomenon of the identity crisis among Muslim youth. Although it obviously mattered in general how Muslims viewed the United States, what bore most on our goal of defeating Al Qaeda and groups like it was how Muslim youth thought about *themselves.*

Helping Muslim youth to resolve their identity crisis was an ambitious goal, but not, I felt, an unrealistic one. With focus and determination, we could mobilize efforts by credible voices (as judged by the youth themselves) while simultaneously destroying the terrorist organizations on the battlefield. The point was to listen to what was going on in the lives of these Muslims, to understand what they were feeling and why, to help connect them with like-minded individuals in their local areas and across Europe, to provide role models, and, vitally, to help these credible voices build local resilience to foreign ideologies. By mobilizing bloggers, social entrepreneurs, media mavens, political visionaries, enlightened business leaders, artists, musicians, and many others, we could create a vast and powerful army of individuals who were alerting their peers 24/7 to extremism's danger and steering them to resolve their identity crises differently. Traditional public diplomacy was centralized and institutionally driven, proceeding from the top on down. CVE as I envisaged it would be entrepreneurial and bottom-up. If regular people at the grassroots level didn't fight back against harmful ideas infiltrating their communities, we would never remove Al Qaeda's ideology or its appeal.

When I described for Secretary Clinton some of our grassroots efforts within Muslim communities, she was taken aback. Turning to Dan Fried, who was seated right next to her, she said, "You did *this* in the Bush administration?"

The room erupted in laughter. Dan smiled. He looked over at me and then to her, seated right next to him. "You know, when Farah leaves—"

She placed a hand on Dan's arm and pulled it back slightly. Edging forward, she pointed to me. "Where are you going?"

I think my heart may have stopped. The room went silent.

I told her about a new job I was about to start at a think tank working on a new CVE effort.

Grinning, she gestured in my direction. "We'll see about that."

I felt confident that Secretary Clinton understood the importance of our CVE agenda in Europe, but I didn't think she was serious about keeping me on. She didn't know that I was a Bush appointee, or that years before I had worked in the Bush 41 administration. When she found out, I thought there was no way she would want me on her team.

As it turned out, she did. A few days later, I was in my office on the sixth floor of the Harry S. Truman Building clearing a diplomatic cable, surrounded by government-issued file cabinets and piles of paper on my desk. I received an e-mail from Patrick Kennedy, the undersecretary of state for management (basically, the department's chief operating officer) asking to meet with me. When I arrived at his office, I found him happy to see me. "Farah," he said, "I have been told to ask you: what will it take for you to stay on?"

I was speechless. Since 9/11, I'd become outraged that a terrorist organization was trying to portray America as a country aligned against Muslims—it was not at all what I experienced growing up. But manifold other aspects of extremist ideology also repelled me. My mother had instilled in me a deep respect for diversity, and had expected me to show kindness to all people, irrespective of their background or beliefs. Having traveled often to India to visit family, I had become alert from an early age to the multiplicity of identities, and to the notion that people are more wonderfully complex than any hateful stereotype of them we might create. Extremism was an affront to everything I stood for. And as a Muslim, I was infuriated by extremists' attempts to define "real" Islam. Who were they to tell me how to be Muslim? This constellation of reactions motivated me to find a way to serve again in government, and I was truly honored now to have that opportunity.

"Pat," I finally said, "when the secretary of state asks you to serve your nation, you salute."

Pat smiled. "Excellent."

Days later the contours of my new job became clear. In conversations with Cheryl Mills, Secretary Clinton's chief of staff, I learned that the secretary wanted me to "do what I did in Europe but to do it around the world." In particular, I would have a mandate to build and spread the kinds of pilot programs I had already been executing. Secretary Clinton felt that the U.S. government needed to focus on inoculating Muslim youth worldwide against extremist ideologies. She sought to create a new, senior-level position for me with my own office, Special Representative to Muslim Communities. Reporting directly to her, I would focus on engaging with Muslim youth and building networks of like-minded thinkers to push back against violent extremism in a wide range of ways.

I couldn't have been more delighted. Most State Department

bureaus had focused exclusively on other aspects of the War on Terror, and had shunned CVE. Toward the end of Bush's presidency, with Undersecretary of State for Public Diplomacy and Public Affairs James Glassman taking the interagency lead on CVE, we had finally gotten traction, and the initiatives piloted across Europe were seen as a way forward in other parts of the world. But since our approach was experimental, since it threatened power centers within State, and since it deviated from conventional wisdom, we had lacked the funds and commitment to go "all in" on CVE. Now, with Secretary Clinton's support, I felt optimistic that this support would be forthcoming. We'd be able to take our existing approach and scale it up dramatically, igniting what I would eventually call a "youthquake" in Muslim communities.* By puncturing extremism's appeal, we would prevent armies of extremist recruits from forming. That would complement the important strategic efforts taking place on the battlefield, in terrorist finance, and law enforcement. A *combined* approach of hard and soft power would spare cities across the world untold bloodshed. It would provide stability, save billions in military expenditures, and prevent trillions in economic costs.

MISSED OPPORTUNITIES

From the very beginning, CVE didn't flourish the way I had hoped. Congress didn't fund it, and the media all but ignored it (military action makes for better TV than conversations held at community centers). Meanwhile, my appointment as special representative sparked

* I began using this term in early 2009. In 2017 the Oxford Dictionaries made "youthquake" its word of the year. As the *Guardian* reported, youthquake denotes "a significant cultural, political, or social change arising from the actions or influence of young people." Sian Cain, "'Youthquake' named 2017 word of the year by Oxford Dictionaries," *Guardian,* December 14, 2017, https://www.theguardian.com/books/2017/dec/15/youthquake-named-2017-word-of-the-year-by-oxford-dictionaries. As Cain details, *Vogue* editor Diana Vreeland first used the term circa 1965 to refer to different cultural changes then taking place.

resistance at the White House. As dedicated and thoughtful as most new White House policy staffers were, most lacked on-the-ground experience in Muslim communities and therefore didn't understand the scope of what was happening among youth in Europe, and as I suspected, in communities globally. But there was a deeper problem. To its great credit, the Obama administration was seeking to reset relations with Muslims, and in particular, to counter perceptions that the United States was "against Muslims." In the weeks following Obama's election, Denis R. McDonough, deputy national security advisor, chaired a meeting at the White House, soliciting ideas about how to expand engagement with Muslims and usher in a new era of mutual understanding. Among these ideas was giving more prominence to Islam's important role in American history, a theme that was then showcased in timeline form on the White House website. But some key White House staffers thought only about the damage done to America's image by the Iraq War. Since many Muslims perceived that President George W. Bush had been "out to get" them, the United States now had to distance itself from anything that seemed to conflict with their theme of "a new beginning." Advisors feared that Muslims would bristle at open conversations about rising extremism in their communities. They didn't believe that you could do two things at once—extend a hand in friendship to Muslims, and speak honestly with them about violent extremism and how to solve it.

Three weeks after Obama's June 2009 speech in Cairo, in which he explicitly advanced a shift in U.S. relations with Muslims worldwide, the State Department announced my appointment in a press release. A White House official called my direct line to express displeasure. "You need to know," he told me a little nervously, "that I have been told to tell you that we do not consider you to be part of this administration." He instructed me not to present myself as a "U.S. representative" in the course of my work.

"What are you talking about?" I asked. "Do you think when I'm traveling around the world defending our president and our country, dealing with people face-to-face, I'm going to be representing Nicaragua?" I was stunned by the request, having been treated so differently by Secretary Clinton and her team. I felt disrespected, and really angry at the position in which the request placed me.

I decided to resign—the last thing I wanted was to arouse controversy and become a burden for Secretary Clinton. It was former Bush colleagues who advised me to stay and deliver on what the secretary had asked of me. The White House would come around, they said, because officials there would soon realize the grave threat posed by extremist ideology and the importance of taking grassroots action. I was not so sure. I asked for a meeting with Secretary Clinton's senior staff and will never forget what transpired. These key aides told me that Clinton had my back. "Just do what you do, Farah," they said. Subsequently, the secretary herself delivered a similar message. Minutes before I was to begin my first official press briefing in the State Department press room, I was standing in the secretary's suite preparing with her staff. She emerged from her office, gave me a hug, and said, "I have confidence in you, Farah."

For the next five years, I pursued the work that Secretary Clinton (and then Secretary John Kerry) had requested of me. I no longer expected to have a close, working relationship with the NSC, as I had in the Bush administration. Rather, I was collaborating closely with my colleagues across State and with the secretary's senior team. I traveled to more than eighty countries, met with youth, and designed new networks and other efforts to lift credible voices within local communities. Yet the tension with the White House never dissipated. Worse, staffers there had no firsthand exposure to what we had learned in Europe, what we were learning about the crisis of identity globally, and why the CVE approach required more attention.

As the years passed, the idea of building resilient communities capable of fighting back against extremist ideas became stuck in a tortured political dance. Senior Obama advisors acknowledged that we needed to stop recruitment and that local ideas mattered, but the National Security Council was not given sufficient personnel devoted to CVE, nor was it creating an integrated global strategy for dealing with extremist ideology. Some senior policy advisors within the NSC were as frustrated as I was, aware that old thinking was guiding many of the administration's programs. But they were as powerless as I was to direct more resources or attention to CVE.

Unfortunately, the nightmare scenario that I'd been warning against largely came to pass. Online and on the ground, extremists exploited an ideological vacuum in Muslim communities. By the time I left government in early 2014, thousands of young Muslims in Europe and around the world had grown sympathetic toward violent extremist ideology, and some of those people had become radicalized. Months later, the world learned that a group calling themselves the "Islamic State" had proclaimed a so-called caliphate and occupied large swaths of Iraq and Syria. Even then, while governments were floating new collaborations to stop recruitment, no real system existed for fighting back against this type of ideology.

Only toward the end of 2014, when a series of horrific videos of beheadings circulated on the Internet, did American policy makers begin to address recruitment in earnest. And in 2015, when the United States began seeing "lone wolf" attacks in cities like San Bernardino and Orlando, a new era of public discourse began around the need to prevent radicalization. At the 2015 CVE Summit held at the White House, I listened as President Obama's team set forth certain concrete policy proposals that many of us in the CVE space had been espousing for years (several former Bush colleagues were also in attendance). Lisa Monaco, assistant to the president for homeland security and counterterrorism; Amy Pope, deputy assistant to the president and deputy homeland security advisor; and others at the National Security Council had already been analyzing this issue, examining what was going well, what could be scaled, and what other creative tactics we might deploy to help on the ideological front.* Despite this recognition and attention, no deep policy accomplishments followed, nor did anyone manage to unlock the kind of financial resources needed to expand local CVE initiatives so that they could saturate communities. During the last two years of Obama's presidency, America succeeded mainly in creating a large, ineffectual CVE bureaucracy within our government and a massive infrastructure globally. Many government offices across the interagency were now tasked with CVE programming, alongside an increased focus by the State Department's Counterterrorism Bureau. These offices had lines of financial resources tied to it, which allowed for more scope and power within the interagency. Yet by the time Obama left office, only a handful of really sharp, small-scale CVE programs existed to stem the appeal of extremist ideologies. Ironically, it was several programs launched during the Bush administration in partnership with then-unknown nongovernmental organizations (NGOs) that gained prominence as the go-to examples of noteworthy CVE efforts.

Today, almost every week brings news of a new terrorist atrocity perpetrated around the globe. In the United States and countries around the world, mounting fear has sparked a harsh xenophobic backlash. Donald J. Trump and other candidates ramped up anti-Muslim and anti-Islam rhetoric during the 2016 presidential election, unleashing a wave of racism and anti-Semitism and emboldening white supremacists.[4] During his campaign, Trump called for "a total and complete shutdown of Muslims entering the United States" and immediately following his election, he issued a presidential order that prevented citizens of a number of Muslim-majority nations—first seven, then six—from entering the country.[5] With the rise of so-called Islamic State, the Syrian refugee crisis, and more

* During the second term of the Obama administration, I had a much closer working relationship with the National Security Council.

frequent terrorist attacks in Europe and the United States, the issue of extremism has clearly become "top priority." And yet, almost all of the money still flows primarily to military solutions, which also snare the lion's share of the public's attention. Stopping the appeal of the ideology seems intractable, generations long, and something best left for Muslims themselves to manage.

In this fluid context, government simply can't build a big enough "cultural listening" machine, nor can it do it fast enough. Government must therefore do what it does well, working with outside partners to execute where it lacks capacity. Fortunately, such partners do exist. I'm talking here not simply about grassroots-level influencers or NGOs, but also actors in the business community. Large corporations and the communications agencies that serve them have been studying millennials for years and are well practiced in communicating with them. That we have barely begun to harness private sector expertise in our fight against extremism is a travesty. And as we shall see in subsequent chapters, this is but one of the ways that private sector companies might help. The fight against extremism will not be won with the efforts of government alone. We need business to step up as never before, for the public interest as well as their own.

Here's the truth: we're in part responsible for the present situation. We could have done a great deal more to prevent the appeal of the ideology from mushrooming into a serious global threat. Countries like Afghanistan and Pakistan remain unstable, and the Syrian disaster remains a source of instability well beyond the Middle East. Huge numbers of Muslim youth are growing up as refugees, with unknown implication for the identity crisis and recruitment. We might have inhibited the so-called Islamic State from turbocharging its appeal and attracting thousands of foreign fighters. Indirectly, we might well have helped to prevent the wave of Syrian refugees coursing into Europe, as well as the resulting political and cultural fallout. Through two administrations, we have seen the global growth of the extremists' "us versus them" narrative. We've watched extremists exploit the crisis of identity and develop millennial-friendly ways to recruit their armies. Neither administration deliberately ignored the ideological fight, but rewarding policy execution on the ground has been painfully slow. By the latter part of the second Bush term, we understood the ideological threat and had tested some promising methods. In the end, with a few exceptions and despite so many terrific people in our government working so hard, we lost the next eight years of valuable time in which our CVE capacity essentially languished.

Others might counter that the Bush and Obama administrations worked hard to go after terrorist groups, and that they notched some important battlefield wins. They are right. Killing Osama bin Laden, diminishing Al Qaeda's strength, denying safe havens, reducing the extremists' financial resources, and protecting the homeland from another 9/11 attack are all critical accomplishments. Still, we did not do nearly what we could have done to prevent the terrorist problem from worsening. All along, the bad guys recruited new members using tools that we had in our own arsenal. We might have mobilized them on our own behalf—but we didn't. We lacked the extremists' strong ideological focus. That we didn't act more boldly when we could have will go down in history as, at the very least, a tremendous missed opportunity.

TOWARD A NEW START

In his inaugural speech, President Donald Trump proclaimed that he was going to defeat "radical Islamic terrorists." His administration then issued his "Muslim travel ban," sparking protests and legal challenges, and prompting top counterterrorism experts to publicly challenge the intellectual rigor behind the plan. Several weeks later, Trump traveled to Saudi Arabia and helped inaugurate a glitzy center dedicated to countering extremism—yet another big, expensive PR stunt diverting funds that might otherwise have been spent on actual civil society measures. In a speech given to a few dozen Muslim-majority nations, Trump articulated his desire to defeat the so-called Islamic State and pointed to the need to undermine the ideology of extremists. Yet, in the days that followed, his administration actually removed money budgeted for CVE programs at both the State Department and the Department of Homeland Security. The administration gave no public airplay to the importance of stopping recruitment, or to discussing specific measures that would accomplish this. If our CVE policy was a big mess by the end of the Obama administration, it was dead in the water under President Trump.

Notwithstanding this stern judgment, I've written this book out of hope, and dare I say, optimism. Extremist groups remain surprisingly vulnerable, despite the gains they've made. We *can still defeat them,* in the sense of disabling violent extremists as a significant geopolitical threat. We can reduce terrorists' ability to recruit, turning a new generation of Muslim youth against their corrupt ideology. We can do this in relatively short order—in as little as a decade. And we can do it for a tiny fraction of what we spend on military and police actions, without creating a mammoth new bureaucracy. It's not too late to pursue CVE in earnest, the way it should have been pursued in President Obama's first term. It's not too late to make a sustained and full commitment to taking away the lifeblood of extremist groups: their ability to recruit and retain young Muslims.

In the wake of 9/11, observers assumed that terrorist attacks on the United States reflected a visceral hostility toward our country. "Why do they hate us?" they asked.* But posing this question won't help us understand the full phenomenon of extremism. Although this phenomenon does exist on the level of political argument and

* Fareed Zakaria famously posed this question in an October 2001 *Newsweek* essay. Afterward, people responded by probing political sentiment in the "Muslim world" or the "Muslim street," paying special attention to political tensions in the Middle East. From the very beginning, however, politics in the Middle East and beyond formed only part of the picture. Muslims around the world cared about many other things as well.

ideology, it's fundamentally emotional in nature, not rational. This is why I don't start this book by recounting every grievance I've heard Muslim youths utter as a rationale for violence against the West. Before we can make sense of such rationales, we must first understand more broadly what has happened to Muslim kids growing up post-9/11. How have they come to experience the world? What factors have shaped, influenced, and informed their perspectives? What's the *cultural context,* in other words, in which political grievances take form and are expressed? These are the essential questions that accounts of extremism have all too often ignored.

We have hardly begun to mobilize our forces in this ideological battle. And I'm not talking about engaging in a messaging war on Twitter or disseminating U.S. government-made videos that policy makers think are great. I'm talking about government, the private sector, and civil society working together to mobilize citizens in new ways. I'm talking about helping parents and especially women understand extremist tactics so they can educate their children and protect the community. I'm talking about supporting the hundreds of grassroots ideas and initiatives in our own country and around the world that reject extremist ideology. I'm talking about working closely with mental health professionals to understand the adolescent mind and to develop programs aimed at youth that can help stop radicalization. I'm talking about encouraging the teaching of global histories that give a comprehensive view of religion and that dispel the idea of a monolithic Islam. I'm talking about preserving human heritage sites worldwide that the extremists, seeking to create the illusion of a monolithic Islam, threaten to destroy. Most broadly, I'm talking about changing global discourse so that the cultural and intellectual system that underpins extremism becomes starved of oxygen.

I've written this book to share what I know about the extremist threat, and to issue a call to arms to government, the private sector, and civil society. I begin in the first chapter by describing in more detail how CVE took shape within our government in the decade after

9/11. Then I go on to identify the basic generational phenomenon underlying the extremist scourge—not economics or conflict within Islam, not disillusionment with the United States or its policies, but the global identity crisis afflicting Muslim youth. As I discovered through my travels, a vast cultural, ideological, and economic system has grown up around this identity crisis, perpetuating it to this day. In chapters 2 through 6, I dissect this system, describing its primary elements, explaining how each element helps facilitate the extremist threat, recounting how extremists have used each element to their advantage, and providing ideas for how we can win. As we'll see, this system includes among its core elements a vibrant consumer culture that privileges conservative ideology and translates it into readily consumable products and practices, an economic and intellectual patron of extremist ideology (Saudi Arabia), a set of beliefs and assumptions about the United States, and a new, technologically mediated way of experiencing religion. Many CVE advocates emphasize one part or another of the system, failing to understand that you need to address the entire system in order to make inroads.

With the underlying problem of extremism properly in focus, and the basic contours of a solution laid out, I continue in chapters 7 through 9 to suggest how important actors in our society can best mobilize themselves to wage the ideological war. As I argue, CVE isn't a task for government alone. It's a task for all of us: government (chapter 7), business (chapter 8), and local communities of interest and philanthropists (chapter 9). I close the book by explaining how this approach diverges from the ways in which scholars, policy makers, and others have thought about not just extremism but global challenges in general. We're used to persuading others to do what we want by using hard power (military might) or soft power (achieving goals by appealing to shared values rather than coercing people or paying them off).[6] In the epilogue, I describe the approach to extremism I outline here as a new variant of soft power, what I call "open power."

Ultimately, this book offers a comprehensive program for combating extremist ideology—the program I wish we'd followed all these years. It's a book for anyone who has ever wondered why extremists always seem to be one beat ahead of us, and what we can do to change that. And it's a book that conveys a humanistic approach to global affairs. How we treat other people matters. What we say about identity matters. Ultimately, CVE entails reaffirming the ability of every human being to claim a place in our communities, whether they pray or live or believe like us or not. This is a cause that every one of us can further, in ways big and small, no matter where we live or our station in life. The stakes couldn't be higher. In 2010, one-fourth of our planet—1.6 billion people—was Muslim, and 63 percent of those Muslims were under thirty years of age. By 2030, the Muslim population will number 2.2 billion.[7] Although the overwhelming majority of these Muslims pose no threat, the demographic trends still represent a potential bonanza for the bad guys. Even if extremists only comprise one-twentieth of global Muslims, that was still 80 million people in 2010.

RATIO OF MUSLIM YOUTH TO GLOBAL YOUTH IN YEARS 1990 AND 2030. AGES 15–29 YEARS.

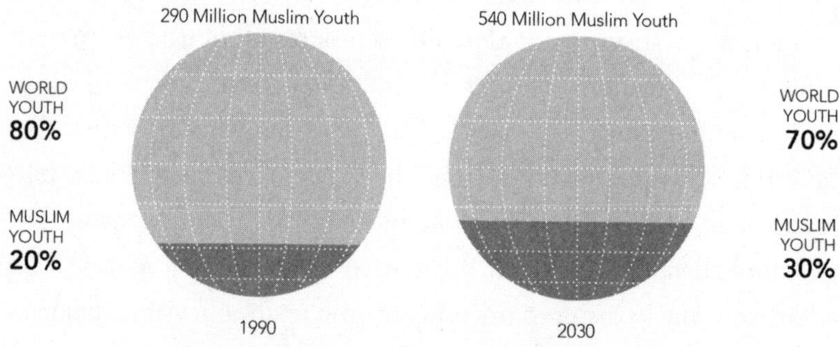

The population of Muslim youth is expanding dramatically.

Pew Research Center's Forum on Religion and Public Life, *The Future of the Global Muslim Population, January 2011.*

Illustrated by Nafisa Nandini Crishna

President Trump's first year in office has brought a drastic change in the way America deals with anticipating and preventing terrorist attacks. Beyond shifting our terminology from "CVE" to "terrorism prevention," the administration has slashed funds for community-led programs originating in State and Homeland Security, and instead is focusing on law enforcement. Further, the administration's refusal to engage with our own existing wealth of intelligence, grassroots and academic research, forward-leaning insights, and partnerships means we have gone backward in the fight to stop recruitment. Over the next three to five years, if nothing is done, the identity crisis underlying extremism will worsen, and younger Muslims will grow up perceiving extremism as an ever more credible ideology on the rise. We will see many more episodes like the Boston Marathon bombing or the *Charlie Hebdo* massacre. We'll see thousands more youth—including far more Americans—flocking to conflict zones and then returning home to set off bombs in suburban shopping malls. We'll see a world dramatically more unstable, more fearful, and less prosperous.

It doesn't have to be this way. We can win. This is how.

CHAPTER ONE

A FIGHT WE'RE LOSING

On November 13, 2015, I was sitting at home when a friend texted me. "Turn on your TV—*now*." My stomach tightened, and I felt a sense of dread. I grabbed the remote and turned on CNN. Terrorists had struck Paris, France, in a series of coordinated attacks. A sports stadium, a music venue, cafes, restaurants—all had been hit by either suicide bombers or gunmen wielding assault rifles. The situation was fluid, but it appeared that hundreds of people were killed or wounded.

I watched, slack-jawed. My mind flashed to a visit I'd made to Paris eight years earlier as a U.S. government employee. I met with groups of Muslims in cafes very much like the ones that were attacked, sipping coffee and talking about their lives. My tablemates were typically French, their dress and ideas indistinguishable from that of their fellow countrymen. None of them thought much about Al Qaeda. To them, terrorism seemed a faraway threat that didn't affect their lives. However, they had noticed more violent, extremist views circulating in their communities—the notion that attacks on Muslims and non-Muslims were justified, or that killing secular

Muslims was the only way to "teach" them—and this had concerned them.

As the news continued to come in, it became clear that the so-called Islamic State had organized and inspired the Paris attackers. By hitting and severely paralyzing the city, the so-called Islamic State would show both opponents and potential recruits that it could wreak destruction far beyond its nominal "caliphate" in Syria and Iraq. With fundamental French values in mind, the attackers had targeted cultural installations, seeking to inflict the maximum amount of emotional distress. And the attack had been an "inside job," executed primarily by French-born Muslims who had been radicalized (six of the attackers were French, two Belgian, and two of unknown nationality). The message to the French and other nations opposing the so-called Islamic State was terrifying: "We've got small cells of sympathizers hidden inside your countries. No matter how strong you are, we can mobilize them at will to cause major damage. Nobody is safe." As Paris mayor Anne Hidalgo said, lamenting the violence visited on her city in 2015, "This was an attack against the foundations of our democracies."*

As distressed as I was to watch images of dazed and bloodied civilians fleeing mayhem in a European capital, I was also profoundly frustrated. Since the 2006 Danish cartoon crisis, members of the policy establishment had been concerned that an attack like this—coming from within Europe, aimed at soft targets—was possible. We had known that the extremists were attracting youth by crafting an appealing ideology. But rather than directing significant resources toward countering this ideology, we had downplayed it as a threat.†

---

* Anne Hidalgo, remarks at the White House Countering Violent Extremism Summit, February 18, 2015, https://www.c-span.org/video/?324398-102/white-house-summit-countering-violent-extremism. Though she articulated this sentiment in response to the January 2015 attack against *Charlie Hebdo,* her remarks are certainly applicable to the even more destructive events that transpired later that year.

† France has especially downplayed this, even though it has the largest Muslim population in Europe and boasts one of the best traditional law enforcement capabilities. In 2007, a senior French law enforcement

Radicalization had taken place unimpeded, to the point where it now menaced many countries. The attacks on Paris were, paradoxically, a predictable surprise—and entirely preventable.

Today, two groups—Al Qaeda and the so-called Islamic State—stand as the dominant sources of global terrorism. Al Qaeda emerged during the 1980s, fighting the Soviets in Afghanistan.[1] Osama bin Laden sought to exploit anti-Soviet "jihadi" momentum in the region to globalize Al Qaeda's cause, providing disparate terror movements elite training facilities, weaponry, and other logistical support.* By the 1990s, he and his compatriots had refocused their hatred from local antagonists to one common enemy: the United States.[2]

The so-called Islamic State, by contrast, took shape in the unrest that followed America's intervention in Iraq in 2003. At the time, Abu Musab al-Zarqawi affiliated his group, Jama'at al-Tawhid w'al-Jihad, with Al Qaeda, creating Al Qaeda in Iraq (AQI).[3] Zarqawi himself was unenthused about the alliance, but it proceeded, proving beneficial to both organizations. As Daniel L. Byman, Brookings Institution senior fellow and former counterterrorism official, explains, "Bin Laden got an affiliate in the most important theater of jihad at a time when the Al Qaeda core was on the ropes, and Zarqawi got Al Qaeda's prestige and contacts to bolster his legitimacy."[4] Disputes persisted, however, as Al Qaeda remained focused on U.S. targets, while Zarqawi used increasingly brutal means to target "apostate" Sunni Muslims in the Iraqi region. Tensions and ideological disagreements only escalated until the so-called Islamic State, under the leadership of Abu Bakr Al-Baghdadi, severed any ties with Al Qaeda in 2014.

---

official told me that his organization knew that foreign ideologies were influencing some French citizens and were monitoring them carefully.

* According to a 2010 CIA report, prior to 9/11, Al Qaeda had financial requirements of $30 million per year: Juan Miguel del Cid Gomez, "A Financial Profile of the Terrorism of Al-Qaeda and its Affiliates," *Perspectives on Terrorism* 4, no. 4 (2010), http://www.terrorismanalysts.com/pt/index.php/pot/article/view/113/html.

Subsequently the two groups became rivals vying for leadership in the global terrorist movement.[5] In June 2014, the so-called Islamic State shocked the world by suddenly redrawing the map of the modern Middle East, capturing vast swaths of Iraq and declaring a "caliphate" under the leadership of al-Baghdadi, the self-proclaimed "leader of Muslims everywhere."[6] The group's dominance, fueled by black-market fossil fuel dealings, cash stolen from banks in captured territories, antiquities trafficking, protection rackets, robust tax collection, and lucrative ransoms for captive Westerners, attracted sympathizers the world over.[7] As a 2016 Council on Foreign Relations profile details, "Insurgent groups in Afghanistan, Bangladesh, Egypt, Indonesia, Nigeria, Pakistan, the Philippines, Saudi Arabia, and Yemen have sworn allegiance to Baghdadi. In 2015, the group seized territory in Libya that spanned more than 150 miles of Mediterranean coastline between Tripoli and Benghazi."[8] Heeding Baghdadi's call, others far from those battlefields emulate the group's tactics in "lone wolf" attacks, such as that perpetrated against a Florida nightclub in June 2016.[9] Al Qaeda, meanwhile, had extended its recruitment and affiliation channels into India, Tunisia, and the Caucasus. Both currently vie for supremacy in Libya, Pakistan, Sinai, Yemen, Algeria, and elsewhere.[10]

The rift between the two groups is profound, extending to strategy, philosophy, and tactical approach. Al Qaeda maintains a "far enemy" stance, focusing on the United States, while so-called Islamic State is more invested in the "near enemy," which includes Yazidis, Iraqi Shia, the Lebanese Hezbollah, and others it deems heterodox.[11] Al Qaeda's foremost objective is to orchestrate another spectacular terrorist incident in the United States along the lines of 9/11, the 1998 bombings of the Kenyan and Tanzanian embassies, or the attack on the USS *Cole* in 2000.[12] Through symbolism and spectacle, it hopes to attract new sympathizers to the brand and instill terror among enemies. The so-called Islamic State, by contrast, proactively and enthusiastically claims responsibility for many of its destructive acts, seeking to leave an exaggerated impression of its global reach. Tactically, Al Qaeda operates with a somewhat gentler touch, using persuasion to lure local Muslims to its cause, while the so-called Islamic State uses crucifixion, rape, and beheadings to force submission and allegiance.[13] Consistent with this approach, Al Qaeda has shown clemency toward U.S. aid workers and journalists. The so-called Islamic State, by contrast, has shocked the world by brutally slaying journalists and aid workers.[14]

On a number of occasions, the U.S. government has celebrated its ability to dismantle Al Qaeda.[15] Such proclamations have been premature. Al Qaeda hasn't simply survived—it has thrived. Not only has the organization recovered from military setbacks sustained during the early twenty-first century, it now boasts nearly twenty-five local "franchise" organizations, along with tens of thousands of fighters who have carried out attacks throughout northern Africa, the Arabian Peninsula, and elsewhere.[16] And while the so-called Islamic State is internationally famous for its digital savvy, we shouldn't discount Al Qaeda's command of these technologies. As Richard H. Shultz, professor of international politics at Tufts University's Fletcher School of Law and Diplomacy, observes,

> Since 9/11 al-Qaeda's use of the World Wide Web in several languages, innumerable blogs and bulletin boards, and other Internet tools has burgeoned. Collectively, these tools provide al-Qaeda with the capacity to circumvent both the mainstream global media, which is dominated by Western media outlets, as well as the media in Muslim countries that are largely controlled by authoritarian governments.[17]

Writing in 2017, Bruce Hoffman, former director of Georgetown University's Center for Security Studies, observed that the "16th anniversary of the terrorist attacks of Sept. 11, 2001, might be less mournful if we could say that the threat of jihadist terrorism had receded or disappeared. But that is far from the case." Instead, he affirmed that "Al Qaeda has been quietly rebuilding, after ceding the spotlight for several years to Islamic State. . . . Taken together, these two groups—with their expanding capabilities and multiple branches across the globe—pose a security challenge for the U.S. and its allies every bit as perilous as what they faced immediately after 9/11."[18] The power of Facebook, YouTube, Twitter, Instagram, Flickr, and WhatsApp has facilitated communication between extremists, would-be recruits, and potential benefactors. Former FBI director James Comey described the challenge in the following terms: "We are looking for needles in a nationwide haystack, but we are also called up to figure out which pieces of hay might someday become needles."[19]

Even as the sources and motivations underlying radicalization become ever more elusive, we are still plagued by fundamental problems of misunderstanding. The media and public at large, for example, are prone to understanding terrorism as irrational, senseless, and rooted in textual literalism and antiquated history. In 2004, Brynjar Lia and Thomas Hegghammer, two specialists working at the Norwegian Defense Research Establishment's Transnational Radical Islamism Project, challenged this perception, publishing a critical appraisal of Al Qaeda's *Jihadi Iraq,* a document detailing the terror organization's military strategy against its Western enemies in Iraq. Characterizing the terrorist document as "secular in style, analytical in its approach, and pragmatic in its conclusions," Lia and Hegghammer liken the text to a sophisticated intelligence memo that military strategists in the West might produce. It was, in their estimation, "strikingly similar to Western strategic studies," and not the misguided apocalyptic machinations of an irrational cult.[20]

Still, notions of the terror organizations' irrationality persist. In December 2015, *New York Times* reporter Rukmini Callimachi described the so-called Islamic State's motivations in terms of medieval, literalist soothsaying: "The group bases its ideology on prophetic texts stating that Islam will be victorious after an apocalyptic battle to be set off once Western armies come to the region."[21] Such analysis is widely accepted—surely, it seems, there can be no discretion and sagacity in conducting suicide bombings or in facing off against much more powerful enemies. As Hoffman observes, by failing to acknowledge how adept and logical terror groups are, "governments remain enmeshed in spiraling cycles of violence and campaigns with no end apparently in sight."[22]

To date, we've also mostly conceived our battle against terrorist organizations as a matter of what the political scientist and author Joseph Nye has termed "hard power." Nye defines hard power as the use of military and economic tools to compel action from other states, either by punishing them or by rewarding their compliance. The mere threat of some form of military action, up to and including war, or of economic measures like sanctions, trade deals, and tariffs, constitutes the wielding of hard power.[23] In regards to extremism, we've deployed numerous hard power tactics, including following and cutting the financing of extremist groups, using drones and special forces troops, boosting our intelligence capabilities and our coordination with other countries, and adopting law enforcement policies that let us track potential terrorists better. Most recently, the Trump administration has cracked down on would-be extremists through law enforcement actions that focus on immigration (Trump calls it "extreme vetting")—another hard power tactic, with results that are perceived to be both measurable and effective. The Department of Homeland Security, which led these law enforcement actions, has also prioritized building a physical wall on the southern border (the 2018 federal budget adds $4.7 billion to DHS but trims $600 million off antiterrorism capacity).[24]

As Nye argues, hard power is not the only way governments can achieve their objectives. Governments can also persuade, attract, influence, or motivate others to behave in ways we like—what Nye calls "soft power." As he explains, governments can "shape the preferences of others" so that they *want* to behave in desired ways. Practically speaking, soft power encompasses any number of tactics that build affinity for a government and its objectives, including the use of media, art, literature, language, policies, institutions, and so on. As Nye explains, "The Soft Power of a country rests heavily on three basic resources: its culture (in places where it is attractive to others), its political values (when it lives up to them at home and abroad) and its foreign policies (when others see them as legitimate and having moral authority)."[25] The precise impact of soft power tactics is frequently difficult to measure, but these tactics afford a flexibility and nuance that states can't achieve with hard power, and they are especially well suited to broader goals like "promoting democracy, human rights, and open markets."[26] As Nye has noted, "Much of American soft power has been produced by Hollywood, Harvard, Microsoft and Michael Jordan."[27] Beguiled by our culture, individuals and governments have been more inclined to embrace our values and behave in ways we find desirable.

As Ambassador Nicholas Burns, director of the Future of Diplomacy Project at Harvard's Kennedy School of Government, told me, "Sometimes when you hit a brick wall, your citizens can be an effective way to try to make a connection that might lead to something bigger. President Nixon did this with the ping-pong team in 1971 that was sent to China."[28] Another example arose in 2005, when Secretary Condoleezza Rice and Ambassador Burns, then undersecretary of state for political affairs, sought to create a nondirect path of engagement with Iran. U.S. policy didn't allow for direct communications between its own government officials and their Iranian counterparts. In "trying to figure out how to achieve an opening with the Iranian people, because we had been isolated from Iran since the hostages were taken in 1980," Burns said they turned to soft power tools.[29] Their soft power approaches included opening up a virtual embassy with lots of content in Farsi and supporting the sending of "American doctors and nurses to Iran, along with the American national wrestling team."[30] Wrestling is the national sport of Iran, and citizens there know our American team through global competitions, so the choice was particularly well conceived. Said Burns: "We wanted to meet them halfway and the best way to do that was through soft power, and through American citizens that had no connections to our government."[31]

When it comes to extremism, we've achieved some successes by focusing almost exclusively on hard power. We've cracked down on terrorist financing. We've arrested and killed terrorist leaders. We've pushed back the so-called Islamic State in Iraq and Syria, liberating vast swaths of territory. Yet terrorist attacks have proliferated. In 2001, terrorism killed almost 8,000 people worldwide. In 2015, it killed more than 38,000.[32] On a single day in February 2016, terrorists struck in Syria, Cameroon, Somalia, Pakistan, Bangladesh, and Egypt.[33] The ravages go beyond lives lost. As the 2016 Center for Strategic and International Studies (CSIS) CVE Commission report noted, "Violent extremists are altering the political landscape and erasing national borders, and in so doing, destroying evidence of people, history, and cultures that threaten their world view."[34] "Lone wolf" attacks have also spread to the American homeland. On April 15, 2013, Dzhokhar and Tamerlan Tsarnaev detonated an explosive device at the Boston Marathon, killing three and injuring over 260.[35] On June 12, 2016, Omar Mateen opened fire at an Orlando nightclub, killing forty-nine and wounding fifty-three.[36] Other tragic attacks have taken place in San Bernardino (2015) and at Fort Hood (2009).

More ominously for the long-term outlook, the global recruiting of new extremist soldiers continues apace. Hard power might stop terrorists from launching specific attacks, but like a weed, terrorism shoots back up, stronger and more pervasive. Such resilience has spawned pessimism among policy makers and the American public, a sense that we're winning specific battles but losing the broader war. In a 2016 survey fielded across eight countries, 61 percent of

Americans queried regarded terrorism as a "major problem" for the United States, while 80 percent judged it as a major problem for the world. Almost all U.S. respondents (89 percent) believed an attack was "very likely" or "somewhat likely" in the next year. And 74 percent of U.S. respondents felt that extremist groups would "acquire and use" weapons of mass destruction.[37]

Most people today also assume that we will always face terrorism inspired by Al Qaeda– or so-called Islamic State–like ideologies. People shake their head at a problem that seems so big that it is impossible to manage. In the spring of 2015, General John Allen proclaimed (using the Arabic term for the so-called Islamic State) that "defeating Daesh's ideology will likely take a generation or more." He further warned of "more groups like Daesh" in the future if we don't defeat extremism.[38] Other observers have warned that it could take "years" to defeat the so-called Islamic State militarily, and that we face a "long campaign ahead."[39]

MODERN TERRORISM AND THE "HARD POWER" RESPONSE

To understand why we're coming up short against extremism, it helps to reflect on the broader history of terrorism and our fight against it. The term "terrorism" first surfaced during the French Revolution, where it connoted democracy and virtue—rupture from a corrupt Old Regime. Today, of course, the definition has become inverted, and terrorism is widely associated with evil, perversity, and organized destruction. The *Oxford English Dictionary* provides a useful starting point, defining terrorism as "the unlawful use of violence and intimidation, especially against civilians, in the pursuit of political aims."[40] This definition allows for a diversity of terrorist phenomena, encompassing an array of ideological perspectives, funding models, tactics, justifications, and organizational frameworks. With its broad language and the absence of any reference to nation-states, the definition encompasses violence perpetrated by non-nation-state actors lacking in international legitimacy. Certain terrorist organizations bear characteristics of nation-states: robust politico-religious ideologies, advanced weaponry, money, soldiers, territorial dominion. Terrorists can even fight nation-states or particular elements therein. But they always lack legitimacy.*

Terrorism has evolved considerably over the past century and a half. As David Rapoport, professor emeritus at the University of California, Los Angeles, observes, the late nineteenth and early twentieth centuries saw an "anarchist wave," in which lone operators belonging to a nonhierarchical movement used assassinations to effect regime change in Russia, Armenia, Poland, and other global hot spots.[41] By the mid-twentieth century, terrorism had broadly shifted. With empires disintegrating and local self-determination movements rising, an "anticolonial wave" of terrorism took shape, with nationalist groups in Ireland, Algeria, and elsewhere targeting civilians in an attempt to build international support for their causes. These nationalist movements continued to operate during the 1970s and 1980s, but the world also saw the rise of a "new left wave," in which self-understood revolutionaries used assassinations, kidnappings, and especially bombings to achieve ideological objectives.

Beginning in the 1990s and continuing to the present, terrorism

---

* The U.S. government has its own definition and designations. Under the Immigration and Nationality Act, the State Department may designate certain groups as foreign terrorist organizations (FTO), and under the aegis of Executive Order 13224, it may classify a broader array of entities, groups, and individuals, such as financiers and front companies, as specially designated global terrorists (SDGT). The State Department's Bureau of Counterterrorism identifies and evaluates various individuals or organizations. FTOs are foreign organizations that have either engaged in terrorist activity or have the capacity or intention of doing so, which undermines national security. The Department of State is authorized to designate FTOs and SDGTs, while the Department of the Treasury may only designate the latter. For more on these designations, please see "Terrorist Designations and State Sponsors of Terrorism," U.S. Department of State, https://www.state.gov/j/ct/list/index.htm, and "What are designations?" U.S. Department of the Treasury, https://www.treasury.gov/resource-center/sanctions/Pages/designations.aspx.

entered a new, "religious wave." During this time, the three Abrahamic religions, particularly Islam, have dominated ethno-national conflicts. Movements such as the Muslim Brotherhood in Egypt and the internationalists in Afghanistan both inspired so-called jihadis to wage *holy war*. While such movements had locally rooted political objectives, they envisaged their struggle as universal in scope—a tendency especially evident in Afghanistan. As French political scientist Olivier Roy suggests, "Jihad in Afghanistan was aimed at setting up the vanguard of the Ummah," and soldiers throughout the world flocked to that country's underground training facilities, later operated by Osama bin Laden.[42] In 1996, Osama bin Laden allied his movement with the country's Taliban regime, increasing the reach, complexity, and sophistication of his operations, all of which were showcased to the world on 9/11.[43]

Rapoport's scheme is neither exhaustive nor definitive, but it helps us to identify terrorism's primary historical shifts. As we might expect, the U.S. government's response to terrorism has changed over time as well. Compared to the international community, America's engagement with terrorism has been relatively brief. While the United States didn't figure prominently in any of the first three historical waves of terrorism, the events of September 11, 2001, brought America decisively into conflict with the current fourth wave. As Bruce Hoffman has noted, the United States hadn't before "faced an adversary who believes their mission is divinely decreed and therefore ceaseless alongside the fact that [Al Qaeda] operates internationally. Even if in the past we faced recalcitrant, determined adversaries, their geographic base and ambit were far away and constrained to that location."[44]

To meet this challenge, America responded with sweeping legislation and institutional reform, including the Patriot Act (2001), the Homeland Security Act (2002) (the largest governmental restructuring in the modern era), the Intelligence Reform and Terrorism Prevention Act (2004), and the formation of the Terrorist Threat

Integration Center (2003), renamed the National Counterterrorism Center in 2004. President George W. Bush also announced the "War on Terror" and initiated two prolonged military engagements in Iraq and Afghanistan to prosecute this war."[45]* As terrorism expert Brian Michael Jenkins has observed, the notion of combating any threat, including terrorism, suggested an ongoing struggle with no clear end. "War," however, suggested a clear mission, with a concrete antagonist, and a finite ending point. It also implied that once we defeated those behind 9/11, all would be well.

This counterterrorism strategy was partially successful. America's two military expeditions have helped prevent another domestic terrorism incident of the size and scale of 9/11.[46] In the decade following 9/11, as Daniel Byman said in testimony before the Homeland Security Committee, "the U.S. relentlessly pursued Al Qaeda, targeting its leadership, disrupting its finances, destroying its training camps, infiltrating its communications networks, and ultimately crippling its ability to function."[47] The power of the Al Qaeda brand diminished as well, following the leadership of Ayman al-Zawahiri (a much less formidable and magnetic a leader than his predecessor Osama bin Laden) and the organization's inability to replicate another major attack in the West.[48]

Still, U.S. security specialists keenly understand the inadequacy of this strategy, especially following the emergence of the so-called Islamic State. As late as 2014, Major General Michael K. Nagata, the special operations commander for the United States in the Middle East, expressed bewilderment about the so-called Islamic State and its ability to attract adherents: "We have not defeated the idea," he said. "We do not even understand the idea."[49] In January 2014, President Barack Obama was similarly uncertain, explaining the

* The National Counterterrorism Center was originally known as the Terrorist Threat Integration Center: "The Terrorist Threat Integration Center One Year Later," Federal Bureau of Investigation, April 30, 2004, https://archives.fbi.gov/archives/news/stories/2004/april/threat_043004.

so-called Islamic State's significance to *The New Yorker*'s David Remnick in terms of a crude sports analogy: "The analogy we use around here sometimes, and I think is accurate, is if a J.V. team puts on Lakers uniforms, that doesn't make them Kobe Bryant."[50] The analogy would soon falter as the so-called Islamic State's advance across Iraq continued. By June 2014, the so-called Islamic State controlled much of Iraq's Anbar Province and was advancing toward Baghdad.

Obama, who criticized his predecessor George W. Bush for his unilateralism and campaigned to substitute military intervention with multilateralism to fight terrorism, seemed to contradict this campaign promise throughout 2014, authorizing air strikes in Syria and providing assistance to Syrian rebels.[51] In September 2014, Obama amped up his rhetoric, delivering threatening messages to the so-called Islamic State. "It was unclear whether Mr. Obama's tougher tone meant he had fundamentally rethought his counterterrorism strategy," mused the *New York Times,* "or was responding to an American public shocked by the beheadings of American hostages by Islamic extremists."[52] In June 2015, when he broached the topic of combating the so-called Islamic State to the Group of Seven (Canada, France, Germany, Italy, Japan, the United States, and the United Kingdom), Obama was still unsure, saying "we don't have, yet, a complete strategy," and noting that "the details are not worked out."[53] A "complete strategy" would have involved a deep and comprehensive evaluation of our goals and how to reach them. Like our responses to the SARS and Ebola outbreaks in 2002 and 2014, respectively, a complete strategy would have engaged all elements of our national power to ensure the homeland was protected. Directives would have been in place in a sequential system to ensure the strategy was deployed correctly, that money and personnel were allocated, and that the results were measurable and accountable. The Trump administration has essentially continued this practice of navigating without a compass.[54]

A lack of precision in counterterrorism strategy is understandable. After all, the world's dominant terrorist threats aren't solely composed of clearly defined organizations that can be easily targeted and weakened. Sleeper cells and loose clandestine affiliations have spread across the globe, aided and abetted by social networking technologies. Geography is only one part of the equation. Some onlookers, observing the diminishment of the so-called Islamic State's territorial power, have mistakenly expressed relief. Even before his "caliphate" began to crumble, the group's leader, Abu Bakr al-Baghdadi had instituted contingency plans, creating and establishing relationships with nearly two dozen other affiliate branches of his organization elsewhere in the world and directing would-be adherents to gravitate there. They have heeded his call, orchestrating further attacks.[55]

The United States and other targeted countries routinely attempt to thwart these strikes in an endless game of Whac-A-Mole. That has proven more difficult as attackers learn about the so-called Islamic State's tactics over social media. According to Bruce Hoffman, "Islamic State has now perfected a third, hybrid option, known among security experts as the 'enabled attacker.' Such terrorists operate independently, like lone wolves, but also receive guidance and direction from jihadist commanders whom they have never met or previously interacted with. Those instructions contain specific directions and detailed intelligence about particular targets—thus making such attacks faster, more lethal and harder to thwart."[56]

JOINING THE IDEOLOGICAL FIGHT AGAINST EXTREMISM

After 9/11, when the terrorist threat abruptly coalesced for policy makers and members of the public, the enemy was "violent extremists" writ large, albeit in the specific form of Al Qaeda. Members of the policy establishment grappled with the novelty of a nonstate actor dealing a harsh blow to the greatest power on earth. Who was Al Qaeda? What were their capabilities? What did they want?

Some inside the U.S. government focused on the ideological dimension. President Bush regarded the War on Terror as both a military and ideological conflict, remarking in an address to a joint session of Congress shortly after 9/11: "We have seen their kind before. They are the heirs of all the murderous ideologies of the 20th century. By sacrificing human life to serve their radical visions . . . they follow in the path of fascism, and Nazism, and totalitarianism."[57] Over the next several years, this thinking became so entrenched that the 2006 National Security Strategy stated, "From the beginning, the War on Terror has been both a battle of arms and a battle of ideas—a fight against the terrorist and against their murderous ideology."[58]

Matt Bryza, who served as a member of the National Security Council during the early 2000s and later as the United States ambassador to Azerbaijan, remembers, "Everyone who had a solid head on their shoulders in Washington was thinking about what are the so-called root causes of terror." Yet most conversations about extremist ideologies were not terribly sophisticated. "We stumbled around, people hadn't thought about it, there was a lot of defensiveness at first, elsewhere in the world people were saying, 'How did the US bring this upon itself?' The discussions were not very enlightened in the beginning."[59]

The "immediacy" of the terrorist threat on the ground in countries like Afghanistan, Pakistan, and Iraq made it hard to focus on the ideological side, and the lack of clear precedents for addressing a twenty-first-century ideological challenge also made quick action difficult. Extremism didn't match the kind of ideological threat we faced during the Cold War. As Juan Zarate told me, "It's a little bit of the anarchist movement meets the Bolsheviks meets the Palestinian national terrorists, all combined with a theological narrative.

How do you combat that ideology, and how do you do it as the US government?"[60]

In Washington, an effort to organize ourselves bureaucratically against the extremist threat soon took hold. The new Department of Homeland Security was an enormous accomplishment that announced to the world and to ourselves that we were taking the extremist threat seriously. We invested billions, building a complex, multifunctional organization from the ground up, and adding a cabinet-level position. To provide more of the quality intelligence we needed, we created the National Counterterrorism Center, another multimillion-dollar entity. We created the Transportation Security Administration (TSA) to help secure air travel. All in all, we "created or reorganized" more than 260 government bodies.[61] But although these organizations were critical to defending the homeland (which included stopping recruitment), none of the institutions in the "white world" (the public, transparent parts of our government, as opposed to the secret, "black" world of spycraft, special operations, and the like) were tasked with building practical tools that would stanch the spread of extremist *ideology*, such as networks of people within local communities bent on fighting extremism, psychological interventions, or educational programs. It wasn't even clear who should spearhead the building of such tools: the White House? The State Department? The Department of Defense? The Department of Homeland Security? "We could never quite figure out how to organize as a government [against extremist ideology]," said Zarate. "The issues were international, related to military, related to intelligence, related to law enforcement, they related to mental health issues, they were related to education programs, to state and local authorities and communities, to the very fabric of our society. How do you organize around an issue like that?"[62]

What efforts were made to fight ideology were extremely limited. Perceiving that America had, among other things, an "image problem" with Muslims worldwide, the administration resolved to engage with Muslims in hopes of convincing them to change their "hearts and minds" about America and its values of democracy and freedom. If we could get Muslims to perceive the United States differently, the thinking went, we would "solve" the extremism problem. The goal was to rebrand America, reminding the general public and Muslims in particular that we had a legacy of partnership, and that America had a Muslim population that enjoyed life just as any other Americans. We also sought to affirm that Islam was compatible with democracy—that one could be a proud American and a proud Muslim. Al Qaeda was branding America as Islam's enemy, so it seemed logical to expose their lies and spin. Al Qaeda used a selectively culled collection of our foreign policy choices to "prove" their contentions about our implacable hostility to Islam. As a result, we needed to try to explain those foreign policy choices, eroding the conspiracy theories about our policies that prevailed on the "Muslim street" and even within the ministries of foreign affairs of our closest partners and allies.

Our initial attempts during the George W. Bush administration's first term didn't go well.* Senior members of the administration knew that the U.S. government didn't have the talent on hand to produce a high-quality, credible, compelling campaign, so the president's team turned to Madison Avenue,[63] bringing in Charlotte Beers, a respected ad executive, and appointing her undersecretary of state for public diplomacy and public affairs. The job made her, in the words of one commentator, "the de facto international PR representative for the US."[64]

Beers created a $15 million campaign called "Shared Values" in

---

* As Elliott Abrams recalled at the time, the NSC wanted a definition of this phenomenon and advice for how to balance its military and ideological dimensions. The agency knew that the United States "actually used to know how to do this during the Cold War." With no federal information agency in existence, "occasionally we would have . . . a free conversation about how it would be recreated . . . but that argument . . . that's a bureaucratic argument. That's not the critical thing. The critical thing is what would you do? What is it that you think is missing?" Elliott Abrams, interview with the author, Washington, D.C., April 11, 2016.

which American Muslims touted their ability to practice their religion and live freely in the United States. Unfortunately, the ads were seen within Muslim communities as superficial and contrived—all the more so since national Muslim prejudice in the United States had indisputably increased since 9/11. Criticized as too "simplistic," these ads aroused the ire of several Muslim-majority nations, which refused to allow them to be broadcast.[65] In addition, the Department of State set up a third party called the Council of American Muslims (CAMU), which seemed to take ownership of the ads but came across as inauthentic and propagandistic. In her defense, Beers faced serious challenges in her job, including excessive red tape, a "demoralized" staff, skeptical officials inside and outside the State Department, and a budget that was "equal to what the Pentagon spent in a day."[66] As we'll see in chapter 7, her office also lacked the kind of cultural or ethnographic "listening" capacity that would have led to better, more relevant communications. The ads that were launched in Indonesia then ran throughout the Middle East and Pakistan were canceled, and in March 2003, after less than two years on the job, Beers stepped down.[67]

Her successor, Karen Hughes, fared little better, despite enjoying a great deal of influence due to a close relationship with President Bush. As Kurt Volker, who was a director for European and Eurasian affairs during the first George W. Bush administration at the time, remembers, Hughes "totally got [the need to fight extremist ideology], and was completely thwarted in pursuing them by the bureaucracy and the State Department."[68] Opposed to policies connected with the president's War on Terror, and fearing that Hughes's portfolio was impinging on their own work in other policy areas, some rank-and-file State Department employees who couldn't refuse to do her bidding without losing their jobs stonewalled her.

As we'll discuss in detail later, the very idea of government-produced public information campaigns as remedies for extremist recruitment was misconceived. Beers herself recognized limits to the U.S. government's ability to project its message convincingly, pointing to the need for third parties to speak authentically on the government's behalf, and counseling "that we should approach our subjects with a certain amount of humility."[69] By then, millions had been wasted and the campaign had come across as a political act designed to show the American public that we were taking action against extremist recruitment. This same pattern would lead many subsequent counterterrorism efforts astray. Domestic politics and optics carried enormous weight when it came to some of our crucial strategy decisions—and still do.

A persistent challenge facing the U.S. government was that of preventing Al Qaeda from spinning news events about U.S. government action and policies to their advantage. Consistently, we found ourselves caught by surprise and outmaneuvered, forced on the defensive to respond to negative publicity drummed up by our adversaries. In some cases, we made it easier for our adversaries. In 2004, when the Abu Ghraib scandal gained international attention, I was working for USAID and living in Kabul, Afghanistan. There I witnessed the violence and loss of life that took place after images of Muslim prisoners, stripped naked and humiliated, flashed across the global media. In an instant, our efforts on the ground were irreparably damaged.

In 2005, Hughes created the Rapid Response Unit (RRU), a team intended to neutralize Al Qaeda's daily agitprop. The RRU later expanded and became the Counterterrorism Communications Center (CTCC), a rapid response unit that "produces strategic communications plans, develops effective narratives and themes to undermine and counter terrorist messaging, and produces specific messages for use by State and DoD communicators." Within the CTCC, a Digital Outreach Team would "go into chat rooms and on interactive websites, in Arabic, Farsi, and Urdu (and, we had planned, Russian), to explain U.S. policy and refute lies and distortions."[70]

After Hughes's departure, the CTCC lived on, renamed the

"Global Strategic Engagement Center." In 2011, President Obama refreshed it and created a new body, the Center for Strategic Counterterrorism Communications (CSCC), to coordinate social media efforts to counter extremism.[71] Envisioned as "a war room in a political campaign," the CSCC had a budget of only around $5 to 6 million, sums that, as the *Washington Post* noted, "barely [register] on Washington's spending scale," and that are paltry compared with the Pentagon's $150 million annual budget for public relations initiatives, and the CIA's cumulative $250 million in spending "to monitor social media and other 'open' sources of intelligence." Given its budget, it was no surprise that the CSCC didn't make much impact. Although it attempted to take on the so-called Islamic State, its posts on Twitter "were often drowned out by the volume of Islamic State messages."[72] Even when not deluged, it was unclear whether the CSCC's tweets made any difference. In 2016, the CSCC was in turn replaced by a Global Engagement Center (GEC), charged with disseminating communications that "[undermine] the disinformation espoused by violent extremist groups, including ISIL and al-Qaeda, and that offers positive alternatives."[73] The GEC was again quite small by Washington standards: By late 2017, it had only about seventy staffers, with four foreign service officers.[74] In the end, the effort probably changed initials more than minds.

Even outside the GEC's work, government funding for CVE programming was quite meager. According to the CSIS CVE Commission Report, "State and USAID had roughly $100 million to $150 million in FY 2016 for CVE programming and staffing," and total "soft power" CVE spending equaled "roughly 1/10th of 1 percent of the resources dedicated to military, law enforcement, and intelligence efforts to combat terrorism."[75] As of 2016, only about *.0138 percent* of money spent fighting the so-called Islamic State had been spent on "soft power" (that is, nonmilitary) measures.[76] Even CVE community grants initially created during the Obama administration have been channeled by the Trump administration toward law enforcement programs (hard power) rather than softer, community-based programs.

BIRTH OF A DISCIPLINE: COUNTERING VIOLENT EXTREMISM

Ultimately, as enshrined in the national counterterrorism strategy of 2006, the Bush administration concluded that we would have to mobilize both "hard" and "soft" power against the extremists. As Zarate told me, "one of the defining features of that period of the Bush administration and the US government was the concentration on the fact that we were not going to solve this problem through military means alone. I think everyone understood that plainly. And we also understood that we were applying all elements of national power: law enforcement, diplomacy, economic, financial power, intelligence and military force."[77]

As Bryza remembers it, those officials interested in soft power had only a general sense that an "ideological struggle" was occurring *between* Muslims, as opposed to a more binary *Muslims versus Americans* viewpoint. Recognizing that the U.S. government couldn't fight extremism directly due to its lack of credibility among Muslims, we would need to take "an invisible hand approach," partnering "with people who think the way we believe we would want people to think, how we would empower them and how we'd work with other governments to make that happen." But, although the National Security Council staff developed a strategy with specific programmatic ideas, these ideas met stiff resistance in several parts of the State Department, and as a result the actual policy decisions remained vague. Should the government directly develop education programs that would head off extremist ideology? Should the government actively preserve local religious traditions that conflict with extremist narratives and make Muslims around the world aware of them? Should the United States promote ideas and practices, such as increased human rights, that radical preachers disparaged? In the absence of an accepted, overarching strategy, a dominant belief still persisted that "as long as we communicate and show them our country, the extremists will just melt and love our country."[78]

By 2005, intelligence reports increasingly suggested that the situation on the ground in Muslim communities in Europe was worsening. Foreign imams were entering Muslim communities and attracting youth to their anti-Western worldview. Muslims were experiencing a backlash in their daily lives that made them feel even more like "the other," and European governments weren't doing enough to address the increasing resentment.

A small, informal "brain trust" of interested officials at the National Security Council—again including Dan Fried, Elliott Abrams, Kurt Volker, Matt Bryza, myself, and a few others—began to think more strategically about how to push back against Al Qaeda's narrative and expose the group's faulty reasoning.* Yet almost any innovation, it seemed, was frowned upon. The culprit was conventional "big government" bureaucracy, with its culture of protocols, risk aversion, and careerist thinking. Some officials were protective of their budgets and didn't want to part with any of it to fund experimental initiatives. Others didn't want to depart from "business as usual" and take bold action. We knew we couldn't wait for a grassroots movement against extremism to arise within these communities—we had waited for four years since 9/11, and that hadn't happened in a significant way. In sum, we needed that "invisible hand" approach, whereby we partnered, in Bryza's words, "with people who think the way we believe we would want people to think." This approach would have us "go right at the things that

* At the time, the interagency was stuck in older policy frameworks, and Bryza was attempting to guide it through a process that would allow us to think differently about the ideological dimensions of the War on Terror.

[the extremists] hate, the things they see as a threat, and support [those things]."[79] Possible initiatives included increasing Muslim youth's awareness of Islamic history, giving a megaphone to younger Muslims who wished to speak out against extremism and to Muslim victims of terror, helping mothers speak out about the radicalization of their children, and many others.

Just as it seemed like key decision makers in the national security apparatus were seeing the wisdom of a newer, more sophisticated approach, *U.S. News & World Report* published a scathing article portraying our government's initiatives since 9/11 to battle extremist ideology as chaotic and dysfunctional. There was, the article asserted, "no one in charge, no national strategy, and a glaring lack of resources. From the CIA to the State Department, America's once formidable means of influencing its enemies and telling its story abroad had crumbled, along with the fall of communism." One former ambassador quoted in the article declared that, "in the battle of ideas, we unilaterally disarmed."[80] While much in the article was true, it didn't help our efforts. Key decision makers within the interagency grew defensive, and discussions became more political than ever. What appetite had existed to depart from traditional, Cold War–era ideological tactics evaporated.

In early 2006, the Danish cartoon crisis erupted, validating our worst fears. Rioting and other violence erupted in Muslim communities around the world, fueled by outrage at the publication in the Danish newspaper *Jylland-Posten* of cartoons lampooning the prophet Muhammad. Shock waves reverberated inside the interagency and the governments of our allies. None of us had seen ideas "go viral" before, rocketing around the world in a matter of days. It was a new reality we didn't quite understand.

Conversations within our brain trust, which now included Zarate, who had arrived the month after the *U.S. News* article, grew more urgent. What could we do to help local Muslims speaking out against extremism? Might we approach some of the larger Islamic organizations to help us undercut Al Qaeda's ideology? Could we create a special envoy to the Organization of the Islamic Conference, the international body of Muslim-majority states?* What role could American Muslims play on the national and global stages? We looked methodically at every lever at our disposal, steps we currently weren't taking to debunk extremist narratives. In particular, we took a hard look at every existing Muslim organization, considering how we might build stronger, more trusting relationships so as to enhance our influence on the local level.

In June 2006, I had an opportunity to engage firsthand with European Muslim communities.† Dan Smith, Karen Hughes's chief of staff, asked me to work with their bureau on a program that would allow us to bring American Muslims into the European conversation in a new way. As before, the administration sought to showcase real stories of regular Americans. Eager to play a constructive role, the administration wanted to broaden European Muslims' perspectives on the compatibility of Islam and democracy by exposing them to the reality that American Muslims were well-off and integrated. Hopefully, that American "model" could inspire new, more positive

* The Organization of the Islamic Conference (OIC), now called "Organization of Islamic Cooperation," was composed of Muslim-majority nations and was based in Jeddah, Saudi Arabia. America interacted with the OIC largely through the U.S. ambassador in Saudi Arabia, and members of our consulate in Jeddah were also charged with following the OIC's work and reporting back to Washington. At the time, the OIC was highly political and did not engage with the United States in consistently productive ways. Sensing an opportunity to build stronger ties, the United States sought to change this dynamic and use this partnership to pursue the following goals: (1) represent the interests of minority Muslim populations (Muslims were a growing minority population in America); (2) gain access to the OIC's deliberations (we thought that the OIC's statements condemning violence in the name of Islam could help us in the War on Terror); and (3) position ourselves to take advantage of future diplomatic opportunities. We thought that the unprecedented move of naming a full-time American diplomat as a U.S. envoy to the OIC would send a powerful signal of our interest in building stronger connections with Muslims around the world. After extremely careful consideration, the president believed it was important to send such an envoy. Other nations like the United Kingdom followed our example and sent envoys of their own in subsequent years. In the fall of 2018, a senior OIC official told me that many envoys—including Canada, Sweden, Australia, Italy, and Russia—had become a regular and important part of the consultation process.

† This was my second trip to Europe in a matter of months. Earlier, I had traveled with Dan Fried to meet with Danish government officials immediately after the cartoon crisis.

expectations among European Muslims for their futures. Unlike the failed "Shared Value" campaign, this new program had as its central pillar two-way dialogue between American Muslims and their European counterparts. The Citizen Dialogue Program, as the effort was known, brought together a small group of American Muslims sponsored by other State Department bureaus or by themselves and chosen by the public diplomacy bureau. These Muslims initially included a Lebanese American imam, an Iraqi American second-generation millennial, a Syrian American businessman from California, and myself. Touring Denmark, Germany, the Netherlands, and Belgium, we would meet with local Muslims, describing our own experiences in America and hearing their views.

The exchanges that took place weren't easy. I'll never forget our visit to a community center in Berlin. As the four of us sat perched on stools, a young German of Turkish background asked us bitterly if the U.S. government was paying us to speak to them. "Why are you coming here telling us how great life is in America? Can't you see how we have to live here? The Germans think we are filthy and will never accept us as German!" Throughout our trip, we heard similar expressions of anger about the treatment Muslim immigrants received in Europe. We also discovered that the Muslims we met knew little about American Muslims' experience. They thought that all Western Muslims were experiencing the same hatred and hostility. In fact, they weren't. The four of us could happily portray a very different, more welcoming climate prevailing in the United States. We did meet some European Muslims who were well assimilated, but the stark differences between our opportunities in America and Europe were clear to us all.

Back in Washington, National Security Advisor Stephen Hadley and Secretary of State Condoleezza Rice had come to understand that we could no longer wait for a lengthy bureaucratic process to work itself out before fighting the ideological war. With their blessing, my colleagues and I began pursuing the completely independent, more experimental policy approach I sketched out in the introduction. Led by Zarate, Abrams, and Fried, we considered new kinds of partnerships with civil society actors—arrangements that would let us provide support, while local NGOs and others were actually executing the tactics. We also explored how we might help to connect local individuals and groups with one another to fight extremism more effectively. At a time when the rest of the U.S. government was pouring money into Iraq, Afghanistan, and Pakistan, we looked to Europe's 44 million Muslims, seeing this population as a place where extremists might make future gains if no action were taken, and conversely, where a success with Muslims might prove a turning point in the global war of ideas.*

In 2007, I moved from my position in the White House to the State Department to become senior advisor to Dan Fried. My job: focus on policies bearing on Muslim communities in Europe. I sought to understand European Muslims better at the grassroots level and devise new ways of connecting with these communities. Nobody had ever had this job, and it put me on what within a decade would become the front lines of global terror. Because I had direct backing from both Hadley and Secretary Rice, not to mention the support of my direct boss Fried and close collaboration with Zarate and Abrams, I had unprecedented license to "operationalize" our ideas with a minimum of bureaucratic clearances and other hassles inside the State Department. I also had a license to experiment, and to fail if need be in the interests of maximizing creativity. Specifically, I could engage with bloggers, imams, activists, and others in

* As Ambassador Kurt Volker related to me in an interview on March 7, 2016, "President Bush was hosting the G-8 summit in 2004 and so we . . . made it the centerpiece set of initiatives at part of the G-8 . . . we started unpeeling and unpeeling a civil society component, a government component. . . ." Though the initiative initially showed promise with the Forum for the Future in Morocco, various creative partnerships between Middle East nations, as well as the G-8 and other civil society organizations, it eventually lost strength as the war in Iraq began to go badly. "The way I thought of it," said Ambassador Volker, "instead of the terrorists infecting these communities in Europe and giving us bigger problems, we can actually be working with them to infect the terrorists with open ideas."

Muslim communities who had never before interacted directly with the State Department.

Unsurprisingly, Washington resistance blossomed. Within the State Department, some found it outlandish to focus on Muslims in Europe as opposed to the Middle East. Certain colleagues suspected that I had a secret agenda and was working on President Bush's behalf to whitewash the Iraq War. Others criticized me for involving myself in "religious matters" that should be, they thought, beyond the government's purview. The reaction elsewhere was mixed. In Europe, some government officials and journalists perceived us as presumptuous and arrogant, lecturing them, in effect, about how to engage with "their" Muslims. European Muslims were more positive. Although they deplored American actions in Iraq and Afghanistan, they appreciated that the U.S. government was trying to listen to them at a time when their governments were not.

Proceeding with our approach, we conceived and created a number of small, pilot programs to engage "credible voices" within European Muslim communities to serve as activists on our behalf. These projects, some of which I will discuss later in this book, included efforts to build networks of Muslim change makers and to address issues of identity facing Muslim youth in Europe. I had been looking for "black holes," areas of need that the Europeans themselves were not addressing, and where we might be able to offer help. Our pilots were designed to fill these black holes as best we could.

CVE UNDER BUSH AND OBAMA

Astonishingly, on Capitol Hill, staffers judged the appeal of extremist ideology an insufficiently large problem to warrant allocating significant new funds—an argument that infuriated me then, and even more so in retrospect. As our elected officials saw it, Muslims "needed to figure out this problem for themselves," and there was no point in America getting involved. Within the executive branch, the vast majority of officials steered clear, grumbling that the only reason Muslims were becoming radicalized was Bush's policies. They didn't want to risk their careers by seeming to collaborate on CVE programs. Officials in two agencies in particular—the State Department and the United States Agency for International Development (USAID)—opposed CVE with great zeal. Although Secretary Rice and USAID administrator Andrew Natsios understood the need to puncture Al Qaeda's "us versus them" ideology, functionaries deep in the bureaucracy of these two bodies didn't. They fought my colleagues and me every step of the way as we sought to gain support for projects aimed at stopping recruitment.

Some USAID mission directors insisted that they were in the business of delivering economic and humanitarian aid, not helping in the War on Terror. Wary lest the rest of their work become "tainted," they resisted diverting precious resources from regular programming to prop up credible voices in local communities. In their minds, it was enough to build stronger communities by alleviating poverty and supporting education and women's rights. Such initiatives, they reasoned, would quell sympathy at the grass roots for extremist ideas.

Officials inside the State Department didn't like CVE for any number of reasons. First, Congress had earmarked no funds for it, so allocating money within the State Department's budget to counter extremism meant depriving other programs of funds. State Department officials also felt that their job was diplomacy or "soft power," and they equated CVE with counterterrorism—in other words, "hard power." They feared that if they asked embassies in Muslim-majority countries to work on CVE initiatives, they would come across in local communities as "targeting" Muslims. Indeed, governments in many Muslim-majority countries were claiming that they weren't seeing the spread of extremist ideology, and thus might regard CVE programs as insulting, even accusatory. The resulting alienation, officials feared, would prevent an already stretched State Department from making progress on other priorities, like stopping nuclear proliferation or protecting human rights. Finally, many State Department officials simply found CVE confusing. What kind of officer in an embassy—already deluged with an assortment of tasks—would do CVE, and how on earth would he or she measure success? None of this was clear.

If CVE had gained traction inside the State Department, the approach might have worked like this: Each of the State Department's regional bureaus would have appointed a liaison responsible for designing and building credible voices and networks of likeminded thinkers in its region. The State Department would have requested much more money for CVE, and would have lobbied for it more aggressively. Speeches by senior State officials would have explicitly pressed for more money for the building of grassroots programs, and bilateral and multilateral discussions would have included serious strategies for making CVE stick. Finally, each embassy would have been allocated personnel and additional funds to build these programs.

Alas, none of these actions materialized. It is true that some U.S. ambassadors in European countries did respond well. These officials deserve special recognition and praise because they engaged with CVE initiatives without receiving any extra money or staff. Often, in private conversations, these colleagues would describe to me how hard it could be to convince their teams to take time away from other priorities. They made headway, they said, by avoiding the term "CVE," and instead referring to the endeavor as simple "engagement" with Muslim communities. I also encountered many outstanding foreign service officers and local hires who went to great lengths to convince colleagues to share knowledge and to engage themselves with local Muslims. Some used money in their own budgets to help with my projects. (One foreign service officer even used her annual leave to travel with me into local Muslim communities to meet with potential partners.)

Overall, furthering CVE in the face of entrenched resistance was torturous. Still, my colleagues and I stuck with it. By the time of President Obama's election in 2008, we understood quite well the cultural and psychological factors that made youth vulnerable to recruitment online and offline (covered in depth in later chapters). The concept of CVE had begun to penetrate into regional bureaus at State and elements of the Department of Defense that had initially bypassed it in favor of "hard power" solutions. But most policy makers still hadn't backed these kinds of experiments, unable to envision how we could develop organic, local voices that could push back against Al Qaeda's ideology. Furthermore, officials believed that ideological tensions would naturally dissipate now that Bush was out of the equation and a more "Muslim-friendly" president had taken office. Without broad support, we couldn't obtain more than token funding to push forward CVE initiatives.

Obama himself was thought of as someone who understood Muslims. His own father was Muslim, and his presidential campaign had made much of the fact that he had spent part of his youth in Indonesia, the world's largest Muslim-majority nation. Once in office, his policies seemed to bear out the prevailing interpretation. Obama took steps to engage with Muslims, seeking to "win hearts and minds" and forge a "new beginning" in America's relations with Muslims, most notably in his June 2009 "Cairo Speech." As the thinking went, such grand gestures backed by policy changes and a spirit of constructive listening would finally solve our ongoing "image problems" with Muslims. Administration officials spoke not of CVE but of "mutual interest and mutual respect."

During the first two years of Obama's administration, we seemed headed in the right direction, building considerable goodwill with Muslim communities. As I've related, I helped take the

CVE framework I had deployed in Europe and expand it to other countries around the world. Still, our efforts were tiny compared with the magnitude of the challenges we faced, and administration officials weren't always clear on the basic meaning of CVE. Regular briefings, interagency meetings, and discussion papers defined CVE well enough, but each department or agency spun the ideological fight to fit into its own mandate. Like certain members of the Bush administration, some Obama administration officials also thought CVE was about "brand America" and "winning hearts and minds." They didn't understand the identity crisis that had taken shape within Muslim communities, and they therefore didn't see CVE as a way of addressing that crisis. As I noted in the introduction, because CVE had been developed under President Bush, Obama administration officials tended to avoid it, assuming that it had to be bad policy. While embassies were working with local NGOs, faith leaders, and a handful of organizations specifically dedicated to CVE, they weren't taking steps like building large networks, developing and mobilizing youth leaders, or aggressively promoting the idea of Islam's traditional diversity.

Our CVE efforts were also frequently thwarted by a lack of curiosity and a superficial approach to the problem. On one occasion, I asked a senior Obama aide if I should brief her on CVE. "What's CVE?" she asked. I told the president himself that I had been in forty countries and wanted to share disturbing trends I had uncovered, and he directed, "Come brief me." The meeting never happened. Most strikingly, Obama's emphasis on engaging with Muslims in a "friendly" way led to a ludicrous series of senior personnel appointments. In one instance, Obama's team picked a person for a key position who had not studied the issues, had no experience at the community level, and had been known to be disrespectful to Muslims. He "looked the part"—he had dark skin, hair, and eyes—but that was about it.

Although our thinking and our actual innovations significantly outpaced those of our European allies, our lack of knowledge at top levels of government all too often translated into bad policies. Some of the administration's new appointees were content to put out images of women with headscarves or to quote a verse from the Qur'an to show how "sensitive" we were to Muslim concerns. Predictably, we made little headway against recruiting.

By Obama's second term, the rise of violent extremism became too grave to ignore. The so-called Islamic State had emerged on the world stage—seemingly out of nowhere, people thought*—and was growing uncontrollably, recruiting new members in Europe, America, the Middle East, Australia, and elsewhere. Despite having appreciated the appeal of violent ideology for years at this point, we were caught off guard. We simply could not keep up with the English-language magazines, Instagram appeals, YouTube videos, or hashtag wars on Twitter.

Even as the first American-born citizens turned up in the Middle East to fight for the so-called Islamic State, the U.S. government still didn't mount a respectable CVE effort, just the appearance of one. With recruitment now receiving media attention, the State Department, USAID, Department of Homeland Security, and Department of Defense all scrambled to get a piece of the action. Layers of bureaucracy arose around CVE—oversight bodies, dozens of conferences and regional summits, white papers, countless unproductive meetings of interagency task forces and working groups. Few saw the irony, but I did. Precious little money had been spent to date on actual CVE programs. (Domestically, the organ of the Department of Homeland Security charged with coordinating with members of local Muslim communities received only $10 million in funding

* If we had actually been paying attention to the signs and listening closely to what was taking place in Muslim communities, we would have predicted the so-called Islamic State's rise. Instead, experts were looking at extremism in a fragmented way. They were paying attention to specific countries or regions, and they weren't looking for patterns and "connecting the dots" globally. As I'll explore later, it's precisely this comprehensive view we need to cultivate in order to drive our policy.

for fiscal year 2016 allocated to grant programs, as compared with billions in antiterror funding allocated to the FBI and TSA. A similar situation existed internationally.)[81] With recruitment now a hot issue, you might have thought the government would scale up CVE pilot programs that had proved successful, but it didn't, nor was it investing in the thousands of Muslim entrepreneurs, activists, and other thought leaders who had participated in our networks, nor did it put money into research, or into creating and launching new programs, nor did it design a comprehensive strategy. Instead it squandered millions on overhead costs. To show the world that we were taking action to stanch recruiting, we put on high-profile events designed to showcase its CVE prowess. Once again, it was all a big advertising campaign.

What real action there was didn't have much of an impact. In 2016, the Obama administration updated yet again the idea of a single, centralized entity to handle messaging, establishing the Global Engagement Center (GEC), described earlier. A "command center" charged with fighting the war of ideas online, the GEC seemed like a tremendous asset. If we cannily responded to the so-called Islamic State propaganda in the viral world, the thinking went, we would stop recruitment. But we had long ago realized that CVE was far more than a messaging war. It had to unfold across government, including our embassies around the world as well as departments that touch local communities in our homeland. If CVE wasn't expansive and coordinated, it wouldn't work. As of this writing, the GEC has suffered one PR disaster after another, suffocated by leadership that, with a couple of exceptions, has been ill-equipped for the job.

Meanwhile, legions of interested diplomats and contractors have flocked to the CVE effort. With each new attack, the professional opportunities for those connected to the Obama administration expanded. CVE became the "flavor of the month," and a whole industry cropped up around it, including massive initiatives that were designed to convey gravitas but that accomplished very little.* Officials who once ran from CVE now outdid one another to show that they were "doing CVE." So-called experts appeared everywhere, including on panels at conferences and as commentators on television. Most never worked with Muslim communities at the grass roots to build authentic programs. Can you imagine what would happen if Washington had people working on emergency response, cybersecurity, or Ebola "just because" it seemed like a nice career move? That's exactly what happened with CVE.

In 2016, the Center for Strategic and International Studies issued a "new comprehensive strategy for countering violent extremism." The bipartisan report, on which I advised and served as a commissioner, listed the "conceptual challenges" that have hamstrung U.S. administrations in their CVE policies. Policy makers "underestimated the allure of violent extremism"; they "failed to provide leadership and vision"; they struggled to tackle extremism without "alienating Muslims"; and they failed to see it as a "global, generational struggle." Further, the report notes that CVE practitioners themselves haven't agreed on the basic definition of the field, much less on best-practice tactics and strategies; that scholars are still mapping out the radicalization process in its specifics, as well as strategies for countering it; and that "civil society actors are unclear" about whether or how they might solve the problem.[82] Much as we might want, we can't pin CVE's failure to date on any one administration, branch of government, government official, department, government process, or policy decision. We can't—nor should we—even pin CVE's failure on the United States exclusively. Our allies in Europe, the Middle East, and elsewhere also came up short in fighting extremism (and arguably, their responsibility for their own

* For example, the Global Community Engagement and Resilience Fund was a public-private partnership that was supposed to provide grant monies to grassroots programs. Months of work in advocacy for the program resulted, as of 2016, in broad-based support, which included twelve governments, $30 million in funding, a large bureaucracy, and no private sector partners.

communities of Muslims exceeds the U.S. government's). Overall, it has been a system-wide failure, one fed by many factors, personalities, and circumstances, and producing the gravest of consequences.

EXTREMISTS ASCENDANT

Some people love what's happened to CVE: the terrorists. The armies we're supporting in Iraq and Syria have eaten into so-called Islamic State–controlled territory, and such battlefield setbacks coupled with better policing has dramatically slowed the flow of new recruits into the so-called caliphate. Yet the extremists are still winning the war of ideas, gaining both sympathizers and soldiers. Sympathizers are bad enough, as they help nurture, fund, and perpetuate the ideology, allowing the virus to spread further. But so-called Islamic State and affiliated groups are also continuing to convince young people around the world to leave their homes and join the so-called caliphate in Iraq and Syria, albeit in smaller numbers, and to conduct attacks on soft targets at home, such as the one on the Ariana Grande concert in Manchester, United Kingdom. They are further winning in the sense that they have succeeded in branding themselves and creating a forceful movement on the ground.

As a government official once told me, "Al Qaeda is the dissertation. ISIS is the sound bite." What this means is that Al Qaeda laid down the basic ideological framework for extremists, but so-called Islamic State has taken it to the next level, operationalizing the ideology, bringing it to the masses via social media, making it a part of pop culture in Muslim communities, mobilizing Muslim youth on a mass scale, creating a viable global movement. The so-called Islamic State's propaganda machine is saturating the media in real time, speaking in a sophisticated visual language that millennials and their younger cohort, Generation Z, understand and appreciate. This machine is appropriating the latest platforms and tactics as

A sample meme.

soon as they become available. As for cultural memes, they've got them in spades:

Memes seamlessly connect violent "jihad" to global youth culture. Countless others are circulating right now on the Internet, and they are joined by *Dabiq,* the so-called Islamic State's magazine; millions of social media messages (some 90,000 per day, according to one 2015 estimate)[83] put out across tens of thousands of Twitter accounts; podcasts; blogs; and other communications aimed at recruiting youth. In comparison, only about two hundred people in the U.S. government were fighting back against this onslaught online.[84]

These communications are stunningly effective. It is estimated that more than 40,000 foreigners from over 110 countries traveled to

Iraq and Syria to join the so-called Islamic State.[85] Although recruitment of so-called Islamic State soldiers across the West dwindled in 2016, this likely represented a pyrrhic victory, since so-called Islamic State had begun encouraging sympathizers to stay home and engage in "lone wolf-style" atrocities. As a Europol report noted, so-called Islamic State's "involvement with potential violent jihadists in the West seems to be shifting from 'training' to 'coaching' primarily self-taught operatives."[86] When a twenty-four-year-old Canadian man, Aaron Driver, sought to detonate a car bomb in August 2016 in Ontario, he cited this very motivation. As Canadian journalist Stewart Bell has remarked, "Europe is concerned that as ISIL continues to suffer battlefield losses, foreign fighters will return to their home countries, bring wives and children who have also been radicalized."[87]

In the United States, the extremist threat has shown few signs of receding. According to the George Washington University's Program on Extremism, every American state harbored ongoing extremism activity. As of November 2016, a total of "111 individuals have been charged in the U.S. with offenses related to the Islamic State (also known as IS, ISIS, and ISIL)—since the first arrests in March 2014."[88] Significantly, fewer than half of these had tried to travel abroad to join the so-called Islamic State, and almost one-third (30 percent) "were accused of being involved in plots to carry out attacks on U.S. soil."[89] The so-called Islamic State was hardly the only inspiration for extremist activity. Since 2007, "more than 25 Somali-Americans left to train to join al-Shabaab," the Somali branch of Al Qaeda.[90] And a good portion of extremist activity wasn't inspired by or related to any particular group. "While group affiliation matters," one research report noted, "the draw of the . . . ideology that al-Qaeda, IS, and other like-minded groups adhere to is equally important when analyzing the jihadist threat to America."[91]

A month after the GWU report, the incoming director of the United Kingdom's MI6 intelligence agency proclaimed terrorism the "most immediate" threat to the country, and noted that the scale of the threat was "unprecedented."[92] When I interviewed Juan Zarate in January 2016, he was very clear: "We're not going to win it . . . as we're currently configured. There's no question in my mind that we are underresourced, not as well organized as we should be, and lack the mechanisms to create meaningful partnerships in the ideological domain." Zarate went on: "There will be a son of Daesh that's probably going to be just as dangerous and more virulent. The ideology is going to continue to adapt just like a virus. And absent getting this right in the environment, creating the antibodies, we are in for a long slog."[93]

When Donald Trump was elected president in November 2016, the so called Islamic State–affiliated media outfit al-Minbar Jihadi didn't miss a beat. "Rejoice with support from Allah," the network proclaimed. "Trump's win of the American Presidency will bring hostility of Muslims against America as a result of his reckless actions, which show the overt and hidden hatred against them."[94] Since then, Trump's hard stance against "radical Islamic terrorists" has seemed to play into the so-called Islamic State's own narrative, and beyond the terrorist group's wildest imagination. Trump's muted responses to acts of terror against Muslims has been duly noted, both in the United States and abroad. In May 2017, when two Americans in Oregon were killed defending a person who appeared to be attacked because of her Muslim faith, a firestorm erupted because the president did not condemn the violence.

As grim as these assessments may sound, we can derive an optimistic message from CVE's checkered history to date. We might have failed to mobilize a coherent and effect CVE strategy, but we can still mount one now. If we do—if we go "all in" against extremist recruiting, committing sufficient financial resources, and staying focused—we stand to make rapid gains. Extremist ideology is not an insurmountable problem. We have everything we need to contain it. What we've lacked is the will to do CVE right, as well as clarity about the nature of the underlying problem. With these two elements in place, we'll arrive at the right package of policy solutions, and we'll see them through to execution.

Extremists are not nearly the evil geniuses they appear to be. They are merely *competent,* and driven. We don't need to be geniuses, either. If we are merely competent and driven, our far superior resources will lead us to victory—not in a hundred years or fifty, but in as little as ten. To borrow a medical metaphor, we won't eradicate the cancer or achieve a full remission in ten years. But we'll shrink it so dramatically that it threatens neither the health of the organism or its well-being. I'm not alone in thinking this, either. As Matt Bryza has told me, "We're going to have to live for decades with terror in our midst, as the UK did with the IRA for years. It's going to be scary. But the ISIS caliphate will be gone and we'll have this slow burn for a long time. If we stay awake to these ideological challenges and then do more than just fight violence, I'm actually optimistic."

CHAPTER TWO

MILLENNIALS ADRIFT

In 2006, when I traveled to Europe as part of the Citizen Dialogue program, I had an opportunity to meet with Danish Muslims in Copenhagen. I was thrilled to be there, and eager to learn. I hadn't spent much time in Europe before—just a stint in France during my junior year in high school, and a college summer spent studying International Law at Trinity College, Oxford. Neither experience had exposed me to Western Europe's large Muslim population. I also hadn't thought much about issues involving immigrants, assimilation, and what it was like for Muslims to live as minorities. Although my family had emigrated to the United States from India, I had never felt the need to defend my religion or ethnicity while growing up in Massachusetts during the 1970s and 1980s, nor did I ever feel "different" or marginalized.

On this trip to Copenhagen, I was in for quite an education. At one of our conversations, held in an old mansion's elegant salon with high ceilings, floor-to-ceiling panels, and elaborate crown moldings, about fifty teens sat chatting with one another, waiting for the program to begin. I circulated among them, introducing myself and engaging in friendly conversation—they all spoke English. Then I strolled to the front of the room and sat beside an American Muslim leader, Imam Talal Eid,* who happened to have been my local imam at a mosque in Quincy, Massachusetts, during my childhood. Two other Americans were with us, a Syrian American businessman and a recent Harvard undergraduate and Iraqi American who worked as a staffer at State.

The room fell silent as we began the program and invited the teens to ask questions about what it was like to live as a Muslim in America. Amid nervous laughter, several hands shot up. The teens peppered me with questions: As a Muslim, did I feel uncomfortable living in the United States? Could I practice my religion freely? How could the United States allow a Muslim to serve at the White House? Did I face discrimination? Were Muslims in America well-off financially? Were there mosques?

As I answered these questions, the teens listened attentively and respectfully. One girl sitting perched near a windowsill raised her hand. She wore jeans, a white T-shirt, sneakers, and a dark blue cardigan sweater. "I'm Sanam," she said.[1] "I need to ask you something, but my English is not very good." She paused and said something in Danish to her friend.

I smiled at her. "That's no problem. Please do not worry."

She paused, pushed her long black hair behind her shoulders, and then said, "My imam says I'm not a Muslim. I don't know what I am then."

The room fell silent.

"What do you mean?" I asked.

She pointed to her clothing and gave me a knowing smile. "Well, look at me."

Everyone in the room looked at her.

---

* In 2007, President George W. Bush appointed Eid to the U.S. Commission on International Religious Freedom, making him the first imam ever to serve on the commission.

"I'm sorry," I said, "I don't understand."

"Look at me," she said again, a bit defiantly.

I was completely befuddled. I had no idea what she was talking about. "I'm really sorry, could you explain?"

Again, she gestured toward her clothing. "*Look* at me. My imam tells me that if I dress like this, I'm not Muslim."

I looked over at Imam Eid, who chuckled.

"He said my jeans are not Islamic. He said I should wear Moroccan clothing."

I asked her about her imam. It turned out he was from a small village in Morocco, had recently arrived in Europe, and barely spoke Danish (he spoke with her in Arabic).

"How did you respond to him?" I asked.

Her lips quivered. "I didn't know what to say. I . . . I can't understand how to behave. How to be Muslim. He is older than my parents, and he tells us all to keep to our traditions. I feel like I do not belong anywhere. How am I supposed to be Muslim if my imam tells me I'm not? My friends tell me not to listen to him, but my family says I must listen to him because he is the imam. But he doesn't understand. My friends are Danish. And I'm Danish, too."

I nodded, along with everyone else in the room. We had all been taken by her sincerity and honesty.

She took a deep breath to compose herself. Managing a polite smile, she asked, "If I don't listen to him, does that mean I am not a real Muslim?"

I looked over at her friend, who put her arm on her shoulder. Another teen behind her whispered supportively in her ear.

Imam Eid thanked Sanam for sharing her story. "I don't want to disrespect your imam," he said. "I also do not have the right to tell you what to do. We are here as visitors to your country to talk with you. But, I do know something about this subject, because I myself have experienced this, because youth ask me these same questions all the time. You need to live in the society you are in and adapt to its culture. You are a Danish Muslim and only you can define what that means. You don't need to dress the way people dress in that Moroccan village to be Muslim."

At this, tears streamed down her face, while the other kids in the room erupted in spontaneous applause.

I've had hundreds of conversations like this, with Muslim kids of diverse cultures, languages, and socioeconomic backgrounds. Consistently, these conversations have illuminated the profound pain and uncertainty young Muslims experience around their religion. Muslim kids began feeling adrift after 9/11, when every news headline seemed to contain an unpleasant or negative message about their religion. Can you imagine what it must have felt like to grow up perceiving that you were under constant suspicion not because of anything you personally said or did, but because of your name, the way you looked, or your ethnic background? For a generation of Muslim youth, global issues over which they had no control were not abstract or distant. They impinged directly on their personal, everyday experience. Today, they still do. With terrorist attacks in Europe, the United States, and elsewhere perpetually in the news, Muslim youth feel as marginalized as ever—singled out, feared, maligned.

Muslims in the West and in some other parts of the world are also living as immigrants, a status that exposes them to further distrust and gives them the sense of being unwanted "others." But whether they are immigrants or native born, Muslim millennials become easy fodder for extremists simply by virtue of their uncertainty about their religion and how to square it with modern life. Extremists lure in youth with promises of a clear identity and a sense of purpose and belonging. They ask youth to embrace a seemingly authentic religious identity. All of a sudden, youth experience a new sense of certainty about who they are, and they feel like they fit in. Whereas before they felt confused and conflicted, now they feel powerful, ascendant. They have a mission and are driven to fulfill it.

Often, government policy makers, global television and cable news outlets, and Hollywood have ignored the identity crisis among Muslims, perceiving the spread of extremist ideology as a by-product of something more fundamental—poverty, lack of education, lack of hope, or a fight within Islam. However, as Professor John G. Horgan, a terrorism researcher and psychologist at Georgia State University, has noted, "Terrorism today involves men, women and children from all walks of life, all socioeconomic backgrounds and all levels of religiosity and ideological commitment." It follows, then, that if we want to understand terrorist recruiting, we need to look beyond the more easily quantifiable categories—something relatively few scholars have attempted. As Horgan (one of the few who have investigated this dimension) relates, "there is so much we don't know about terrorist psychology. For too long, psychologists haven't really tackled the question of terrorism seriously."[2]

My grassroots-level experience points clearly and more specifically to an identity crisis as the root cause of extremism's spread. For Muslim millennials growing up post-9/11, the central question has become, "What does it mean to be a Muslim?" And for far too many, the most appealing answers have come from extremist sources. Economic and political factors certainly feed into recruitment, increasing the odds that some individuals will join the extremist fight. Yet these factors aren't the most basic or profound cause—the identity crisis is.

EUROPEAN MUSLIMS IN TROUBLE

I only came to appreciate the importance of the identity crisis affecting Muslim millennials because of the unusual opportunities I had to visit diverse Muslim communities, first in Europe in 2007 and 2008 and afterward around the world. This travel, conducted over an eight-year period, afforded me a unique vantage point on the experiences, emotions, and perspectives of thousands of Muslim youth. Rather than working on a specific country or region, as many people within our government do, I was tasked with understanding a particular demographic stretching across communities, languages, and cultures. I also wasn't rooted in a specific discipline, such as human rights or economic policy, and I had no particular assumptions about what I was seeing.

My direct observation of Muslim youth started in the wake of the 2006 Danish cartoon crisis. The cartoons' original publication in September 2005 by the newspaper *Jyllands-Posten* sparked protests among Danish Muslims, but Western governments took little notice, regarding this as a fairly standard battle over freedom of speech within Danish society. The situation changed a few months later in January 2006 when the Norwegian magazine *Magazinet* republished the cartoons. By the end of that month, protests had erupted across the Middle East, and European countries bolstered security at their embassies in the region.* Many Middle Eastern countries condemned Denmark and boycotted Danish goods.[3] In a show of solidarity with their Scandinavian counterparts, other European newspapers took the bold step of reprinting the cartoons. In Friday sermons in Saudi Arabia and other Muslim-majority countries, imams railed against the cartoons and urged confrontation.[4]

The speed with which these protests spread was stunning. Social media was new—we had Facebook, but not Twitter, Snapchat, Instagram, or today's other popular platforms. In this context, seasoned American officials had not imagined that dissent could spread so quickly—that something that happened in Copenhagen could have a rapid and direct impact on a life in Kabul. And yet, this was happening. By early February, protestors were marching and burning

* Security efforts increased following the kidnapping of a German national in Nablus, a city in the West Bank. See Ewen MacAskill, Sandra Laville, and Luke Harding, "Cartoon Controversy Spreads Throughout Muslim World," *Guardian*, September 4, 2006, https://www.theguardian.com/world/2006/feb/04/muhammadcartoons.pressandpublishing.

Danish flags in Jakarta, "attacking the Danish and Norwegian embassies in Tehran," rioting in Libya, and attacking a NATO base in Maymana, Afghanistan.[5]

It wasn't clear if a particular person or group was orchestrating the grassroots response on the part of Muslim populations, or if the response amounted to an organic and spontaneous reaction. But either way, many Muslims were incensed not merely by the publication of cartoons deemed insulting to the prophet Muhammad, to Islam, and to Muslims, but by the Danish government's initial refusal to take action and even to meet with diplomats from Muslim-majority countries about the controversy.[6] The cartoon crisis prompted violent threats against staff at *Jyllands-Posten,* attacks on churches, and at least two hundred deaths worldwide. Denmark's total exports fell by more than 15 percent for a period of months thanks to the economic boycotts.[7]

Inside the White House, officials were alarmed at the intensity of anti-Western sentiment sparked by the cartoons, viewing it as a threat to our troops in Afghanistan and our interests around the world. Like the Danes, Germans, British, and others, our government wondered what precisely was happening—why this cartoon, and why now? Was Al Qaeda stoking Muslim hostility? If not them, who? We hoped the uproar would die down, but this was uncharted territory. The Danes had long been known for their humanitarian and development efforts—how could this be happening *to them*?

In a meeting on the sixth floor of the State Department in the days after the crisis, Dan Fried, assistant secretary of state for European and Eurasian affairs, and other senior diplomats, including Ambassador Adam Ereli, the deputy spokesman for the U.S. Department of State, discussed a variety of implications, including diplomatic security at our embassies and the consequences for free speech. Those present also discussed how to show respect to nations outraged by caricatures of the prophet Muhammad, as well as what statements Secretary of State Rice might make or actions the U.S.

government might take to help countries across Europe, starting with Denmark. Fried decided to travel to Denmark to offer our assistance and sympathy and to share what some in our government were thinking about Muslim engagement. Specifically, he wanted to suggest ideas for how the Danes could mobilize local Muslim voices to counter impressions of Western hostility to Islam. Dan asked me to come along on the trip and share my work. Initially limited to Denmark, the trip was eventually expanded to include stops in Belgium and the Netherlands. Though we had gone to impart our own insights, the experience marked a turning point in the way the U.S. government looked at the issue of Muslims in Europe.

At the time, I was a director at the National Security Council working on Muslim engagement in the Near East and North African Affairs Directorate, reporting to Elliott Abrams. There was no one at the Department of State doing CVE at this time. Collaborating with others in the State, Treasury, Homeland Security, and Commerce Departments as well as at the Justice Department, I was charged with helping the United States government improve its outreach with Muslim communities working across agencies and departments. Initially, we had sought to make sure that the U.S. government "did no harm" in how it spoke to and engaged with Muslims. Afterward, reviewing what kinds of outreach were then underway, and hearing complaints from American Muslims that the U.S. government wasn't listening to them, we went further, organizing events at home and abroad, ranging from *Iftars* hosted by various departments, agencies, and embassies to more substantive policy roundtables with Muslims. The latter especially allowed Muslims to share their concerns as well as their ideas on how best to stop Al Qaeda's ideology from spreading. Reaching out to established American Muslim organizations, start-up NGOs, and individuals who were stepping up in their communities to combat extremism, I found that these actors sought to talk to their government in respectful ways, and on topics that went far beyond law enforcement. They wanted to broadcast Islam's diversity, countering the widespread conflation of "Muslim" and "Arab" in the minds of Americans.* While we were far from successful in such outreach, we were certainly further along than anyone else, so I hoped that in meeting with the Danes I could convey the importance of methodically opening channels of communication with Muslim communities.

Arriving in Denmark, we met with a serious-looking senior official who was accompanied by several others in the foreign ministry. The official greeted Dan as an old friend and offered me a curious but polite smile. The two, and our ambassador to Denmark, James P. Cain, launched into conversation, with Dan empathizing with the Danes and also underscoring the importance of freedom of speech. The tone of the meeting was extremely grave—the government official quite upset. "What have we done?" he asked us. "We've never done anything to deserve this. We give aid all over the world. We've been so good to Muslims everywhere."

The duo considered security questions and the broader impact of the cartoon crisis on European Muslims' receptivity to extremist ideology. The official asked me what we had been doing at the NSC since 9/11 to engage Muslims, and in particular why President Bush was leading on this. Did I feel confident that reaching out and engaging with Muslims was the right approach? What, he wondered, were American Muslims saying about the U.S. government's efforts to work with them to fight Al Qaeda in particular? Were American Muslims reacting to the Danish cartoon the way European Muslims

* To further build connections with Muslim communities, we had planned a large White House summit for American Muslims, scheduled to take place in 2006. For the first time, senior leaders from a number of government agencies would have a chance to hear a diversity of American Muslim perspectives and engage in substantive dialogue. Despite considerable effort on our part, the event was canceled due to a carefully constructed political play by a member of the American Muslim diaspora. The summit required months of bipartisan planning and efforts to solicit buy-in. By making this about politics, this individual sabotaged a tremendous, unprecedented opportunity for American Muslims to visit the White House and meet with high-level officials. Four cabinet members would have attended, as well as half a dozen other senior officials in the White House and across the interagency.

were? And how did I know that local Muslim leaders could in fact serve as helpful partners in the effort to stop extremism?

Fielding these questions, I found myself wondering how welcome Danish Muslims actually felt living in Denmark. Although the Danish government provided generous development aid to Muslim-majority countries, the way this official was speaking gave me pause.* The cartoon crisis was, quite understandably, a traumatic event. He portrayed the Danes as a minority being persecuted by Muslims worldwide, remarking, "Now I know what the Jews felt like in Europe during World War Two." Yet he kept referring to Muslims as "them": "We've welcomed them in," "we've given them a good life." His discourse seemed to keep Muslims at a distance. It identified them as the "other," a kind of alien species.

Despite my lack of experience with Europe or its Muslims, it was clear to me that something significant was happening here. That belief deepened later in the trip as we visited our embassy in Belgium. Our ambassador there, Tom Korologos, organized a discussion about the cartoon crisis with a group of local Muslims—about twenty of them, young and old, men and women. As we gathered around a long, polished dining room table in Korologos's residence, a Muslim of Pakistani descent raised his hand and said something that hit me hard. "How do you expect us to live here? God is dead here. *God is dead.*" I was stunned. Growing up in the United States, I had never come close to thinking or feeling such a thing, nor had I ever heard anyone else make such statements. The entire table turned to look at him, and many nodded their heads in agreement. I remember looking at Dan wondering how in the world the United States could even begin to get inside of these issues. Dan responded kindly to the man, asking him: "Do you feel like you can be a Muslim here?"

---

* Denmark now ranks among the best examples of a country that has been proactive and engaged vis-à-vis CVE, having invested substantial financial and political resources in programs that show great promise.

"We have no choice," the man responded. "We do our best. But we are not at ease here."

These initial encounters got me thinking more deeply about the experience of Muslims in Europe—how emotionally charged their perceptions of themselves and the West were, and how these perceptions were quite possibly being transformed before our eyes. But I hadn't yet connected it to youth or perceived it to be a generational phenomenon. That happened months later, when I returned to Belgium to participate in a two-day conference about the West's engagement with Islam.

I was sitting again in the living room of Ambassador Korologos's residence with a group of Muslim youth, talking about what it was like to grow up Muslim in Europe. These young people had all been born and raised in Belgium to immigrant parents. The young men and women were dressed in Western clothing. Some of the women covered their hair, while others didn't. Many of them expressed surprise that the United States had invited them to the embassy to hear about their experiences. All, however, were excited to talk about being Muslim in Belgium. As one young man said to me, "You can't really succeed here if you're an immigrant. Nobody in power is Muslim. We have no role models to aspire to. People think of us as second-class citizens. We just don't really have a chance to be successful here because we are always different." Another man described the sense of cultural isolation he felt, the sense that he and his cohort were floating in space. "We don't really know a lot about our home countries. We've just learned about it from our parents. We don't have a good sense about our religion. Actually, I'm a little ashamed of being Muslim."

The other young people nodded their heads at statements like these, adding similar reflections. In addition, they all seemed convinced that America was "at war" with Islam. They shared their belief that our country pursued anti-Muslim policies, most notably as regards our strong ties with Israel. "How is it possible for Muslims to be Muslim in America?" they asked me. They couldn't conceive of it. Were we allowed to pray? Where were the mosques? Could Americans wear clothing that covered their heads if they wanted to? What happened to Muslims if they were discriminated against? Having learned about America online, and from Hollywood movies, popular music, and CNN, as well as from parents and religious teachers, they assumed all Muslims must experience discrimination in America. They certainly couldn't have imagined that the U.S. government would have allowed a Muslim like myself to represent our country.

Listening to these young people, I was struck by how open European Muslims were to speaking with representatives of the American government. As I saw it, their ability to share seemed especially poignant given that their own governments had, in their view, never tried to solicit their opinions. It was a strange situation, because while the country they viewed as being at war with them was actually reaching out, many European governments were retrenching around the issue of free speech and immigration.

The following year, 2007, I went to work for Dan at the State Department. Coordinating with our embassies, I held hundreds of meetings just like the ones in Belgium and Copenhagen. Wherever I went, I had largely the same conversations. In Helsinki, Finland, for instance, I spoke with a group of Somali youth who had recently immigrated and who had been hosted by an NGO called International Cultural Center Caisa.* Having learned to speak Finnish, they told me that they felt far removed from Somalia. They had taken to joking that the very idea of sun and sand seemed alien to them. Finland was their home. And yet they didn't feel they truly belonged. Wherever they went, people noticed their skin color and let them know—

* "Caisa is a cultural center for art, people and ideas from around the world. We build the international future of Helsinki together with our partners with performances, meetings and networks as building blocks. Caisa's heart beats for everyone—in the center of Helsinki." "Caisa Moves," accessed April 7, 2018, http://www.caisa.fi/en/frontpage.

sometimes quite directly—that they weren't Finnish. So, who were they? These youth felt frustrated and confused.

As far as Muslims were concerned, I noticed that the experience of an identity crisis was primarily relegated to millennials. In Paris, Frankfurt, Rome, and Barcelona, many of the millennials with whom I spoke echoed a sense of disillusionment with Western society. More than that, they weren't sure what to think about their identities. Young Muslims heard imams from foreign countries like Turkey, Egypt, and Saudi Arabia say that the Europe where they lived was not their home, and that they should approach non-Muslims cautiously. Were these imams right? What was the "correct" way of living as a Muslim? How did that square with living in their particular European country? Could they form friendships with non-Muslim kids? Could they sit at the same table if non-Muslim peers were drinking beer (traditionally, Islamic practice forbids the drinking of alcoholic beverages)? How in particular were they supposed to reconcile religion with the demands of modernity? What religious beliefs were they supposed to hold? Did they have to fast during Ramadan even if they had exams? And how were they supposed to behave politically? Could they date non-Muslims? Would they still go to heaven if they did? These were just some of the many, tormented questions about daily life with which these kids were struggling.

As my travels continued, I found that this identity crisis was by no means limited to Muslims. Native-born Europeans were debating a range of identity-related issues, such as their shared value of freedom of speech, what it meant to be part of the European Union, the history and meaning of the Holocaust, and how to assimilate immigrants into the public schools. Europeans' uncertainty about identity was extremely personal. While visiting an Italian church, I met an old man who told me with disdain that as the population of "real" Italians shrank, the immigrants were "now taking care of them," and Italians in turn were teaching them "Italian ways." The

Poster appearing around Switzerland advocating the banning of minarets. The posters were disseminated by the conservative Swiss People's Party in advance of a 2009 national referendum on the issue.[8] I saw these posters on multiple occasions during a trip to the country in 2008. Note how the silhouettes of the minarets also evoke the shapes of rocket launchers. This photograph appeared in the *Daily Mail.*

Tunisian immigrants in Naples were learning to make cannolis better than "real" Neopolitans, he said with a wistful shrug. Most of the time, members of the older generation expressed sadness that their homelands were changing. With so many immigrants, who would carry on their traditions? And how could Europe afford to be so generous with social benefits? On many occasions, I encountered posters and graffiti telling immigrants to "go away" and to "go fuck themselves." Some European countries I visited placed legal bans on the construction of minarets, the wearing of any kind of head or face covering, and other elements of cultural expression.

I took an informal survey in every country I visited, asking native-born Europeans what it meant to be part of their nationality. Most of the time, I received pained, confused, or superficial answers. When I asked a native-born employee of our embassy in Switzerland what it meant to be Swiss, he seemed flustered and then said he'd have to get back to me—he just didn't know. At the end of my trip, he approached me and said he had finally come up with an answer: "If you are a real Swiss, it means you like football." Other Europeans equated their national identity with a liking for native foods or other parts of European culture. Muslims, too, gave me similar answers. In Lyon, a well-assimilated Muslim professional in his forties told me that, "Being French is being French—knowing and loving our culture and art and history. We are proud and we are French." One idea seemed clear to many of the non-Muslim Europeans I met: Muslim immigrants represented the "other." These Europeans articulated their expectation that Muslim immigrants would take on "European" ways *completely.* And they expressed puzzlement that Muslims didn't feel more at home given how much Europeans had ostensibly done to welcome them.

Older people I met sometimes echoed these ideas, but in general the sense of rootlessness marked a significant generational divide. Parents, teachers, and religious leaders sensed this malaise in their children, too. Over and over again, they made a point of warning me that "something is going on with our kids." In Palermo, Italy, a mother of Tunisian descent remarked on how strange it was to see her daughters asking questions about being a "real" Muslim and how they could fit into Italian society. "When I was young," she said, "I just took my identity for granted. We never even thought about being Muslim, my sisters and I. But not these kids. All of a sudden, they're talking about the proper way to wear a headscarf, all this anxiety, all this angst, as if it matters so much. I don't get it." What made the situation especially disconcerting for this mother was that she didn't feel she had the answers. Although a "practicing" Muslim, she said, she wasn't an expert on Islam. She knew what she knew. She believed what her parents believed and dressed and acted like her mother. Instead, she was baffled that her kids were so unsettled, and she felt bad that she couldn't help them navigate what they were experiencing.

I gained further perspective on her position and that of others like her one morning in Barcelona, Spain. I was meeting with a group of women convened by the consul general. The woman sitting across the table from me asked where I was "really from," and I told her I was born in India. She told me that she was a recent immigrant from Pakistan. I had learned from a member of the Catalonian government that some 40,000 immigrants from Pakistan lived then in Barcelona, about 80 percent of them single males. As our conversation continued, this woman remarked that she was very worried about her son, who was not at ease in Barcelona. "Back home," she said, "if my child had asked these questions, there were so many people around who could talk with him and show him by example. But here, I have nobody, and I am unsure what will happen." In Pakistan, members of this woman's family observed Islam in a variety of ways. Her son could have found a style of observance that felt natural to him and left it at that. Here, his questions seemed to be leading him in more unsavory directions. The woman explained that her son was growing more intolerant of non-Muslims, and more vocal about groups like Al Qaeda. Weren't they champions of Islam? he asked her. His mother attributed this to what her son saw and heard from others when she was not around. "There are no mosques here," she lamented. "The government will not allow us to build them. So, we have all these 'garage mosques' where the men go—who knows what my son is learning there? No one is clear on what is being taught."

Many of the parents I encountered during such sessions were not only deeply pained by their children's angst but admitted feeling at least partially responsible for it. In Aarhaus, a city outside Copenhagen, I spoke with immigrants at a community center. After the session, a father approached me with tears in his eyes. "I don't know what to do," he said. "I left Turkey because I wanted to give my family a better experience. Now here we are. What have I done? I have taken them away from their home, but here, they don't fit in." He looked around the room at the others, Muslims of many cultural backgrounds and countries of origin. "We're here in a country that doesn't accept us. My son will never belong. They feel different, like they're less human. They don't know what to think about themselves. And it's all my fault. I brought them here."*

TRACKING A GLOBAL PHENOMENON

I assumed that this identity crisis among millennials was a European phenomenon, linked to immigrants' difficulties adapting to unfamiliar and sometimes unwelcoming cultures. This vision would soon be tested. Beginning in January 2009, when Secretary of State Clinton asked me to continue my work engaging with local communities, but to do it on a global scale, I traveled throughout Asia, Africa, South America, and the Middle East. I met with youth, community, political, and religious leaders and held conversations with groups of local youth. For the first time, many of the countries I was visiting were either Muslim-majority or had Muslim communities that were centuries old. To my great surprise, I was hearing the *exact same themes* about youth articulated there that I'd heard in Europe. It didn't matter whether I was talking to professional

* At Humboldt University in Germany, I learned that Germany did not officially accept Islam as a religion. Upon asking a professor there how the German government expected their Muslims to feel at home, he acknowledged that this was a major hurdle. I also wondered why the German government had allowed Turkey to decide what imams it would send to teach German youth. I would recall this conversation in Kosovo in 2012, when an older man, describing the changes that had happened in his country, said to me, "It is the small things that will break us. It starts small then becomes an avalanche."

Kazakhs in a restaurant in Almaty; or less affluent high school students in Cairo, Egypt; or youth in cities in places like Saudi Arabia, Morocco, Argentina, Tanzania, or Nepal; or twenty-somethings in more rural places in Indonesia, Mauritania, or China. It didn't matter whether I was talking to Sunnis, Shiites, Bohras, Ahmadiyyas, Sufis, or Ismailis. The topics of conversation among the youth were always the same. And I mean *always:* literally every discussion among the thousands that I had across cultures and geographies followed the same script. As a professor in New Zealand told me, there was a "major identity crisis" going on there.*

In part, this congruence reflected a phenomenon I'll consider more fully in chapter 5, the connectedness of Muslim youth in our age of smartphones and the Internet. Not only were pop music and movies the same across the world; ideas, information, and cultural reference points were as well, zipping instantly across oceans and time zones. In 2008, for instance, I met with a group of youth in Zanzibar's Stone Town, and participants expressed concern about a statement an American senator had made just days earlier equating Islam and Al Qaeda. "Why do Americans think Muslims are responsible for Al Qaeda?" one of them asked. It was possible that the young people assembled before me were more aware of what a politician in Washington had said than his own constituents.

That's not to say that local cultures, issues, or interests didn't influence people's beliefs. They certainly did, sometimes in colorful ways. When I visited the Maldives in 2010, teachers, youth counselors, heads of women's social groups, and student leaders told me about the many difficult questions being posed by younger people, and they also reported that extremists were stepping in to fill the void with their own ideology. "It's a confusing time to be in the Maldives," one leader said. The community was becoming much more conservative in ways that broke with local religious traditions.

* I visited New Zealand in 2011.

Women were being pushed to drop out of school, stay at home, wear non-Western clothing, and bear children, and the population at large had begun to accept this. At a police academy for women, new cadets dressed in crisp dark blue uniforms and shiny black shoes spoke to me about the growing reluctance of citizens to accept female officers. The cadets felt at risk even though they were officers trained to protect communities.

On a number of occasions, locals recounted to me the legend of Islam's arrival in the country some eight hundred years ago. The ancient people of the Maldives had to appease a sea monster that used to eat people and destroy ships. The only way they could survive was to strike a deal with the monster. They would sacrifice a virgin girl each year on the same day—the price to pay for security and peace. One year, a wooden boat was shipwrecked and the survivor, an Arab, landed on the beach. A family took care of him and nursed him back to health. As it happened, the family's daughter had been chosen for sacrifice that year. The Arab, upon learning of this sad situation, grew upset and made the elders of the community an offer. "I will dress as a girl and be sacrificed instead. I am a Muslim and I have a noble and just God. I do not fear death. I will go instead." The elders agreed. The man dressed up and on the appointed night lay on the beach ready to be eaten. The next day, the people found him on the beach alive and well. They instantly converted to Islam, saying that his God was the right one. They followed his faith and became Muslims.

Fast-forward to 2010. Rising sea levels were threatening to inundate the Maldives. Several years earlier, in 2004, a terrible tsunami had hit (called "the Great Tsunami of 2004"), destroying several islands and drastically impacting the country's tourism industry.* The arrival of this "sea monster" had left the Maldivians feeling besieged,

---

* In 2009, the newly elected Maldives president Mohamed Nasheed held a cabinet meeting underwater to dramatize the effects of climate change. "We're now actually trying to send our message, let the world know what is happening, and what will happen to the Maldives if climate change is not checked," he said. "Maldives Cabinet Makes a Splash," BBC, October 17, 2009, http://news.bbc.co.uk/2/hi/8311838.stm.

and they perceived that God was angry with them. As they saw it, the people bore responsibility for their own misfortunes. If they practiced their faith in the "right" way, perhaps bad things wouldn't happen to them. They'd find favor with God. The sea monster wouldn't return.

Practicing in the "right" way meant that young Maldivians had to leave the country and go to places where they could experience "real" Islam. A local imam living in Malé, the capital, described this to me as a "religious revival" sweeping the country. While we were speaking, as if on cue, a group of women in black loose-fitting, full-length robes and face coverings appeared outside the mosque and huddled together. The imam explained that money, scholarships, and exchange programs funded by wealthy Pakistanis and Saudis were making the revival possible. When young Maldivians returned, they spread the supposedly "authentic" Islam in which they had been indoctrinated—never mind that Maldivian culture already had eight centuries of Islam informing it. Here, then, was the same basic insecurity or uncertainty about religious identity that I'd seen in Europe and many other places in the world. But it came inflected with local beliefs and concerns that were authentically Maldivian.

This insecurity would have terrible consequences that extended far beyond these beautiful islands. A few years later, the Maldives would go on to supply, according to some estimates, "the world's highest per-capita number of foreign fighters to extremist outfits in Syria and Iraq."[9] What was causing this rift between younger and older generations? Why were Muslim millennials questioning everything about their lives and their faith, when their parents and grandparents hadn't in quite the same way?

9/11 AND THE MAKING OF A GENERATION

I began to notice a pattern: Kids throughout the world weren't merely asking questions about their religion. They were feeling defensive about it, even when Islam was the dominant religion in their countries. A Turkish man, a natty dresser in his twenties, put it memorably at a gathering I cohosted with Hannah Rosenthal, U.S. envoy to combat and monitor anti-Semitism, in Ankara in 2012: "We see Muslim identity as a bigger issue than our parents ever did. Because we are bombarded everywhere with questions about Islam. Constantly, in the media, everywhere, we're being asked: How do you feel about being Muslim? What are your emotions? What does the religion mean to you? It's an unfair burden to put on our generation."

By this time, I already understood: The reason millennials were so on edge about their religion had to do with the messages they were receiving daily, even hourly from politicians, conventional news outlets, and on social media. It had to do more precisely with the legacy of this generation's defining moment: 9/11. Since 9/11, we Americans have been fixated on that horrible day, in addition to the threat posed by terrorists. This is understandable: The trauma was and remains massive, the terrorist threat real. But because we were attacked and remain under threat, we have also reverted to an "us-versus-them" way of understanding the world. We thought that *we* were wounded, and *they* were the perpetrators. Because we focused on the "we," we forgot that some Muslims were part of this we, and we didn't spend very much time trying to understand what was happening in Muslim communities in the United States and beyond. Policy makers were not talking to Muslims in Kazakhstan and Argentina and Tanzania and Malaysia and Norway about how 9/11 affected them. Our media wasn't paying much attention to Muslim communities, either, other than to report on possible terrorist attacks or to assess non-Muslim perceptions of Muslims. As a result, we have largely failed as a society to understand the impact of 9/11 on Muslims. We have failed to understand that 9/11 was also traumatic for Muslims globally, and in particular for Muslim millennials.

Whenever I asked Muslim millennials how old they were when they began to think about their religious identity, they always pointed to 9/11 and the period immediately following it. The attack on America seemed to mark the beginning in their minds of a time when Muslim identity came unmistakably and relentlessly into question. In Muslim-minority countries, digital natives told me that at about this time, they began encountering negative messages about Islam and Muslims as they went about their daily lives. People would look at them funny or move away from them in grocery store lines. They would hear elected officials speak of "Moose-lems"* and "Izz-lum" as if they were biology students trying to pronounce the name of obscure bacteria. At school, non-Muslim kids would inquire about Al Qaeda and Osama bin Laden, expecting Muslim kids to explain what had happened and speak up on behalf of their religion. Muslim youth hadn't done anything wrong—they'd never heard of Osama bin Laden before 9/11. An American Muslim grandfather of South Asian descent once told me at an event on Capitol Hill how his eleven-year-old grandson had been called on by a teacher to tell the class "why Bin Laden attacked our country." "Can't people see that these are just children," the grandfather said to me, tears in his eyes. "They are absorbing all this—it makes them feel bad."

Academic research has documented the harsh emotional impact that 9/11 had on Muslim youth in America. In 2003, in one of hundreds of similar studies performed after the attacks of September 11, 2001, Lori A. Peek, professor of sociology at University of Colorado at Boulder, interviewed sixty-eight college students across seven educational institutions located within a short distance of the World

---

* After the inauguration of Donald J. Trump, *Saturday Night Live* produced a skit featuring Melissa McCarthy as Sean Spicer, the White House press secretary. In the skit, McCartney mocked the White House with a stuffed animal of a moose and lamb saying, "The president will not be deterred in his fight against radical moose lambs."

Trade Center towers.* Although most interviewees appreciated the sensitivity of their college faculty and administrators,[10] nearly all of them expressed grave concern about life beyond their college campuses. Most found taking the subway especially harrowing. Others found traveling by themselves on any form of transportation difficult, citing instances of hostility.[11] Many felt pressured by their families to modify their appearances so as to seem less "Muslim." Women had to stop wearing headscarves, while men were encouraged to shave their beards.[12] The students were upset that self-proclaimed Muslims had perpetrated the 9/11 attacks, and they feared for their future,[13] but they were most distressed by how the media, public, and governments portrayed them. They lamented the ubiquitous references to "jihad" and felt that Muslims were being mischaracterized, presented as outsiders in American culture.[14]

The experiences of these students were far from unique. Following the 9/11 attacks, it was not uncommon for American Muslims to hear murder threats, to have "Osama" shouted at them, or to experience spitting, egg-throwing, headscarf desecration, and ethnic jokes. Some American Muslims were even assaulted or killed. In 2003–2004, Louise A. Cainkar found that interviewees felt unsafe, unfairly persecuted, and constantly on edge.[15] Since the election of Donald Trump, such concerns have skyrocketed amid a wave of violent attacks and acts of hate directed at Muslims.

In Muslim-majority countries, 9/11 served equally to inflict trauma and define a strong sense of generational awareness. To younger people especially, it seemed that the outside world was relentlessly and negatively fixated on Muslims and Islam. A 2002

* Lori A. Peek, "Reactions and Response: Muslim Students' Experiences on New York City Campuses Post 9/11," *Journal of Muslim Minority Affairs* 23 (2003). Research has also documented shifts in behavior among the general public after 9/11, with more people showing interest in politics and community service: Morgan G. Scott, Daniel C. Wisneski, and Linda J. Skitka, "The Expulsion from Disneyland: The Social and Psychological Impact of 9/11," *American Psychologist* 66 no. 6 (2011): 447, http://search.proquest.com.ezproxy.library.tufts.edu/docview/882618201/fulltext/A2366380287640D4PQ/1?accountid=14434.

Gallup survey of people in Muslim-majority countries found "overwhelmingly negative perceptual barriers between the people of Islamic countries and the West," in particular a sense among Muslims that the United States and other Western nations lack "respect for Arabs or for Islamic culture or religion."[16] Youth in these countries felt stigmatized—it seemed as if the world was blaming them for what Al Qaeda had done. They faced a wrenching question: how *should* they feel about what had happened on 9/11? It was awful to see the loss of innocent life in the name of a religion that they held dear, and that they had always regarded as nonviolent. What did it mean? How should they think about their relationship with their heritage and with the West?

The events of 9/11 triggered something akin to a collective existential crisis, one that has actually intensified over time. A 2011 Pew Research Center survey found that almost a third of U.S. Muslims (28 percent) felt that others regarded them with suspicion. Just under a quarter (22 percent) reported being called offensive names, and 21 percent say they've been singled out by airport security. Almost 40 percent reported being bothered by their sense that American Muslims were singled out for greater government surveillance. These numbers seem especially meaningful when you consider that most U.S. Muslims are assimilated into American society. This same poll found that 82 percent were generally satisfied with conditions in their lives and that almost that number saw their communities as great places to live. A majority said that in their view, most Muslim immigrants to the United States wanted "to adopt American customs and ways of life."[17] A 2017 Pew poll found similar results, with almost half of respondents reporting "at least one instance of religious discrimination in the past year," even as more than 90 percent reported being "proud to be an American" and 80 percent being "satisfied" with their lives.[18]

At a 2016 session I conducted with Muslim and non-Muslim

millennials hosted at George Washington University by the deputy director of their Program on Extremism, Seamus Hughes, I asked participants what it felt like to grow up in a post-9/11 environment in America. One bright young woman of Middle Eastern descent didn't hesitate. "Before," she said, "it was almost like my identity as being Middle Eastern didn't really mean anything, it didn't really exist. I was just like another person in my high school. After, 9/11 the same people . . . started looking at me a bit differently. All of a sudden, I was an 'other.' And I was angry. And because I felt that I . . . was automatically rejected, I had to align myself with something that rejected them."*

This woman's specific experiences might feel unfamiliar to Muslim millennials living in Muslim-majority countries, but the general sense of feeling marginalized and burdened by 9/11 is universal. In my engagements with Muslim teens, I frequently saw them not only raising questions about their religion and how they should behave in their daily life but also groping for interpretations of 9/11. These defensive interpretations often included vile conspiracy theories that were then circulating in Muslim communities. In Pakistan, Brazil, Australia, and Jordan, for instance, many young Muslims recoiled at the suggestion that people calling themselves Muslims bore responsibility for 9/11. The whole tragedy, they thought, was orchestrated by the United States itself—it was an event staged by Hollywood, or by Israel's Mossad spy agency, or by both. Some youth went as far as to assert that there was no such thing as Al Qaeda. A blogger in Bangladesh told me that there was "no

* "Muslim Millennial Roundtable," George Washington University's Program on Extremism, March 8, 2016. Research has found that among American Muslims, women feel more concerned than men about "the place of Muslims in U.S. society." "U.S. Muslims Concerned About Their Place in Society, but Continue to Believe in the American Dream," Pew Research Center, July 26, 2017, http://www.pewforum.org/2017/07/26/findings-from-pew-research-centers-2017-survey-of-us-muslims/?utm_content=buffer8b97c&utm_medium=social&utm_source=twitter.com&utm_campaign=buffer.

proof" that Al Qaeda existed, and an imam in Bahrain dismissed the notion that such an organization could even be allowed to exist. "If there was such a group," he said, "wouldn't America have killed them all by now?"

You might wonder how Muslim youth could possibly think that the United States and Israel produced 9/11. According to some with whom I spoke, it was to insult Islam by tarring it as a religion of mass murderers, or to justify attacks against Muslims, or to justify invading Arab countries and taking their oil, and so on.* Other younger people I met with differed, arguing that Muslims themselves were to blame by supporting Bin Laden and not doing enough to stop extremists—often foreigners—from coming into their neighborhoods and stirring up trouble. Muslims had created a monster, and now it had come back to haunt them by attacking America. I will examine these hateful and incorrect ideas in more detail in chapter 6. For now, it's worth noting that these ideas helped Muslims, and Muslim youth in particular, process what had happened in a way that felt individually nonthreatening. Conspiracy theories reflected nothing if not deep-seated defensiveness and uncertainty about their own religion.

Even in less tumultuous times, adolescents of all ethnicities have a pretty rough time of it. These are the years when we begin to craft adult identities for ourselves, when we question certitudes we grew up with as children, when we try to figure life out, and, as the psychologist Erik Erikson and others have theorized, when some of us experience painful "crises" of identity.† Adolescents experience

---

* A 2006 Pew Research Center poll found that "majorities in Indonesia, Turkey, Egypt, and Jordan say that they do *not* believe groups of Arabs carried out the September 11, 2001 terrorist attacks." "The Great Divide: How Westerners and Muslims View One Another," Pew Research Center Religion & Public Life Project, June 22, 2006, http://www.pewglobal.org/2006/06/22/the-great-divide-how-westerners-and-muslims-view-each-other/.

† Studies have shown that adolescents struggle with their identities during high school, not just during college, as some scholars had previously assumed: Wim Meeus, "Studies on Identity Development in Ado-

a powerful "need to belong"—a primary reason why gang members might regard "membership into an often dangerous and self-destructive collectivity" as a "welcoming experience."[19] But at the exact moment when hundreds of millions of Muslim millennials were passing through this developmental phase, a horrific criminal attack on the world's superpower made these normal struggles with identity unfathomably more difficult, more charged, more painful. Ever since 9/11, the world's attention has been fixed on what had happened and by the terrorist acts that continue to transpire. Every new terrorist attack in our post–*Charlie Hebdo* world reignites the stigmatization, making it just as real for younger teens today as it was for those who came of age in the years immediately following 9/11. Every day, Muslim youth have been bombarded by negative news, messages, and imagery about their heritage. It is constant, unescapable. As a kid, what do you do with that?

We Americans often feel as if we "own" 9/11, by virtue of having been victimized. I wouldn't dream of minimizing what we Americans suffered and lost on 9/11—not for a single moment. But Americans alone don't own 9/11. Citizens of fifty-seven countries were killed that day—these countries all "own" it, too.[20] And Muslims worldwide "own" it, in the sense that the event comprised a generation's defining moment. When those airplanes crashed into the twin towers, the Pentagon, and a field in Shanksville, they destroyed buildings and bodies and a sense of innocence among Americans everywhere (including American Muslims). For Muslim youth, they destroyed a sense of innocence as well: a largely untroubled belief in their faith, their heritage, their identity.

---

lescence: An Overview of Research and Some New Data," *Journal of Youth and Adolescence* 25 no. 5 (1996): 569–70, https://link-springer-com.ezproxy.library.tufts.edu/article/10.1007/BF01537355. For more on identity crisis, see Erik H. Erikson, *Identity, Youth, and Crisis* (New York: Norton, 1968), and for an application of Erikson's theory to extremism, see Cally O'Brien, "Eriksonian Identity Theory in Counterterrorism," *Journal of Strategic Security* 3, no. 3 (2010).

THE EXTREMIST "SOLUTION" TO THE IDENTITY CRISIS

As scholars have shown, people often use ideology to help them feel better about their lives—less uncertain, less anxious, less isolated.* At its most benign, ideology can help foster friendships and broader civic and community relationships. But people also marginalize themselves and join cults because they yearn even more intensely and urgently for meaning in their lives, for answers to basic questions they have.[21] This unmooring has increased in recent decades. According to anthropologist Scott Atran, "Young people unmoored from millennial traditions flail about in search of a social identity that gives personal significance and glory." Liberation from past webs of reciprocity and demarcation can be a wonderful, progressive thing. Yet it can also result in precarious detachment. "This is the dark side of globalization," Atran continues. "Individuals radicalize while seeking identity in an increasingly flattened world. We have replaced vertical lines of communication between generations

---

* "Psychologists often point to the uncertainty-reducing function of ideology in seeking to explain its motivational potency (for example, Dember 1991; McGregor and Marigold 2003). For instance, Hogg (2007) has argued that ideologies "arise under uncertainty and prevail to ward off uncertainty" (103) and that this explains the "zealotry and the cult of the 'true believer' in the thrall of ideology" (69). Ideology is also motivating because it confers existential security, as emphasized in the writings of Becker (1975) and terror management theorists (Greenberg et al., 1986). The purpose of ideology, according to this view, is to cope with anxiety concerning one's own mortality through denial, rationalization, and other defense mechanisms. Presumably, people are also drawn to socially shared belief systems for reasons of affiliation, as suggested by social identity (Tajfel and Turner 1979) and shared reality (Hardin and Higgins 1996) theories, among others. It has been suggested, for example, that "religion is a fraternity," insofar as it "brings people together, giving them an edge over those who lack this social glue" (Bloom 2005). In an effort to integrate these perspectives, Jost et al. (2009) proposed that ideology possesses motivational structure and potency because it serves underlying epistemic, existential, and relational needs. In other words, political and religious ideologies offer certainty, security, and solidarity. John T. Jost and David M. Amodio, "Political Ideology as Motivated Social Cognition: Behavioral and Neuroscientific Evidence," *Motivation and Emotion* 36, no. 1 (2012): 55–56, http://www.psych.nyu.edu/jost/Jost-Amodio-2012.pdf. For an analysis relating specifically to extremism, see John Knefel, "Everything You've Been Told About Radicalization is Wrong," *Rolling Stone,* May 6, 2013, http://www.rollingstone.com/politics/news/everything-youve-been-told-about-radicalization-is-wrong-20130506.

with horizontal peer-to-peer attachments that can span the globe, but paradoxically within ever-narrower channels for information."[22]

Rather than a "clash of civilizations," as Samuel Huntington put it,[23] Atran perceives a "collapse of communities"—and on that score, he's absolutely right. Understanding young Muslims' vulnerability, extremists prey on them, adroitly offering narratives about a clear, simple, unproblematic Muslim identity. Bifurcating the world into "us" and "them," extremists assert that as custodians of "the truth," they are fighting an epic war with The Rest of the World (not just the West). Islamic imagery and mythology, conspiracy theories about America, Christians, Jews, Hindus, Buddhists—these and other motifs convey the notion that if not for The Rest, purity and peace would reign.*

The Middle East itself, of course, has played an important role. Many youth, even those who stay at home and plot attacks in their own communities, have found it validating to see the "powerful and victorious" so-called Islamic State armies march, train, and behead on Arab lands. They have fervently believed that so-called Islamic State and others are launching a new chapter in human history. The presence of a "caliphate" in the heart of the Middle East has served as a tangible, physical "solution" to the problem of identity. Matthew Levitt, director of the Washington Institute's Stein Program on Counterterrorism and Intelligence, has observed that extremist recruiters in Belgium offer youth "a fast track from zero to hero" by offering the prospect of life in the "caliphate." Instead of experiencing marginalization "living among the infidels" in the West, they can go to the Middle East and live as "true" Muslims.[24]

But more than the "caliphate" itself, it's the nexus of ideas that underlie and accompany it that allows extremists to resolve issues of

* Portions of text in this section originally appeared in a chapter I authored titled, "Extremism in the Middle East and Beyond Fighting and Winning the Ideological War," in *Blind Spot: America's Response to Radicalism in the Middle East* (Aspen, CO: Aspen Institute, 2016), 33–45.

identity for Muslim youth. As scholars have noted, human beings harbor a latent bias toward simplicity—we like to see the world in black and white.[25] Extremists exploit that bias, perpetuating a notion that has been spreading for years in Muslim communities that there is only one "right" version of Islam, and that its norms should govern all of life—how a person eats, thinks, prays, interacts with others, and so on. Extremists do not tolerate diversity of thought or practice within Islam, and in this respect, they're changing the very nature of Muslim communities the world over. For individual youth, including preteens as in the case of the so-called cubs trained by the so-called Islamic State in Syria,[*] the notion of an authentic Islam affords a binding sense of identity, a sense of belonging to a global community of Muslims who are similarly dedicated to living in "proper" ways and spreading the word to others.[†]

A WINNING STRATEGY

Conflict between Muslim-majority nations and organizations and specific countries in the West had certainly existed before 9/11. Muslim communities were touched by tensions with former colonial powers, and they were upset by policies pursued by the United States and others. Likewise, notions of a "pure" or "authentic" Islam had existed for centuries among specific Muslim sects, most notably the Salafists of the Arabian Peninsula.

---

* "What to Do with Islamic State's Child Soldiers," *Economist,* June 17, 2017, https://www.economist.com/news/middle-east-and-africa/21723416-cubs-caliphate-are-growing-up-what-do-islamic-states-child?fsrc=scn/tw/te/bl/ed/whattodowithislamicstateschildsoldiers. One mother told the *Economist* of what it was like dealing with her twelve-year-old boy once he had fallen under the thrall of the so-called Islamic State: "I was scared to wear a T-shirt inside my own house. He told me these things were forbidden under Islam. They washed his brain."

† On extremism's ability to satisfy the need for belonging, see Randy Borum, "Psychological Vulnerabilities and Propensities for Involvement in Violent Extremism," *Behavioral Sciences & the Law* 32, no. 3 (2014), doi:10.1002/bsl.2110.

Yet it was the extremists who, post-9/11, understood the centrality of angst around identity. The so-called Islamic State, Al Qaeda, Boko Haram—these specific groups are ultimately not that important. What is most important is the way that they collectively manipulated the notion of "pure" or "real" Islam to turn diverse local grievances into a single set of global grievances. Of course, extremists have to be able to "prove" the accuracy of their storytelling. To do so, they manipulate facts and connect them to emotion. It doesn't matter to America's bottom line if a blogger in Rabat believes America is at war with Islam, but it absolutely does matter if he or she brings youth along to do something about it. The us-versus-them narrative has grown exponentially because of the extremists' vast audience and the megaphone the extremists possess to sell it. It has also grown because the notion of a common adversary is extremely powerful, giving youth a galvanizing mission in life that they had previously lacked.

What's the answer? Should we fight back by simply communicating a different message: that America is not the "bad guy" here, that the extremist narrative is wrong? As discussed, that approach hasn't worked, not least because the U.S. government doesn't have credibility among Muslim youth. But there's another, critically important reason why simply blasting out government propaganda has failed. To solve the problem of extremism, we can't just convince Muslim youth of abstract ideas. We must do nothing less than influence the way that youth are processing and resolving their identity, day in and day out. We must get ideas into their minds from all directions and at all times, and from people they know and trust.

Let's acknowledge the complexity at work here. Examining terrorism through the lens of identity, professors Seth J. Schwartz, Curtis S. Dunkel, and Alan S. Waterman break identity down into three relevant components: "personal, social, and cultural identity."[26] Terrorism, in their view, arises out of the "confluence" of these components, in particular an "authoritarian" personal identity, or one that is "diffused and aimless"; a social identity defined by opposition to some threatening "other"; and a cultural identity "strongly based in collectivism and in fundamentalist adherence to religious or cultural principles."* To battle terrorism, we must appreciate each of these levels, as well as the interplay between them. As Schwartz, Dunkel, and Waterman note, "disenfranchisement, when coupled with fervent adherence to traditional, dichotomous us versus them religious principles justifying violence against those perceived to threaten one's religious or cultural group, a strong prioritization of the group over the individual, and a belief that one's group is morally superior to the group being attacked, may combine to make terrorism considerably more likely."[27]

This confluence of factors means matters of identity cannot be resolved with a single advertisement, or even a whole series of them. They're resolved over time as individuals live their lives and interact with people and organizations around them. Our interventions must address each of the three levels, as well as their interactions.† But that means closely understanding the experience of youth at all three levels. Who are the kids we're trying to influence? What kind of support systems exist in their communities that value diversity? Do these kids understand how their families practice religion and why? What kinds of personal emotions do they experience as regards to their heritage, their parents and relatives, and their own lives? Which peers in the local community or online influence these kids?

In light of this complexity, a government program here or there can't possibly "fix" the problem of identity. Instead, we need con-

---

* For more on social identity and its relationship with extremism, see Dina Al Raffie, "Social Identity Theory for Investigating Islamic Extremism in the Diaspora," *Journal of Strategic Security* 6 (Winter 2013), http://scholarcommons.usf.edu/cgi/viewcontent.cgi?article=1242&context=jss.

† "If identity is indeed central to the nature of terrorism, it follows that techniques for reducing the threat of terrorism should be identity-related, including efforts to reduce terrorism promoting interactions among identity elements. Because terrorism involves aspects of identity at the cultural, social, and personal levels, the possibility exists for interventions to be delivered at all three levels as well." Schwartz, Dunkel, and Waterman, "Terrorism," 551.

certed, multidimensional, evidence-based action, addressing the entire period of adolescence as well as all factors that shape how young Muslims think about themselves. Such a comprehensive response would by necessity draw upon the insights of a number of academic disciplines that concern themselves with youth, including psychology, neuroscience, sociology, and ethnography. We know, for instance, that emotional control is influenced by brain development. How might this render them susceptible to recruiting, and how might we respond?[28]

As we'll see in the chapters ahead, the kind of response I'm envisioning would also draw upon a range of actors, including government, business, and civil society. In essence, we need to do nothing less than redesign the emotional experience of youth, "complicating their thinking" and enhancing their critical awareness. That way, in the process of forming their identities, they'll reject simple us-versus-them thinking and move away from extremism's orbit.

Extremists promote their ideas by exploiting a cultural, technological, and economic *system* that has existed informally in Muslim communities worldwide. I think of this system as fluid but pervasive, the "ether" that exists in these communities, as prevalent as the air people breathe. Just because you have contact with parts of this system—as virtually all young Muslims I met did—doesn't mean you'll join an extremist group. But it does mean that you will be exposed to potent extremist narratives.

Nobody rules this system—it isn't controlled by a central power. But that is not to say that some people and groups don't wield undue influence. Some do, on account of the billions of dollars of funding they provide. Remember that African imam in Denmark who wrongly told young Sanam that she wasn't Muslim? How was it that he had come to live in a European community and espouse his hard-line views? I never found that out exactly—he might have come on his own initiative and with his own financial support. But as I discovered elsewhere, wealthy patrons often paid for such imams, as well as the instructional materials they used and the mosques in which they taught. As I'll describe in the next chapter, extremist ideology would never have taken root and flourished over decades without strong, systemic, and sustained financial backing from one of our most erstwhile partners, the Saudis. By avidly spreading the teachings and practices of an ultraconservative form of Islam, the Saudis along with other Gulf states have helped perpetuate the identity crisis, creating fertile soil for extremist groups to take root and spread.

CHAPTER THREE

PLAGUE FROM THE GULF

In March 2010, when my special assistant Sarah told me the news, I nearly leaped out of my chair. I couldn't believe it—I had managed to get a visa to visit China! My colleagues at State were shocked as well. The State Department's Human Rights Reports regularly called out China for its treatment of its minority Muslim populations, and one ethnic group in particular, the Uighers. China saw the Uigher issue as a domestic terrorism problem, and our public highlighting of it as an affront to their Chinese identity. As a result, they were reluctant to hold diplomatic conversations about Muslims. Understanding this, I had abandoned any hope of going to the country as a diplomat. Still, an opportunity had arisen—an invitation to speak at an event in China hosted by the Asia Society, a global nonprofit organization founded by John D. Rockefeller III and devoted to increasing partnerships and alliances across several disciplines, including education, arts, history, policy, and business. I had submitted a visa request on the off chance it would be accepted, and it had. I had to be careful about what I did and whom I saw, but working with our embassy, we designed a trip that would allow me to talk to young Chinese Muslims in Shanghai, Nanking, Kunming, and elsewhere.

A highlight of the trip turned out to be a visit to a small town I had never heard of: Shadian, located in the southern part of the country, about 150 miles from Kunming.* It was a clear, warm day when I arrived in Yunnan Province, where a population of Hui Muslims have lived for more than a millennium. My team and I drove for hours through lush countryside, cruising along dusty roads through villages replete with mom-and-pop storefronts and skinny white lampposts. The scenes I passed were familiar—I could have been in any Asian country: Grocers sold fresh produce on the side of the road, their apples and leafy vegetables piled in perfect pyramids. Stray dogs and cats milled about, and Chinese-language signage promoted medical products. These sights were so regular—rhythmic, even—that I found myself lulled by them.

Our arrival in Shadian jolted me from my reverie. Turning a corner, we came face-to-face with a glorious pedestrian boulevard, rows of majestic palm trees planted down the middle. At the end of those trees stood a huge, modern structure made of what appeared to be white marble and topped off by a light green dome. Fountains and two tremendous Jumbotron screens framed its entrance. I was mesmerized. What was all this? Then I glimpsed what seemed to be minarets flanking a prayer hall, and I knew: it was a mosque.

I couldn't believe it. The mosque was so dramatically out of place. The buildings that surrounded it were older, more modest structures made of cement, mud, or wood. In Saudi Arabia, Qatar, Kuwait, or the United Arab Emirates, a mosque as new and grand as this would have fit right in. But here?

Seconds later, we pulled up at my hotel, and I checked in. I couldn't help but think that I had been magically transported to the

* According to Chinese census data, the town had a population of 13,793 as of 2002. "Shadian District Overview," *Xinhhua,* accessed April 7, 2018, http://www.yn.xinhuanet.com/nets/gj/zj/xzzb-jj08.htm.

Middle East. My hotel was called, to the best of my recollection, "the Muslim Hotel" (and in fact, the most memorable part of the hotel, I would later discover, was a bright neon sign right outside my hotel room window that bore the hotel's name in English and blinked on and off all night). Hanging near the reception desk were pictures of the Kaaba, Islam's most sacred site, located in Mecca, Saudi Arabia. I also spotted books on "Islam and His Prophet" and wall hangings in Arabic that read, *Bi'smi'Llah al-Rahman al-Rahim,* or "In the Name of God, the Compassionate, the Merciful." Though the receptionist was a Chinese man, he was dressed like a Saudi in a white long robe.

When I stepped outside to stretch my legs, I found many other elements of a Middle Eastern urban scene. The small shops surrounding the hotel sold the same "religious" knickknacks you'd find in an airport anywhere in the Middle East: incense, "pure Arabic" soaps (whatever that meant), cheap plastic prayer beads, mannequins outfitted with brightly colored headscarves, and long gowns for men and women that screamed "modesty, modesty, modesty." The stores also sold educational materials, including DVDs of Saudi religious authorities reciting the Qur'an or offering opinions about Islam, and the requisite pamphlets on how to be a good Muslim. It was one-stop shopping for the religious-oriented tourist.

The next day, a professor at a local Islamic university, an ethnic Chinese who identified as Hui, graciously hosted me for lunch at his home. I was treated to a delicious, multicourse meal prepared by his wife. She and several other women were covered from top to bottom in black, wearing flowing, floor-length garments over their bodies and tightly fitted headscarves around their faces. They brought out dish after dish, placing them in the middle of the round dining room table. Although they hovered around me to make sure I had taken generous portions of food, they did not eat with us. They, too, seemed to be Hui, although their style of dress was clearly not.

Throughout the meal, my host talked about Islamic education—how important it was for Muslim kids to learn about the religion and mix with other Muslim students, and how few proper Muslim universities existed. He also related that local youth sought to learn about Islam by studying in the Gulf countries. After our meal, we continued our talk in a nearby sitting room outfitted with faux leather couches, a television, and a laptop. Here, too, religion was a dominant presence. On one wall hung a giant map of the Middle East. The clock on the television set was set for Mecca time as well as local time, and the television was tuned to a Saudi channel. Another clock featured a large picture of the Kaaba, as did a tapestry hanging on the wall.

We left my host's house and went to tour the inside of the large mosque I had seen when I first arrived. It was called the Great Mosque, and six years after my visit an article in *The New Yorker* claimed it cost $19 million to build, the amount funded entirely by private donations.[1] My host seemed excited and proud to show the building to me, and he emphasized how important it was that the local population had such a magnificent place to pray. He left me alone for a few minutes, encouraging me to stroll the grounds and peek inside the gleaming structure. I did so and found the mosque quite impressive. It boasted a huge prayer hall, high ceilings, and ornate floral decorations on the walls and archways. The few faithful praying at the time seemed tiny inside this grand space. I did not see any women praying inside.

Reemerging outside, I found my host, and we proceeded down a walk lined with palm trees. I remarked that this vast marble space and in fact the whole complex closely resembled mosques in the Gulf. He seemed taken aback by my statement. "We designed the mosque to be in the 'modern style,'" he said.

"Did Saudi money fund the mosque?"

"No, no," he said, shaking his head.

As respectfully as I could, I asked how a small community like his could raise the funds to build this kind of structure, and if the Chinese government had actually paid to have this built.

He scowled and looked away. "This area of China has money from minerals. The Muslims here built the mosque out of religious devotion."

I asked if he could take me to see a more traditional mosque from this region of China. Although we had been conversing in English all this time, my embassy colleague, who spoke Chinese, now broke in and went back and forth with my host. It was clear that he didn't want to show me a traditional mosque. Finally, he agreed to do so.

We took a short drive, no more than five minutes. When we got out, all evidence of the Gulf had vanished. I stood on a dirt road lined with modest houses and shops. My host pointed toward a compound surrounded by a tall wall covered over in painted terracotta. "Here it is." We proceeded through the entrance into a small courtyard, an oasis of fruit trees and flowerpots, the perfect site for prayerful contemplation.

The mosque itself was much simpler than the Gulf-style mosque had been, made of wood and reflecting the themes of traditional Chinese architecture. The structure's roof curled outward at its edges, while its open doorways permitted a view of the faithful praying inside. The religious services it housed conformed to what I was told was the ancient Sufi devotion mingled with traditional indigenous Chinese customs. Although I did not know for sure, I suspected that these services were quite different in style and content from what was practiced in the newer mosque.

At the entrance to the open-air prayer room, dozens of pairs of shoes belonging to the faithful had been placed in a neat line. I approached a group of elderly women sitting nearby. Instead of long black robes, they wore loose-fitting cotton pants and simple, tunic-like shirts as well as loose headscarves. I told them I was visiting from the United States, and that I was interested in learning about the clothes they wore to pray. They indicated that they wore the traditional garb of Chinese Muslims. And what about the shiny mosque around the corner? "Oh," they said "that is foreign Islam."

As my host and I walked back toward the garden, he indicated his displeasure at Sufi observance. "This isn't the real Islam," he said. "This isn't who we are."

I challenged him on this. "Well, what about the traditional history you have? Sufism has been in China for over a thousand years!"

"We have to get rid of the Sufis; it's what we must do." I asked what he meant, and he said, "They're not real Muslims."

Many Americans think that all Muslims are the same, and that they all share the same beliefs. In truth, Islam has historically been inflected by local customs and cross-cultural interactions in every corner of the globe. Extremists would *like* you to think about Islam as homogeneous or monolithic. As they exploit the global identity crisis among Muslim youth, they propound a very particular set of ideas about Islam and individual purpose—ideas that originate in the Gulf region and Saudi Arabia in particular, and that include a claim to represent the only true Islam. This form of Islam, called Wahhabism, is rigid, intolerant, highly dogmatic, puritanical, and contrary to liberal values. In recent decades, it has proliferated thanks to a very important sponsor: the Kingdom of Saudi Arabia.

Saudi Arabia—the Kingdom of Backwardness, Nicholas Kristof has called it[2]—has emerged as one of the key elements of the global system underlying extremism. We can't understand the global system underpinning extremism without surveying the pivotal role played by the Saudi government as well as private organizations and individuals within the kingdom. In recent decades, the Saudis have spent up to an estimated $100 billion spreading Wahhabism and perpetuating the notion that they are Islam's caretaker.[3] Their methods to persuade and influence run the gamut and include the funding of mosques, schools, textbooks, imams, imam learning centers and exchanges, cultural institutions around the world, and more. The Saudis don't simply want their extreme form of religious practice and belief to prevail. They want to destroy other, local traditions within Islam. To that end, they are rewriting history, erasing evidence of the past to favor their own narrative—a move that ideologically aligned extremists in many parts of the world have since copied.

The relationship between the Saudis and extremism is not merely one of affinity. The Saudi government and Saudi individuals have directly supported terrorist groups in the Middle East and beyond.* At the same time, quite paradoxically, the Saudi government has also served as a staunch ally in the fight against terror, sharing intelligence and military assets and helping to rein in terrorist financing. It also serves as a valuable counterbalance against Iran's influence in the Middle East. Puzzling, isn't it? Such is the canny strategy that has served the Saudis so well for so long.

Beyond direct support, Saudi efforts at indoctrinating young Muslims worldwide have rendered them highly vulnerable to recruitment by extremist groups, including those formally unaligned with or even opposed to the Saudi regime. Extremism would not have become the pervasive threat it is had it not had a patron awash in trillions of dollars of oil wealth and happy to spend it so as to secure hegemony for an extreme, uncompromising, and literalist interpretation of Islam. According to Will McCants, a counterterrorism expert and former senior State Department advisor, so-called Islamic State in particular would not have existed "in the configuration that we see them today." The group justifies its violence by recourse to Wahhabi tenets and teachings that "have been pushed by the Saudi state."[4] McCants goes on: "It's the Saudis that really put this on the map. [The so-called Islamic State] certainly gets its theology from the Wahhabi and also its approach to jurisprudence

* "Hillary Clinton on National Security and the Islamic State," Council on Foreign Relations, November 19, 2015, https://www.cfr.org/event/hillary-clinton-national-security-and-islamic-state. In 2016, news broke that German intelligence had discovered financial links among Saudi Arabia, Gulf countries, and extremist groups in Germany. Lizzie Dearden, "Saudi Arabia and Gulf States 'Support Islamic Extremism in Germany,' Intelligence Report Finds," *Independent,* December 14, 2016, http://www.independent.co.uk/news/world/europe/saudi-arabia-gulf-states-fund-islamic-extremism-germany-salafism-wahhabism-qatar-kuwait-islamists-a7473551.html.

and law. Culturally it is very much a descendant of the kind of Islam you find in Saudi Arabia or Wahhabism."*

Given this history, the single most important step we can take toward eliminating extremism would be to combat the supremacy of Saudi ideology worldwide by cutting off the Saudi money that funds it. It's vital, too, that we take action to buttress local Muslim cultures and traditions. Otherwise, a generation of Muslims risks falling under the sway of a pernicious ideology that presents itself as authentic and absolute, and humanity risks losing a true and full record of its rich, Islamic past. Finally, we must address the ignorance of governments and individuals who quite innocently (perhaps) perceive the Saudis as Islam's legitimate arbiters. Whether they realize it or not, they are part of the problem as well.

WHAT THE SAUDIS DON'T WANT YOU TO KNOW

Before we can understand the power and influence of Saudi money and the significant threats they pose, let's briefly examine the reality of Islam's rich complexity and local variation. As Ziauddin Sardar, scholar, author, and editor of the *Critical Muslim,* has written, "the reality of the Muslim world is its immense diversity."[5] The way Muslims pray, the construction of mosques, the way Muslims interpret holy texts, and the way they conduct themselves differ dramatically depending on where you practice Islam and what teachings and hadiths[6] are emphasized. Even pious Muslims who pray five times a day don't often agree on all elements of the faith. How could they? Differences are part of the human experience, even

---

* In an interview with David Weinberg, former senior fellow for the Foundation for Defense of Democracies, in Washington, D.C., June 28, 2016, this point was further emphasized. After printing their own books, they have continued to rely heavily on the early teachings of Saudi Wahhabism.

among people who generally accept the teachings of a religion like Islam.

If you're a non-Muslim, you might wonder whether one form or variety of Islamic practice takes precedence over others. Is there a single, "correct" way of being a Muslim? The answer is a resounding no. A Filipina reciting a prayer as she begins her Halal meal and the tattooed Tajik drinking vodka in one hand while fingering prayer breads with the other are both natural expressions *to those followers*—as natural as the Bahraini with a long beard and robe and the Senegalese poet wearing traditional dress. In America, this rich variety is on constant display: our country is home to every kind of Muslim on the planet. Looking at Muslims in cities from Los Angeles to Lexington, you quickly understand that 1.6 billion people simply aren't going to practice their religion uniformly.

Yet for many people, Muslims included, the notion of diversity within Islam seems novel. The concept of the Umma, the worldwide community of believers, emphasizes unity, the notion that all Muslims are joined by common doctrine, ritual observance, and so forth. Most non-Muslim Americans likewise have little idea that not all Muslims follow the same customs and beliefs. Frankly, that's because they usually lack knowledge about the religion itself or its long history throughout the world and, specifically, the United States.*

American ignorance about Islam is legendary. When I spoke to a group of Indonesian Muslims in Jakarta in 2012, a student said to me, "Ma'am, how come you are coming to visit us in Indonesia? Americans only think Arabs are Muslims." In Sri Lanka, I got the same sentiment, this time from a religious scholar who sternly told me that "until Americans begin to give dignity to all kinds of Muslims, they will continue with the troublesome caricature that plagues them. They only know *Lawrence of Arabia* and Disney's *Aladdin*."

---

* Most Americans know little about Islam's long history in the United States, and even fewer know how it has evolved elsewhere in the world.

In Uganda, a social entrepreneur said to me: "Ms. Farah, even these children here know that African Islam is ancient and important; why doesn't your country know this?"

Regrettably, the U.S. government has done little to dispel such impressions. For instance, American policy makers and officials speak of "the Muslim world," usually implicitly referencing Arabs in the Middle East, when in fact Muslims live in every country—there is no unifying "Muslim world."* Inside the State Department, the Bureau of Near Eastern Affairs wields the most influence over matters concerning Islam, as if what is said in the Middle East were what everyone outside the region does.

This is not to say that some within our government aren't deeply knowledgeable about and respectful of Islam. During my service at the National Security Council, respect for the religion dominated our work. In Elliott Abrams's directorate, several of my colleagues were Muslims from different ethnic or cultural backgrounds, and across the NSC, senior officials were determined that our country do more to engage with Muslims and acknowledge Islam's diversity. When President Bush held his annual Iftar at the White House, he included not merely diplomats from Muslim-majority states, but in an unprecedented move, those from countries in which Muslims were a minority. (At one point, the White House received a call from a European embassy to say their ambassador had been invited to Iftar by mistake. "No mistake," the White House said.) The move irked some Arab ambassadors, who were used to thinking of themselves as Washington's "go-to" Muslims.

It might seem strange to worry so much about acknowledging Islam's diversity, but this isn't just a matter of diplomatic protocol. The diverse and colorful local traditions of Islam are part of our global

* For a critique of the "Muslim world" concept and a discussion of its genesis, see Anver M. Emon and Daniel Steinmetz-Jenkins, "How the Muslim World Was Invented," *Foreign Affairs*, June 2, 2017, https://www.foreignaffairs.com/reviews/review-essay/2017-06-02/how-muslim-world-was-invented?cid=int-lea&pgtype=hpg.

heritage, adding a layer of richness to the soil of human culture. Furthermore, a widespread homogenization of Islam is under way, one not merely tolerated but reinforced by some of those Arab ambassadors and their governments. To understand why, we must shift our gaze to the Arabian Peninsula. There we find a particular variety of Islamic practice and belief in place, one known for its strictness and rigidity as well as its intolerance of other Muslim traditions. This variety of Islam seeks to spread its allegedly "authentic" brand of Islam and to smother all others. I'm talking about Wahhabism.

WAHHABISM: THE ENEMY OF DIVERSITY

In his intellectual genealogy of Al Qaeda, scholar Quintan Wiktorowicz ties the "global jihadi movement" to a long-standing Islamist movement known as "Salafism." The Arabic word *salafi* designates people "who follow the example of the companions (salaf) of the Prophet Mohammed." According to Salafis, these companions imbibed Islamic teachings in an unmediated way from the ultimate source—the Prophet.* As a result, their own conceptions of Islam were purer or more valid than those originating in later centuries. To practice authentically, the Salafis say, Muslims should return to the ideas and practices of Muhammad's companions, and they should also pay close heed to the words of the Qur'an and the *Sunna,* as the Prophet's own traditions are called.[7] Significantly, Salafism does not necessarily promote violence. It merely advocates for a "puritanical approach" to Islam, one that disallows other potential interpretations. Explains Wiktorowicz: "Salafis believe that by strictly following the rules and guidance in the Qur'an and Sunna . . . they

---

* As Wiktorowicz writes, "All Salafis share a puritanical approach to the religion intended to eschew religious innovation by strictly replicating the model of the Prophet Muhammad." "Anatomy of the Salafi Movement," *Studies in Conflict & Terrorism* 29, no. 3 (2006): 207.

eliminate the biases of human subjectivity and self-interest, thereby allowing them to identify the singular truth of God's commands. From this perspective, there is only one legitimate religious interpretation; Islamic pluralism does not exist."[8]

In Saudi Arabia over the past couple of centuries, Salafists have given rise to another, related group known as Wahhabists. "Wahhabism" denotes a Sunni Islamic reform movement that seeks to return to the seventh-century teachings of the prophet Muhammad and his followers. Wahhabism grew out of the teachings of Muhammad ibn Abd al-Wahhab (1703–1792),[9] whose followers believed they were charged with the task of restoring an unadulterated, pure, "authentic" monotheism. The movement gained traction in modern Saudi Arabia, which encompasses the territory where the Prophet lived (and died). Today, many associated with Wahhabism decry that moniker and prefer to be called *salafi* (that is, one who follows the teachings of the original Muslims), or *muwahhid* (one who expounds on the unity of God).[10] Saudi leaders in turn have dismissed criticisms of their religious indoctrination by claiming that Wahhabism doesn't exist[11]—a ridiculous bit of sly theological gymnastics. The fact is that what the Saudis call "true" Islam clearly reflects the intolerant and exclusionary doctrine of Ibn Abd al-Wahhab.[12]

Besides Ibn Abd al-Wahhab, other thinkers have also helped inspire radical ideas among modern Wahhabis, including the twentieth-century Egyptian intellectual Sayyid Qutb* and the fourteenth-century thinker Taqi al-Din Ibn Taymiyya. The latter was famous for regarding the minority Shiite branch of Islam as apostate.[13] As journalist Nicolas Pelham has written, Ibn Taymiyya was "a bit-player in his time," but more recently "the Salafists have elevated him to centre-stage today, ranking his teachings alongside the Prophet's in Saudi Arabia's core curriculum."[14] Wiktorowicz notes that Saudi Salafis were radicalized during the 1980s thanks to the

* Qutb, in fact, inspired radical ideas among Wahhabis and non-Wahhabis alike.

war in Afghanistan, which exposed them to more extreme and intolerant ideas from elsewhere in the world.

What distinguishes Wahhabism from other sects or forms of Islam is the rigorous orthodoxy it enforces, and also its intimate connection with the Saudi royal family and the modern Saudi state. "Saudi Islam or Wahhabism," Will McCants told me, "seeks to return the believer to an authentic, pristine form of the religion that is deracinated or disconnected or purified."[15] Since the establishment of the modern Saudi state in 1932, Wahhabism and the ruling family have become intertwined, seeking to combine "orthodox proselytization with political domination" so as to "engender a moral society."[16] Wahhabi doctrine forms the basis of the laws and social mores, judiciary, and educational practices of the desert kingdom. Religious education in the country emphasizes obedience, duty, proselytizing to others, and defending Islam against "the enemies."[17] Wahhabi textbooks I have seen outside the kingdom teach practices for cultivating spiritual "purity." They fail to mention vital Islamic concepts that endorse respect for diversity, and they specifically endorse isolation from and even hatred of other religious groups.[18]

As I've also seen, Wahhabis are obsessed with banning any kind of "suspicious" behavior in everyday life. For instance, they follow specific rules about the length of a man's pants or beard, or the type of fabric he can wear. Violate these rules and you are living in an "impure" or "forbidden" fashion. The Saudis have funded local presses as well as publishing facilities of their own, ensuring that Wahhabi literature is published and that materials from other Islamic practices and teachings are suppressed.[19] A taxpayer-funded report commissioned by the State Department in 2011 revealed that Saudi government textbooks had been discovered in use as far afield as Africa, Europe, and East and Southeast Asia.[20] A textbook I once encountered in the British city of Leicester explained how a good Muslim was supposed to watch television. Another time, in Malaysia, someone handed me a Saudi textbook in English that contained teachings about the duties of Muslim women—when they should get married, when they should have children, the ways they should obey their husbands, how they should speak to male members of their family. I recognized that by the standards articulated in that textbook, I was neither female nor Muslim. Official government textbooks "teach that LGBT individuals and converts from Islam should be executed and that women shaking hands with men or traveling unsupervised causes adultery and spreads moral corruption. Jews are depicted as inherently treacherous, and Christians as waging a modern-day crusade against Islam."*

In 1979, a group of extremists took over the Grand Mosque in Mecca. Saudi rulers felt they needed permission from the country's Wahhabi clergy before retaking the mosque militarily. After receiving that blessing and recapturing the mosque, they gave the clergy much greater influence over the direction of the country, giving Wahhabi social conservatives even greater say over everyday life in the kingdom and redoubling efforts to export Wahhabism abroad.† And spread Wahhabism the Saudis did. As scholar Karen Armstrong observes, "The soaring oil price created by the 1973 embargo—when Arab petroleum producers cut off supplies to the US to protest against the Americans' military support for Israel—gave the kingdom all the petrodollars it needed to export its idiosyncratic form of Islam. The old military jihad to spread the faith was now replaced by a cultural offensive."[21] Elliott Abrams told me that, "if you go back to previous decades [before 9/11], every Saudi embassy had a religious attaché who was just handing out money to Salafi mosques and madrassas

* David Weinberg, "How to Build a More Sustainable and Mutually Beneficial Relationship with Saudi Arabia: Blueprint for U.S. Government Policy," Human Rights First report, March 2015, 5. Such incitement remains in Saudi textbooks as the 2017–18 school year: David Weinberg, "Congress Must Act to End Incitement in Saudi Textbooks," Huffington Post, December 5, 2017, https://www.huffingtonpost.com/entry/Congress-must-act-to-end-incitement-in-saudi-textbooks_us_5a26b5bbe4b0e383e63c3cae.

† Yaroslav Trofimov, *The Siege of Mecca: The 1979 Uprising at Islam's Holiest Shrine* (New York: Anchor Books, 2008), 100–101; 240–43.

everywhere."[22] Indeed, as various diplomats and intel officers have told me, this practice still occurs in numerous parts of the globe.

In exchange for endowing chairs at the top American and European universities and other cultural institutions,[23] the Saudis have often selected individuals with Wahhabist training or sympathies to fill them. They have also leveraged multilateral organizations and created others to teach their brand of Islam, making it difficult for non-Wahhabi imams to compete. The Organization of Islamic Cooperation (formerly the Organization of the Islamic Conference), its subsidiary the Islamic Development Bank, the World Muslim League, and the World Assembly of Muslim Youth have all served as vectors for the global dissemination of Wahhabism.[24]

A favorite tactic of the Saudis is to deliver Wahhabism under the guise of charity for local communities. In the early 1990s, while traveling in the Middle East for USAID, I held dozens of conversations with local representatives of NGOs who informed me that they had new schools or educational materials because of the generosity of "the Saudis." These conversations also occurred while I was traveling in Afghanistan in 2004. The representatives often could not describe exactly where the money came from—the Saudi government or private philanthropic donations—with good reason: as I discovered, the Saudis sometimes support specific charities around the world, then transfer that donor money to local NGOs. This charitable network allows them to discover local needs and fill them, while simultaneously covering their tracks and working to spread Wahhabi ideology. A 2015 Human Rights First report cites a Saudi magazine estimating "that the government's efforts wholly or partially financed the construction of 210 Islamic centers; 1,500 mosques; 202 colleges; and nearly 2,000 religious schools for children in 'every corner of the world.'"*

* Weinberg, "How to Build." As Carol Choksy and Jamsheed Choksy have written: "According to the Saudi monarchy's official websites, Wahhabi charities and royal trusts, including that of another Saudi ruler, the late King Fahd, spent millions of dollars recruiting students to more than 1,500 mosques, 210 Muslim centers, 202 Islamic colleges, and 2,000 madrassas and on staffing those institutions with nearly 4,000

I first became aware of these efforts in 1994, when I spent the summer in Srinagar, Kashmir, India, interviewing militants for my master's thesis. A young doctor I'd met wanted to thank me for coming to obtain a firsthand account of the region's political complexities. He placed a heavy object in my hand. I thought he had given me a traditional, painted papier-mâché box, an art form that has long been the pride of Kashmiri people. However, I felt metal in my palm. Looking down, I spotted a two-inch-wide disk with the Saudi flag on it. "What is this?" I asked.

My friend smiled. "It will remind you of true Islam. Not like what is happening here in this place. The people have lost their way. My wish is to go to Saudi and forget this place. They take care of their people and Muslims worldwide."

I was shocked. "What do you mean? Why are you looking to the Arabs?"

He shook his head, "You have a lot to learn. This isn't the real Islam we have here in Kashmir. We should look to the Saudis to help us regain our identity."[25]

I received such keepsakes in a good number of the countries I've visited, but these were literally trinkets compared to a much greater and more sinister project. Another important Saudi tactic is to disseminate translations of the Qur'ans with translations that favor hard-line, Wahhabi interpretations of the holy text. As Ziauddin Sardar notes in his book *Reading the Qur'an: The Contemporary Relevance of the Sacred Text of Islam,* Muslims and non-Muslims alike have translated the Qur'an in ways that favor specific ideological interpretations.[26] But the Saudis seem to have taken a particular interest in this exercise. A Saudi Arabian religious propaganda organization called the Presidency of Islamic Researches, Ifta, Call,

---

preachers and missionaries in non-Muslim nations in central, southern, and southeast Asia, as well as in Africa, Europe, and North America. Adherents to Wahhabism used Saudi control of four-fifths of all Islamic publishing houses around the world to spread their fighting words into faraway places." Choksy and Choksy, "The Saudi Connection."

and Guidance painstakingly revised Abdullah Yusuf Ali's standard interpretation of the Qur'an into English, altering specific words and phrases to lend authority to hard-line Wahhabi interpretations. One verse in Ali's translation (43:23), for instance, read: "No reward I ask of you for this except the love of those near of kin." In Ali's view, "love of kindred" signified "the love of our common humanity, for all mankind are brothers descended from Adam." In the hands of the Saudi editors the line was deleted entirely. And the Saudi editors go even further, as Sardar highlights: in explaining 45:14, "it is for Him to recompense (for good or ill) each people, according to what they have earned," Ali states that, "it is not right for private persons to take vengeance even for the cause of right and justice. . . . Nor is it permissible even to a group of persons to arrogate to themselves the championship of the right." As Sardar notes, "The editors of the revised version have done precisely this: arrogated to themselves the right to decide exactly what is and what is not right. So out goes the part of Ali's commentary that questions their authority."[27]

Sardar also notes that a relatively recent English translation of the Qur'an contains language "suggesting that polytheists and apostates, by their very nature, have committed crimes that are on a higher plane than carnage; and hence they are legitimate targets for killing."[28] Bearing a "certificate of approval from the late Grand Mufti of Saudi Arabia, Sheikh Bin Baz," this version has "been distributed largely free and extensively through mosques, seminaries, religious organizations and Muslim bookshops throughout the Muslim world."[29]

The ability of a Qur'anic translation to support a particular ideological view might not seem so apparent at first glance, but it's real. Scholars of the Qur'an debate the precise meaning of words and spend years examining layer upon layer of historical and literary context. Even native Arabic speakers must carefully study the Qur'an and accompanying scholarly commentary to glean the Qur'an's meaning. Most Muslims don't pay much attention to the version of the translation they are reading. They do not presume that there might be alternatives, nor do they comprehend how much those differences can affect the meaning of the text and guidance it presents concerning human conduct.

The Saudis have published almost 300 million Qur'ans with translations that favor hard-line, Wahhabi interpretations of the holy text.[30] They have sent those Qur'ans all over the world, including America (and even America's prison system, where we've seen increased levels of radicalization). Overall, Saudi investments in the diffusing of their ideology has been estimated to be in the "tens of billions of dollars," and most likely is significantly higher.*

Through the donation of books, schools, mosques, cemeteries, professorships, and even medallions and the sorts of keepsakes I received during my travels, the Saudis have managed to dominate global conversations about Islam.† In the Maldives, locals told me that the Saudis were sponsoring Hajj trips and building mosques and houses. In New Zealand, clerics told me that their society was becoming "more conservative with money"—that thanks to Saudi grants and subsidies the local Muslim communities were becoming more conservative as a result. In Kazakhstan, I learned that Saudi

---

* Others have observed that the Saudi government "has spent up to $100 billion spreading its fundamentalist interpretation of Islam around the globe." Lawrence Pintak, "An Idiot's Guide to Islam in America: A Memo to the President-Elect about the People He Fears," Foreignpolicy.com, December 8, 2016, http://foreignpolicy.com/2016/12/08/an-idiots-guide-to-islam-in-america-donald-trump/. Government officials and other experts have confirmed to me that it is extremely difficult to quantify Saudi investments in spreading Wahhabism. The true number may be $100 billion or more. See Joseph Liu, "The Global Spread of Wahhabi Islam: How Great a Threat?" Pew Research Center Religion & Public Life Project, May 2, 2005, http://www.pewforum.org/2005/05/03/the-global-spread-of-wahhabi-islam-how-great-a-threat/. See also Carol Giacomo, "A Warning About the Secret 9/11 Pages," *New York Times,* April 27, 2016, https://takingnote.blogs.nytimes.com/2016/04/27/a-warning-about-the-secret-911-pages/?mcubz=3&_r=0. As Giacomo notes: "The 9/11 report was critical of Saudi Arabia: It cited the government's funding of schools and mosques that fanned an extreme form of Islam known as Wahhabism, as well as contributions by some wealthy Saudis to Islamic charities with links to terrorism."

† Citing "a State Department cable released through wikileaks," *New York Times* columnist Nicholas Kristof reports that extremist schools in Pakistan "offered impoverished families a $6,500 bounty for turning over a son to be indoctrinated." "Obama in Saudi Arabia, Exporter of Oil and Bigotry," *New York Times,* April 20, 2016, https://www.nytimes.com/2016/04/21/opinion/obama-in-saudi-arabia-exporter-of-oil-and-bigotry.html.

Qur'ans were being translated into Russian so that local citizens could learn the Wahhabi version. "The Saudis demanded religious conformity in return for their munificence," Karen Armstrong has observed, "so Wahhabi rejection of all other forms of Islam as well as other faiths would reach as deeply into Bradford, England, and Buffalo, New York, as into Pakistan, Jordan or Syria: everywhere gravely undermining Islam's traditional pluralism."[31]

Judging from their actions, the Saudis' larger goal seems to have been to perpetuate the fiction that "Muslim" is synonymous with "Middle East" or "Arab." In this, they have largely succeeded.

"AUTHENTIC" ISLAM FROM THE PERSPECTIVE OF MUSLIM YOUTH

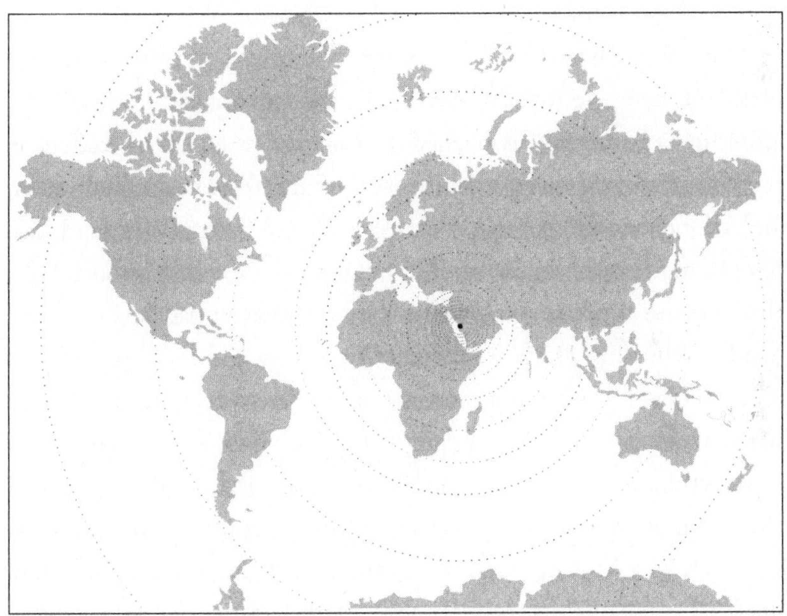

I noticed that the farther away from Mecca I got, the more insecure Muslims were about their identity. Even if an Islamic culture was hundreds of years old, or contained some of the largest populations of Muslims in the world, it seemed to youth that they were not practicing "authentic" Islam. The perception that Saudis knew more than anyone else was a dominant theme during my travels.

Illustrated by Nafisa Nandini Crishna

Even though only about 20 percent of Muslims truly are Arab, both Muslims and non-Muslims alike equate Middle Eastern Arab customs with "authentic" Islam.[32] As one observer remarked in 2008, the spread of "Arab culture" risked burying Islam and its traditional diversity. Pushing back on such "Arabization," this observer boldly pointed out, "It is possible to be Muslim without being Middle Eastern, without having a name like Mohammed, and without wearing *dishdashas* (the long robe worn by most men in parts of the Arab world) or *niqabs*."[33] Thanks to the Saudis, hundreds of millions of Muslim kids today would beg to differ.

OVERLOOKING THE THREAT

In May 2017, when President Trump took his initial overseas trip as president, he made Riyadh, the capital of Saudi Arabia, his first stop, attending a conference convened for him and attended by leaders of more than two dozen Muslim-majority states. The move sent a clear and very dangerous message: that the United States recognized the Kingdom of Saudi Arabia as the spokesperson for all of Islam. Further, Trump announced a $400 billion investment package with the Saudis, rebuffing many intelligence experts who have been calling on the United States to do more—not less—to rein in Saudi support of extremist ideology.[34] From media reports, there was no indication that Trump extracted any concessions from the Saudis regarding their support of extremist ideologies. On the contrary, and without so much as a hint of irony, he praised them for their efforts and presided at the opening of their new, "state-of-the-art" digital center, named Etidal (which means "moderation" in Arabic), for countering extremist ideology.

As unfortunate as Trump's actions were for anyone who cares about defeating extremism, they are broadly consistent with decades of U.S. policy toward the Saudis.* The fact is, Western governments haven't concerned themselves much with Wahhabism. Outside of the intelligence community and aid workers, most U.S. government officials over the last three decades didn't perceive Wahhabism as a salient threat to U.S. interests and global security. Elements of Wahhabism such as its treatment of women and its application of sharia law might have seemed unpalatable, but until recently it has been hard to find evidence that U.S. officials comprehended how directly Saudi investments in spreading Wahhabism might have been contributing to the radicalization of a generation of young Muslims worldwide, helping to cultivate the global terror we're experiencing today. As Elliott Abrams told me, the U.S. government saw Saudi support for Wahhabism as a problem, but no one imagined the kind of impact it could have. And, after 9/11 U.S. government officials generally assumed that the Saudi government would rein it in. "I guess we were a little bit optimistic that they would understand the ideological side of it," Abrams said. "And it was exactly wrong in the sense that they doubled down on the ideological side as another form of self-protection, and I guess we didn't see that coming."[35] Saudi assurances certainly weren't borne out by action. In 2005, for instance, the Saudi king claimed that his country had fixed the textbooks it was sending around the world. Almost a decade later, they remain very nearly just as bad.[36]

I myself didn't understand the dangers of the Saudi influence on local Muslim communities when I first started my government service. In fact, I didn't know much about Saudi Arabia or Wahhabism at all. Growing up, I rarely heard Saudi Arabia mentioned in our local mosque, nor was there even a hint of the Wahhabi intolerance for

---

* Indeed, none of the deals identified in Trump's $110 billion sales commitment were new. They all began under the Obama administration. Bruce Riedel, "The $110 Billion Arms Deal to Saudi Arabia Is Fake News," Brookings Institution, June 5, 2017, https://www.brookings.edu/blog/markaz/2017/06/05/the-110-billion-arms-deal-to-saudi-arabia-is-fake-news/.

other forms of Muslim observance. Muslims the world over prayed at our mosque, dressing and observing the Islamic holidays differently. Sudan, Albania, Trinidad and Tobago, Egypt, India, Iraq, Lebanon, Somalia—all these countries were represented in our little mosque community, and we all got along. I went to Sunday school before midday prayers at the mosque with these kids, and we never discussed what a Sunni or Shiite was, or the "right" way of practicing. The teachers who led classes on Islamic history or Qur'anic reading were parent-volunteers whose family paths to Massachusetts had begun just like our neighbors of different faiths all over the world. These volunteers often discussed the difference between religion and customs as well as the importance of respecting Islam's diversity. The only controversy I can recall occurred during my teenage years when a visitor from the Gulf expressed his displeasure at seeing women and men praying together in the same room. He told the mosque board that they should build a wall so that they could pray separately. That didn't go over very well, and he soon moved on.

My first inkling of the dangers that the Saudis posed both to Islam and to Western interests came during the years immediately after 9/11. In the wake of the attacks, some decried the Saudi educational system's function as a vehicle for the spread and inculcation of Wahhabism in the country and the fact that Osama bin Laden was Saudi. Meanwhile, the Bush administration attempted to confiscate the assets of a Saudi charity that the U.S. government believed was diverting money to Al Qaeda terrorists.[37] "We take a new step in the war on terrorist financing, making our first joint designation of a financial supporter of terrorism," Treasury secretary Paul H. O'Neill said in mid-March 2002. "Since September 11, the U.S. has blocked more than $34 million in assets of terrorist organizations. Other nations have also blocked more than $70 million. The funds captured only measure the money in the pipeline at the time the accounts were shut down, which is a small fraction of the total funds disrupted by the closing of the pipeline."[38] The charity, with a presence in fifty countries, was the Riyadh-based Al-Haramain Islamic Foundation.

In my own travels and conversations with people, I started to hear murmurs about the Saudis' harmful role. In 2003, during a USAID trip to Lebanon, an aid worker I met told me he had noticed that the Saudis were increasingly present and that they were trying to displace local cultural traditions with their own, monolithic brand of Islam. The turning point in my own thinking came in 2007 and 2008 as I visited Muslim communities across Europe. Speaking with representatives of local communities about my work, I was consistently told about Saudi Arabia's efforts to dominate discussion about the meaning of Islam. Whether I was in Belgium or Italy, Britain or France, I heard that the Saudis weren't just building schools or mosques; they were also seeking to disseminate pernicious teachings that left local youth insecure about their parents' traditions and also deeply alienated from the Western societies in which they lived. Preachers spouting Wahhabi teachings would tell these youth that their parents' practice wasn't "real" Islam, and that members of other religions were infidels. As community leaders told me, millennials were adrift, they had nowhere to turn—except to the Saudi-funded preachers themselves, and to extremists they found online (discussed in chapter 5).

Over the next couple of years, while I was working in the White House on the national security staff, I saw how hard it was to get the Saudis to engage with us against extremist ideology. Many Arab countries had pledged support for the Bush administration's Broader Middle East and North Africa Initiative,* and for the war against Al Qaeda, but behind the scenes the Saudis were putting up roadblock after roadblock. They resisted the entire idea of reform and even the process of being told that reform was something that needed to be

* As described in chapter 1, the BMENA initiative sought to advance reform efforts throughout the region by encouraging cooperation among civil society, the G8, and Arab governments.

prioritized. Quietly, they told others (as did the Egyptians) not to cooperate with us. They also refused to attend the Sea Island Summit, where the initiative was launched in June 2004, and urged others to skip the summit in an attempt to actively undermine it. Their justification for all this was that the initiative was a Trojan horse to attack their culture. It was no such thing.

So, why haven't we compelled the Saudis to cooperate? Our need for their collaboration on a wide array of political issues in the Middle East, our need at various times for access to Saudi oil, our need for lucrative markets for U.S. defense companies,* our deference to Saudi Arabia as Islam's chief "caretaker"—all this and more inclined (and still inclines) U.S. policy makers not to push the Saudis overtly, and instead to try to exert gentle pressure behind the scenes. During the first term of George W. Bush's administration, we asked the Saudis to help us crack down on private money from the country flowing into extremist coffers, separate from the fight against terror finance per se. According to Abrams, "The Saudis did nothing."[39] Years later, when President George W. Bush left office, the Saudis still hadn't established a requested commission controlling charitable giving. Keep in mind, the Saudi population is not that large—about 30 million, with Saudi citizens comprising only about two-thirds of that number (the rest are foreign workers). If the government wanted to, it could closely track its citizens' charitable activities. "We

---

* During the Obama administration, the United States sold roughly $115 billion in arms to the Saudis. In May 2017, President Trump announced an agreement with Saudi Arabia for an additional $110 billion, which likely included many preexisting initiatives from the Obama administration and a Saudi wish list for future items. In June 2017, ABC reported that Congress was only notified about $23.7 of the $110 billion of the newly announced arms sales. Mark Landler, Eric Schmitt, and Matt Apuzzo, "$110 Billion Weapons Sale to Saudis Has Jared Kushner's Personal Touch," *New York Times,* May 18, 2017, https://www.nytimes.com/2017/05/18/world/middleeast/jared-kushner-saudi-arabia-arms-deal-lockheed.html?_r=0; Bruce Riedel, "The $110 Billion Arms Deal to Saudi Arabia Is Fake News," Brookings Institution, June 13, 2017, https://www.brookings.edu/blog/markaz/2017/06/05/the-110-billion-arms-deal-to-saudi-arabia-is-fake-news/; Elizabeth McLaughlin and Conor Finnegan, "The Truth About President Trump's $110 Billion Saudi Arms Deal," ABC News, http://abcnews.go.com/International/truth-president-trumps-110-billion-saudi-arms-deal/story?id=47874726.

let them get away with it," Abrams says. "They never did it."[40] Nor did the Obama administration do much better. Although it worked closely with the Saudi government to curb incitement, the action on the ground never equaled what the Obama administration had promised.

It's difficult even to get government agencies and individual policy makers to speak out against Saudi support of extremist ideology. In 2011, the State Department commissioned a formal report on the Saudi link to extremism. Unlike similar reports on other topics, this one—critical of the Saudis—was withheld from the public despite reports that the State Department had intended to release it. It only came out three years later, when the *New York Times* filed a Freedom of Information Act request.[41]

Such silence stands in marked contrast to the behavior of European government officials, who on a number of occasions have publicly rebuked the Saudis for supporting extremism. The Finns, the Germans—even Iceland's leader promised to refuse Saudi funding in response to terrorist attacks. "Why can't we do that?" an American colleague asked me. "Are we less brave than the Finnish? And do we have less power, let alone more responsibility, given our relationship with the Saudis?"

Like many foreign countries, the Saudis have paid handsomely for former diplomats, public relations gurus, and consultants of all kinds for help gaining access and favor in Washington. These consultants have also helped the Saudis project an image of themselves as compassionate and progressive. Per Washington norms, elected officials of both parties in Congress and across the legislative branch have opened themselves up to Saudi perspectives on an array of issues. As David Weinberg notes, the Saudis and other Gulf states have donated money to a number of Washington think tanks. Until 2015, witnesses testifying before the House of Representatives weren't required to disclose their acceptance of Saudi funding, and those testifying before the Senate still don't have to.[42]

At the same time, doubt lingers in official circles about the precise role played by the Saudis. Some intelligence analysts have regarded Wahhabism as the root cause behind groups like Al Qaeda and so-called Islamic State, while others have seen it merely as a factor and not a catalyst. "The intel community," Will McCants observes, "hasn't tried to really answer this question in a sophisticated way."[43] As a former NSC colleague explained, "you would have to train assets on [how much money they spent on selling Wahhabism] to collect that information." Getting the right answers means asking the right questions.

Focused narrowly on terrorism as opposed to its ideological roots, intelligence agencies haven't tried to document some of the most basic facts about the Saudi link to extremism, such as exactly how much money the Saudis have devoted to spreading Wahhabi ideology, or how many mosques they have helped build, or how many young people or religious leaders travel there every year to receive religious instruction.[44] The lack of such data in turn has made it easier for the United States not to take a harder line with its Saudi allies, and to prioritize securing Saudi cooperation on the military front.[45]

In addition, the Saudi government doesn't have to fund extremist groups directly in order to further their cause. As Human Rights First has noted, "hardline clerics are granted impunity by the state to propagate the sorts of hatred against other sects and religions that encourage Sunni sectarian extremism and legitimize terrorism by ISIL, al Qaeda, and other such groups."[46] Perhaps because of such incitement, thousands of young Saudis have gone to fight for so-called Islamic State in Iraq and Syria. Further, Saudi Arabia has continued to allow expressions of religious and ethnic hatred in those official textbooks I've mentioned, even though so-called Islamic State has reportedly used those textbooks to teach kids under its control.[47] As Nicholas Kristof suggests, Saudi Arabia isn't "intentionally spreading havoc, more that it is behaving recklessly; it has made some painstaking progress in curbing extremist financing, but too slowly."[48] Other observers are more damning. Commenting in 2015 on a group of hostages held by so-called Islamic State, former State Department official and counterterrorism expert Alberto Fernandez tweeted: "Saudis should pay the ransom given all they've done to promote Salafism and Jihadism for decades."* Will McCants has told me that so-called Islamic State is "very much a descendant of the kind of Islam you find in Saudi Arabia and Wahhabism." The "easiest proof of this" was so-called Islamic State's use of Saudi state textbooks in the Syrian city of Raqqa once so-called ISIS had brought Raqqa under its control.†

A GLOBAL PHENOMENON

As I continued my travels around Europe and the pattern and impact of Saudi involvement became clearer, I grew indignant. What gave the Saudis the right to come into communities and spread their destructive ideas? European Muslims were never going to return to their parents' or grandparents' countries. They would need to create their own identities as German or Dutch or Belgian Muslims. Instead of feeling confident and independent, instead of feeling that they had a viable future in these countries, they were made to feel marginalized—caught between their own, allegedly impure traditions and the West's alleged "godlessness." What gave the Saudis the right to turn people against their adopted countries and against their own traditions? What gave them the right to intensify and amplify the emerging identity crisis?

---

* Alberto Fernandez, "Twitter Post," October 8, 2015. Fernandez was the vice president of the Middle East Media Research Institute and the former coordinator for strategic counterterrorism communications at the State Department.

† Will McCants, public policy manager at Google, interview with the author, December 14, 2016. Even Adel Kalbani, a prominent Saudi cleric who preached at the Mecca Grand Mosque, admitted as much. See also Ben Hubbard, "ISIS Turns Saudis Against the Kingdom, and Families Against Their Own," *New York Times,* March 31, 2016, https://www.nytimes.com/2016/04/01/world/middleeast/isis-saudi-arabia-wahhabism.html.

Local leaders and their communities truly were in a bind. I remember a conversation I had with an imam in northern England who was urging his fellow Muslims not to take Saudi money. Community groups in the country that ran after-school programs for Muslim youth were taking it anyway because they were desperate—it was the only money available. People in these communities wanted their kids to learn about Islam. They didn't want them growing up without a religious background, so something was better than nothing. In addition, many Muslims maintained a kind of insecurity complex around the Saudis. Residing in the physical birthplace of Islam, Saudis seemed to have a privileged perspective on the religion. Who were Muslims in far-flung parts of the world to disagree with and critique the Saudis?*

In some ways, of course, the Saudis were helping. As they didn't hesitate to emphasize, they were doing charitable works, serving as self-appointed "custodians" of Islam around the world. But rather than functioning as broad-minded, liberal custodians of the faith, they were surreptitiously fomenting a narrow, sectarian view that threatened to inflame and alienate the youth.†

My indignation only increased as I continued to travel as special representative to Muslim communities. In July 2010, for instance, while visiting Kazakhstan, I was driving with some companions through the beautiful countryside. There was nothing around—just mud structures and simple, concrete-block houses. Up on a distant hillside, I spotted a shiny, glitzy structure. I asked the driver what it was. "Oh," he responded, "that's the mosque." I remarked that it seemed so out of place. "Well, the Saudis built it."

A few months earlier, I had visited a mosque in Timbuktu, one

* The irony, of course, is that the Saudis weren't the historic custodians of Mecca and Medina's two holy mosques—they merely conquered those sites by force in the 1920s.

† The Saudi king Fahd claimed the mantle of supreme spokesperson for both Islam and the country. The claim was based solely on geography. There is no religious justification for this claim, as the shrines in the holy cities belong to Muslims all over the world, not just the Saudis.

of Africa's oldest and most iconic. Built hundreds of years ago, the structure's simple design was consistent with the local architecture and utterly unlike a mosque built in the Gulf style. I had never seen anything like it. A local guide told me how important this mosque was across the region, yet he confided, "Things are changing. People are scared. The Saudis are trying to come here and take away our African Islam and they have no place here. We don't want them. They are not welcome." He was desperate to make sure that I understood that there was a distinct tradition of African Islam and that the Saudis were chipping away at it. He was not alone. Near the mosque stood a small library housing ancient Qur'ans. As the chief librarian told me, locals had hid these precious texts from the extremists, who wanted to destroy them.*

When I went to Burma in 2012 as part of a larger, historic diplomatic opening between the United States and Burma, the abuse of the Muslim minority, the Rohingya, was in the news. Numbering about a million, the Rohingya had lived in Burma since the fifteenth century, practicing a form of Sunni Islam influenced by Sufism.[49] In Yangon, citizens told me that the Rohingya felt under attack and forgotten by the world. What the media hadn't reported directly enough was that the Saudis had established a strong presence in this country as well, offering to protect the local Rohingya population and telling them that only they, the Saudis, were "authentic" Muslims. I met with aid workers from the United Nations and other organizations who were concerned because they had seen the impact of Saudi money elsewhere and understood what would likely happen in Burma. Yet the fact remained that this money was needed. As one UN worker asked, "Who is going to take on the Saudis when they are giving aid to these people in need? They are getting inside

---

* Years after my visit, violent extremists did: Rebecca Hersher, "Militant Who Destroyed Mali Cultural Sites Pleads Guilty to War Crimes," NPR, August 22, 2016, https://www.npr.org/sections/thetwo-way/2016/08/22/490962861/militant-who-destroyed-mali-cultural-sites-pleads-guilty-to-war-crimes.

the hearts of these people." Other countries weren't doing anything about it.

The Saudi influence was also apparent in 2012, when I traveled to the Balkans. The United States had helped stabilize the region, brokering peace between Bosnia and Herzegovina, Croatia, and Serbia and supporting the new, predominantly Muslim nation-state of Kosovo. Our early recognition of Kosovo's government helped debunk the notion that somehow the United States did not want Muslims to succeed. For that reason, I was especially excited to meet younger people there and include them in the new networks of "credible voices" that I was building across Europe. I was also eager to accept a personal invitation I had received from President Atifete Jahjaga, a young, dynamic female Muslim whom I had met during the launch of the Women in Public Service Project ceremony at the Department of State in December 2011.

During our discussion, President Jahjaga proudly recounted Islam's long presence in her country. Despite a history of violence, including Serbia's brutal campaign of ethnic cleansing waged upon Albanians living there, Kosovo has been for the most part a religiously moderate place. Forming part of the Ottoman Empire for five hundred years, Kosovar Muslims followed in the liberal Hanafi Islamic tradition, embracing different faiths and cultural practices.[50] Women rarely veiled, and the sexes commingled both in public and schools—in general, Muslims expressed their strong faith with a light touch.[51]

That said, some ominous signs were visible. Shortly after the end of the war in 1999, a younger generation of Wahhabi preachers came into conflict with older, more moderate Kosovar imams. In one mosque, an Albanian flag proudly commemorated the liberation struggle the country had successfully waged. Violence broke out when a young student tore down the flag (certain adherents of Wahhabism consider depictions such as these to be blasphemous) and then abducted and beat the mosque's moderate imam.[52]

A few days after President Jahjaga's welcome, a group of us from the embassy drove out of the capital, Pristina, to see evidence of Kosovo's Islamic history for ourselves. We went to a charming town in a rural part of the country. Driving on streets lined with wood-framed houses and shops, we stopped at a beautiful old mosque set back from the street. Behind and beside the mosque was a cemetery with gravestones hundreds of years old, and in front of the building was a stone water fountain that the locals presumably used to perform ablution before going in to pray. The Arabic on the stones around the fountain sparked a conversation between the men acting as my tour guides and myself. They wanted to be sure I understood how important it was that we kept this old mosque intact. They worried that "outsiders" were making headway across their country getting rid of historic sites, taking down evidence of Kosovo's Islam and inserting new models of religion. In fact, as I was snapping pictures of the quaint courtyard, one of them remarked that I would "never see such beautiful buildings in Pristina because of the Arabs."

Afterward, I visited a nearby compound surrounded by high walls. A religious man from a minority sect indigenous to the region had asked me to meet with him. He was elderly, with a white flowing beard, long robes, and a bulbous turban. In an unexpected moment that still makes me laugh, he offered me a homemade alcoholic beverage—not something most pious Wahhabis would ever countenance. Then he spent time recounting all the efforts to indoctrinate the youth coming in from Saudi Arabia and others in the Gulf. "We're taking their money," he said, "but we're not going to teach our kids to be any different from what we already are." The Saudis "think they can come in here and buy us by financing our way of life and keeping up our buildings. We know their game."

I heard similar sentiments throughout my global visits. In countries like Pakistan, Senegal, Guyana, and Indonesia, leaders told me that they understood Saudi Arabia's true motives and were only superficially playing along. They didn't want to accept Saudi money at all, but they had no choice. In accepting the funds, they thought they could control the impact of Saudi ideology, preventing it from taking root in the culture. What emboldened them was the notion that Wahhabi traditions were foreign to their local culture, and thus something that would never resonate with local people. They were wrong. As I saw myself, Islam was in the process of becoming homogenized, rendered more synonymous with Wahhabism and Arab culture generally. In the words of Ziauddin Sardar, the "view of Islam and Muslims that is solely derived from the Middle East" was in many of these places now.[53]

THE LINKS WITH VIOLENT EXTREMISM

Around the world, such creeping "Gulfiness" has contributed both directly and indirectly to extremist recruitment and violence. What has happened in Kosovo is typical. A 2016 *New York Times* investigation documented much of what I saw on the ground there myself years earlier: the deliberate and surreptitious spread of Wahhabi extremism in the country, "using an obscure, labyrinthine network of donations from charities, private individuals and government ministries."[54] Saudi charities offered Kosovars scholarships to study in the desert kingdom, and the young people returned to their homeland with the missionary zeal of the newly converted. According to townspeople and officials, "From the outset, the newly arriving clerics sought to overtake the Islamic Community of Kosovo, an organization that for generations has been the custodian of the tolerant form of Islam that was practiced in the region."[55]

I must say, I was thrilled to see the *Times* run this piece. Upon seeing these developments years earlier, I had grown frustrated that others in government and beyond weren't paying attention. My briefings, memos, and specific requests for resources to address these issues were continually received as noncritical. Back in 2012, in fact, a U.S. embassy official in Pristina told me that local authorities had to reengineer traffic flows because under the influence of Saudi-trained clerics, so many people were now coming to the mosques that they were forced to pray in the street for lack of space. By 2016, Kosovo had in excess of eight hundred mosques, a quarter of them constructed since the war—prime loci for the inculcation of Wahhabism. To make room for their new religious institutions and ideologies, vestiges of a more tolerant past were swept away: "In some cases, centuries-old buildings were bulldozed, including a historic library in Gjakova and several 400-year-old mosques, as well as shrines, graveyards and Dervish monasteries, all considered idolatrous in Wahhabi teaching."[56] Wahhabi preachers then proceeded to promote strict interpretations of their own sharia law[57] as well as the murder of dissenters. Saudi charities financed religious courses held at these institutions, requiring recipients to attend sermons and for women to strictly veil in return. And it wasn't just the physical landscape that was changing—in the newly transformed Kosovo, members of older generations were trying to cope as young women refused to shake hands or converse with their male relatives, and young men joined the ranks of those promoting violence in the name of Islam.

Moderate imams had become accustomed to abuse that included the shouting of insults during their homilies, beatings, kidnappings, and even death threats. Idriz Bilalli, an imam of a mosque in Podujevo, was among those who suffered on account of their moderation, eventually losing his job. Bekim Jashari, who assumed his post around 2008, continued Bilalli's efforts, blocking a radical from opening a new mosque by preventing a transfer of 20,000 euros from Saudi charity Al Waqf al-Islami. Al Waqf al-Islami's Balkan branch was incorporated in 1989 and was backed by Saudi Arabia and other Gulf States. The Financial Intelligence Unit of Kosovo found that its Pristina-based office, with a staff of twelve, spent 10 million euros between 2000 and 2012. Much of that money has gone unaccounted for, though we know that a scant 7 percent of the budget was dedicated to tending to orphans (the charity's explicit mission).[58] In 2014, Kosovo authorities shut down Al Waqf and twelve other charities and made forty arrests. The damage was done, however: since 2014, 314 Kosovars (two suicide bombers, forty-four women, and twenty-eight children) have joined the ranks of the so-called Islamic State—the highest rate in all of Europe.

Again: it's not that we haven't known the basics of this toxic network until now. The link between Saudi Arabia, Wahhabism, and extremism was so pronounced back in 2007 that Stuart Levey, then the undersecretary of the Treasury responsible for tracking terrorist financing, was quoted as saying: "If I could somehow snap my fingers and cut off the funding from one country, it would be Saudi Arabia."[59] As of September 2013, " 'hundreds of millions' of dollars were still flowing to Muslim terrorists from private donors in the Arabian Peninsula."[60] In 2014, the United States revealed that the peninsula was the largest source of private donations to the original Al Qaeda terrorist group, or core Al Qaeda as it's called (as opposed to Al Qaeda's subsequent offshoots in various countries).[61] And make no mistake, that money was bringing death and destruction. The French-Algerian Kouachi brothers, perpetrators of the *Charlie Hebdo* massacre, were radicalized by Al Qaeda operatives in a mosque located in Paris's nineteenth arrondissement, as well as in a French prison.[62] While the Kouachis' allegiance was to Al Qaeda, their counterpart (who around the time of the *Charlie Hebdo* attack targeted a Jewish grocery store) did so in the name of the so-called Islamic State. Their weaponry can largely be traced back to terrorist operations and outfits financed, ultimately, by Saudi Arabia.

In Asia as well, the Saudi financial link to extremist groups has been significant. It has been estimated that approximately $100 million per year from Saudi Arabia and the United Arab Emirates went to fund "jihadis" in Pakistan.[63] For decades, the Saudis have also been spending heavily to bring Salafist teachings to Indonesia, the world's most populous Muslim-majority country, building some 150 mosques and providing books and teachers to 100 schools. As Din Wahid of Syarif Hidayatullah State Islamic University (UIN) in Jakarta said, "The advent of Salafism in Indonesia is part of Saudi Arabia's global project to spread its brand of Islam throughout the Muslim world."[64] As of 2017, members of the Indonesian government were concerned that some youth who attended Saudi-sponsored educational institutions were becoming radicalized. And several years earlier, in 2014, about one hundred recruits from Indonesia had come to the Middle East to fight on behalf of the so-called Islamic State. Saudi charities have also supported Jemaah Islamiyah, the Indonesian terrorist organization.* Meanwhile, "Salafi TV, YouTube channels, Facebook groups, and Telegram channels have become a fertile ground for female extremists and ISIS sympathizers in Indonesia in the last few years."[65]

THE ERASURE OF HISTORY

In striving to disseminate Wahhabi doctrine, the Saudis and extremist groups influenced by them aren't just seeking to influence ideas today. They're trying to make the hold of Wahhabi ideas permanent by effacing evidence that other forms of Islam ever existed, or that other religions prevailed in a given local area. Around the world, they are rewriting history, destroying architecture, art, and other historical evidence that doesn't support their narratives. I saw such destruction not merely in Kosovo, as I've recounted, but in dozens of communities around the world. The Saudis place no value on

* The Saudi government subsequently shut down the charity accused of providing support to Jemaah Islamiyah.

human history if it does not support the fairy tales they tell about Wahhabism and Islam's supremacy.*

As I discovered, recent Saudi efforts to rewrite history merely continued a process that they had begun decades ago in their own country and in Islam's holy city of Mecca. During the early nineteenth century, armies jointly led by the sons of the founder of Wahhabism and Muhammad ibn Saud captured Najaf and Karbala, the holy cities of Shia Islam. In the process, they destroyed the grave of Husayn ibn Ali, the founder of Shia Islam. They then captured the holy cities of Mecca and Medina (1803–4). Once in Mecca, notes Irfan Ahmed, "They executed a campaign of destruction in many sacred places and leveled all the existing domes, even those built over the well of Zamzam."[66] (The well of Zamzam is a biblical reference to the well that miraculously materialized when Abraham's son Ishmael was thirsty—it is a popular destination on the Hajj.) Their far-ranging ravaging of Mecca included the grave sites of Fatima, the prophet Muhammad's daughter, as well as other graves of close friends and family of the prophet, which had been meticulously maintained and venerated by the more permissive and tolerant Ottoman Turks.[67] The prophet Muhammad's own grave was nearly destroyed, sparking worldwide outrage. Sadly, no action was taken against those responsible.

In the twenty-first century, the holy cities of Mecca and Medina continue to come under ferocious assault. As the birthplace of Muhammad and location of the Kaaba, a black granite structure thought to have been constructed by the prophet Abraham, Mecca's

---

* Muhammad ibn 'Abd al-Wahhab, the Wahhabist movement's founder, "attacked the popular practices of worshiping saints and making pilgrimages to tombs and monuments in their memory, advocating the destruction of sacred sites as symbols of idolatry. These aspects of Wahhabist ideology (merged now with Salafism) lay at the root of the Taliban's destruction of the Kabul Museum and the Bamiyan Buddhas in Afghanistan in 2001, among many other cases, not only in the Middle East." Edek Osser, "Why Is Saudi Arabia Destroying the Cultural Heritage of Mecca and Medina?" *Art Newspaper,* November 19, 2015, http://old.theartnewspaper.com/comment/why-is-saudi-arabia-destroying-the-cultural-heritage-of-mecca-and-medina/.

significance for Muslims is unrivaled. Each year, millions of devout Muslims converge on this city in a holy pilgrimage called the Hajj, a religious observation required of all able-bodied Muslims at least once in their lifetimes. Many such pilgrims could once view the Kaaba, "encircled by arched porticos erected some three centuries ago by the Ottomans, above dozens of carved marble columns dating back to the 8th century."[68] Today, these columns, porticoes, and other remains in which the precincts were once ensconced are now completely gone, replaced by structures designed to affirm Saudi munificence to the world. Much of Mecca was paved over during the 1970s, turned within a few short years into "a 'modern' city with large multilane roads, spaghetti junctions, gaudy hotels and shopping malls."[*] In 2011, the Saudis launched a multibillion-dollar expansion of the holy site itself, constructing a Western-inspired complex that features a Royal Mecca Clock Tower (modeled after London's Big Ben, and one of the world's tallest structures), mammoth shopping malls, mega-hotels, parking structures, and a royal palace, built in honor of King Abdullah.[†] The list of priceless historical monuments destroyed in the erection of this monumental complex includes, "an 18th-century Ottoman fortress and the hill it stood on,"[69] "500-year-old Ottoman columns, commemorating the Prophet's ascent to heaven,"[70] the house of Muhammad's first wife, Khadijah (leveled and replaced by public toilets), and the house of Islam's first caliph, Abu Bakr.[71] Most of this destruction happened

---

* Ziauddin Sardar, "The Destruction of Mecca," *New York Times*, September 30, 2014, https://www.nytimes.com/2014/10/01/opinion/the-destruction-of-mecca.html?_r=0. See also Osser, "Why Is Saudi Arabia Destroying the Cultural Heritage of Mecca and Medina?" "Two years ago in Mecca the 1,300-year-old house of Hamza, the uncle of the prophet, was bulldozed to make way for a hotel. The house where Muhammad was believed to have been born in AD 570 has also been demolished for a skyscraper."

† According to one source, "more than 90% of the old quarters of the holiest cities of Islam has been razed to make room for a new urban landscape of hotels, shopping centres and apartment blocks. . . . Recent major projects include the $15bn Abraj Al-Bait, a hotel, shopping and residential complex; its Fairmont Makkah Clock Royal Tower hotel boasts the world's largest clockface and is the third tallest building in the world. Meanwhile, a 10,000-room 'mega-hotel' aims to be the biggest in the world when it opens in 2017." Osser, "Why Is Saudi Arabia Destroying the Cultural Heritage of Mecca and Medina?"

in the dark of night, when the world's eyes were averted.* A monument might have stood at dusk only to have disappeared from the landscape the following day.

As Ziauddin Sardar, author of the book *Mecca: The Sacred City*, has written, "The 'guardians' of the Holy City, the rulers of Saudi Arabia and the clerics, have a deep hatred of history. They want everything to look brand-new."[72] Confronted with such criticism, the Saudis insist that their motives are pure—given the increased numbers of the faithful each year, they simply must improve local infrastructure.† Still, it is hard not to see them cashing in on this extremely lucrative opportunity. "The Saudis know the oil is going to run out," Sardar said. "Hajj is already their second major source of income, after oil. They look at Dubai, and Qatar, and ask 'what are we going to do?' And they say, 'We have Hajj, and we're going to exploit it to the max.' "[73]

Regardless of the Saudis' motives, the destruction they've wrought is both unconscionable and breathtaking in its scope. The Gulf Institute, a Washington, D.C.–based self-described think tank, estimates that, "up to 95 per cent of Mecca's millennium-old buildings have been destroyed, to be replaced with luxury hotels, apartments and shopping malls."[74] As for the kingdom as a whole, the Islamic Heritage Research Foundation estimates that more than 98 percent of its patrimony has been decimated since 1985.[75] "It's as if they wanted to wipe out history," says Ali al-Ahmed, of the Institute for Gulf Affairs in Washington, D.C.[76]

He is not the only one to think that. In early 2010, shortly after President Obama's famous speech in Cairo, I went to Alexandria, Egypt, and visited the Alexandria Biblioteca, a spectacular new museum of Islamic art. As I toured the facility, marveling at its col-

---

* Photographs of the destruction have been heavily censored. See Osser, "Why Is Saudi Arabia Destroying the Cultural Heritage of Mecca and Medina?"

† Over the years, many have perished in overcrowding incidents during the Hajj.

lection of old, gilded Qur'ans, a prominent local leader told me how important it was to keep and preserve a lot of Islamic artifacts, "because soon, there won't be any." I asked him what he meant, and he specifically cited Saudi Arabia's deliberate and systematic efforts to remove or destroy antiquities.

In fact, the situation is much worse than even this gentleman imagined. Ziauddin Sardar has posited a connection between the Saudis' gutting of Mecca and the rise of extremism. As he writes, "The spiritual heart of Islam is an ultramodern, monolithic enclave, where difference is not tolerated, history has no meaning, and consumerism is paramount. It is hardly surprising then that literalism, and the murderous interpretations of Islam associated with it, have become so dominant in Muslim lands."[77] Nor is it surprising that extremist groups such as Al Qaeda, the Taliban, and so-called Islamic State have also sought to rewrite history by selectively destroying historical artifacts. The world first caught a glimpse of this in 2001, when the Taliban decimated the famous Buddhas of Bamiyan. After 1,500 years in existence, these priceless monuments—one standing at 120 feet, the other at 175—came plummeting to the ground, lost to posterity.[78] As Mullah Mohammed Omar, the spiritual leader of the Taliban at the time, said, "How could we justify, at the time of the Last Judgment, having left these impurities on Afghan soil?"[79] Six years later, as they campaigned across the Swat Valley, the Taliban defaced another 1,500-year-old Buddha stone engraving located in the town of Jahanabad in northwest Pakistan. Dating back to the sixth or seventh centuries, it was one of the largest and most impressive such statues in South Asia.[80]

More recently, so-called Islamic State has overseen the methodical looting and destruction of priceless historical relics in territory under its control. In 2015, the world watched in horror as so-called Islamic State destroyed the temples in Palmyra, Syria, and Nimrud, Iraq, as well as Judeo-Christian and Sunni Muslim sites.[81] An Antiquities Coalition was formed to bring awareness to such cultural racketeering and looting and to construct a comprehensive and interactive database of past destruction.[82] "Cultural crimes represent much more than the 'destruction of property,'" Deborah Lehr, chairman of the coalition, says. "The destruction and looting of heritage sites are recognized as war crimes. The looting of heritage sites represents a significant source of financing for terrorist activities."[83]

As of 2016, much of the so-called Islamic State's wealth and power was derived from cultural racketeering. Like the Saudis, the group justified cultural destruction by insisting that certain artifacts were sacrilegious. According to Loveday Morris of the *Washington Post,* "The group's looting has become so systematic that the Islamic State has incorporated the practice into the structure of its self-declared caliphate, granting licenses for digging at historic sites through a department of 'precious resources.'"[84] "They steal everything that they can sell, and what they can't sell, they destroy," said Qais Hussein Rasheed, Iraq's deputy minister for antiquities and heritage.[85]

After taking control of Mosul, Iraq's second-largest city after Baghdad, so-called Islamic State destroyed the tomb of the prophet Jonah, a holy and beloved figure to Jews, Christians, and Muslims alike.[86] They proceeded to wreak havoc on the Mosul Museum, Iraq's second-largest collection, destroying many of its treasures. Some of these treasures were replicas of originals kept in Baghdad, while others were priceless early modern manuscripts and books from the Ottoman Empire. In fact, the museum contained 173 pieces it was preparing for its reopening prior to the so-called Islamic State's invasion,[87] including the mighty stone-winged bulls adorning the gates of the ancient city of Nineveh, capital of the mighty Neo-Assyrian empire.[88]

Going to the source, the so-called Islamic State decimated the UNESCO world heritage site of Hatra, an ancient fortress city located in Nineveh. Flourishing under the Hellenistic Seleucid empire, founded by Seleucus I (312 BC–64 BC) after the death of Alexander the Great, Hatra had been among the best extant examples of a Parthian city.[89] UNESCO decried its devastation by the so-called Islamic State as "cultural cleansing," while other reports noted that the destruction of Nineveh brought an end to centuries of peaceful commingling and religious diversity in the region.[90] The so-called Islamic State then used sledgehammers, bulldozers, and explosives to destroy the three-thousand-year-old Assyrian city of Nimrud, located outside Mosul,[91] and close to Dur Sharrukin, once a flourishing Assyrian city.[92] The fourth-century Mar Behnam Monastery, along with the Imam Dur Mausoleum, were eradicated as well.[93]

Just as the dehumanization of religious minorities has led to their attempted extermination in places like Syria and Iraq, so, too, have Salafist extremists exterminated the cultural heritage sites of these minorities.[94] Such destruction represents a catastrophe for humanists everywhere, dramatically reducing our ability to understand who we are and how our societies have evolved. Such destruction should also deeply concern anyone interested in squelching the extremist threat. The extremists are rapidly erasing any evidence that diverse strains of Islam and diverse faiths besides Islam once coexisted and flourished in the lands in which they operate, in effect projecting backward in time their simple, monolithic view of Islam. In the absence of such physical evidence, it becomes that much harder to contest the extremist narratives.

A WINNING STRATEGY

Thanks to Wahhabi expansionism, an entire generation of global Muslims has grown up fostering negative attitudes toward other faiths, as well as a narrow, unyielding view of their own. Their mindset constitutes a fertile ground that extremists can exploit, including "unqualified freelancers" like Osama bin Laden. Karen Armstrong refers to Bin Laden as unqualified because in the past, extremism was kept in check by learned opinions of scholars (known as the *ulema*). Since Wahhabism has its own ulema, distinct from that recognized by most global Muslims, Bin Laden, the so-called Islamic State, and other forces of extremism, all having their roots in Wahhabism, are now permitted to flourish. And flourish they have.

Rather than holding the Saudis responsible for redressing a longer-term, ideological problem, we've opted to secure their cooperation on short-term issues, and to defer to them as the supposed arbiter of all things Muslim simply because they are the self-proclaimed custodians of Mecca and Medina. We've treated the Saudis the way we do the Vatican, assuming that they have the right to tell all the Muslims what to do. But the Saudis don't have this right. Ideology matters. The Saudis might be helping us fight terrorist groups, they might be helping us counter the influence and power of Iran in the region, and they might be buying billions of dollars of weapons systems and commercial products from us, but they are simultaneously taking actions that feed extremism and help it to grow. The Saudis are "both the arsonists and the firefighters," Will McCants has said, partnering with us on counterterrorism while fomenting "a very toxic form of Islam that draws sharp lines between a small number of true believers and everyone else."[95] And our tolerance of their behavior signals to other Gulf countries—the United Arab Emirates, Qatar, and Kuwait—that they can get away with their own, lesser support for extremism.

So, what should we do? As a general proposition, we should push toward three goals identified at the outset of this chapter: eradicating the spread of incitement through Saudi ideology, buttressing local cultures (including Islamic), and demolishing notions of Saudi Arabia as Islam's legitimate arbiters. Let's briefly consider each of these goals in turn.

If we want to fight back against Saudi ideology, all branches of our government must contribute, with prompting from the president. The missions of the departments of Defense, State, and Homeland Security all lend themselves quite well to the goal of eradicating ideologies that promote violence. Congress should pass legislation requiring the State Department and intelligence agencies to report on and publish data about the Saudis' exportation of extremist ideology via the governmental and private funding of mosques and textbooks. State and USAID should cease all partnerships and joint programs with the Saudis until we formally ensure that they are not spreading extremist ideology. In addition, the Treasury should implement a broader system to assess the funding sources behind problematic schools, training programs, community centers, and digital vehicles, providing our government a basis for halting any support we might be giving these programs. Tracking second- and third-tier funding sources will allow us to disrupt and dismantle all pertinent financial networks, large and small. The U.S. government should also require Saudi Arabia to "buy back" all their Qur'ans, textbooks, and other materials globally, with the money going to seed a new fund dedicated to historic preservation.

In March 2018, Crown Prince Mohammed bin Salman made a historic trip to Washington, making the case that America needs Saudi Arabia as its trusted regional ally, and touting Saudi Arabia's 2030 vision of a new, more moderate society. Rather than simply taking him at his word, we ought to create a master list of desired Saudi actions relating to CVE, up to and including establishment of a formal buyback program. Developing that initiative at scale and making it both transparent and measurable would require that the U.S. Department of State work collaboratively with the U.S. Department of Treasury, the United Nations, Saudi Arabia, and other countries to, among other things, create an extensive network of "stations" attached to banks. At these locations, citizens could turn in Qur'ans and textbooks supporting extremist ideology and receive cash for them on the spot.

But these governmental measures are just the beginning. The U.S. Commission on International Religious Freedom Report, operating under the International Religious Freedom Act (IRFA), should increase its advocacy for sanctions against Saudi Arabia, reassessing the wavier that has been granted to the country since 2006 despite its status as a "country of particular concern" (CPC).[96] Saudi Arabia desperately needs and wants the United States as a close and trusted partner. The country's political leadership wants us to consider them as our go-to source in the region, and they crave our praise. They want access to our thinkers and innovators, our education tools, our equipment, our military (through which they receive training and intelligence briefings), and our partnership on specific policy issues (or "joint alliances," as it's called). Simply put: they look to us for excellence and want to sit by our side when we conduct our diplomatic activities. This in turn gives us valuable leverage, which we can and must exploit.

There are also a wide range of potential actions that we could take to persuade Saudi Arabia to take action relative to CVE. We could build up other allies as "Muslim Centers," reconsider our broader relationship with Iran, deny visas to Saudi students, discontinue our close collaboration with the Saudis around the Palestinian issue (thereby creating unrest within the kingdom), and withdraw support for Egyptian president Abdel Fattah el-Sisi (thereby hobbling one of their client states). We could impose sanctions related to terror financing, challenge Saudi Arabia's membership in the World Trade Organization, sanction specific royals who support extremist causes, undermine Saudi interests in Iraq, and oppose Saudi Arabia's war in Yemen. The list goes on and on.[97]

The U.S. government likewise should spearhead the creation of a Cultural Coalition Force, comprised of governments, multilateral organizations, and NGOs, to help oversee the cleansing of Saudi extremist ideology globally. We should also create incentives for the Organization of Islamic Cooperation (OIC), a body of fifty-seven Muslim-majority countries (including Saudi Arabia), to collaborate with our government to develop a program for rooting out Saudi-funded ideology, from schools to imams. I can imagine, for instance, the creation of a credit or certification program, with cooperating OIC countries given special status toward bids, commercial or educational partnerships, U.S. grants, or study programs if they have taken steps to help stop the flow of Saudi incitement. Such a measure would build on the OIC's own mounting awareness of the Saudi challenge: In October 2017, after all, the OIC announced the creation of "an online messaging center designed to counter extremist propaganda and deconstruct violent ideologies," in partnership with an influential academy of Muslim clerics.[98] As one expert has written, "The OIC's unique access, socio-political legitimacy and track-record in representing the diversity and breadth of the Islamic world makes it a natural body to support this goal of addressing the radicalization toward violent extremism that has led to terrorist groups like ISIS."[99] Ultimately, we need to make it easy and advantageous for countries to work with us. Individual countries will always undermine one another, but to succeed with diplomacy, we must cannily provide more carrots rather than deploying sticks and waiting for them to have an impact. I know that many Muslim-majority countries cower publicly before Saudi Arabia, but privately they come to America and ask us to do more to stop Saudi ideology from entering into their countries.

Domestically, we need to evaluate the best, most socially and legally acceptable ways of blocking extremist incitement. In the United Kingdom and elsewhere, debates about how far to take government action against extremist ideology are already raging. Should governments prosecute people for accessing inciting material online?[100] Should they close down mosques where imams have incited followers toward extremism? Leaders in countries such as Germany and Iceland have already taken public stands against Saudi funding for extremist ideology.[101] In Belgium, public pressure has led the country to reclaim oversight of its Grand Mosque, which had previously been placed under Saudi supervision.[102]

In the United States, we desperately need a public reckoning about Saudi ideology and the lengths that we as a society are willing to go to contain it.[103] Over time, Americans have learned about the dangers of secondhand smoke and have mobilized for laws against public smoking. Likewise, we must make the American public aware of our decades of close relations with Saudi Arabia, as well as of the implications these relations have had for our fight against both terrorism and extremism. We have long given the Saudis a pass because most Americans have remained blissfully unaware of Saudi behavior. The time has come for the American people to assess whether our past arrangements are worth sustaining into the future. With pressure from citizens, the U.S. government might be more inclined to join NGOs and local communities and speak loudly and clearly about Saudi actions, articulating what we expect in the present and future.

Beyond these big-picture moves, our government should consider a number of other tactics. These include:

- Providing monetary rewards to schools, mosques, and NGOs for the replacement of inciting textbooks that appear in the United States and elsewhere. Replacement texts should be publicly cleared through a designation mark by the U.S. Commission on International Religious Freedom or the Department of State's Bureau for Democracy Human Rights and Labor.
- Developing education programs through grassroots partnerships with local NGOs and global publishing houses in Western countries. These programs should teach parents about the ideological implications of the translation of Qur'ans.
- Publicly outing and closing foreign-sponsored training centers for imams. We must create norms of pluralism and mutual respect, and enforce those norms with legal measures.
- Forcing the Saudi government to develop an internal system that prevents their clerics from issuing extremist fatwas.

Those clerics that persist would risk losing student visas and other U.S. benefits.

- Raising awareness about Saudi religious television broadcasts in America. If necessary, we should apply public and shareholder pressure on U.S. parent companies to root out extremist ideology.
- Mobilizing like-minded countries to cut off financial support to religious figures and organizations that use their authority to incite violence.

We cannot truly eradicate extremism without acting on the local level as well. Mayors and governors should enforce bans on incitement to violence and advocate for more public discourse around accepted community norms, while upholding a constitutional right to freedom of speech. They should also work with educators, parents, religious leaders, and others to build awareness programs and fire or deport teachers, scholars, and imams from foreign countries that inspire followers to violence.

Besides fighting back against incitement, a second important way to counter Saudi-funded ideology is to buttress local Islamic cultures and human heritage. First, I advocate forming a formal U.S. strategy for understanding the global problem of cultural destruction, remedying it, and preventing it from happening in the future. Second, and relatedly, we should create a Cultural Heritage Defense Authority (CHDA), a formal body of scholars that would compile and share information about past cultural destruction while monitoring ongoing developments. This body should include top historians, archaeologists, preservationists, art historians, and theologians, as well as representatives from libraries, museums, NGOs, partner governments, multilateral organizations, and agencies like UNESCO. At present, several international organizations and nonprofits work in this area, but no single, authoritative body exists to certify cultural destruction and help governments levy consequences against governments, individuals, or terrorist organizations. In order to bring perpetrators of cultural crimes to justice and to help our government execute a strategy of cultural conservation, we need ongoing, reliable documentation of those crimes. The CHDA would also help rebuild destroyed artifacts where possible and at the very least help us "rebuild digitally" by creating digital maps of destroyed artifacts.*

Interestingly, since 2007 cultural crimes are enforceable through the Department of Homeland Security's Immigration and Customs Enforcement (ICE) program. Working with the Smithsonian Institution, agents are trained to spot antiquities smuggled illegally into the United States and are "assigned to domestic and international offices [to] partner with federal, state and local agencies; private institutions; and foreign governments to conduct investigations."[104] These agents could work with the International Criminal Court, which can try individuals for war crimes regarding cultural destruction. In this case, the ICC would have a partner in the CHDA.

Who would pay for the formation and operation of the CHDA, and for execution of the strategy described above? That's easy: the Saudis. In the wake of the Valdez oil spill in Alaska, Exxon had to pay to remediate the damage it had caused. The same logic holds here. And there is a more direct precedent. At one time, it was unimaginable that Libya would compensate the U.S. families and victims of attacks perpetrated in the 1980s, including that on Lockerbie Pan Am Flight 103. Yet in 2008, the United States and Libya created a system for terrorist reparations, and Libya settled litigation

---

* American Muslims could buttress these cultural preservation efforts by creating a formal body charged with vetting various translations of the Qur'an for use in Muslim communities, weeding out those inflected with extremist ideas. Philanthropists, universities, technology companies, and governments could create innovation labs charged with creating new local programs that deploy artificial intelligence and other technologies to increase awareness of Islam's historical diversity and how different cultures have historically intermingled. Framed as public-private partnerships, these labs would draw on a variety of industries and academic disciplines to draw youth away from extremist concepts and thinking and to help them foster strong, stable identities.

in U.S. courts, paying out nearly $2 billion for terror-related events. Of course, it's impossible to quantify the loss of human history and heritage. But while any costs the Saudis assumed for the kind of organization I'm proposing would likely pale in comparison to the damage they've caused, those amounts would almost certainly constitute a massive contribution.

In addition to creating a CHDA, we should take a number of companion actions, including:

- Rebuilding cultural heritage sites decimated by the Saudis, to the extent possible. Where rebuilding isn't possible, we should build museums and write and/or make available literature, films, and textbooks to help spread knowledge about what was destroyed.
- Create a public global index of Saudi cultural destruction over the past forty years.
- Fund a global public awareness campaign on Islamic diversity and the meaning of local Islamic traditions.
- Establish cultural diversity commissions within specific countries to monitor the preservation of diverse heritages and histories. Acting as a first-alert system, countries can operate in tandem to stop potential harm to historical treasures by levying sanctions and undertaking other formal actions.

Historical diversity is vital to countering extremism. As Juan Zarate and I have argued, societies must "embrace and defend historical diversity like antibodies as a bulwark against modern extremist division. We must save persecuted minorities and the threatened sacred sites—from revered tombs and ancient monasteries in the Middle East to temples and statues in Asia."[105] To help with this task, we should expand the United Nations Blue Helmet Force and deploy it to preserve rich cultural and historic sites, with funding from corporations and individual philanthropists as well as government.

As a final plank in the battle against Saudi-supported ideology, we should demolish the prevailing and insidious notion of Saudi Arabia as Islam's ultimate arbiter. Saudi Arabia has furthered this notion and wielded power commensurately, even though nothing in Islam justifies special status for the country. The U.S. government needs to take a stand here, treating all Muslims equally rather than giving special weight to Saudi viewpoints. That means, for starters, avoiding the standard diplomatic language that describes the Saudis as "custodians of the two holy mosques." In framing policies that affect Muslims, the U.S. government should also engage scholars from all branches of Islam and all ethnic heritages, and it should consult Muslims from across the globe, not merely from Riyadh or Cairo. Privileging diversity in general will dilute Saudi influence and prevent us from conflating them and their traditions with "real" Islam.

President Bush's team developed a wide range of strategies for expanding America's commitment to Muslim engagement, including naming an Ismaili envoy to the OIC and ensuring that we had balanced meetings of multiple practitioners of Islam in those meetings. This created an important signal about how our government accepted Islamic diversity. Just as we focused on changing norms overseas, we must do more inside the halls of government. The Department of State's Bureau of Near Eastern Affairs should no longer maintain jurisdiction over all things "Muslim" simply by virtue of covering a geographic area that includes Saudi Arabia. All regional bureaus should have equal standing in developing policies that affect Muslims, unless an issue is specific to those regions—then they should have primary oversight. More generally, the U.S. government must take steps to de-Arabize American policy making and render it "Islam-neutral." Rather than treat Arabic expressions, religious norms, and foods as "Muslim," we should be clear that these perhaps are simply Arab, and that Muslim cultures are far broader and more diverse. Given our power in the world, the U.S. role is very important here. If we play favorites when it comes to the Saudis and their

Arab allies, most others will, too. The world must know that the Saudis are not some divinely anointed people.

A MATTER OF NATIONAL SECURITY

In connecting Saudi Arabia to extremism, I can't quantify all of Saudi Arabia's global activities, nor can I perfectly document a pervasive, decades-long link between the country's government and private donors and extremist groups. Some estimate that the Saudis have spent $100 billion promoting Wahhabi ideology. Whether or not that's true, I can personally attest to the link between Saudi Arabia, Wahhabi ideology, and the savage violence that has resulted, because I have seen it consistently and over many years with my own eyes.

The good news is that we have leverage today, perhaps more than we've had in decades. As of 2017, Saudi Arabia faced an array of serious challenges, including low oil prices, regional conflict, shifting geopolitical alliances, Congress's Justice Against Sponsors of Terrorism Act, and potential exposure to billions of dollars in lawsuits from 9/11 victims, their families, and businesses affected by the attacks.[106] The government unveiled its "Vision 2030" plan,[107] an ambitious program to reform Saudi society economically and socially in light of demographic shifts.* As regards extremist ideology, the country had taken two high-profile steps. With President Donald Trump in attendance, King Salman launched the new global center to fight extremist ideology mentioned earlier.[108] Working across languages and dialects, the center would "develop artificial intelligence technology

* "More than 60% of the Saudi population is aged under 30 and among that demographic are large numbers of disenfranchised youngsters dissatisfied with the current social contract, which is bound up in rigidly conservative rules governing social interactions." Via Martin Chulov, "Saudi Society Is Rigid, Its Youth Restless. The Prince's Reforms Need to Succeed," *Guardian,* September 2, 2017, https://www.theguardian.com/world/2017/sep/02/saudi-prince-reforms-society-rigid-youth-restless.

to determine geographical spots that incubate terrorism in order to reach the roots of extremist ideologies. The center also planned to create an informational content that encourages tolerance and moderation under the supervision of a high committee that consists of thinkers and Muslim scholars from different countries."[109] The heir to the Saudi throne, the young crown prince Mohammed bin Salman, also went on a public relations offensive, proclaiming his intent to "return the country to 'moderate Islam.' " As he told the *Guardian:* "What happened in the last 30 years is not Saudi Arabia. What happened in the region in the last 30 years is not the Middle East. After the Iranian revolution in 1979, people wanted to copy this model in different countries, one of them is Saudi Arabia. We didn't know how to deal with it. And the problem spread all over the world. Now is the time to get rid of it."[110]

Such statements make for good copy, but the results have not been forthcoming. And make no mistake: we need results, and we need them now. If we allow the Saudi-funded monolithic view of Islam to prevail, extremists will continue to find fertile ground for recruitment in local communities. Indeed, when the so-called Islamic State is defeated, other extremist groups will crop up in their place with equally harsh, unyielding ideologies, because the roots—the identity crisis that prompts youth to look outside their communities for answers—will remain. David Weinberg has it right: "If the United States fails to address the underlying sources of radicalization that emerge from Saudi Arabia, it could eventually win the battle against ISIL but lose the broader war against violent extremism."[111]

Whether Saudi Arabia will continue to invest in projecting ideological influence beyond its borders remains to be seen. In light of its past behavior, we can no longer give the country the benefit of the doubt. We also have to understand and account for another key dimension of the global system underpinning extremism, a dimension that grows out of extremist ideology but to some extent exists independently of it. For younger generations of Muslims, Islam isn't simply a set of beliefs to subscribe to. It's a process of displaying and expressing religious identity through fashions, products, and digital media. In the next chapter, I'll describe how this process has pushed young people toward enmity, with every bit as much force as the plague from the Gulf.

CHAPTER FOUR

HALALIZATION

HALAL—adj. 1. denoting or relating to meat prescribed by Muslim law; 1.1 religiously acceptable according to Muslim law. Origin mid-19th century: from Arabic "halal," according to religious law.[1]

HALALIZATION—noun: the process by which Muslim individuals and societies have adopted new, seemingly "purer" religious norms and lifestyles, replacing local or ancient cultural religious expressions.

During Ramadan 2010, I joined a group of Brazilians for a reception at São Paulo's Lebanese Center. At one point during the evening, I happened to stand beside a glamorous young woman dressed in tight black pants, open toed, high-heeled couture shoes, and a long tunic fringed with bling at the cuffs and neckline. Holding a glass of something sparkling in her hand, she leaned over to me and pointed across the room. "You see that girl over there?" she asked. "Last year, she told her parents she wanted to be more Muslim, like her friends were. So, she went to YouTube and learned how to tie that scarf on her head like that."

The object of this fashion gossip was an attractive, petite woman in her late teens. Smiling and talking with her friends, she evoked confidence and style, although clearly not the type that made my company happy. The woman standing next to me sighed and sipped her drink. "I don't know. It is like that everywhere. These girls are learning this from YouTube." She shook her head. "This is not Lebanese! I don't know what they are thinking. Who told them to be like this? This is totally against our culture. We don't do it like that—it is like the Gulfies."

I turned to my stylish interlocutor. "Well, what is your culture? Is it just one thing? What is it about her scarf that you don't like? Is it because she is covering her hair and you are not?"

My companion waved her finger. "Of course not. It is not about head coverings. It is about the reason she is covering herself. She thinks that this is what you have to do to be Muslim. It is a false gesture, like she is wearing a uniform."

I had heard this sentiment many times over the previous few years. Across the world, women and men alike had wondered aloud to me why members of the younger generation seemed so consumed not just with Muslim identity, but with the way they *wore* their Muslim identity. Among Muslim youth, Islam had become a consumer subculture similar to other subcultures, such as punk rock, heavy metal, and DIY. Even as the Saudis were foisting a monolithic Wahhabi ideology on the world, a rising generation of Muslims was reinventing Islam as a lived experience mediated by consumer culture.

Both trends reflected a basic impulse on the part of young Muslims to seek relief from their underlying identity crisis. In general, consumer products allow people to make public statements about their identity. If you wear a Fitbit, use an iPhone, or sport a Prada bag, you implicitly convey elements of your personality, and position yourself as a member of a particular "in group" of consumers who share affinities and membership in a socioeconomic class. Just as a hipster might express his identity through a sculpted beard, or a biker through a Harley-Davidson tattoo, so young Muslims broadcasted their identities through consumer choices big and small. And they did this precisely because their identity had become destabilized and uncertain. As author and Muslim marketing expert Shelina Janmohamed notes, consumer culture especially entranced young Muslim women, perhaps because they were still largely excluded from more traditional modes of religious expression.[2]

The vast majority of Muslim millennials I encountered didn't harbor extremist beliefs, but they were still recasting every conceivable part of their daily lives so as to demonstrate an austere devotion to "authentic" Islam. Uncomfortable with local cultural practices and traditions that felt increasingly dated and irrelevant, they embraced common practices that made them feel "Muslim" and that let them project that identity. The performance of Islamic identity often became more important to these youths than the theology underlying it.[3]

I came to call such performance, as well as consumer trends that accompanied it, the "halalization" of everyday life. Every practice, behavior, or consumer purchase had to be or seem "halal," or conforming to a doctrinal interpretation of how a "real Muslim" should act.* Traditionally, "halal"—which means "lawful" or "permissible" in Arabic—had a meaning similar to the Jewish concept of "kosher." It referred to practices of eating and drinking that conformed to sharia law (the loose system of local Islamic laws based on the Qur'an and other texts), primarily when it came to the slaughter and consumption of animals. The government of Malaysia's halal

* As a girl at a school in Guyana told me, she had her expression of Islamic identity down to a checklist. Hijab—check. Islamic ringtone—check. Islamic-themed posters on her wall—check. She wanted to make sure she didn't miss anything, that she got her Islamic identity "right."

guidelines, which enjoy broad currency throughout the globe, begin with a definition of halal as "things or actions permitted by Shariah law without punishment imposed on the doer."*

Halalization was both more comprehensive and confined than what had come before. Mirroring broader commercial tendencies, the merchandising of "halal" extended far beyond diet, extending even into the most intimate corners of life. At the same time, buying into halalization implicitly negated the diversity of community, affirming an awareness that one standard or set of choices defined the proper "Muslim lifestyle," and that deviation from that standard was unacceptable. Sporting a Prada bag might have attached you symbolically to a certain kind of glamorous subculture, with its own beliefs and norms. But it didn't suggest that membership in this subculture was the only kind of identity you should have. Halalization did.

Superficially, the practices associated with "halalization" constituted a cultural extension of Gulf religious norms. The Gulf Arabs had colonized not merely the mosques and teachings of their coreligionists, but daily life itself. Non-Muslims had unknowingly reinforced these interpretations; for instance, using Arabic words and expressions instead of vocabulary from local cultures could help mark the speaker as connected to the presumed power center. Yet language and slang are perhaps the subtlest element of the promotion of a specific Gulf-inspired lifestyle that could appeal directly—

* "Halal food Production, Preparation, Handling, and Storage General Guidelines," Federation of Malaysia, Edict of Government (MS 1500 [2nd rev.], 2009), 1. As the International Trade Center remarked in 2015, "Traditionally, halal was seen to refer only to meat and poultry, specifically with reference to the method of slaughter. More recently, the definition has grown to include non-meat foods such as dairy, baked goods, snacks, confectionery, ready-made meals and other processed food and beverage products." For this reason, the International Trade Center report identifies halal as "a new horizon of opportunity" in the global economy—a great source of revenue for Muslim and non-Muslim countries alike." Or, as the *Borneo Post* put it, "No longer is 'halal' viewed solely a religious obligation or observance for Muslims, but a new engine to drive the economy." International Trade Center, *From Niche to Mainstream: Halal Goes Global* (Geneva: International Trade Center, 2015), 21; Yvonne Tuah, "Rise of the Halal Flavor in Global Food Sector," *Borneo Post Online*, May 22, 2016, http://www.theborneopost.com/2016/05/22/rise-of-the-halal-flavor-in-global-food-sector/#ixzz49bFQ93bf.

and compellingly—to youth. Other elements were more overt—like fashion.

DRESS LIKE THE GULFIES

When I first coined "halalization" as a quick way to summarize what I was seeing, I thought I was simply describing a general trend toward externalized expressions of devoutness. Visiting European Muslim communities in 2007 and 2008, I noticed that young girls and women seemed to be embracing many new habits, including covering their hair with headscarves in the same, uniform way. Traditionally, there are many ways a Muslim woman might cover her hair. In some parts of the world, a woman might don a scarf that loosely covers some of the hair. Elsewhere, she might wear a type of shawl that settles on the head and shoulders—again, loosely. In still other locales, she might tightly wrap a scarf around her head, leaving only the face exposed.

But what I saw among younger Muslims during my European travels in 2007 and 2008 was a tendency to cover *all* of the head and sometimes the neck, too, because they had been told that this practice was more "authentically" Muslim. In addition, like men choosing which kind of knot they would use on a tie, these women, from Sweden to Sicily, had settled on one style of head covering in particular—a *khaleeji* in Arabic, literally, "from the Gulf." As one cultural observer has noted, this fashion "emerged from the shopping malls of Kuwait and is characterized by a rounded bulge emerging from the back of the head, which is supposed to give the impression of a cascading mane of hair that's been neatly coiled up into a bun." Defined by the head covering's cone shape, the use of little pins to secure it around the head, and the specific way the scarf was wrapped, the angle and tilt of the cone marked the garment as "stylish," thanks to a tightly packed cotton cushion that the women wore atop their heads and underneath the fabric. The longer, bigger, higher and more pronounced the cone shape was, I was told, the more visible it became as a fashion statement. If you recall the beehive hairdos common during the 1950s, you've got a pretty good picture of what I was seeing, except without hair, just material whose colorful hues perfectly matched or complemented the women's accompanying garments and jewelry. As the observer went on to detail, "Early adherents used milk cartons and yogurt cups to achieve the desired volume. Now, it's all about 'bumpit' gadgets and hair donuts."[4] From the Middle East the fashion spread to Europe, but it hardly stopped there. Over the past decade, I've seen it all over the world, including America.

As a Gen Xer growing up Muslim in America, I hadn't known a uniform way to dress in order to appear authentically "Muslim." If you were a woman, nobody judged you if you decided to cover yourself up or go uncovered. From a sartorial standpoint, there were literally dozens of ways to appear Muslim, none better or worse than any other. When I attended the Quincy, Massachusetts, mosque during the 1970s and 1980s, I never heard a discussion about "Muslim fashion," nor did my Qur'anic school classmates or teachers spend a moment talking about "lifestyle" in the high-concept sense that defined personal image in those decades. Most of us probably would have found such a conversation strange or offensive.

The *khaleeji* hijab was hardly the only fashion trend I observed among Muslim youth during my travels. Two other trends were veils in general, and face veils in particular (the latter known in Arabic as the *niqab)*. Walking the streets of Leicester in Great Britain, I was shocked to see young girls aged four or five wearing face veils. A generation ago, you would have found these coverings only among Muslims and non-Muslims in specific tribes and cultures, mostly from Africa and the Middle East. Not long before that, all veiling seemed to be going out of fashion. Albert Hourani, one of the most distinguished American scholars of Middle East history, predicted in 1955 that the veil would soon disappear.[5] Likewise, when Harvard Divinity School professor Leila Ahmed departed her native Egypt in the late 1960s, few urban women wore hijabs. She regarded this as a positive development—as an Arab feminist, she saw the dress as symbolizing patriarchal dominance in general, and indicative of the repressive and violent nature of extremist ideology saturating certain Muslim communities.[6] Like Hourani's, Ahmed's predictions about the hijab's demise proved incorrect.

I want to be clear: I take no position on whether a woman *should* "veil." Many scholars have studied Islamic modesty, and they've taken positions both pro and con. Indeed, while researching her 2011 book *A Quiet Revolution: The Veil's Resurgence, from the Middle East to America,* Leila Ahmed came to see the veil differently—not as a return to a patriarchal past, but as a powerful marker of identity, one that affirmed "pride in Muslim identity."[7] My purpose is simply to note the trend I saw during my European travels, where it was becoming more mainstream to cover girls, not just something one would see in small, conservative, rural villages.

In some European communities, I found young people combining more conservative, Gulf-style dress with traditional garments in ways that were strikingly incongruous. In Scotland, Muslims created a special tartan to evoke Scottish heritage and "Muslim fashion." They used this tartan not just on kilts, but on tunics and headscarves. One Muslim Scot characterized the tartan as ideal for younger members of the community. Instead of representing a fraught relationship between two identities, it conveyed harmony, "a tightly woven blend of tradition and heritage."[8]

At a community center in Barcelona, I met a woman wearing a *shalwar kameez,* a traditional South Asian outfit consisting of loose pants and a long tunic. Traditionally, both Muslim and non-Muslim women in the region would pair this indigenous ensemble with a *dupatta,* a shawl-like garment that could be worn in a variety of ways including spread loosely over the head. This woman wore a *shalwar kameez* with a *khaleeji* hijab. Struck by the inconsistency, I asked her why she wasn't wearing a *dupatta*. She laughed. "This is what we do here."

"But why?" I asked.

"This is the style. It just shows that we're good Muslims. This is the way we're supposed to dress, and I feel like it's important for me to fit in."

I had similar conversations with women across Europe, and beginning in 2009, around the world. Perhaps because I was a Muslim woman myself, girls and women felt comfortable discussing their fashion choices with me. And what they uniformly told me was that they wore what they did because they wanted to broadcast their Muslim identity to the world. Conservative fashions had an air of "authenticity" to them—a word young Muslims consistently used. They wanted to feel like they were plugged into something "real" or true, and even more important, they wanted others to see that they were plugged in. Such self-display didn't merely reflect the presence of peer pressure, but also of advertising that promoted "authentic" Muslim clothing. Further, appearing authentically Muslim was chic partly because parents were sometimes uncomfortable with such fashions. As we'll see in the next chapter, posting images of yourself in "traditional" Muslim dress on social media was even cooler.*

At one point during my visit to Leicester in 2007, I sat in a large, carpeted room enjoying tea and cookies with a group of young mothers in their twenties and thirties. A sprinkling of older women in their sixties and seventies, most of South Asian origin, were also

---

* In Argentina, I visited a school maintained by the country's small Muslim population. Every girl wore some style of veil. I spoke with one teacher, a woman in her early twenties who wore western clothing as well as a headscarf in the *khaleeji* fashion. When I asked about the trend toward more conservative fashions, she told me how important she thought it was to embrace one's religion as a kind of social statement. "I really want to be proud of my Muslim background," she said. Describing her headscarf, with its characteristic hive in the back, she related that she wore it because it was "very obvious. It's a very clear way of showing who we are. We're young, this is very fashionable, and we're showing people that we're the young Muslims, not part of the older generation."

present. The younger women wore Western dress and *khaleeji* headscarves tightly around their heads. The older women dressed in the traditional *shalwar kameez,* which obviously included a *dupatta.* Some had thrown it loosely over their shoulders, others had placed it tidily but loosely on their heads, and still others had draped it around their shoulders. The two generations stood in stark contrast, their clothing choices reflecting a clear difference in sensibility. Members of the younger generation were trying to express their individuality, and specifically their Muslim-ness. Their elders were simply dressing the way tradition in their communities dictated.

This generational shift was not limited to women. Men were also displaying strong Muslim identities, sometimes by wearing ethnically inspired trousers cut above the ankle, but primarily through their beards. The prophet Muhammad was thought to have worn a beard, and traditionally they bear strong associations with piety. More recently, beards have been associated with the rising Salafi and Wahhabi presence around the world. In embracing longer beards in communities with more secular traditions, Muslim men whom I met were showcasing their identities in ways that their parents found foreign.

In numerous communities I visited, older Muslims expressed puzzlement at the habits of the youth. They simply didn't understand why girls were wearing Gulfie hijabs, especially in instances when they had been raised in resolutely secular households. When I visited Kano, Nigeria, in 2009 during my inaugural trip overseas as special representative, men explained that the hat or *kufi* they wore with traditional outfits served not merely as a religious marker, but as a designation of tribe and local neighborhood. These traditions were centuries old, and the weaving, embroidery, and overall design were specific to their community. In their view, youths were eroding their rich cultural heritage by affecting a uniformity of outward Islamic expression. Older Muslims seemed relatively powerless to fight this tide.

On occasion, I encountered some young Muslims who articulated similar misgivings. At a school I visited in Senegal, some of the women had covered their hair using traditional African tribal prints. As they were quick to explain, their headgear and specific wrap indicated their tribal heritage. The Saudis, they claimed, had tried to tell them to change their traditional outfits because they were not "appropriate," but these youth were not having it.

Likewise, at an American Center* in Tajikistan, a woman dressed in modern fashions (pants and a loose top, with no head covering) openly wept at the disrespect people around the world had shown for Islam since 9/11. When she regained her composure, she said that for a time after 9/11, she had worn a headscarf because she wanted to show her pride in Islam. Observing her outfit, I asked why she had decided to stop wearing a headscarf. Her answer: "Because I realized that our Islamic traditions in Tajikistan are important, and I want to be a proud Muslim in other ways."† She was not alone, though not all of her fellow Tajiks had reverted voluntarily. Citizens there told me over and over again that police seeking to push back against "radicalism" and "foreign" influence had shaved thirteen thousand beards. They also "convinced more than 1,700 women and girls to stop wearing headscarves."[9] These were powerful public actions but, frankly, cutting off one part of the cultural system is not enough. More important, these actions led to an unhealthy blowback by citizens angry that their self-expression was being dictated by the State. As a group of women in Dushanbe told me, some people became more fiercely interested in theology as a result.

On the surface, you might take "Muslim fashions" as an expression of the strength of Muslim identity. But I perceived that this

---

* "American centers" around the world often provide libraries and shared space for lectures and gatherings. The library usually stocks books on American history as well as resources for those wishing to study in America. As I routinely found, such centers are important venues for public diplomacy.

† Such gestures did not exist in a vacuum. As I found, external political pressure often prompted kids to become more deeply involved in identity politics so as to normalize their Muslim identities.

outward expression of piety or devotion was very much the opposite—it indicated identity's *fragility*. For millennials after 9/11, religious identity had to be continually expressed and validated. Salafi teachings, Wahhabism, and access to previously unknown expressions of Islam gave millennials an ideological frame and a language for this self-affirmation of identity, but it wasn't enough. Young Muslims also had to act out this religious identity in the real world. They simply couldn't conceive of a notion put forth by one cultural anthropologist and fashion writer who remarked that "God is not something we can see in the way we dress, we can see it on the inside."[10]

The global mass market for more modest, "Muslim" clothing has grown rapidly and is expected to top $500 billion by 2019.[11] In May 2016, the first-ever "Modest Fashion Week" was held in Istanbul, Turkey, featuring seventy designers, including many from Muslim-majority countries. Meanwhile, Western brands such as H&M, Dolce & Gabbana, DKNY, Tommy Hilfiger, Oscar de la Renta, and Uniqlo have been "creating and marketing collections for Muslim women, especially those living in the Middle East."[12] These lines have featured "special Ramadan collections" as well as "more modest versions of their standard wares, with lower hemlines and longer sleeves." Other brands such as Marks & Spencer and House of Fraser have launched modest Islamic swimsuits and headscarves intended for use during exercise.

THE NEW HALAL

Muslim youth whom I met weren't only performing their identities through what they wore. They were also doing it through what they were eating, how they decorated their homes, and so on. The vast consumer culture that sprung up to enable young Muslims to project their sense of belonging to Islam—what ethnologist and Muslim fashion expert Leila-Karin Österlind has coined "Muslim cool"[13]—

produced a burgeoning array of standard, readily understood signifiers that individuals used to project their status as authentic Muslims.

During my 2007 travels, I saw early signs of this emergent consumer culture in the tchotchkes and knickknacks people possessed. I noticed watches on the wrists of young people that showed the local time as well as the time in Mecca, or that chimed loudly when it was time for prayers, thus alerting everyone in the room to the seriousness of one's religious devotion. Across Europe, I spotted mirrors, panels, posters, pens, and stickers with Islamic phrases on them: "Being a good Muslim means that you love your family," or "Islam is the call to prayer, Islam is peace." In China, I not only saw white marble mosques built in the Gulf style but candies that originated in the Gulf and that were fabricated with symbolic water (called *zumzum)* and thus were allegedly "authentic." In Pakistan, it became fashionable to equip your car so that it played Surah Al Fatihah, the Qur'an's opening chapter, when you started the engine. In New Zealand, I met an entrepreneur selling (incredibly) halal *water.*

I also started seeing important changes in how young people thought about everyday life. Confronted with seemingly minor consumer decisions, young Muslims were asking themselves what the "right" or "correct" choice was. Although the Muslim youth I spoke with used the word "halal" to speak of dietary restrictions, they also used it much more broadly to designate *anything* in daily life that seemed to conform to a strict, Gulf-inspired interpretation of Islam. The precise way you do your laundry could be "halal," or the way a couple got to know and date one another, or the way you exercised, even though clear doctrinal norms did not necessarily exist around these practices. "Halal" was becoming a catch-all for anything "authentically" Muslim.

Instances of this new, broader way of using the word "halal" popped up all over social media. Simply type "love" and "halal" into Pinterest and you'll find a seemingly endless stream of images that depict strong, loving relationships between Muslim couples as correct or "halal." Venturing on the site in the summer of 2016 (for research!), I spotted images of loving couples with accompanying messages such as "Halal love stories," "be with God: Halal is more beautiful and blessed," and "Halal family." These captions meant something quite different than, say, "Muslim love stories" or "Muslim family"—they replaced a theologically well-founded category with one that until recently would have seemed bizarre theologically. Further, if you were projecting halal, that meant you were not *haram*—that is, not doing something contrary to Islam. This tension between right and wrong, *halal* and *haram,* took on a new cultural importance that far transcended what previous generations would have considered as "normal" religiosity.

Discovering millennials' desire to express their identities through a "halal" lifestyle, entrepreneurs and established firms have jumped in the fray, attaching "halal" to all kinds of consumer goods and via aggressive marketing. Malaysia has emerged as an informal administrative center for the extensive industry of halal merchandise, programming, and paraphernalia that has appeared in recent years. This is no accident: According to the Halal Industry Development Corporation (HDC), operated by Malaysia's Ministry of International Trade and Industry, "Malaysia is the only country in the world whereby the government provides full support in promoting the Halal Certification process on products and services. Halal certification bodies in other countries are either developed by the individual provinces or states or backed by their non-governmental organizations (NGOs)."[14] Dozens of companies exist in Malaysia and elsewhere whose endeavors connect to halal, and whether the owners have a religious agenda, are in line with the Wahhabists, or are simply capitalists, their numbers are growing. The HDC features new applications for users to download onto their smartphones, created the "world's first Halal widget" for people to organize and share information about halal-based products and services, advertises World Halal Conferences, and even promotes a *Halal World* TV series, which began in 2011.* The series aimed to increase awareness of the halal agenda and encompassed thirteen episodes, each one giving viewers an overview of the halal industry, with a focus on health care, food, and beverages.[15] Thanks to government support and subsidy, Malaysia has become a crucial incubator not only for specific enterprises but for the very idea that "halal" as a category can expand beyond its original meaning.

The halal craze is by no means limited to or dependent upon Malaysia. A freewheeling market can be seen everywhere, from a halal food truck that opened in Seattle,[16] to popular halal food festivals celebrated in the suburbs of Toronto,[17] to the expansion of the nationally acclaimed Halal Guys food business to both coasts of the United States,[18] to the attempt of a small Brunei village to get their local chili sauce certified halal so it could sell better.[19] A company called Noor Pharmaceuticals has launched halal vitamins and has forged lucrative contracts with mega-retailers like Walgreens and Whole Foods to sell them.[20] The cosmetic industry has gotten in on the action, marketing halal makeup.[21] A British entrepreneur has launched a halal-complaint website marketing a variety of sex toys.[22] And Ibraheem Toy House, London's first and exclusive Islamic toy store, sells a variety of popular merchandise including Qur'an memorization card sets, the ninety-nine names of Allah boxed card set, and giant puzzles depicting holy sites in the Muslim calendar.[23] While halal food has been available for decades in cities around the United States, the leap into multiplatform "marketing" of halal begets a latent need for its consumers to tangibly express themselves as Muslim, and speaks to the larger identity crisis experienced by Muslims around the world.

In speaking of halalization, it's important to note that these products can serve to empower people without serving to distinguish

* All of these features are prominently displayed on the Halal Industry Development Corporation website: http://www.hdcglobal.com/.

morality in a harsh, binary way. Hop on the Internet and you can find the "Hijarbie," a modestly dressed alternative to the iconic (and scantily clad) blond-haired and blue-eyed Barbie.[24] Nigerian Haneefah Adam sought to create a Muslim doll that young girls could look up to. As she said in an interview with CNN, "I thought I had not seen Barbie dressed in a hijab before so I decided to open an Instagram account and dressed Barbie up in the clothes that I made. I thought it was really important for a doll to be dressed like how I would be."[25] Having attracted eighty thousand followers on Instagram, Adam has created a range of modest wear for the Mattel doll and plans to market the modest doll online.[26] In the opinion of one analyst, "The Hijarbie is part of a growing trend among fashion-conscious Muslim women who want to fit into mainstream society while adhering to the tenets of their religion."[27] More to the point, it's for Muslim women who want to *express* their identity. Their identity has become dislodged, and so it must constantly be reconstructed, reimagined, and reconfirmed visually. What we are seeing is that more and more millennial Muslims are moving in the direction of saying "I will buy that latte because it says 'Muslim' on it." They are choosing to *be* Muslim in very public ways—to express an identity, not necessarily to commit to specific religious beliefs and a binary way of looking at the world.

For young Muslims eager to express their identity while traveling, a thriving halal-based travel industry has emerged. Since 2011, CrescentRating has provided annual rankings of "Halal-Muslim-friendly holiday destinations"—sending travelers to comfort zones in which they don't have to see or deal with things that are not "authentically Muslim."[28] Beginning in 2015, MasterCard partnered with CrescentRating to create the Global Muslim Travel Index. GMTI describes their report, issued in 2016, as "the most comprehensive research done on the Halal/Muslim travel, tourism and hospitality market."[29] Significantly, the website generally makes "halal" functionally interchangeable with "Muslim." By 2020, halal travel was expected to bring in $200 billion for companies globally, driven by growth in the Muslim population.[30]

We cannot do justice to the rise of a consumer culture around Muslim identity without mentioning the huge amount of media that now caters to young Muslims. Countless websites are aimed at Muslim audiences, including prominent blogs such as Muslimmatters.org, Feel Islam, and Darvish. Predictably, there are Muslim TV shows, podcasts, Web channels, magazines, bulletin boards, comedy shows, and of course, dating sites. In 2000, Adeem Younis founded SingleMuslim.com, which now boasts more than two million members worldwide.[31] Another popular site, Muslimmatrimony.com, allows users to search based on doctrine, sect, and language, while HipsterShaadi.com advertises itself as able to find you someone who likes to "write poetry and dance in the rain," but who also won't offend your parents.[32] Now under ishqu.com, it markets itself for liberal women looking for feminist men or a "Rumi-and-granola-loving Muslim" partner.[33] One Muslim Internet dating pioneer, British-Pakistani Azad Chaiwala, even created several polygamist websites, including SecondWife.com and Polygamy.com.[34] Though originally intended only for Muslims, the sites attract Muslims and non-Muslims alike, from Canada, Britain, Australia, America, and the Gulf states.[35]

HALALIZATION AND EXTREMISM

How exactly does halalization relate to extremism? If halalization, as we've seen, tends to perpetuate conservative Gulfie fashions, ideas, norms, and beliefs, should we condemn it as a radicalizing element?

The phenomenon of halalization stands as a vital component of the global system of extremism, but the connection is by no means simple. I can't stress it enough: Halalization is not, in itself, bad or evil. Just because a kid dresses like a hipster or a gangster doesn't mean he is one. Just because you wear a Fitbit or take yoga classes doesn't mean you're a fitness freak or subscribe to Hindu beliefs. Likewise, just because a Muslim youth chooses to dress in a particular style or wear a watch that emits a ringtone when it is time to pray, or plays with a Hijarbie, doesn't mean that this person subscribes to extremist beliefs. It doesn't even mean they are particularly religious. Consider, for instance, "cosplay" in Malaysia, a growing phenomenon whereby girls use their head coverings to dress up as their favorite characters from popular culture: Elsa from Disney's *Frozen* in a silver headscarf with a perfectly braided wig and a flowing shimmery blueish gown, or Captain America in a patriotic headscarf and a tightly fitting bodice.

This practice is about fun, personal expression, and even sexuality, not religiosity—yet it makes use of religious garb.[36] As cosplay and other practices I've described in this chapter suggest, halalization is first and foremost a matter of aesthetics. It is a screen on which youth project identity and through which they achieve a sense of belonging and validity. Solid beliefs need not underlie or inform the effort.

Throughout my travels, I met numerous youth—both young men and women—who were extremely unobservant. They drank alcohol, ate bacon, did not pray, smoked pot, and watched porn. And yet they dressed like "devout" Muslims because it was "cool." In 2011, for instance, I lunched with a group of young, Muslim, professional women in Kuala Lampur, Malaysia. We had gathered to discuss millennial life among women in this majority-Muslim country, and some of my guests came dressed in colorful outfits with beehive-styled scarves on their heads. Although older Malaysian women still donned headscarves in the traditional way, these young women sought to be on the cutting edge and, as one woman related, "glamorous, like *Sex in the City*." Another woman stated that it "didn't matter" that they were not actually that religious in practice (she said she did not pray five times a day, and that she drank alcohol). What was essential was that her Muslim-ness was overt.

I asked these women whether the tight suits, jewelry, and makeup they wore alongside their headscarves sent conflicting messages. Giggling, a young woman with dramatic eyeliner on her eyes and a very pretty smile said, "Ms. Farah, we are young! We want to be stylish! We love fashion! We don't want to dress like our mothers!" Fair enough. Young women here were no different than any others around the world. And the same was true of young men I met during my travels who adopted "Muslim" fashions and practices.

And yet, just as police departments regard a "sudden change of dress style" and the wearing of gang symbols as a warning sign of "possible gang involvement,"[37] recognizing the role that presentation plays in creating powerful "in group" identities among youth, so we should be concerned about the ways in which halalization can help create an environment in which extremist ideology can thrive. In a few short years, Muslim identity has evolved from a novelty item to the focal point for an avalanche of products and experiences. Muslim youth are now expressing their identities on a daily basis and in a "surround sound" environment that encompasses everything they might wish to do, eat, watch, read, or otherwise consume. Although events like 9/11 might have destabilized identity, this destabilization has been exacerbated by the very steps taken by Muslim youth to attenuate it. A dynamic has taken hold: the more Muslim youth try to establish themselves as "authentic" via consumption, the more they must *continue* to do so. As theorists and critics of late capitalism suggest, the work of identity construction via consumption is never done.

Accelerated by a romanticization of the success of the Gulf states, halalization perpetuates a homogenized, monolithic Islam rooted in conservative practices. Instead of perceiving Islam as a religion of diversity, millennial Muslims are channeled toward certain expressions of Islam, and away from others. Their views becomes narrowed, provincial, inward-looking. And since the underlying ideology encourages a more rigid sensibility, subtle (and sometimes not-so-subtle) elements of that rigidity become embedded in the minds of young Muslims worldwide. A cultural basis has been laid on which extremists can easily build—an extremist edifice atop a halal foundation. And in fact, extremists have often policed fashion in areas under their control, specifying the fabric, color, and other features of "legitimate" dress, and punishing those who don't comply.

Indeed, an allegedly "authentic" halal lifestyle that in most parts of the world includes fashions, travel, and toys can quite easily come to include ritual rape and other atrocities in the hands of an extremist group.[38] As a *New York Times* exposé uncovered, so-called Islamic State has condoned and encouraged rape on the part of its members on the grounds that it is "halal." Consider the memories of a twelve-year-old girl who had been raped by a so-called Islamic State fighter before escaping: "He said that raping me is his prayer to God. I said to him, 'What you're doing to me is wrong, and it will not bring you closer to God.' And he said, 'No, it's allowed. It's halal.' "[39] The entire ordeal was choreographed in a religious way, the rapist beginning and ending his violence against the girl with prayers and prostration.

Again, there is nothing wrong with young men and women trying to connect with Islam in a way that makes sense to them, nor is there anything fundamentally wrong with businesses trying to profit by advancing this trend. Just because a Muslim buys halal towels online does not mean he is about to join the so-called Islamic State. Still, because elements of halalization conform to extremist ideology, and because youth are seeking out Muslim identities, the halalization trend allows extremists to manipulate their emotions and sincere curiosity about religion more easily. Halalization is not directly complicit in extremism, but by often seeming to reinforce specific elements of extremist ideology (namely, the notion that there is a single, correct way to be Muslim, that Islam is a one-size-fits-all monolith lacking in diversity, and that there is an "us and them"), it leaves Muslim youth more vulnerable. The halalization trend comprises one of the general cultural conditions necessary for extremism's global spread. In that sense, it is part of the global system underlying extremism. As a Turkish imam once told me, heightened religiosity in everyday life "may be good or may be bad—time will tell."

In fact, many young men and women partaking in halalization might be more susceptible to extremist ideology than they realize. Take gender roles. Despite the Internet's democratization of religious knowledge and decision making, the expansion of halalization has coincided with more conservative social practices relating to gender.[40] In virtually every Muslim society I visited, social relations were becoming stricter and more visibly Wahhabi in nature. In Morocco in 2010, I dined with a young couple at a charming old restaurant with stained glass windows and intricately carved mouldings overlooking a main square. As the waiter brought our food, I glanced out the window and commented on how many young couples were lingering in the square below. My hosts laughed. "You think they are young lovers, don't you?" the male asked. "There was a time when friends could hang out in cafes without anyone calling them names. Today, young women are more conscious. They don't want to be screamed at for being improper. They go out with their male brothers and cousins now." What was acceptable before was apparently not acceptable now—a common refrain in other places I visited.

Around the world, husbands and fathers have begun to prohibit girls and young women from attending school and building careers. Formerly coed schools and civic events are now segregated by gender, and prepubescent girls are required to wear a face veil or head covering—a practice that paradoxically *sexualizes* young girls through the very choice to cover them.* In May 2016, Turkish pres-

---

* In a discussion with my colleague Jared Cohen and a group of Muslims gathered for dinner in a private home, I mentioned my surprise at seeing such a young girl in a face veil. Someone at the table remarked, correctly, that "they are bringing the customs of their village to the high street."

ident Recep Tayyip Erdogan proclaimed that women who pursued careers or otherwise worked for a living were "half persons."[41] He suggested that family planning methods were wrong, that women were morally and religiously obligated to reproduce,[42] and that women who didn't pursue and/or achieve motherhood were deficient.[43] As I saw firsthand, in places like the Maldives, communities that had long allowed men and women to learn together were now teaching them separately, for the sake of propriety and modesty.

We might expect young Muslim women to feel alienated by such conservatism, but many embrace it as an additional opportunity to articulate "authentic" identities. In the past, the desire for authenticity has defined other consumerist forms aimed at young people. Hip-hop, for instance, originally was seen as the authentic expression of underprivileged African American youth in urban settings, and youth everywhere could tap into that authentic experience by purchasing hip-hop music and fashion. A similar dynamic has emerged here.[44] And it is crucial to note that this category of "Muslim youth" extends beyond high school. After all, someone who was starting high school on 9/11 would be in their early thirties today, and possibly parents themselves by now. As some of these mothers have migrated over the intervening years toward being more "religious," they've tended to alter the environment in the home, rejecting more "liberal" practices for more authentic piety. As I would discover through dozens of private conversations, such mothers thirsted for information about how to live as a good Muslim woman. What was required of them? What did the Qur'an say? Whom could they trust to tell them how to behave? Were some women out there educated about this stuff, or were men the go-to sources?*

---

* As time passed, I began to look more closely at the issue of women and extremism, as I was seeing a rapid change in the way women were expressing their Muslim identity. In a series of memos and meetings, I made my concerns clear to colleagues in the intelligence and counterterrorism parts of the U.S. government. It was challenging to gather precise data about trends, but colleagues could see aspects of what I was describing nonetheless. We lacked a women-centered framework to examine the comprehensive changes happening

Extremist groups have not hesitated to incorporate this nascent conservatism into their "sales pitch." In 2014, the so-called Islamic State opened a wedding center in al-Bab, Syria, presenting an allegedly Islamic version of a Western-style, "marriage tourism" lifestyle. Widows and single women could register through the center in al-Bab, at which point a member of so-called Islamic State would travel to her home and propose. The office offered other marriage-related services, such as a honeymoon in the "caliphate." Departing from Raqqa and going to Iraq's Anbar, the buses ran twice per week, played militant songs, and were of course gender segregated: men in front, women in back.[45]

Seeking to explain how Western women could possibly be attracted to an ideology that curtails their freedom so extensively, Western media outlets have perpetuated the "jihottie" thesis. Women are attracted to these groups, the theory goes, because the extremists' "traditional masculinity" is sexy and alluring. Bordering on misogynistic and patronizing, such analyses miss the point entirely. Although there is no, single "type" of woman who joins this terrorist group, women in general are attracted by a chance to claim and express to the fullest the "authentic," incarnate "halal" Muslim identity that they had been cultivating all along. As criminologist Simon Cottee has argued, women who join the so-called Islamic State are not "duped," but rather committed to the cause, just as men are. "What they want is to live in a properly authentic Islamic state in which [their understanding of] Islamic law—sharia—is fully implemented." Specifically, they want to live under the "caliphate," which, they believe, it is their divine duty to support. What they do not want is to live in the West, for a multitude of reasons."[46] Anthropologist Scott Atran calls women who join so-called Islamic State "post-

---

inside and outside the home. As soon as I left government in 2014, I asked the London-based Institute for Strategic Dialogue to create a new initiative focused on women and extremism. The institute's early research on female radicalization helped substantiate my observations and further underscored the need for a systematic assessment of the global phenomenon I described to my government colleagues as far back as 2010.

feminist and post-adolescent." As he suggests, these women buy into so-called Islamic State's mission because they see it as a final and permanent solution to the identity crisis they had been experiencing: "They are tired of a seemingly endless, genderless, culturally indistinct coming of age. The Islamic State and al Qaeda provide clear red lines: Men are men, and women are women."[47]

A strange juxtaposition follows: Shielding themselves behind face veils, women protect themselves from pollution by the modern world, espousing the purity of the sexes. At the same time, they revel in twenty-first century technology, embracing iPhones and Twitter accounts (and posing for selfies in their face veils). Initially puzzling, but if we see it as the logical conclusion of an ongoing process of identity creation and projection, it makes perfect sense.

For both men and women, halalization creates cultural conditions whereby adherence to specific groups like the so-called Islamic State seems understandable, even natural in a modern context. As Michael Kugelman of the Woodrow Wilson Center has argued, the rise of self-radicalized, "lone-wolf" attacks attest to so-called Islamic State's broad-based "brand recognition" and persuasiveness. He's right: within the cultural environment defined by halalization, the so-called Islamic State essentially represents a full-fledged, compelling complete lifestyle brand, including a logo, an extensive online brand presence, brand ambassadors, a brand mission and ideology, and so on. In this sense, Amedy Coulibaly, the man who killed Jews in a kosher supermarket, Syed Rizwan Farook and Tashfeen Malik, who devastated a Christmas party in San Bernardino, and Omar Mateen, who perpetrated Pulse nightclub's gruesome killing spree, are so-called Islamic State brand ambassadors. As British anti-radicalization specialist David Kenning has remarked, "The Islamic State brand is empowering. It tells you you're a victim and offers a license for revenge. And, through social media, it offers you celebrity, a chance to be somebody rather than nobody. Anyone who thinks a theological argument could counter this is simply naive."[48]

An entire generation is caught in a dynamic in which consumption seems to address underlying needs for self-understanding and belonging but simultaneously perpetuates and exacerbates that need. By perpetuating this bind, halalization keeps Muslim youth vulnerable to the extremists who purport to offer a stable, grounded identity. That halalization does bear a connection with extremism is evident in efforts by governments and cultural authorities in some Muslim-majority countries to counteract it. Earlier I mentioned Tajikistan's beard removal program. Government officials and imams told me that "halal" fashions constituted a "dangerous craze" that had enveloped countries such as Afghanistan and Pakistan, whose populations had become more overtly religious, and they wanted nothing to do with it. Government officials I spoke with across the globe confirmed their fears about halalization, even if their governments were not formally banning women from their beehives and men from wearing long beards. The Egyptian government has banned face veils from college dormitories.[49] The late sheikh Mohammed Sayyed Tantawi, a former Egyptian grand mufti and grand imam of Egypt's Al Azhar University—a venerable center of Muslim scholarship hundreds of years old—scolded a young woman for wearing a face veil while visiting the college.[50] Insisting that she remove it, he insisted that such attire "has nothing to do with Islam and is only a custom." In Comoros, an elderly imam pulled me aside and told me that he was watching the youth take part in "one of the worst chapters of Islamic history."

A WINNING STRATEGY

So, what should we do about halalization? Should we rush to restrict face veils and other outward displays of consumerist Muslim piety? Not at all. First, as we've seen, these particular articles of clothing are not the root of the problem—the identity crisis is, coupled with the willingness of extremists to exploit it. Second, it would be very difficult in the United States to internally restrict dress and other behavior associated with halalization, given First Amendment challenges. (Although some localities have banned gang clothing in school,[51] some of those bans have not survived scrutiny.[52]) Third, repressive policies risk backfiring. In the aftermath of the French government's ban on veiling in public, pictures of veiled women being forcibly removed from French beaches went viral, coupled with other images that showed French nuns allowed to swim publicly while wearing habits. It was a public relations disaster for the government, opening a deep wound among French Muslims, alienating them and putting their French identity further into question.

The failure of bans does not mean that we lack effective options. Societies can respond to the complex threat posed by halalization by taking a more nuanced approach. The more that Muslim youth and members of the general public understand Islam's historical and present-day diversity, the more they'll reject the extremist narrative as a solution to the crisis of identity. Government can fund and execute programs that educate communities about Muslim religiosity around the world, contesting rigid extremist assumptions, affirming the crucial point that there is no one way to be Muslim, and bolstering the conviction that anyone who makes that claim is wrongheaded and not the least "authentic."

A proper response to halalization goes well beyond government to include business and civil society. As we saw earlier in the book, parents, schools, and other community institutions have an important role to play in shaping how adolescents navigate the problem of identity. As regards halalization, civil society actors again can make a difference by framing mainstream messages about the diversity of Islam. For example, when cities celebrate diversity, they should not just draw images and stories about Islam from the Middle East (it's standard practice for public murals and forums to check the "there is a Muslim" box by showcasing a stereotype in a head covering or inside a mosque praying). Rather, they should adopt the more sophisticated and nuanced approach to storytelling deployed by international nonprofit organizations like Facing History and Ourselves, whose educational tools have been deployed in New York, Los Angeles, London, and other major metropolitan areas. Further, politicians and other elected leaders should think carefully about how they speak about Muslims in their community, refraining from using terms like "the Muslim world." Mosques should reinforce in their religion classes the many ways Islam is practiced around the world, not just the usual "Sunni and Shia." More broadly, communities need to fight back against all kinds of extremism, including right-wing extremism, affirming that any rigid worldview built around the exclusion of others has no place.

Corporations also should become more aware of the impact they're having with their "halal" products and services. Although their concern to make a profit is certainly legitimate, they can do that while also taking more responsibility for how products and services are conceived and marketed. In offering products and services to consumers, they should affirm the diversity of Islam, steering consumers toward healthy expressions of their identity. Just as Mattel's Barbie doll has evolved to emphasize the diversity of female body shapes,[53] so we need far more products that showcase Islamic diversity and attempt to puncture the "standardization" of Muslim form.

Finally, Muslims themselves need to engage in a new dialogue about halalization. We should encourage young Muslims to talk peer-to-peer about what halalization is doing to their generation, and how it relates to their own, personal identity struggles. Just as millennials and members of Generation Z talk openly about the need for a different kind of consciousness regarding issues such as organic or sustainable agriculture, a balanced lifestyle, or fair-sourced clothing, so Muslim consumers should have conversations about the commercialization of religion, and whether to participate in it. So far, these conversations haven't happened in any sustained way, and they certainly haven't happened at scale. If they did, young Muslims might form a more nuanced and critical view of their own behavior that could help shield them from extremist recruitment.

THE CULTURAL TECHNOLOGY OF EXTREMISM

As a mass cultural phenomenon, halalization is not new. Americans might put bumper stickers on their car proclaiming their belief in aliens or their devotion to skiing or their love of cats. Everywhere you look in modern societies, you see outward expressions of identity through consumerism, and you also see consumers attaching themselves to brands and products in an effort to express their ideals and advance social missions. What's striking about halalization is the speed and force with which it has emerged. Unlike their forebears, Muslim youth are intensely preoccupied with representing their own Muslimness to themselves. "I'm an authentic Muslim—I'm part of team Islam," they shout—not literally, but through their dress, their diet, their dating habits, their banking habits, and so on. This practice of expressing identity becomes stubbornly self-reinforcing. The more others do it, the more *you* want to do it. And your public expression of Muslim identity cajoles others to embrace halalization in turn.

Given halalization's connections with extremism, we must ponder an array of worrisome security implications. As the trend continues to spread, will we see new lifestyle brands akin to the so-called Islamic State? Will these brands be even more developed and compelling? The so-called Islamic State lacks a charismatic youth friendly leader or front man. What happens should an extremist lifestyle brand emerge around such a figure? And what happens when extremist lifestyle brands begin to set forth iconic heroines for Muslims worldwide to adulate and emulate?

Other possibilities are less obvious, but no less disturbing. As time passes and halalization becomes even more widely entrenched, we might see a generation of youth who know little about their faith's historical diversity, and who as a result are more insular and rigid in their beliefs, less likely to associate with people unlike them. As this generation gains more political power throughout the world, will they have a harder time relating to and interacting with other religious groups? Halalization represents a wholesale shift in attitudes, beliefs, and practices. To think that it won't resound in the political arena is naïve and foolhardy.

Ultimately, halalization represents a new kind of "cultural technology" for the display of identity in Muslim communities. If the identity crisis and extremist ideology comprise the "inside" of the millennial Muslim experience, halalization is its shiny, eye-catching outside. Yet halalization also depends on actual technology to spread and evolve. Previous generations experienced religion primarily in their local communities, face to face, in the flesh. For young Muslims today, the experience of religion—both as ideology and as social practice—is mediated by the Web, and social media in particular. As I'll describe in the next chapter, we can't understand how extremists can recruit young people around the globe unless we also understand a set of online practices that I like to call "Sheikh Google."

CHAPTER FIVE

SHEIKH GOOGLE

In 2008, before the age of social media and mobile computing, I had an occasion to travel to Lankaran, a small town in Azerbaijan near the Iranian border, accompanied by foreign service officer Jonathan Henick. As we made the long drive from Azerbaijan's capital of Baku, I spent hours entranced by the rich history I saw reflected in the buildings we passed along the way. Baku had possessed many new hotels serving travelers drawn by the country's booming oil industry, but out here I spotted many buildings that exhibited architectural flourishes from neighboring Iran. I pestered Henick for as much background as he could tell me about this region, which I was surprised to learn had been inhabited since the Neolithic era.

When we arrived at Lankaran, I found the town simple but charming. Surrounded by scenic mountains and fields, it comprised numerous wooden houses, some with small yards. Older women strolled the streets, headscarves tied under their chin as seen in old European paintings. A fountain in the town square boasted newly installed jet streams of "dancing water" illuminated with colored bulbs. As the mayor proudly told me, he had seen such a fountain while traveling in the United States and had been so impressed, he just had to erect a similar one in his hometown because it "was a sign of success."

The mayor took me to a school, a cement structure with drab, spartan classrooms. The kids we encountered wore the standard uniform of their millennial counterparts around the world—torn jeans, baggy pants, T-shirts, baseball caps. I led a conversation in which the kids expressed great curiosity about the United States and what it was like to live as a Muslim there. I asked them about their lives, their hopes for the future, and their thoughts about current events. I also asked where they went to learn about their religion. I was expecting that they would cite their parents, relatives, or teachers. They had another answer: the Internet.

"How do you know that the people who are answering your questions online know what they're talking about?" I asked.

"Well, we know because friends tell us to go to certain websites—that the people on there are good. They know."

"But you don't really *know* that these people really are legitimate scholars, right?"

The teens were quick to jump in. "We see they are popular, and they seem like they know. So, we believe these people are good."

We wrapped up the discussion, and I went on to meet with a number of teachers at the school. What they told me was disturbing. They said that these kids, who were so quick to believe what they saw online, were changing their behavior in dramatic ways, such as beginning to fast on certain holidays that, traditionally, were not observed by locals. "For these kids, it's all about Google," one of the teachers told me. "Whatever Google tells them, they do. It's beyond our control."

We all know that millennials are the "wired generation," and we've been inundated with media reports about how extremists are seducing kids online. According to one study that examined only Arabic tweets, supporters of the so-called Islamic State send out more than twice as many tweets per day as their opponents.[1] With tens of thousands of tweets produced each day by extremists in various languages, social media has clearly become a serious and dangerous means of indoctrinating youth about violent ideologies. In addition, the use of social media by both extremists and millennials has evolved, both in terms of the technological platforms used and online behaviors. Yet as we dissect the constantly changing so-called Islamic State recruiting machine, what many people don't realize is that the group's online success in recent years is part of a much larger set of technological habits that have developed since 9/11.

As I've traveled the world over the past decade, I've had numerous encounters like the ones in Azerbaijan. Collectively, they've taught me that technology does not just serve as a conduit for Muslim identity formation through consumption. It also allows for the dissemination of a particular type of Islamic doctrine to nearly all parts of the world. Driven by their identity crisis, Muslim youth have gone online for answers, seeking information about Islam and opportunities to share their religious beliefs online. In their innocence, they have found a dangerous space largely dominated by conservative interpretations of Islamic texts. Whereas the belief systems of individual families once were most influential in shaping how youth thought about religion, now youth look to what a global "family" has to say about proper religiosity. As a young person in Mauritania assured me, "It's okay to be Muslim and use the Internet."

I glimpsed this trend unfolding as early as 2010. That year, at a mosque in the tiny country of Brunei, I discovered a computer kiosk similar to ones you find in airports, stores, and other public places around the world. This one was different: You wouldn't use it to print out your boarding pass or find out what aisle of the superstore stocked detergent. Rather, you'd use it to find answers to burning questions you might have about Islam. Enter a query, and this religious counselor would spit out a quick answer.

As I typed questions into this kiosk, I pondered what it might mean that young people might have such a device—or that they might *want* to have one. It occurred to me that for this generation, technology might have an authority of its own, helping to define for youth not merely how they should dress to be good Muslims, but what they should *think*. Urs Gasser, executive director of the Berkman Klein Center for Internet & Society at Harvard University, supported my suspicion, noting that young people frequently turn to digital technologies as sources of information, whether it's Wikipedia or instructional videos on YouTube. He agreed that "the level of sophistication is not equally distributed . . . even within the population of young people," with socioeconomic factors influencing skill and knowledge levels.[2]

This lack of sophistication was also borne out during my travels. Wherever I went, I found kids who not merely struggled with deeper questions about their identities and heritage in the wake of 9/11, but who turned in ever more numerous ways to the Internet for practical, everyday guidance. Were they really not allowed to drink alcohol? When should they get married? Can they become friends with non-Muslim classmates? What does Islam say about their responsibilities to their families? Did Islam have anything to say about the political issues of the day? Instead of parents or imams, instant gratification held the most sway. Knowledge about religion had to be easy for millennials to understand, and it had to be ready and available at the precise moment that kids desired it. Religious exploration no longer meant going to the old man with the longest beard and highest hat. Nor did it necessarily mean extensive reading followed by close reflection. Rather, it meant going to Sheikh Google or a kiosk, where easy, simple, and unambiguous answers were there for the taking.[3] And, as has become increasingly clear (especially in the dissection of the 2016 presidential election), search engines are not as neutral and broadly encompassing as myth would have it.

Michael Leiter, former director of the National Counterterrorism Center, said during a hearing on Capitol Hill that the fight against extremism should be based on "factual and truthful analysis of radicalization."[4] He noted that the radicalization was not generally happening in mosques in America, as commonly believed. But extremists from groups like so-called Islamic State are hardly the only ones to mobilize technology to establish their authenticity and attract youthful followers. Right-wing extremists have as well. Self-proclaimed "identitarians" seeking to "defend" Europe against non-Christian immigrants have spread across the continent. Like the so-called Islamic State, they seek to create a global culture that is hip, attractive, and available to youth across geographic and linguistic divides.[5] To that end, they've established a presence on an array of platforms, including Twitter, Gab, and the gaming app Discord. As one European researcher told me, "The connectivity of gamers, co-conspirators and the manosphere and anti-immigrants all converge in the Trump era, precisely because [the identitarians] had a vehicle to do it." According to a 2017 report from the Institute for Strategic Dialogue, "Alternative online platforms, some created explicitly for use by the extreme right, provide mechanisms for transnational knowledge exchange, fundraising and coordinated information operations. . . . Their strategic, tactical and operational convergence has allowed the extreme right to translate large-scale online mobilization into real-world impact."[6]

Policy makers, educators, and even mathematicians have hazarded explanations and tried to "model" the process by which a young person who ventures online is radicalized.[7] General patterns emerge, though the specific elements and sequences remain hard to determine with absolute certainty. One truth seems apparent, however: if we are to compete with the extremists, we have to better appreciate the broader implications of how millennials and Generation Z use technology.

In consulting this "Sheikh Google," many Muslim millennials haven't critically analyzed arguments about Islam. They've assessed these arguments superficially, in short bursts, visually, and via peer-to-peer transmission. Technology entrepreneur Shahed Amanullah, who formerly served as my senior advisor for technology and new media, has told me that millennials "don't reflect the way previous generations do" because they don't have that opportunity in online contexts. "If you ask a millennial to stay in a room for a couple hours with no sensory input, they won't be able to handle it."[8] These kids are used to finding quick answers. According to one scholar of online behavior, "teens are likely to have less patience and poor research skills," and they "lack skills in evaluating material they find online."[9] With traditional authorities (local imams, religious schools, parents, etc.) absent by virtue of being perceived as useless and out of touch, young Muslims have become more vulnerable to bad actors peddling dubious ideology. As Amanullah remarks, kids "now can let themselves get immersed by whatever messages are coming in [online]. The more provoking and exciting and colorful and evocative, the better. That's the opportunity that extremists have [exploited]."[10]

Yet the solution isn't to ban Muslim millennials from the Internet, or to censor harsh interpretations of Islam we dislike. The European Union and the United Kingdom have leaned hard on Facebook, Google, Twitter, and other technology platforms to take down bad content. And while they and others can and must do more to prevent extremists from showing beheadings online in real time, for instance, or from advertising their violent wars using words and images, they don't represent the entire solution. After all, material that is taken down tends to go back up in other ways, often driving followers to dark channels that are harder for authorities to trace. One authority, Joanna Shields, former British minister for Internet safety and security, told me that "we need to reach [extremists] when they are fishing for recruits, because once they get one they move to encrypted areas and we lose touch."[11]

Rooting out all terrorist recruiters would certainly help, but while we're waiting for that to happen, we must do something else: find ways to project more credible, moderate voices online. If impressionable youth encounter a multiplicity of ideas and not just conservative ones, they'll have a healthier perspective on their religion and apply a more critical gaze. So long as millennials' underlying identity crisis remains unsolved, and mainstream ideologies don't dominate online, we can expect extremist groups to garner recruits. Even if we defeat the so-called Islamic State as an organization, we can't kill their ideas. Other groups will crop up to peddle hateful ideologies, using tactics and platforms that have yet to be invented. Phenomena such as fake news will further play to extremists' advantage. Indeed, a large part of the problem is that digital technology and behaviors online are changing faster than governments and law enforcement experts can keep up—and the pace of change will only increase over time.[12] By constantly flooding online spaces with the right kind of messages, we can give kids a fighting chance against those who would recruit them, no matter which extremists are operating, what ideas they're peddling, and what specific recruiting tactics they deploy.

CHEATING GOD

In 2010, I attended a dinner with young Muslim bloggers in Kazakhstan, a country that had formerly languished under Soviet rule. As my dinner companions recounted, the Soviets had prohibited religious practice, and as a result, the local youth continued to lack knowledge about Islam. "We have a hard time connecting to any understanding of the Qur'an," one said, because their parents grew up without instruction, and so there was nobody around to teach them. Kids were going online, where they were encountering radical strains of Islamic theology.

Yet Sheikh Google was not only figuring prominently in the lives of kids who lacked access to local sources of information about their religion. During Ramadan in 2011, I visited a school for orphans in Indonesia. A young musician gave me a tour of the facility. He was in great spirits: some talented youth had played a concert for me, and he was very pleased that I had enjoyed it. As we passed through a humble wooden house, we viewed the dormitory and some simple classrooms. And then, pausing on a balcony overlooking the school courtyard, I asked him how he and his peers connected to being Muslim. For this teen, with his big smile and friendly manner, it was easy: on Facebook. I wondered how he had access at this poorly funded orphanage, where the kids did not have their own computers. "We do have one computer," he said. "We like to go on there and see what Muslim kids are doing, and how they spent their time during Ramadan." On this same trip, I met with a group of kids in another Jakarta school. A young man remarked that it was "easier to get what you need from the Web" than to try to look it up in a book. "We don't have the time," he said. "If we want an answer, we get it instantly."

Not everything on the Internet inevitably pushes an extremist viewpoint. Indeed, disconnection from local authority can be liberating. The following year, during a visit to the gulf nation of Oman, I was talking with a group about twenty kids at the University of Nizwa, about an hour and a half by car from the capital, Muscat. These kids were modern, not merely in their dress but also in their emphasis on education. Some wanted to become doctors, while others studied philosophy and English. They were also curious about the world, asking me all sorts of questions about my travels and conditions in other Muslim communities.

After the event, a few of the girls drove with me back to Muscat. As we drove across the taupe desert landscape, the sky strewn with feathery clouds, the girls spoke about dating, sex, and other personal matters, no longer chastened by the presence of male classmates. "You don't understand," said one girl with a stylish beehive head covering. "People think we're so conservative because we're covering our heads. But all this stuff happens behind the scenes." She proceeded to tell me about how girls often meet up in private with boys, their families unaware. Their tactics were reminiscent of spy thrillers: Cars of boys and girls would drive down a particular street, flashing their lights to signal interest. Balls of crumpled paper would fly furtively through windows bearing phone numbers.

But did these kids stop at kissing? Not at all, even though their culture strictly forbade and punished sex before marriage. As the girls explained, they felt torn between their desires and the demands of their religious traditions, to which they all felt closely attached. They and many of their peers had arrived at a solution. If they officially married a boy, sleeping with him wouldn't be *haram,* or forbidden. So they "tricked God," getting married and then divorced within the space of fifteen minutes or an hour. They did this informally, and without the participation of authorities. All it took was signing a piece of paper and exchanging money. Under one reading of Islamic law, a man and a woman could marry by signing a piece of paper with terms specifying the duration of the marriage. The male partner also had to pay a sum to the female.[13] In the minds of these girls, this practice would allow them to have sex and not sin. "Tricking God" was widespread, these girls assured me, a contention that I have confirmed during visits to other majority Muslim countries. How did these girls learn about this practice? Online—via Google, in chat rooms, on Facebook.

From Muscat to Malibu, the online guidance that kids encounter can be breathtaking, offering points of view that far transcended the parochial confines of their local communities. As one American college student has remarked, "On social media I am friends with family members all over the world and each one will post something religious that I may have never seen before. Each time I learn something new, I feel like I get a little more religious."[14] Sheikh Google was private, beyond the reach of parents, teachers, and other authority figures, and in many cases beyond their comprehension as well. It always had something interesting, peer-relevant, and helpful to say, and traditional authorities were in no position to counter it. Not only did they lack credibility, they were also always playing catch-up, aware of new ideas entering their kids' heads only after the fact.

FOURTH SPACES

What is consistent between those youngsters in Oman and those pushed in a more threatening direction? As a Sudanese blogger was quoted as saying, "The digital revolution has given a voice to young Muslims. It is allowing us to criticize the religious establishment and create our own interpretations."[15] I have heard similar themes in hundreds of conversations, and not just in the Arab world. Parents, teachers, clergy—they all seem detached and unhelpful. But with technology in hand, young people can empower themselves to practice in new, more "authentic" ways.

It's not that the Muslims I met during my journeys weren't going to the mosque or to religious school—they were. But they weren't accepting the messages they heard at face value. They didn't want to part with their roots and were determined to live their religion proudly, to integrate it with the rest of their lives. And while the Islam pushed by extremists was of an ultraconservative sort, it was the local Muslim leadership that was frequently seen by youth as the conservative party, because they were the ones who seemed unwilling to accept that, post-9/11, what was needed was reinvention and adaptation.

Casting about for guidance, younger Muslims were venturing into so-called third spaces, neutral and largely egalitarian institutions outside mosques and households in which practitioners of Islam converge.[16] Washington, D.C.'s Townhall Dialogue Series is one such place. As its founder, Aqsa Mahmud, explained, "the Series is based on the premise that each individual is validated through his or her personal experiences and, by sharing our stories, we build compassion and greater understanding of our diversity."[17] Programs ranged in topic from "Race in a Muslim Space" and "Dating, Talking—Or Whatever," to "Curtain Call—the Gender Performance" and "I accept you, except you: acceptance and exclusion in the communities we choose."[18] When asked about why she created the program, Mahmud offered a telling observation: "I am a Millennial American Muslim who, like many others of my generation, has found that our mosques and formal religious spaces have been overtaken by a mentality that to air our issues would mark us flawed in our Muslim identity. The emergence of the third space reflects the inability of the traditional mosque—its hierarchy and administration—to answer the needs of my generation of Muslims."[19]

But even these alternatives can offer only so much when it comes to younger Muslims. In 2011, when I visited the American Center in Jakarta, I spoke with a group of teens who proceeded to ask me the usual questions about America. Afterward, several approached me to ask if religious websites existed to help American kids learn about Islam. When I inquired about their question, they responded that they liked to go online themselves to learn about their religion, because their parents were too "old-fashioned." Whereas in previous decades, the mosque's call to prayer might have reminded their parents that it was time to pray, these teens could now rely on their smartphones. The technology helped kids feel that they were experiencing religion in a current, cutting-edge way—they were staying abreast of global trends affecting their generation. Also, it felt far more personal. Each of these kids could choose the precise sights and sounds that conveyed the message that prayer time had arrived.

The technological tools themselves have evolved over time. When I first visited European communities in 2007 and 2008, many youth told me that they turned to blogs and websites (including YouTube), where they could watch lengthy recorded sermons and read extended opinions about points of Islamic theology. In France, I also spoke with writers and founders at "Muslim news" outlets like Oumma .com, BondyBlog, and SaphirNews that were then seeking to address religious identity issues with Francophone Muslim youth. As these writers and entrepreneurs told me, there was great demand in Muslim communities for online platforms that seemed to speak about Islam in "authentic" ways. They were confident that once they had captured the attention of this audience, emerging technology would allow even more successful engagement going forward.

By 2010–12, chat rooms and online forums had become popular as a way of gaining exposure to hadiths, fatwas, and other forms of commentary about Islamic theology, followed in turn by social media sites like Facebook, Twitter, Instagram, Pinterest, and Kik. A few years later, smartphone apps such as the popular "Hadith of the Day"[20] had emerged as an example of important, normalized mediums for youth everywhere to learn about their religion. The 24/7 availability of such apps on kids' mobile devices enabled the ideology to go deeper and reinforce behavior changes more easily. Although blogs and websites still loomed large, youth were relying extensively on peer-to-peer transmission of ideas via social media. To take but one example, IslamicThinking circulates uplifting quotes on Twitter from the Qur'an as well as helpful reminders of good religious practice, enjoying a following of more than one million users.[21]

In fact, if there is one thing that defines the generational consciousness of Muslim youth, it is their sense of being connected with their peers intellectually and emotionally via technology.* As Shelina Janmohamed describes it, technology became "the foundation" of a generational identity. Youth could "express what they wear, what they eat, the language they use, their ideas . . . their love and passion

* Non-Muslim youth were also engaging with religion via technology. A 2014 Pew Research Institute survey found that one-fifth of Americans shared their religious convictions and understandings on social media sites, and 46 percent had seen others do so. "Religion and Electronic Media," Pew Research Center Religion & Public Life Project, November 6, 2014, http://www.pewforum.org/2014/11/06/religion-and-electronic-media.

for other Muslims around the world." The notion of the Muslim Umma, the global community of Muslim faithful, took on a new meaning, as youth "are intimately connected to what is happening to other Muslims like them around the world. That actually has consolidated their identity and their pride in their identity."[22]

THE RELIGION OF ME

There's another reason technology appealed so strongly to Muslim youth, and continues to appeal: it allows them a *customized* experience of religion. What defines this generation of Muslims isn't simply their desire to practice religion differently from their parents. It's their determination to practice their religion on an individual basis, as *they* see proper. In this, they fit right in with their non-Muslim peers around the world.* Describing Christian millennials in the United States, *The Atlantic*'s Emma Green has remarked that many have felt alienated from established religious institutions, "[b]ut in terms of people's own religious practices, in terms of praying, believing in God . . . among young people, many are trying to find their own ways of connecting to religious questions and practices even though they're not necessarily attending church in the way that their parents might have."[23]

Millennials of all faiths are used to maintaining control over their destinies in every area of life. They have grown up with technology that allows them to watch and listen to what *they* want to watch, and with a vast array of consumer products customized to their individual needs. They have grown accustomed to breaking with institutions of all kinds that try to lump them together into

* On the topic of technology's transformation of religious practice see Stuart Fox, "Technology Changing Way We Practice Religion," NBC News, July 7, 2010, http://www.nbcnews.com/id/38126658/ns/technology_and_science-science/t/technology-changing-way-we-practice-religion/#.WVZzHxPyvyh.

seemingly arbitrary categories. And they've been empowered by technology to express themselves in ways that would have been unthinkable a generation earlier—by starting their own companies online, broadcasting their own videos, custom-designing their own charities, and so on. In this context, it would be surprising if they didn't actively try to take control over their own religious ideas and beliefs, seeking out options and adopting the ones that resonate with them, while discarding practices and ideologies that don't conform with their values. As Shahed Amanullah puts it, youth "want to make [their lives] mean something on [their] own terms, not based on what other people tell [them]."*

In my conversations with Muslim youth, I consistently found them patching together new, individualized versions of Islam out of disparate ideas, beliefs, and practices. From the outside looking in, such bespoke religion seemed a strange and often contradictory hodgepodge that reflected the specifics of their gender, sexuality, race, demographic status, educational background, personality characteristics, and so on. For instance, I encountered some kids who found the traditional Muslim proscription against eating pork very important, yet who thought it was doctrinally possible to try bacon. I talked to many girls wearing head coverings who didn't hesitate to have sex before marriage—like the girls I'd met in Oman, they'd found a way to rationalize it. Some kids I met understood and accepted that it was wrong under Islam to drink alcohol but found a way to make an exception for red wine—it was "medicinal," and they had found an Islamic teaching online—a hadith (that is, a saying or action of the prophet Muhammad) or a fatwa (a proclamation on a theological point by an established Islamic authority)—that made an exception on that basis.

---

* Shahed Amanullah and Shelina Janmohamed note that Muslim youth use the Internet to explore the boundaries of their identities. Janmohamed, interview with the author, June 14, 2016; Amanullah, phone interview with the author, July 5, 2016.

Everywhere I went during my travels—New Zealand, Bahrain, Kuwait, Sudan, Indonesia, Uganda, European countries, the United States—technology seemed to offer a perfect means of forming a customized religious belief and practice to young Muslims. Millennials felt comfortable going to websites on their own time and in their own way, just as they would do to check restaurant ratings or see what is trending on Twitter. They also were able to see how many comments or "likes" a given religious interpretation might have. Although they might want to develop a personal religious practice, most of them wanted one that they knew had street credibility with their peers.

As Amanullah puts it, youth go online in part out of a "preexisting desire" to be "part of that team—Team Muslim—whatever [that] is."[24] Shelina Janmohamed observes that youths "console" one another in online spaces, giving one another the feeling that they are not alone and that together they can have a voice. In particular, women and others marginalized in traditional Islamic settings can come together online to affirm one another's identities. In this sense, she notes, "the Internet has been a great boon for women and young people."[25] Nor is this phenomenon limited to Muslims. One media report, drawing on the observations of prominent American religious scholars, describes how youths today in many religious denominations are using smartphones to form "virtual congregations" of believers across borders. A scholar mentioned in that report proclaimed that "we have yet to get our mind around a world where some [people get] their whole religious experience through a device."[26] Some of the extremists have.

"I SAW IT ON THE WEB"

How exactly do religious websites and apps that offer teachings about daily practices contribute to the spread of extremism? As we've seen, polls have shown that the vast majority of Muslims globally renounce extremism. Certainly, the youth I've described so far are thinking and behaving in ways that seem inconsistent with strict interpretations of the faith. But don't be fooled: we would not face the threats we currently do were it not for Sheikh Google preparing the way.

Like halalization, the Sheikh Google phenomenon does not turn every young Muslim it touches into a budding extremist. But some are more likely to embrace curated expressions of religion and extremist ideology. As Amanullah explains, extremists are "particularly successful" appealing to youth who "don't have a strong rooting in the religion"—youth who strongly desire to "be" Muslim, but who are cloudy on the specifics of the rules and traditions. "That's the perfect target for extremists," he says. It's "easier to dislodge" people who don't have much knowledge, filling them "with a bunch of nonsense that pushes them over the edge."[27] In this respect, recent converts to Islam might be especially vulnerable to extremist ideas, as many of them might possess enthusiasm for the religion but very little knowledge.

When I visited European communities in 2007 and 2008, in the wake of the Danish cartoon crisis, the paucity of moderate or liberal interpretations available online was apparent. Kids unfamiliar with Arabic and unschooled in Islam would see sources quoted in that language, and they would automatically assume that the opinions presented were "authentic"—more credible than ideas proffered by their parents or teachers offline. Although hard data about the ideological character of websites and blogs was hard to come by, for those of us in government who were alert to the issue, this sample was extremely disturbing. Extremist preachers allied with Al Qaeda could afford to spend their time blogging. In many cases, they had Saudi money backing them. Without support from Western governments, moderates lacked such funding. They couldn't devote themselves professionally to promoting their views, creating an ideological "void,"

Amanullah recalls, "for [the extremists to exploit] the way they wanted to."[28]

The presence of conservative voices was not necessarily bad. The problem was the overwhelming lack of diversity. "Televangelist" Amr Khaled became widely known in 2006 for hosting interfaith dialogue in the wake of the Danish cartoon crisis. Since then, he has sought to encourage progressive community development, linking this project to interfaith dialogue, tolerance, and moderation.[29] In 2007, *Time* magazine honored Khaled by including him on their list of heroes and pioneers. Yet for all of his accomplishments, his popularity paled in comparison to that of the conservative Yusuf al-Qaradawi, a thinker aligned with the Muslim Brotherhood who was regarded as "the most respected and popular Muslim religious figure on television."[30] Khaled also competed with voices like Zakir Naik, who achieved notoriety and an audience exceeding 100 million for his hardline, Salafist views, including the claim that Americans orchestrated 9/11.[31]

In recent years, the volume and breadth of Muslim-oriented materials available online has burgeoned. Today, hundreds of sites deal with Muslim identity, in addition to Facebook groups, Twitter feeds, apps, Pinterest pages, and much else. Popular moderate imams have hundreds of thousands of followers on social media, and in the case of U.S.-based Suhaib Webb, are issuing religious rulings via Snapchat (dubbed "Snapwas").[32] Still, conservative perspectives remain dominant, and a disproportionate share of money is available to fund them.

Even as conservative and extremist views have abounded on the Web, certain elements of the medium have made it much harder for millennials to engage it critically. The ethos of the open Internet is that search results are determined not by careful evaluation of content so much as by popularity. Cascading comments might add context, but sifting through them can efface the immediacy that makes online research so compelling. Without some sort of scale of expert approval, the burden is on kids to determine if what a given person says is credible. But as Urs Gasser observes, critical thinking "is not something that kids [do] just because they're born into" the digital age.[33] When I've spoken with Muslim youth, I've often observed an alarming failure to scrutinize the ideas they encounter online. Sophistication of thinking, rational analysis, and consideration of all sides of an issue represent less of a priority for them than speed and convenience. Decisions about what to believe were made almost instantaneously. If a given image or posting had hundreds of likes or a given imam had tens of thousands of followers, or if a friend had retweeted a picture or an article, that was often enough for them. As Shelina Janmohamed observes, a certain analytical depth and expertise have been lost in online spaces. Kids sometimes "don't even have a clue" how to judge the authenticity or veracity of a belief or practice.[34]

Contributing to the lack of critical awareness among many Muslim millennials is the high esteem with which they hold technology. For kids that I've met, the Internet itself conferred authenticity and veracity to the ideas encountered there. In their minds, Sheikh Google was "authentic," while the local and the offline seemed dubious. I had mentioned earlier that alienated and defensive Muslims often circulated and promoted conspiracy theories involving America, Jews, and 9/11. Kids would tell me that it wasn't Al Qaeda who brought down the twin towers, but the Jews. Or they would say that 9/11 never even happened; Jewish executives in Hollywood created the whole thing. When I asked kids how they knew about these notions, they would frequently say, "I read about it online" or "I saw pictures online." When I would push back, suggesting that these theories were false, those I was speaking with would typically shake their heads and insist that I was wrong. "There's nothing you can say to convince us, because we've seen it. We've seen the pictures." These youth had no concept that images could be Photoshopped, or that some people might cynically post falsehoods to sway others. If they read it online, it was real. Because kids lacked a critical frame, literally *anybody* could post ideas online, and if they spoke with an Arab accent, kids were liable to take their proclamations seriously.

Besides such conspiracy theories (which, it should be pointed out, are not restricted to Muslim communities; the number of non-Muslim Americans who believe the 9/11 attacks were an inside job is shockingly large), I encountered many instances in which young Muslims subscribed to strange ideas that they regarded as authentically Islamic, simply because they'd encountered it online. In Pakistan in 2010, I met a young student who related that he previously hadn't cared about how he prayed and folded his prayer rug, but having gone online, he had learned about a very specific way that "good" Muslims were supposed to fold it—from top to middle and then bottom to middle and then to the side, as if ritually folding a flag. The student had since adopted this practice himself, thinking it an expression of piety. In truth, there was no doctrinal basis for folding a prayer rug the way he indicated. I gently tried to make that point, but he objected. He had read about it on the Internet, he told me, so he knew that it was true.

MUSLIM BUBBLES

Even as more mainstream voices crop up on the Web, another feature of Sheikh Google has prevented youth from questioning some of the objectionable beliefs they encounter. Eli Pariser has written about how platforms that offer a personalized Web experience create "filter bubbles" that seal us in and prevent us from grappling with opposing views.[35] Driven by their prior online behavior, highly sophisticated algorithms, potentially drawing on thousands of pieces of data, present us with content we are likely to find incredibly compelling.[36] In the words of columnist Timothy Egan, we thus are seldom confronted by information that makes us pause and reflect critically on our own ideas, and live in "digital safe spaces closed off from anything that intrudes on [our] worldview."[37] Disseminators of fake news appeal to our emotions, in effect disabling our rational faculties. Pervasive educational gaps only deepen the problem. We become hobbled by ignorance, not knowing what we don't know.

As Baroness Joanna Shields, the former United Kingdom's minister for Internet safety and security and undersecretary of state, told me, algorithms are offering up increasingly accurate bespoke results, giving kids exactly the content that they like or want, and shutting out alternative materials.[38] Of course, we also create our own personal media bubbles online through our preferences, settings, and other choices. As I visited local Muslim communities, I saw ample evidence of this. Youth drifted toward content that confirmed what they already believed, and professed little desire to consume media that brought their beliefs into question. And by now there is so much extremist material on the Internet that Sheikh Google makes it possible for the uncertain to live in the perfect Islamic cocoon of images, ideas, and music.

As a young man I met in Finland in 2008 told me, he got "really offended" when seeing people who were "saying things I don't want to hear. I don't want to read that shit. I want to read people who understand me and share my point of view. It's a waste of my time to hear all these other people." In particular, he sought to avoid thinkers who advocated more gender equality and the ability of Muslim women to work outside of the home. When I challenged him, he asserted that women don't work under "authentic Islam." I replied that the Prophet's wife had been a wealthy businesswoman who had hired Muhammad before he became a prophet. My young interlocutor shook his head. "That doesn't have any relevance for today, and I don't want to hear people who put forward such arguments. They are feminists."

The more communities I visited, the more I sensed that this desire to retreat into a bubble of intellectual comfort and avoid intellectual inquiry was widespread among Muslim youth. In 2011, my colleague Hannah Rosenthal (the former U.S. special envoy to combat and monitor anti-Semitism) and I traveled to several countries to conduct conversations with youth about bigotry and the need to promote respect among people of different backgrounds. We encountered many kids who held sectarian views and who were reluctant to have them challenged. In Baku, Azerbaijan, one young man told us that he could never have "an open heart" to Armenians because of what they had done to his people. In Jordan, a young woman walked out of a roundtable gathering of her peers, professing that she hated Jews and didn't want to speak with one (Hannah is Jewish). In Ankara, Turkey, several young women rejected the idea of accepting people of different faiths, since they had been taught that Islam was the only true religion. In each of these countries we, of course, also found younger people who were more open-minded and eager to discuss and question their beliefs (in Jordan, for instance, several other youths were clearly upset and embarrassed that their peer had treated Hannah disrespectfully). Still, we found a general reluctance to hear dissenting points of view wherever we went.

Muslim youth are hardly the only ones to suffer from such tunnel vision. Commentators have observed a stunning decline in empathy and a rise in narcissism among millennials in general. As Joel Stein related in a 2013 *Time* magazine article, rates of narcissistic personality disorder run three times higher among people in their twenties than for older generations, thanks in part to technology like the smartphone and practices such as the taking of "selfies." According to Stein, "Not only do millennials lack the kind of empathy that allows them to feel concerned for others, but they also have trouble even intellectually understanding others' points of view."[39] By Stein's account, millennials are intellectually stunted because of the peer-to-peer interaction they experience online. He quotes Emory English professor Mark Bauerlein: "Peer pressure is anti-intellectual. It is anti-historical. It is anti-eloquence. Never before in history have people been able to grow up and reach age 23 so dominated by peers. To develop intellectually you've got to relate to older people, older things: 17-year-olds never grow up if they're just hanging around other 17-year-olds."[40] Stein further observes that trends among millennials hold in both developed and developing countries. "Each country's millennials are different, but because of globalization, social media, the exporting of Western culture and the speed of change, millennials worldwide are more similar to one another than to older generations within their nations."*

"IT'S MY JOB TO RECRUIT PEOPLE"

Much has been written about the recruiting efforts of the so-called Islamic State and other groups,† so let me just make a few basic points. These efforts remain massive and growing. In addition, extremist groups continue to expand aggressively into new mediums oriented toward youth, including multiplayer video games and games like Grand Theft Auto and cartoons.‡ The so-called Islamic State posts in multiple languages, and makes use of high-end production techniques, showing "a deft command of varied media," using services such as JustPaste, WhatsApp, and SoundCloud to get its message out.[41] In 2015, the group was disseminating as many as 90,000 tweets a day.[42] It even had a twenty-four-hour "Jihadi Help Desk" system in place, utilizing YouTube and Twitter to help train would-be terrorists in how to evade detection by the authorities.[43]

* Stein, "Millennials." Urs Gasser notes that youth often use technology to establish their own identities vis-à-vis their parents and elders, using coded language, for example, to keep their conversations private. They also engage in other, generationally-based practices online. Interview with the author, August 10, 2016.

† A February 2018 library search revealed more than 410 books, 1,744 dissertations, and 69,488 articles, published between 2014 and 2017, on the subject of the so-called Islamic State's recruitment methods.

‡ The so-called Islamic State experimented with a manga-style comic book in late 2015 (Dr. Matthew Levitt, e-mail message to author, July 29, 2016).

Despite the increased proliferation of liberal or mainstream interpretations, intensive, one-on-one recruitment online has adapted and even intensified. Tales of such recruitment reported in the mainstream media abound. Australian news outlets reported how one French journalist infiltrated a terrorist group, videotaping his interactions. After first creating a fake Facebook account and liking groups affiliated with the so-called Islamic State, so-called Islamic State sympathizers contacted him and asked him to join an encrypted messaging platform. From there, he was personally recruited into a so-called Islamic State cell that was actively planning an attack. (French authorities soon dismantled the terrorist plot.[44]) Another French journalist writing in the *Guardian* recounted a similar episode in which a male extremist personally befriended her and asked her to marry him, thinking that she was a young convert to Islam. "Listen, Mélodie," he said, "among other things, it's my job to recruit people, and I'm really good at my job. You can trust me. You'll be really well taken care of here. You'll be important. And if you agree to marry me, I'll treat you like a queen."[45]

Such encounters online are typical.[46] In an analysis of Americans accused of collusion with so-called Islamic State, the *New York Times* noted that "Twitter, Facebook and other social media platforms played a large role in their recruitment and expressions of support for the Islamic State. Nearly all of the cases involved some form of internet communication."[47] One convicted so-called Islamic State recruit, the American Adam Dandach, was accused by authorities of having "encouraged terrorist beliefs in online chatrooms."[48] His smartphone also contained "jihadi songs supporting Islamic State fighters, maps of areas the group controlled, and Twitter updates on fighting by the terrorist group."[49] The tendency of social media to act as a filter bubble only exacerbates extremist recruiting efforts. Recent research from the London-based counter-extremism NGO the Institute for Strategic Dialogue found that people who search for extremist propaganda or influencers are quickly directed toward additional extremist content through algorithmic recommendations. Searches are quickly translated as preferences and built into users' suggested content within a matter of hours.[50]

Yet social media has also, happily, become a more contested space, with some young Muslims using it to fight back against extremism. Following the horrific Brussels attacks in 2016, when 32 people were killed and over 340 injured after series of bombs were detonated by terrorists in a metro station and airport, the hashtag #StopIslam became popular, with many users adopting the phrase not to express opposition to Islam per se, but to the so-called Islamic State's exploitation of the religion for its own ends.[51] After a 2015 knife attack on the Leytonstone Tube station in which the attacker shouted "This is for Syria," an onlooker retorted, "You ain't no Muslim bruv." The phrase went viral as a hashtag, with many applauding it.[52] In the wake of the devastating terrorist attacks in Paris, Muslims and their sympathizers used the Twitter hashtag #MuslimsAreNotTerrorist to distance mainstream Muslims from extremists and to attempt to stem the tide of Islamophobia in France, Europe, and throughout the world.[53] Other examples include #notinmyname (British youth fighting back against so-called Islamic State) and #sharesomegood, an Australian campaign to fight back against online hate. Yet to date, these efforts have been mere flares. The extremists have called upon a much fuller arsenal.

A WINNING STRATEGY

The phenomenon of Sheikh Google points us to a number of important measures that we should adopt to help us win against the extremists. By "we," I don't simply mean government, but society at large, and large technology companies in particular. If any companies would seem to have a stake in fighting extremism, it would be those in the technology sector. Yet these companies have historically been slow to join the fight, their contributions piecemeal and temporary. Although they have contributed to the struggle against extremism, shutting down accounts of recruiters and helping people in the vicinity of a violent attack let friends and family know they're okay,[54] technology companies have never devoted significant numbers of people or dollars to flooding online spaces with counter-content. Nor have they used their technical prowess to mobilize their massive research-and-development budgets to steer youth away from dangerous voices online, or toward more positive influences. More generally, they have offered little in the way of forward thinking, planning, and investment.

The extent of tech companies' consistent failure over many years to take more strident action has become especially clear as time has passed and the terrorist threat has worsened. Following the gruesome 2015 terrorist attacks in Paris and California, senior U.S. officials bemoaned rampant extremist messaging available online. FBI director James B. Comey claimed that Tashfeen Malik and Syed Rizwan Farook were "consuming poison on the Internet." As he noted, "Twitter works as a way to sell books, as a way to promote movies, and it works as a way to crowdsource terrorism."[55] President Obama explicitly asked for technology companies and Silicon Valley to help curb extremism: "I will urge high tech and law enforcement leaders to make it harder for terrorist leaders to use technology to escape from justice," said Obama, in a live address to the nation, as the country reeled from the California attack.[56]

The reasons for tech companies' sluggish responses vary. In part, it has to do with the strong ethic of individual freedom (often paired with a fear or hostility to government intervention) that has historically existed in Silicon Valley.[57] In general, tech companies don't want to take steps that artificially limit how people think and behave. They certainly don't want to appear as an agent of a "big brother" government, allowing officials backdoor access to smartphones and tablets, as they were called upon to do following the San Bernardino attacks.

Technology executives will often dispute that they contribute to the scourge of extremism. They argue that their products and services are neutral, and that bad people—extremists of all kinds—are turning them to evil purposes. They are merely media platforms, they say, not publishers, and as such they don't bear responsibility for the content on their sites; instead, government should go directly after the extremists who abuse technology, not the platforms themselves. Technology companies have also been slow to perceive CVE as something other than "foreign policy," and hence as something that falls within their sphere of concern. They have even argued that extremists are in some cases political dissidents. If the technology companies responded to one government's definition of a terrorist group or a group inciting hate, they would have to do so for all governments, sending them down a very dangerous Orwellian path.

Only over the last few years, as the use of their platforms for nefarious acts has increased, have companies such as Facebook, Microsoft, Alphabet, and Twitter worked to develop new models to prevent users from not only finding bad content but from using it to ignite violence. Technology companies have strong economic reasons for not wishing to admit responsibility for content posted on their platforms. Extremist content is plentiful, and much of it occupies a "gray area" between legitimate and dangerous messaging. If technology companies bore legal responsibility for the process of removing extremist content, they would have to develop sophisticated technological solutions, at great expense (and in fact, a large majority of content removed now is identified through their automated systems). Sasha Havlicek of the Institute for Strategic Dialogue has been at the forefront of the effort to coordinate CVE efforts between technology companies, governments, and other actors, working extensively with the technology companies themselves. As she told me, "taking responsibility for the nature of the content posted on their platforms, represents a potentially 'existential' challenge to the social media companies' business model."[58]

These companies may not have much of a choice. Legislation passed by the German cabinet in April 2017 threatened to levy millions of dollars of fines on companies that didn't remove offensive content.[59] In June 2017, the United Kingdom and France announced a new, joint initiative to combat extremism, including the possibility of legal liabilities placed on technology companies. At a meeting of the G7 in May 2017, leaders called on companies to "act urgently in developing and sharing new technology and tools to improve the automatic detection of content promoting incitement to violence."[60] And as of January 2018, Germany's "NetzDG" rules threaten companies with potential fines of up to 50 million euros for failure to remove offensive content.[61]

In response to this pressure, large technology companies have announced a range of actions, including, as one media report put it, "suspending accounts, using artificial intelligence to identify extreme content, hiring more content moderators, developing and supporting counter-speech campaigns, and creating a shared industry database of hashes—unique digital fingerprints—for violent terrorist images."[62] In June 2017, Facebook, Twitter, Microsoft, and YouTube announced the creation of the "Global Internet Forum to Counter Terrorism," a new "global working group to combine their efforts to remove terrorist content from their platforms."[63] Facebook announced a collaboration with the Institute for Strategic Dialogue to create the "Online Civil Courage Initiative" (OCCI), a project to train and fund local groups in the United Kingdom, France, and Germany to "track and counteract hate speech and terrorist propaganda."[64] Though the particulars of the funding sums are not public, Facebook did pledge one million euros for the OCCI effort during its initial launch in Germany. That figure also covers their efforts in France and Britain and, notably, includes money to run the initiative and ad credits. Facebook's model of supporting these types of efforts through ad credit is important to state: outside of OCCI, they have also given small amounts—between $20,000 and

$100,000—to NGOs around the world that they feel are fighting online hate speech.

Facebook also announced the creation of a messaging app "that will let parents decide who their children talk to online for kids as young as six," while YouTube "has been trying to combat people from posting violent videos using family-friendly cartoon characters."[65] Google, meanwhile, has announced that it will spend a million British pounds to "promote innovation in combatting hate and extremism" in the United Kingdom, funneling some of this money to established nongovernmental organizations.* As of January 2018, the program received 125 applications for funding, including from Muslim organizations that wished to take action against extremism but were "wary of coordinating with government-affiliated CVE efforts."[66] All of these represent welcome moves—and one hopes, the beginning of a sustained and serious effort to confront extremist ideology online.

What would such an effort entail? Well, quite simply, a lot more than what those companies have currently offered. Technology companies need to devote substantial resources—both financial and nonfinancial—to disrupting the *entire process* by which kids become radicalized online. Technology companies already possess minute-to-minute access to Muslim youth. We need technology companies to go all in in relation to CVE. I'm not primarily talking here about blocking out extremist content. Rather, technology companies should go further in their use and evaluation of their algorithms to flag extremist content for youth. They should adjust search results for youth who might be exploring extremist content, connecting kids with social workers, community programs, and former extremists who can provide help. They should also recognize that algorithms are not

* This British fund formed part of Google's $5 million global commitment: Jane Wakefield, "Google Launches UK 'Anti-Terror Fund,'" BBC News, September 20, 2017, http://www.bbc.com/news/technology-41320171.

enough, and that we also need human eyes and judgment. Certainly, they need to hire many more people to monitor content in different languages, looking for hate speech to flag.* In this last area, Google has already begun to make progress. The company announced in late 2017 that it would "increase the number of content moderators and other employees reviewing content and training algorithms to more than 10,000" in the coming year.[67]

Technology companies should also use algorithms to steer kids toward sites that in some way contravene extremist narratives. If a youth is running a search for "Muslim prayer," what if she were directed away from sites about the so-called Islamic State version of how to pray and act as a Muslim, and toward sites that emphasize the diversity of Muslim traditions and beliefs? If a young person were searching for the meaning of a quote from the Qur'an, what if he were given precise, curated, educated, peer-generated content that taught him how to analyze the Qur'an and its scholarly interpretations? If a youth typed in an image search for "Muslim," what if images came up that reflected the religion's true historical diversity? Both Google and Microsoft have piloted methodologies that advertise positive alternatives or counternarratives in response to extremist searches. The Microsoft project has event-tested directing people searching for extremist content to organizations that can engage with them to prevent recruitment.[68]

To those who might dismiss such proposals, regarding them as overly intrusive and tantamount to censorship, we should remember that the First Amendment doesn't protect all speech. Community standards factor in—and those standards change over time. In 2004, Al Jazeera gave Osama bin Laden valuable minutes to air his

---

* In 2017, Facebook announced that it was hiring three thousand more people to flag suspicious content online. Amber Jamieson and Olivia Solon, "Facebook to Begin Flagging Fake News in Response to Mounting Criticism," *Guardian,* December 15, 2016, https://www.theguardian.com/technology/2016/dec/15/facebook-flag-fake-news-fact-check.

view before the network's viewers.[69] Today no network would do the same for so-called Islamic State leader Abu Bakr al-Baghdadi, because we now appreciate the gravity of the extremist threat. Further, in taking steps to drown out extremist messages, it's essential to recognize that these are private companies who have the authority (on account of the First Amendment) to make the rules for participation on their platforms. To a considerable extent, these companies already curate what people can and cannot see. In 2015, reports surfaced that Google was creating an algorithm (which it has since implemented[70]) for its autocorrect function that excluded the word "nigger."[71] Their search algorithm also already blocks out pornography sites when users input certain search terms. Facebook has experimented* with a function (which is has since begun to roll out) that allows users to flag postings that suggest a suicide risk, triggering experts to review the post and provide help.[72] And in the wake of the 2016 presidential election, technology companies began to get serious about weeding out "fake news" websites, with Google banning such sites from earning advertising money via Google ads.[73]

Technology companies might deliver access to youth for purposes of CVE in a variety of ways. More sophisticated software could detect extremist content as it is posted and provide warning systems to users. Companies could also put systems in place to alert parents that their children have downloaded videos with extremist content. They could monitor usage of their sites and produce regular public reports about online hate speech. They could create easier ways for users to "report" others fomenting extremist ideas. They could review keyword searches to allow platforms to respond better when kids are searching out dubious content. They could support free workshops for parents and kids, educating them not just about online dangers,

* In November 2017, Facebook rolled out a function that allows AI to "spot suicidal tendencies quicker than friends." Leanna Garfield, "Mark Zuckerberg: Facebook's AI Could Spot Suicidal Tendencies in Users Quicker than Friends," *Business Insider,* November 29, 2017, http://www.businessinsider.com/facebook-suicide-prevention-artifical-intelligence-2017-11.

but about how algorithms work to keep their kids and parents inside echo chambers. Google has already invested in the development of a highly innovative digital literacy and engagement program in the United Kingdom called Internet Citizens, developed and run by the Institute for Strategic Dialogue. Rolled out across youth centers, the program equips young people to understand how technology and propaganda—filter bubbles, us-and-them messaging—can dupe and divide us. As of this writing, the project has succeeded in its pilot phase and is in the process of being scaled. We need to expand this program and others like it around the world.[74]

Most of these companies are data driven and thus perfectly placed to sift through the ocean of online information. Technology companies could assemble teams of people far greater in number than the tiny teams that exist today, and farm them out to work directly with NGOs countering violent extremism online. They could also fund, scale, and provide free advertising to dozens of diverse Muslims who disavow extremism and possess followings of their own. In putting a proverbial algorithmic finger on the search scale, these companies could create a digital army that would galvanize kids against extremism—precisely because they have unrivaled access to these kids.

Facebook and Google have both begun to invest in more professionalized, scaled responses to online hate speech and extremism, including the aforementioned Online Civil Courage Initiative in Berlin. Run by the Institute for Strategic Dialogue, and building on ISD research (funded by Jigsaw and Facebook) into the effectiveness of counter-speech, OCCI was launched by Facebook's Sheryl Sandberg in 2016 and is the first online hub designed to "upskill and upscale" counter-speech. The initiative provides a combination of data analytics, targeting, marketing, and donated media support to NGOs working to push back hate online. In light of its initial successes, OCCI has expanded to include France and the United Kingdom, with ISD providing a support desk and communications/technology machinery to drive and measure impact in the counter-speech space.

OCCI brings research partners to the table alongside local NGOs, counter-extremism expertise, and technology/marketing acumen to create a professionalized, full-spectrum response. Yet, at present, OCCI is only in its pilot phase; it would require additional scaling to have a significant impact on extremist recruiting.

Google and Google.org (Google's philanthropic arm) have also now begun investing in scaled work in the counter-speech space, with ISD leading an innovation hub in the United Kingdom that could drive fresh youth-oriented education and counter-speech programming. Designed to build capacity and drive youth responses to extremism and hate on and offline, this program would build the largest evidence base to date on the impact of counter-speech. Again, the challenge is to pump more money and talent into endeavors such as these, so as to bring them to a meaningful, global scale.

Of course, technology companies aren't the only ones that might contribute access to youth for purposes of CVE. If you're a cable news network, newspaper, or a mass-circulation magazine, you could make a point of spotlighting social entrepreneurs who are making a difference against extremism, or educating your audiences about religious diversity. An example of the latter: Vox's 2016 online piece with video titled "What does it mean to be a Muslim? There are 1.7 billion answers."[75] More generally, you could take steps to promote sound civic values and discourage hate. And you could also be sure not to give extremists free airtime. Still other large companies outside of the media industry could mobilize brick-and-mortar resources to gain the ear of youth. With Amazon's data and tremendous attunement to fluctuations in the cultural temperature, its Whole Foods arm is especially well positioned to further our CVE efforts both online and off. Whole Foods, with its reach in hundreds of local communities in the United States, already supports local farms and food manufacturers. It could partner with NGOs to develop programs in local neighborhoods to combat hate and inoculate youth against extremist messaging.

Why Amazon and Whole Foods, you might ask? Their integrated information about who we are as humans connects not just to what kind of book or widget we buy, but what we eat, watch, and are curious about in the marketplace. Such cultural indicators are important to these companies, but they are also important to our larger society. Amazon has a role to play in the cultural cohesiveness of a community and can effect change by mobilizing the information they have about us. With their November 2016 ad centered on a friendship between a priest and an imam, Amazon has already jumped into the global discourse about rising hate.[76] Partnerships with NGOs that fight hate in local communities is an easy next step. (In chapter 8, I'll provide a much fuller account of businesses' role in CVE, describing how we might enlist the entire business ecosystem in this effort.)

When it comes to technology, another intriguing possibility is the use of chatbots—applications that conduct conversations with human users—to intervene with kids whose online behavior suggests vulnerability to recruitment by extremists. Researchers have already deployed a chatbot called Woebot, developed using the principles of cognitive behavioral therapy (CBT), to help people with depression. A clinical trial found that "participants who used the bot over a period of two weeks had both statistically and clinically significant reductions of depression as compared to students directed to a National Institute of Mental Health e-book."[77] Even before humans in the "real" world notice worrisome changes, chatbots could automatically launch and, consistent with the principles of CBT, check in with kids multiple times each day to assess their moods and interests.

AI-powered chatbots have already been unveiled in health settings "to triage patients before directing them to a human doctor or launching a video visit" or to "facilitate communication between visits."[78] Autodesk, a maker of three-dimensional design software, is even creating a full-fledged, three-dimensional digital avatar customer service representative that, driven by cutting-edge AI, can not only simulate emotions but also pick up on interlocutors' emotional states and react to them.[79] With local NGOs providing guidance as to content, such avatars might one day allow vulnerable youth to interact with a neutral entity, who could serve online as a first responder. The potential afforded by such a neutral entity is tremendous. With no judgment or emotional connectivity to the kind of human that is working with you, a user will be able to interface without feeling fear or embarrassment. Digital natives who already interface daily with nonhuman touch points for information might find digital avatars extremely attractive as an easy and familiar source of help.

Of course, as sophisticated as computers are, they don't always get it right. In recent years, Amazon's algorithms have suggested "bomb-making ingredients" to consumers as products that were "frequently bought together," and an AI assistant on Yandex, Russia's equivalent of Google, has pointed viewers to "unsavory opinions," such as support for wife beating.[80] Companies would need to stay alert to the problem and take protective measures when deploying bots for CVE purposes.

There's an educational component, too. The big tech companies should provide funding for "cyber-hygiene" classes for kids and parents to explain how their platforms work and how kids become vulnerable (school districts in turn should make such classes mandatory). Technology companies could also fund graduate-level centers focused on CVE, targeting students in MBA and foreign policy programs and helping them to understand how technology both fuels the extremist threat and might help stop it.

We might wonder whether technology companies would ever willingly agree to devote themselves so fully to the cause of CVE. These are, after all, private companies driven by the profit motive. Can we really expect them to be so public-spirited? The chances, I think, are better than they've ever been. Previously, Silicon Valley had engaged in frequent and often public conversations with government around how to stop extremist content. But they hadn't taken much proactive action, and as we've seen, they had pushed back on the notion that they bore responsibility, citing First Amendment concerns. Government was perpetually "dragging them" into playing a more serious role, and they were perpetually resisting.[81]

Amid concern about hate speech online and Russian manipulation of the American electoral system, and certainly thanks to the congressional hearings into the 2016 election that explored the role of Facebook, Google, and Twitter, the halo that once crowned Silicon Valley appears to have evaporated. Society now expects technology companies to take much more responsibility for their products and services than they did just a few years earlier. The question is no longer whether tech companies will help thwart the proliferation of dangerous content online. It's how far will they go to do so, sacrificing short-term profits for more public safety online. Given popular sentiment, I suspect that the answer is "quite far." You can't stand for nothing. If you pretend to be value-neutral, as the industry largely has, you risk having your platforms overrun by malevolent actors with no such scruples. It's thus increasingly in tech companies' own long-term interests to prioritize CVE, proactively examining every aspect of their role in disseminating content. If they don't take a new tack, they might find large segments of society questioning their very license to operate.

Government can play a role in encouraging tech companies to step up. One option might be to reward companies that take specific steps to make the virtual world safer, offering tax incentives and various forms of public recognition. As regards the latter, we might create a scoring system for technology companies, awarding high ratings to those that take specific actions, or bestowing upon well-behaving technology companies a Better Business Bureau–like seal. More broadly, government must endeavor to serve as a partner for technology companies, aiding and guiding their efforts. For instance, government might spearhead unified industry efforts in which social media platforms band together to coordinate the expulsion of bad actors wherever they operate online. Government in this sense could serve as a convener for the industry, helping companies share knowledge and take collective action.

Inevitably, some companies will continue to resist what they see as government interference. Yet there is a fair and productive middle ground that allows government and respects the tech sector's historical autonomy, while still allowing us to make inroads on CVE. To find this middle ground, government should put its money where its mouth is, sharing the burden with tech companies and refraining from taking an overly adversarial stance. Additional steps to complement the efforts of tech companies, and when necessary, to compel their cooperation might include:

- **Scaling up online detection centers:** Government should train armies of people to scour the Internet for nefarious content, deploying them across the globe using a "call center" model. We need hundreds of thousands of "eyes" on content to spot potentially dangerous situations online.
- **Addressing incitement on social media:** Government should enforce existing terms of service, develop means to track down posters of malicious content, fine and block such posters, and create a public database of inciters akin to those tracking pedophiles, among other measures.
- **Regulating tech companies more stringently in some cases:** We should consider whether it might be possible to fine platforms for allowing hate content to go up, and to require companies to systematically review how bad actors are using their platforms.
- **Providing financial incentives:** Government should offer rewards to NGOs and individuals that identify extremists online and intercede with vulnerable youth.

- **Mapping the threat:** Government should create public databases (using data provided by social media platforms) that map the provenance of bad content online, identifying who is recruiting and posting.
- **Supporting offline interventions:** Online problems require offline help, in the form of local centers where youths can visit when confronted by extremist recruiters online. At present, we lack enough of these facilities. Governments at all levels should help fund their creation and maintenance.

As intriguing as chatbots are, the potential of AI and other technologies in the CVE domain is potentially much broader, and yet to be explored. Sharp minds at the Department of Defense, Department of State, Defense Advanced Research Projects Agency (DARPA), and other government agencies are working hard to get into the minds of youth who are exploring extremist content, but we don't have billion-dollar contracts to amply deploy what they're learning. And we don't have a single, national laboratory for research that would allow government to coordinate efforts and increase their power. Working in collaboration with companies, industry groups, and NGOs, government could bring together engineers and CVE practitioners to develop and mobilize cutting-edge technologies, as well as track and inventory and coordinate the research under way inside and outside government that could be applied to CVE.

"CRISIS MODE"

The global media has tended to focus on the specific, imminent threats posed by groups like the so-called Islamic State, as well as the role played by specific platforms like Twitter in disseminating extremist ideology. Yet these groups and platforms aren't the core of the problem. When specific groups are defeated, as the so-called Islamic State might well be one day, others will crop up to take their place. Likewise, in five years or ten, Twitter might become a relic, replaced by even more popular—and powerful—platforms. The core of the problem—the dynamic that makes recruitment possible—is the mediation of religion by technology. As Joanna Shields has suggested to me, "The genie [of technology] is out of the bottle." We have no choice now but to deal with it.[82]

Dealing with the genie means evolving as technology evolves—since the extremists have been and are doing exactly that. When governments were still making YouTube videos, the bad guys had skipped on to Instagram, because that's where the youth were moving. By the time governments started paying attention to Instagram, the bad guys were already on to Snapchat. As of this writing, government officials were scrambling to respond to the use of encrypted messaging services for recruitment purposes, a technology that was on the horizon for months if not years. Senator Rob Portman went so far as to declare that we are in "crisis mode."[83] An FBI official remarked, "No matter the format, the message of radicalization spreads faster than we imagined just a few years ago. We may see a more dangerous world in the short term."[84] If we don't address the Sheikh Google phenomenon far more directly and aggressively than we have to date, we'll see more extremist content across platforms, in multiple languages. We'll see more kids lured onto encrypted channels that the authorities can't monitor. We'll see extremists using technology such as bots to personalize their messaging to kids, making it even more alluring. We'll see extremists using video games and gaming-related platforms like Twitch to target youth (a natural fit given the violent imagery in many games, and their tendency to socialize kids to actual violence).* We'll see many more attacks broad-

---

* Joanna Shields has told me that "there is now a new era to [the extremist challenge], because people are acting things out live. Symbols, phrases, and semantics of language matter." Interview with the author, April 18,

cast online in real time, including "appointment viewing" incidents in which terrorists announce attacks at an undisclosed location and invite viewers to tune in. As wearable virtual reality technology goes mainstream, we can even imagine that increasingly young recruits will be able to remotely take part in the violence or participate in a realistic simulation designed to make killing seem fun. And of course, we should expect that extremists will eventually hack into the computer systems of Western governments and private companies.

The tactics I've advocated in this chapter can help us avoid these dire scenarios, but even they are not enough. In engaging with technology, we must also take steps to counter some specific political messages about the United States that have circulated in Muslim communities both online and off since 9/11. One reason we're losing the war of ideas to extremists is that a thick fog of ignorance about the United States has settled over young Muslims globally. This fog won't simply go away with another U.S. government publicity campaign to change "hearts and minds." It's perpetuated in part by widespread American ignorance about Muslims, which often leads non-Muslim and Muslim Americans to do and say things that only reinforce stereotyped views. Defeating extremism will require that we operate in new ways to replace stereotypes and incorrect assumptions with truth. As I suggest in the next chapter, we must become much more sensitive to what young Muslims think about us, and then take decisive action on a number of levels to challenge and change those beliefs.

2016. Video games, for example, can alter behavior, and so-called ISIS has borrowed the emotion and design of games like Call of Duty. Jacky Wong, "Tencent Slips in Beijing's Game of Thrones," *Wall Street Journal*, July 4, 2017, https://www.wsj.com/articles/tencent-slips-in-beijings-game-of-thrones-1499171065; Alyssa Abkowitz, "In China, Videogames Will Now Start Limiting Screen Time for You," *Wall Street Journal*, July 4, 2017, https://www.wsj.com/articles/gaming-company-tencent-questioned-over-honor-cuts-kids-play-time-1499173348.

CHAPTER SIX

AMERICA THE BOGEYMAN

The highway linking Afghanistan's capital Kabul with the city of Jalalabad is reputed to be among the world's most dangerous. CNN once gave the road a "death rating" of 9.5 out of 10, citing the "combination of the narrow, winding lanes that climb up to 600 meters through the Kabul gorge" as well as the "reckless Afghan driver."[1]

As an American diplomat being driven down this road in 2004, I worried about another danger: the Taliban. Fearing an attack, the embassy had arranged for us to leave before dawn so that we would reach our destination by early afternoon, when it was safest. Three of us, Joan, KB, and I, were heading to Jalalabad, a day ahead of Ambassador Zalmay Khalilzad's scheduled visit. At the embassy, we all piled into the backseat of an armored SUV. In the front seat sat a former U.S. soldier, nom de guerre Viper. Other cars in our multivehicle convoy were loaded with "shooters," as they were nicknamed by the civilians in Kabul Compound (the area that housed the U.S. Chancery, a historic building that had been closed in 1989 but reopened after 9/11).* The shooters radioed back and forth as we drove, seeming to talk, of all things, about the time. "Four o'clock," a crackling voice said. "Seven o'clock. Two o'clock." I asked Viper what this was all about. He explained that they were signaling the locations of armed men along the road, warning the other vehicles in the convoy. From the sounds of it, the roads were teeming with men with guns. The vigilance of our shooters hardly reassured me.

About halfway through the drive, the car behind us called Viper to say that something was wrong with one of our tires. We pulled off to our left into an open area separating the roadway from the mountain. As we came to a stop, shouting came over the radio. "Fire! Fire! Get out! Get out!" Smoke was billowing from our hood. The first thing I thought of was that our car was about to explode. A shooter appeared and yanked open my door. He pulled me out and pushed a flak jacket into my hands. "Put it on!" he yelled. He led us to unarmored SUV and told us to wait inside while he and some comrades extinguished the blaze. A few minutes later, the fire was out, and we learned its cause: a mechanical problem. That was small consolation. Our vehicle was wrecked.†

Frightened to be stopped in a hostile area, we wanted to leave the damaged SUV behind and continue on our way as soon as possible. The embassy had other plans. Fearing that our SUV would fall into the hands of the wrong people, they instructed us to wait with it—they were sending out a team. I was shocked, as were the shooters, but there was nothing that we could do. We had to fol-

---

* According to one account, the Chancery was closed after street violence erupted and parts of the embassy building were damaged by "government-organized protesters." Kirk Spitzer, "U.S. Reopens Embassy in Kabul with Ceremony," *USA Today,* December 17, 2001, http://usatoday30.usatoday.com/news/attack/2001/12/17/usembassy-usat.htm#more.

† These vehicles, I later learned, were not suited for driving conditions in Afghanistan, but Congress had insisted that the embassy "buy American."

low the instructions of the RSO (regional security officer) back in Kabul.*

So, there we sat, by the side of the road. The SUV was brutally hot. We couldn't turn on the air-conditioning, since we needed to conserve fuel. The shooters were tense, but they tried not to show it. One shooter in the front seat began to sing country music, his M-4 leaning on the dashboard. He teased me for having no idea who the recording artist was. More shooters patrolled outside the vehicles, scanning in all directions. A few of them climbed up into the mountains to get a better vantage on the incoming traffic, radioing messages back.†

Sensing their anxiety, I was scared. This was serious—we were out in the open, an easy target. Every now and then, a bus would lumber toward us, brightly painted, covered over in bold red, yellow, orange, and green colors and pretty, graphic designs of flowers and paisleys, and filled beyond capacity, passengers hanging out the open windows or sitting on the roof. The shooters monitored each bus closely, looking for any sign of a threat. I braced each time one of the vehicles approached and I wondered what might happen. Each time, the bus passed uneventfully.

As the minutes turned into hours, my mind veered into darker places. What if I never made it home? I am not an alarmist, but this time was different. Finding a piece of blank paper in my bag, I wrote a letter to my mother.

After several excruciating hours, help finally arrived. We continued on to Jalalabad, pulling up around dusk at a U.S. compound. On its grounds were several Soviet-built cement buildings and what looked to be a sort of "camp"—an empty swimming pool and several simple bungalow-type structures perched on a small hill.

---

* Every U.S. embassy has a regional security officer as part of the Diplomatic Security Bureau of the U.S. Department of State.

† After we returned from this trip, I threw a tea (which I dubbed, in jest, Operation High Tea) to thank everyone for their care in attending to our safety.

My two colleagues and I were emotionally drained, caked with sweat and dust, and starving. Entering one of the buildings, I ventured to a room that was supposed to be a cafeteria to scope out the offerings. I was disappointed but not surprised to find a couple of tables with military-issue "Meals, Ready to Eat" and water bottles. I turned around and was walking out when a local embassy employee called to me and asked where I was from. Like many Afghans at the Kabul Compound, he had taken me for Afghan. I told him that I was born in Kashmir, India. "Then you are one of us!" he said in English, with a laugh. "Do you want something to eat? Come with me."

He led me outside, around the building, and down a steep hill. We found a group of other local embassy employees huddled around a portable gas stove and eating. It was dark out—at first, I could barely make out their faces. I said hello, and to my great delight, someone handed me a tin plate with *rajma* (spicy kidney bean stew) and naan (bread) on it. It was divine!

As we ate, the locals inquired about my upbringing and what it was like to live as a Muslim in the United States. They wondered about my impressions of Afghanistan. After perhaps twenty minutes of pleasant conversation, as we sat together in the spring night air, our discussion took a more serious turn. The Abu Ghraib scandal had recently broken, with horrifying images of human rights abuses at the Iraqi prison broadcast around the world. One of my dinner companions expressed disgust at what the Americans had done. "We hear Americans talking about how much they respect Islam," he said, "and here you are doing this to Muslims. Nobody deserves to be stripped naked and treated like dogs. You are supposed to be the country that sets the example for human rights."

Another diner observed that if America cared about Muslims half as much as our politicians claimed, Abu Ghraib never would have happened. Others nodded, their anger palpable. As they related, they knew all along that America was against them—Abu Ghraib was simply glaring proof. As for America's intentions in Afghanistan—well, it was clear: The U.S. was pursuing its own interests and cared little about the fate of the country. It was all a big power grab. We saw Muslims as inferior.

I was troubled. These employees weren't trying to disrespect me. They were just conveying what they so often felt but perhaps hadn't been able to express before to a member of the U.S. government. Although I was certainly aware of America's image problems among Muslims around the world, I had never experienced such a frank airing of views by foreign nationals working with us.

I didn't know it then, but that experience previewed the sentiment I would encounter among youth throughout Europe, and later, the world. As I would discover, the belief that America "hated Muslims" was hardly limited to Afghans, or for that matter, middle-aged men and women. Nor did it stem from anger at a particular atrocity, policy, or diplomatic agenda, as observers frequently imply. Although many Muslim millennials admired most aspects of American life and didn't hesitate to consume American food, fashion, technology, or music, those whom I encountered overseas were almost universally suspicious of the United States.

This nexus of anti-American ideology—the wholesale corruption of "brand America" in the minds of many Muslim millennials—forms the final component of the global system underlying extremism. In experiencing and working through their post-9/11 identity crisis, many of the millennials that I encountered weren't simply falling prey to extremist ideology and Saudi influence, partaking of halalization, and experiencing their religion in new ways via technology. Their worldview was also being colored by their alienation from the West, personified chiefly by the great global superpower: the United States. I also spotted a deeper cultural dynamic taking hold, whereby existing biases and stereotypes were validated by subsequent events, policies, political statements, and entertainment. The result was an ideological mind-set that was becoming ever more entrenched as time passed, and ever more difficult to dislodge.

PREJUDICED POLICIES?

In 2012, while on a trip to Jordan, I sat down with a group of Muslim women to talk about their lives and their impressions of the United States. We met at an open-air café, sitting at a long table not far from a large Pepsi cooler. The women were all in their late teens or early twenties and pursuing college degrees. Most covered their hair, some choosing bright red scarves, others patterned or plain white ones. The conversation began pleasantly enough, but as in Afghanistan, it soon grew serious. As the women told me, they knew their country had a good relationship with the United States (Jordan is one of our country's closest partners in the Middle East), and they were glad for it. Still, as one girl asserted, there was a darker reality to the relationship. When I asked her what it was, she replied, "Everyone knows."

I didn't understand her. "Everyone knows what?"

"Everyone knows why you Americans are here."

"And why is that?"

"For the oil."*

Other girls nodded their heads.

"That's the reason you pay attention to the Middle East," another girl said. "Not because you like Muslims, because you don't. You want our oil. All the aid you spend—really it's because you're trying to get us to give you our oil."

"It might seem that way," I said, "but our relationship with the Middle East is far more complex than that." I related that we didn't

---

* This comment was surprising because Jordan lacks conventional oil reserves. It does, however, have oil shale capacity worth billions. See Al Fin, "Jordan's Oil Shale Deposits Contain 500 Billion Barrels of Oil Equivalent," *Oil Price,* October 6, 2010, http://oilprice.com/Energy/Crude-Oil/Jordans-Oil-Shale-Deposits-Contain-500-Billion-Barrels-Of-Oil-Equivalent.html.

maintain strong relationships with particular countries simply because of a resource they might possess. A variety of issues caused countries to align themselves with one another, and in the Middle East, these relationships were especially complex. I went through a list of Arab states where the U.S. government delivered aid, and talked about foreign policy goals of nation-states, mutual relationships and alliances, and global and civil society partnerships and programs related to education, women's rights, the rule of law, and health. If we didn't care about Muslims or want to help them, how come we had been so active in helping to create the Muslim-majority nation of Kosovo? How come we've invested billions on public works projects in a country like Egypt? If our goal was only about "getting the oil," America would not need to create an elaborate array of partnerships and programs around other goals. Our larger vision for the Middle East reflected American values of democracy, freedom, and human rights, as well as our desires for greater regional stability and the formation of friendly commercial and political alliances.

The young woman who had raised this point shook her head. "I don't believe that. All of us know. You want the oil, and so you give us money so that we can have stability in our country, which you need in order to get the oil." At this, the other girls all nodded.

Throughout my travels, I not only routinely encountered the notions that America "doesn't care about," "dislikes," or even "hates" Islam—I encountered it expressed in a variety of ways. Many youth argued for America's hostility to Muslims by pointing to specific American policies that they felt suggested callousness on America's part. Americans were "nice" to some Muslim-majority countries, but for reasons that were strictly opportunistic. We liked Saudi oil. We liked security cooperation with Pakistan. We liked Egyptian moderation toward Israel. And when Muslim-majority governments didn't comply, youth observed, we weren't nice. Some young Muslims pointed to the Iraq War as clear evidence of our hatred of Muslims and thirst for Iraqi oil. Others noted America's repeated military intervention in Muslim-majority countries such as Afghanistan as revealing America's fundamental disdain for Muslims. We weren't routinely invading Christian countries, were we?

And then there was the perception of a strong and particularly revealing double standard in our stance toward Israel. In the view of many young Muslims, Israel and the Jews were malicious actors bent on decimating Muslims in every conceivable way. That we grossly "favored Israel" in their dispute with the Palestinians and Iran constituted prima facie evidence that we loved Jews and hated Muslims. Many youth also spoke to me about the United States favoring Sunni Islam over Shia Islam. And, even worse, they believed, Americans had little value or respect for the many other Islamic sects. In fact, they argued, we talk about Islam in terms of "Sunni-Shia," normalizing this way of thinking, when in fact we should be contesting it. I might have expected to encounter such arguments in Middle Eastern countries, but in fact I found them everywhere.

It was as if the youths were reading from something akin to Mao's little red book. During a visit to Trinidad, I encountered a steady stream of questions about U.S. foreign policy. I was surprised when a group of young, soon-to-be journalists met me in their university and asked why America "put Israel above every other country in the world." Why didn't we recognize Palestinians' legitimate claims? Why did we tolerate Israel's settlement building in the West Bank? Didn't we know that Israel was secretly planning to grab more Arab land—and that we were enabling it? Why were we so uniquely concerned with Israel's security? Why did we give Israel more money than its Arab neighbors? And why did we allow Israel to have nuclear weapons and not a Muslim-majority country like Iran? These students knew all the answers: it was because we hated Muslims and were at war with Islam. One communications student went farther and suggested that our strategy was to beat down any sense of self-respect among the Palestinians. When I pointed out that the U.S. had put significant pressure on Israeli leaders to contain settlement building in Palestinian territories and push for a two-state solution, it had virtually no effect. In Trinidad and beyond, nearly all the younger people I met didn't worry much about the nuances. They just knew America hated them.

Although anger at our policy toward Israel existed everywhere, certain critiques of American policy varied depending on the country or region I was visiting. While traveling in Brazil's tri-border area (a region framed between Brazil, Paraguay, and Argentina), I presumed myself far removed from the conspiracy theories and political dynamics I had encountered in the Middle East and Asia. The city of Foz do Iguaçu, however, harbored a strong Shia community rumored to maintain deep connections with the Hezbollah terrorist group.[2] People there with whom I spoke asked me about America's "double standard" on nuclear arms and their perceptions that we favored Sunnis over Shia. They also cited America's policies toward Iran as evidence that we hated Islam.

In Pakistan, despite the millions of dollars in aid we dispense each year,* youth blamed their country's endemic poverty and instability on the United States. We were the richest country in the world—why didn't we do more to help develop Pakistan? It had to be because we didn't really care about the country—we just used it for our own purposes, such as countering China's influence in the region or helping us fight terrorist groups. During a visit to Timbuktu, Mali, I again encountered young Muslims who blamed the United States for the instability in their country. How was that? Well, America could have intervened for the good of the Malian people, but our leaders chose not to because they "didn't care about Muslims." Christians or Jews were one thing, but when it came time

* America spends about 1 percent of its annual federal budget on foreign aid. "The U.S. has drastically cut aid to Pakistan in recent years, but the South Asian nation still received $383 million in 2016, according to U.S. government data, and $742,200,000 is planned for Pakistan in fiscal year 2017." Ann M. Simmons, "U.S. Foreign Aid: A Waste of Money or a Boost to World Stability? Here Are the Facts," *Los Angeles Times*, May 10, 2017, http://www.latimes.com/world/la-fg-global-aid-true-false-20170501-htmlstory.html.

to help Muslims, we weren't interested because the United States had an apparent interest in sowing instability and suffering in "Muslim lands." In the case of Africa, rather than do so directly, as we did in places like Iraq or Afghanistan, we could just sit back and let other actors get the job done for us. In India, over coffee in a New Delhi hotel, a group of entrepreneurs and bloggers asked about America's disinterest in incidents of violence against Muslim minority groups around the world. Why don't we say more? We had a huge platform and that made us the world's best megaphone for minority rights. I heard similar arguments regarding Burma. Why weren't we intervening to stop the country's Buddhists from persecuting the Muslim Rohingya? Well, because we would just as soon see Muslims put down—Burma's government was saving us the trouble.

In some places, familiar binary criticism—America hates all Muslims—was partly displaced by anger over perceived favoritism. Over dinner in Kuala Lumpur, Malaysia, a diverse group of Muslim leaders posed questions about our tendency to highlight and preference Arab Muslims, while ignoring those from Asia. In Suriname, while at a reception in Paramaribo, a senior foreign diplomat asked me: "Can you speak freely about why your country chose you to be the special representative to Muslim communities? Are you [the United States] making a statement about what kind of Islam you prefer?"

Across the world—from Australia to Lebanon to Greece—I also heard younger Muslims insist that the United States persecuted its own Muslims. According to these youth, American Muslims weren't allowed to wear headscarves or otherwise express their religious beliefs openly; there were no Muslims in senior positions in any field; Muslims were harassed for just walking down the street; Muslims were legally prevented from moving freely about the country; Muslims were constantly monitored by police; Muslims couldn't fast during Ramadan; and Muslims couldn't build mosques. There was no middle ground: in *every* respect, youth thought, American Muslims were second-class citizens. When I assured them that American Muslims could in fact practice their religion freely, more often than not my companions were stunned. They were also stunned to find that I—a U.S. government official—was Muslim. Any evidence that American Muslims weren't wholly marginalized and disempowered in their own country seemed incredible to them. Learning of my Muslim heritage, these youth accused me of being a sellout, a mouthpiece for an exploitative American government.

Making matters worse, these youth had no clue about the history and diversity of Muslims in the United States, or of the efforts of American politicians to recognize them. Many assumed Muslim populations in America had immigrated fairly recently, and mainly from Arab lands. Further, they thought that the American government's outreach to Muslims had only begun with President Obama's famous Cairo speech in 2009, in which he had offered a "new beginning" in our relations with Muslims globally. They had no idea that Muslims, hailing from all over the world and representing a wide array of Islamic practices, exist in America today. Nor did they realize that Muslims have lived in the United States since the republic's founding, or that President Reagan mentioned praying in mosques in a major speech, or that President Eisenhower gave land to Muslims in Washington, D.C., to build a mosque, or that the founding fathers publicly acknowledged Islam's presence in the United States, or that Thomas Jefferson kept a copy of the Qur'an in his personal library, or that George Washington once wrote: "to bigotry we give no sanction." They had no idea that American Muslims owned or co-owned major professional sports teams in the NFL and NBA, or that many had become prominent doctors, had risen to leadership roles in business, and made fortunes in Silicon Valley. In the absence of all this knowledge and more, it was far easier for Muslim youth to believe that our country hated them for their religion.

Such frustration also reflected naïve assumptions about America's place in the world. Almost universally, Muslim youth thought that the United States was all-powerful, blessed with endless riches and resources of every kind, that we could do anything we wanted at all times. Thus, if we didn't do something—like intervene in Mali, or bring peace to Iraq, or force Israel to make concessions to the Palestinians—it reflected a deliberate choice on our part to do harm. Another related myth prevailing among Muslims was that American leaders were all-powerful within their country. So, if America didn't behave in a way Muslim youth desired, it was because the president personally hated Muslims. Still another myth related to the motivations American leaders had in forming their policy. Why did George W. Bush or Donald Trump hate Muslims? Because he was a Christian. Christians hate Muslims. Thus President Bush could ever only hate Muslims.

This logic persisted even in the face of immediate evidence to the contrary. During his presidency, Barack Obama made great efforts to reach out to Muslim communities. Over a six-month period in 2009, he sent signals of warmth to Muslims worldwide in three significant speeches: his inaugural address, a speech given in Ankara, Turkey, and his well-known Cairo speech. In many of his other speeches, he sought to inject a respect for Islamic history, using quotes from the Qur'an and lauding Muslim accomplishments in science, art, and business. Despite that, Muslim youth remained skeptical. Why, they asked, didn't President Obama visit an American mosque? Because he was ashamed of his heritage and did not want people to think he was Muslim. Why, while campaigning for president, did President Obama once remove a woman wearing a headscarf from behind the podium so she would not be in the pictures? Because he did not want to be seen as a Muslim—so the logic went.

An important part of my role was to counter such beliefs, confronting kids with facts they hadn't considered. More times than I can count, I had to comment on the famous "clash of civilizations" theory first put forth by the late Harvard professor Samuel Huntington in his landmark 1993 *Foreign Affairs* essay—the notion that tribal differences rather than ideological rifts or economic competition drive international affairs, and that Islamic culture was fundamentally incompatible with America and with Western traditions of liberalism, democracy, and individualism.* As Huntington wrote in his book *The Clash of Civilizations and the Remaking of World Order*, "The underlying problem for the West is not Islamic fundamentalism. It is Islam, a different civilization whose people are convinced of the superiority of their culture and are obsessed with the inferiority of their power. The problem for Islam is not the CIA or the U.S. Department of Defense. It is the West, a different civilization whose people are convinced of the universality of their culture and believe that their superior, if declining, power imposes on them the obligation to extend that culture throughout the world."[3]

In discussions with kids, I took issue with Huntington's thesis, explaining to them, for instance, that George W. Bush may have been Christian, but he was also the first president to have put a Qur'an in the White House library, and that he had me, a Muslim, as well as many other Muslims working for him in the White House. I pointed out that American laws prohibited religious discrimination, and that legally many large companies had to provide special places for Muslims to pray. I spent a great deal of time trying to help kids understand that Americans didn't make policies in specific countries solely or even primarily through the lens of religion. Our policies toward Morocco or Senegal, say, were not "Muslim" policies, any more than our policies toward India were "Hindu" policies or those toward Spain "Christian" policies. In all cases, I argued, America's

* Samuel Huntington, "The Clash of Civilizations?" *Foreign Affairs* 72, no. 3 (1993): 22–49, doi:10.2307/20045621. See also David Brooks, "Huntington's Clash Revisited," *New York Times*, March 3, 2011, http://www.nytimes.com/2011/03/04/opinion/04brooks.html. Summarizing Huntington's argument, Brooks writes: "People in the Arab world do not share the general suppositions of the Western world. Their primary attachment is to their religion, not to their nation-state. Their culture is inhospitable to certain liberal ideals, like pluralism, individualism and democracy."

foreign engagement reflected many kinds of considerations and many levels of complexity. They couldn't analyze a policy of the United States and simplistically conclude that they were deliberately framed to hurt Muslims.

But the youth I met didn't seem inclined to change their views. They learned about all of these offenses at school, had heard their parents talk about them, had heard their imams preach about American misdeeds, had seen our wickedness discussed on social media. Certainly they weren't prepared to believe me, a representative of the U.S. government. Sometimes, my exchanges with Muslim youth were quite challenging.

Perhaps the most memorable of such encounters occurred during a 2012 trip to Pakistan. I appeared at a number of schools and universities in various cities, arriving on the heels of some particularly complicated diplomatic exchanges between the country and Ambassador Richard Holbrooke's team (Holbrooke was special representative for Afghanistan and Pakistan at the time). In addition to the specific issues straining Pakistan-U.S. relations, Muslims across the globe were incensed about revelations that American troops in Afghanistan had allegedly flushed a Qur'an down the toilet. Everywhere I went in Pakistan, kids were angry. At a well-respected girls' school in Karachi, an auditorium of youth complained about the disrespect allegedly shown to the Qur'an. A mob mentality seemed to take hold, and the girls went on one after the other to lambast the United States over Abu Ghraib, the Iraq War, American policy generally, and the case of a Pakistani woman then being tried for murder in New York. Here, they thought, was a perfect example of America going after Pakistanis.[4] Why did American politicians never say anything nice about Pakistan? Why did we only see Islam as backward and corrupt? Why did we think all Muslims were terrorists?

When I tried to offer counterarguments, the students scoffed, and some booed and tsk-tsked. Strikingly, some parroted the very same hateful views that I'd heard from kids elsewhere around the world, with no reference to or allowances made for the friendly public relationship that had long existed between the United States and Pakistan. After the event, a girl approached me to continue her arguments. "You should be ashamed of yourself," she told me. "You are a Muslim and you are sitting here defending a country that doesn't speak honestly about its beliefs. You are a Muslim! How can you support this behavior?" Other students standing behind her nodded in agreement. The school principal rushed over and begged my apology. "I am so sorry," she said, "this is not how we treat our guests."

The arguments I heard from youth in Pakistan had their origins in a familiar source: extremist propaganda found in textbooks. The U.S. Commission on International Religious Freedom (USCIRF)'s 2011 annual report had noted a "troubling rise in violent religious extremism across Pakistan that targets religious minorities as well as members of the majority Muslim faith," and that "textbooks used in Pakistani primary and secondary schools foster prejudice and intolerance of religious minorities, especially Hindus and Christians."[5] As Harvard professor Amartya Sen confirmed in a 2016 interview, textbooks had conditioned generations of Pakistanis to normalize hatred toward Westerners, regardless of the state of foreign aid or formal diplomatic relations between their country and the United States.[6] In recent years, Pakistani conservatives had embarked on a campaign to "Muslimize" textbooks, replacing "good morning" with "Assalaamu Alaikum," for instance,* and "cleansing" textbooks of intercultural content, "[reversing] changes that had replaced content about Muslims with material about non-Muslims, including American Helen Keller, an author who was deaf and blind, and Hindu ruler Raja Dahir."[7] Ultimately, in the eyes of these girls, it didn't matter that I was a fellow Muslim. I was an Indian-born

---

* *Assalaamu Alaikum* is Arabic for "peace be unto you." In removing any connection to the West and replacing it with a traditional Islamic greeting, they disavow their colonial past and confirm Islamic preeminence and normativity.

representative of the U.S. government. (That I was an Indian-born American didn't help matters—textbooks in the country had long spun a narrative of hatred toward Pakistan's neighbor as well.) That could mean only one thing: I was the enemy, one of "them."

THE TRUTH ABOUT 9/11 (AND EVERYTHING ELSE)

Observers have long remarked on the prominence of conspiracy theories within Middle Eastern countries. As one has written, "Anyone who has spent any time in the Middle East, or even visited it for a brief few days for that matter, invariably will have had some sort of experience with a conspiracy theory in the region."[8] When in 2012 Iranian president Mahmoud Ahmadinejad accused Western countries of causing drought in his country by interfering with the drift of rain clouds, he was building upon a distinct tradition of irrationalism.[9] Yet as I discovered, tall tales and myths—some relatively innocuous, many quite offensive—proliferated not just in the Middle East, but in Muslim communities worldwide.

Why had Americans channeled billions into Muslim-majority countries like Egypt or Jordan? Because, Muslim youth told me, we wanted to establish a Christian presence in these countries and convert good, upstanding Muslims. Why were we paying to vaccinate kids in Muslim communities? Because we weren't really vaccinating them—we were using the needles to sterilize Muslims so they wouldn't reproduce. Why had 9/11 happened? Well, it didn't—it was all an illusion, fabricated by Hollywood. Or if it did happen, it was orchestrated by Jews, conceived as a pretext for the country's expansion into neighboring Arab lands. Did I know that Jews in New York City all got a text the morning of 9/11 telling them to stay home? Or the attack was orchestrated by the CIA—they wanted yet another excuse for invading "Muslim lands" and seizing their oil. How, many of those I met with asked, could a ragtag group of Muslims possibly have hijacked one plane, much less four, without being detected and stopped by the world's most powerful country?*

As for Al Qaeda, some Muslim kids suggested that the terrorist group didn't actually exist, yet another fabrication foisted on the world by Muslim-hating Americans. I heard this even from kids in Muslim-majority countries that Al Qaeda had attacked. Take Tanzania: On August 7, 1998, a suicide bomber drove a truck bomb into the U.S. embassy in the capital, Dar es Salaam, killing eleven and wounding eighty-five. (A simultaneous attack on the U.S. embassy in Nairobi, Kenya, killed 213 and wounded approximately 4,000.) The vast majority of casualties were local residents, not Americans. Afterward the United States carried out reprisal missile attacks on sites in Afghanistan and Sudan. When I visited Tanzania in 2010, a young man in his early twenties told me that the embassy attack had quite possibly been carried out by the U.S. itself. "What do you mean?" I asked. His response: "Well, you guys just did this because you wanted an excuse to attack Muslims."

On multiple occasions, young Muslims I met with told me that America was to blame for the 2004 tsunami that devastated East Asia. This notion, which appears to have originated in an Egyptian magazine called *Al-Osboa'*, held that the earthquake causing the tsunami had occurred because of Indian nuclear testing, made possible by America and Israel.[10] Despite repeated warnings from the Arab world and international experts, both the United States and Israel had allegedly "showed readiness to cooperate with India in

* Conspiracy theories about 9/11 circulate among Muslims of all ages. A 2006 Pew Global Attitudes Project found that "a majority of Indonesians, Jordanians, Turks and Egyptians remained unconvinced that Arabs were responsible for the Sept. 11 terrorist attacks in New York and Washington." A 2011 Pew poll documented that three-quarters of Egyptians denied 9/11 was carried out by Arabs: "Global Public Opinion in the Bush Years (2001–2008)," Pew Global Attitudes Project, released December 18, 2008, http://www.pewglobal.org/files/pdf/263.pdf; Peter Schwartzstein, "Egypt's Latest Conspiracy Theories Target the Country's Syrian Refugees," *The Atlantic*, September 12, 2013, http://www.theatlantic.com/international/archive/2013/09/egypts-latest-conspiracy-theories-target-the-countrys-syrian-refugees/279585/.

experiments to exterminate humankind."[11] In the process, they had succeeded in wiping away hundreds of thousands of people. The kids I met had heard about it from their friends and seen it on social media, so they believed it, just as they might any number of other urban myths and legends.*

What especially startled me about these conspiracy theories was that they came from young people who were saturated in American culture. As discussed, throughout the world, Muslim kids were using American social media platforms like Facebook, Skype, or Twitter (although they knew that Mark Zuckerberg was Jewish, they ignored that). They watched American movies, TV shows and sports, and they listened to hip-hop and other popular music. At a dinner in Suriname, a Muslim parent lamented how hard it was "to compete with Xbox." In Pakistan, the country with the strongest anti-American sentiment I encountered, kids told me that they enjoyed hanging out at KFC. Youth in other places like London, Jakarta, and Mumbai reported liking Starbucks and McDonald's and wanting to wear Nike sneakers. In Amman, Jordan, kids told me they met up on weekends at restaurants that featured "American burgers and fries" or "New York Cheesecake" or "deep-dish Chicago Pizza." One young man in Mauritania told me how important he and his friends thought it was to look like the kids they saw on American television shows. Other kids liked the idea of being free in New York City to live like the characters on the TV show *Friends* did. In Dhaka, Bangladesh, the kids I met with were using Chinese fakes of Apple gadgets, showing off the iconic Apple logo. In Kenya and Indonesia, I saw stores that promoted "American basketball" shoes.

Many of these youths saw no contradiction between loving Ameri-

---

* When I worked at the National Security Council, we (those with whom I discussed this issue) all thought that the notion of American complicity in the tsunami was a spoof. How could people possibly believe that America possessed a "weather button" to create droughts, tsunamis, and floods? In a roundtable in Dhaka, Bangladesh, a young woman explained such reasoning in the following terms: "Americans are rich and they have powerful weapons that can cause us harm. Many believe you made the floods happen."

can culture and even American values such as freedom of expression, and also utterly distrusting the country. These kids often weren't taught to think deeply and critically about the cultural artifacts they encountered. Along with Sheikh Google, social media allowed kids access to a variety of viewpoints, including many that lacked credibility. They often weren't especially self-aware or inclined to probe contradictions in their thinking. They saw life through their TV and computer screens. In Hollywood, they saw adventure and Big Bold America. Yet they also perceived a country dead set against them—a country with great potential and lofty rhetoric that wasn't living up to its promise. In their eyes, America was simultaneously the best of the best and the greatest menace to their Muslim beliefs and identities. It wasn't logical—but it didn't need to be. Anti-American political beliefs were but one ingredient in their amorphous, churning cultural landscape.

THE CULTURAL DYNAMIC OF ANTI-AMERICANISM

How can we explain these pervasive strains of anti-Americanism? Where did they originate? It's tempting to blame specific events in the immediate past, such as the Iraq War or Abu Ghraib, or to see anti-Americanism as the result of longer-term foreign policy choices. While both recent events and the historical context are important, there ultimately is no easy answer. Certainly, anger about specific policy decisions and historical relationships colored the perspective of kids in local communities. But I also found that youth were projecting their own experiences on America. Given that some of their own governments were repressive and behaved in underhanded ways, it was easy for them to believe that America would partake of dark, insidious plotting. Their own political leaders exercised dictatorial powers, so it was easy to believe that American leaders had similar powers.

In addition to these factors, I also came to discern a cultural dynamic in place that seemed to explain a good deal of the anger and suspicion directed at the United States. As I've suggested, 9/11 was a critical turning point for Muslim youth, triggering an identity crisis that continues to this day. But 9/11 and its immediate aftermath didn't occur in a vacuum. Whether thanks to colonialism, the Israeli-Palestinian conflict, or other historical events, Muslims had already nursed grievances of one sort or another toward both the West and the United States. In many countries, these grievances had been further entrenched thanks to decades of propaganda (both from the government and at times from other forces) or to religious figures who saw a theological basis for hating the West. What 9/11 and its aftermath did was fuse these disparate grievances or misgivings toward the United States into a more comprehensive, universal "America hates Muslims" canvas onto which kids could layer local fears, concerns, or grievances about the United States.

When the Abu Ghraib scandal broke, when American troops were reported to have flushed a Qur'an down the toilet, when the United States failed to disavow freedom of expression during the Danish cartoon crisis, when the president seeks to ban travelers and migrants from Muslim-majority countries—young Muslims were primed to interpret these events in a particular way, and each seemingly "negative" event made it more likely that they would similarly and more intensely perceive future events. The absence of strong, credible voices that presented different perspectives on America and its policies guaranteed that Muslim youth would become increasingly entrenched in their distrust of an unease toward America.

THE TERRY JONES EFFECT

We should not conclude that Muslim youth living in other countries would *inevitably* feel estranged from the United States—that there was nothing we could do.* In fact, we could have done many things, first and foremost, behaving differently. Non-Muslim Americans often don't realize just how closely Muslims around the world are watching, scanning for clues about how they are perceived. Given the nature of communications, a statement or behavior offensive to Muslims can spread rapidly to all corners of the globe.

The truth of this was brought home for me in 2012, when I visited a tiny rural village in Cambodia. Getting there required a long drive through dense jungle. Bouncing around on an unpaved road, we passed rice paddies, the occasional villager on a bicycle, children gathering sticks or standing beside their parents working in their yards, and small, impoverished, tin-roofed huts on stilts. Underneath the houses, cows and horses lingered, seeking relief from the stifling heat. Finally, we arrived at our destination. Surrounded by green fields, the tiny village boasted a very simple wooden mosque. On the mosque's covered patio, dozens of sandals lined the walls and, in places, were scattered into piles—a sight similar to what I have found at every other mosque I have visited all over the world.

Dozens of people in this tiny Muslim community had crowded around for the occasion of my visit. The women sat in circles in the back, focused, smiling, and often holding small children in their laps. Many wore headscarves, including several in the Gulfie style, arranged with precision to cover every last hair. The women also wore colorful, loose-fitting shirts over long skirts and what seemed to be loose-fitting pants. Each outfit was joyful, some containing glitter and shiny mirrors, contrasting starkly with the humble village itself. Through a translator, we engaged in a discussion about

* Many young Muslims I met also had positive impressions of some parts of American society, culture, and life. During a breakfast I held in 2010 with Muslim leaders in Norway, a young man named Usman praised America and Europe for their ability to engage with Muslims. "It is difficult generating a Western idea of identity where you are European, and you are Muslim," he said, noting that in America it is easier, since "with Obama you see that there is no black and there is no white." Many young Muslims also identified the boxer Muhammad Ali as an iconic representation of American ideals. Regardless of the country, when I asked the question, "Whom do you think of as the best example of America?" the answer was always Muhammad Ali.

America and the role that I played at the U.S. Department of State. We also talked about Muslims in America, faith in general in the United States, and American foreign policy. Audience members asked the usual questions: Did they *really* have Muslims in America? Do people in America spit on you when they hear you're Muslim? Can Muslim women cover their hair in public? Can they pray, and if so, where?

Then came a question I hadn't expected: Does Terry Jones really represent America? In 2010, this radical, anti-Muslim preacher from Gainesville, Florida, with a congregation of fifty had achieved a brief period of notoriety for threatening to burn a copy of the Qur'an. Most Americans have forgotten all about him (and many Americans probably never paid much attention to Jones in the first place). But here in this remote pocket of Cambodia, the inhabitants had not only heard of and remembered him—they thought he *spoke* for America. Here in this simple and seemingly disconnected corner of planet earth, it stunned me to find that a community of Muslims thought Terry Jones was America and America hated Muslims.*

Think about this incident for a minute. Terry Jones wasn't an important figure in American life. He spoke for nobody save himself and his small flock. Imagine how much greater the impact when, instead of a fringe figure, public figures make statements about Islam that are blatantly false or bigoted. In 2011, former speaker of the House Newt Gingrich declared sharia law "a mortal threat to the survival of freedom in the United States."[12] In 2012, Republican presidential candidate Herman Cain defended his position that Muslims should be banned from the federal bench and prohibited from erecting mosques. In 2011, former governor of Arkansas Mike Huckabee said Christians should refrain from leasing space in their

* During a 2011 interview I conducted with a youth-oriented radio station in Melbourne, Australia, I was also asked about Terry Jones. Just as in Cambodia, these Australian youth thought that Jones spoke for America.

religious facilities to Muslims because the latter were ideologically dedicated to their "obliteration."[13] These are but a few of an unending stream of bigoted statements about Muslims or Islam. When politicians publicly claim that we are at war with Islam, or that there are too many mosques in the United States, or that American Muslims are a "fifth column," or that Arabs should be "ethnically cleansed" from Israel/Palestine, or that Islam is not a religion but an ideology, or that the Qur'an is a "book of war and terrorism," young Muslims notice.[14] And when politicians in other nations, especially in our allied countries, speak out similarly and we do or say nothing, Muslims notice that, too.

Muslim millennials also notice when non-Muslim Americans betray basic ignorance about their religion. And make no mistake, the average non-Muslim American knows very little—and is willing to acknowledge it. In a 2010 study of Americans, Pew found that 30 percent "say they do not know very much" about Islam, and 25 percent claim to "know nothing at all"—numbers similar to those in a 2007 study.[15] Such ignorance comes across in the media, when celebrities, politicians, and others discuss matters having to do with Islam. It also comes across when young Muslims encounter non-Muslim Americans face-to-face. When some Americans seem to suggest that "Allah" is a specifically Muslim God (it's not, just the Arabic word for the monotheistic deity of the Judeo-Christian Bible), or when they betray utter ignorance of the fasting month of Ramadan and other holidays,* or when they are clueless about dietary sensitivities, it sends a signal to young Muslims that non-Muslim Americans don't really care about them enough to know them.

I know firsthand how alienating it can feel to experience obvious cultural ignorance. On one occasion, I was invited to breakfast at

* Ramadan falls on the ninth month of the Islamic lunar calendar. During this holy month, when Muslims commemorate God's revelation of the Qur'an to the prophet Muhammad, Muslims fast from sunrise to sunset.

the U.S. ambassador's residence in a Muslim-majority nation. Only four of us were in attendance, including the ambassador's wife. I was the guest of honor. As the food emerged from the kitchen, I was shocked to smell bacon. When it was offered to me, I politely declined. I happened to look up and see my colleague Sarah's face—she was as stunned as I was. Shouldn't the U.S. ambassador know better? I should clarify that this incident stands out in my mind precisely because U.S. diplomats are normally keenly aware of cultural and religious sensitivities. Still, compare it to an encounter in New Delhi where Muslims and Hindus were gathered together. The host, a Muslim, proclaimed, "We are only serving vegetarian because some of our guests do not eat meat, and we do not want them to feel uncomfortable, we want them to feel respected."

If Terry Jones was bad, he was nothing compared to the damage that Donald Trump and a number of his fellow Republican presidential hopefuls did during the 2016 presidential election campaign. Trump did the most damage, stoking nativist passions with his proposal to ban Muslims from entering the United States, his attack on American Muslim "gold star" parents, his proclamation that Muslims pose a dire threat to the United States, his statement that America should have seized Iraqi oil when it had the chance, his statement that "Islam hates us," and his accusation that President Obama "founded" the so-called Islamic State. Month after month, young Muslims have watched President Trump preaching hate, with about 40 percent of the American population in support. In the minds of many, Trump's words and deeds comprise the strongest evidence yet that "America hates Muslims," an emphatic validation of what they had been told by their parents and what they had come to believe themselves.

Even seemingly innocuous attempts to reach out to Muslims can backfire because of ignorance on our part. As I discussed earlier, Muslim youths see photo ops or glossy marketing materials put out by our government and they spot stereotypical depictions of their coreligionists. They also react to what they perceive as America's arrogant treatment of them. In 2009, while in a cafeteria in Baghdad's Green Zone, I sat with a group of young Iraqi women who possessed PhDs in education. We were discussing schooling in Iraq. One woman turned to me, tears in her eyes, and said that she felt "humiliated." I asked for clarification, and she reminded me that Iraq used to have one of the best educational systems in the Middle East. "I can't believe we're having this conversation. We have to come to you Americans, who are well known for excellence at the university level, but not grammar or secondary school. Your standing worldwide isn't half the standing we had. And your experts are coming in here telling us how we're supposed to run our schools. Are you joking? Do you know how insulting it is to have to hear you tell us how we should work?" So often—and this was but one example—young Muslims shared their perception that we Americans looked down on them, thinking they were backward and knew nothing. There was some truth to this. In many cases, we *were* the ignorant one, unaware of the expertise that did exist. Our ignorance led us to signal disrespect in the eyes of young Muslims, which in turn reinforced impressions of our hostility toward them (such condescension toward others was not unique in American history).

FIGHTING THE "CRUSADERS"

Regardless of how exactly anti-American sentiment has come to exist in the minds of many young Muslims, one thing is clear: extremists have not hesitated to exploit these feelings to attract more recruits. Indeed, the notion of an unresolvable "us versus them" has stood as a persistent justification and rallying cry for the extremist cause. Addressing American Muslims, Al Qaeda's American-born propagandist Anwar al-Awlaki[16] explicitly asked, "How can you have your loyalty to a government that is leading the war against Islam and

Muslims?"[17] On other occasions, al-Awlaki called the United States a "tyrant," regarding this as a "universal fact."[18] Osama bin Laden made similar zero-sum declarations.

As evidence for their claims, the two terrorists pointed to the same specific policies of the United States that also bothered many young Muslims I met. Speaking about conflict between Israel and the Palestinian group Hamas, Osama bin Laden said, "The blockade which the West is imposing on the government of Hamas proves that there is a Zionist-crusaders war on Islam."[19] Truth was dismissed, as al-Awlaki tried to stir up outrage against the American mistreatment of Muslim prisoners, telling his audiences "Every sinister method of interrogation is used against [Muslim prisoners]. They would use against them homosexuals to rape them. They would bring their mothers and sisters and wives, and they would rape them in front of these brothers. The United Nations knows about it. Amnesty International knows about it, and they are doing nothing. In fact, sometimes they are encouraging it."[20] With outrage about American abuses already widespread, it's not hard to see how al-Awlaki's argument might strike a chord among young Muslims.

Other groups such as the so-called Islamic State and al-Shabaab have also picked up anti-Americanism as a rallying cry. The so-called Islamic State's magazine *Dabiq* often refers to both Americans and Westerners as "crusaders," and in fact the notion of a "clash of civilizations" is fundamental to the group's ideology. As a passage in *Dabiq* stated: "O Ummah of Islam, indeed the world today has been divided into two camps and two trenches, with no third camp present: The camp of Islam and faith, and the camp of kufr [disbelief] and hypocrisy—the camp of the Muslims and the mujahidin everywhere, and the camp of the jews, the crusaders, their allies, and with them the rest of the nations and religions of kufr, all being led by America and Russia, and being mobilized by the jews."[21]

The so-called Islamic State propaganda presents extremist violence as revenge for acts of war perpetrated against Muslims. One of their videos, for instance, depicted the murder of a captured Jordanian airman, graphically juxtaposing it with scenes of devastation from coalition air strikes. Yet this brutality is balanced by warmer imagery. A report from the International Centre for Counter-Terrorism identifies "nine core narratives that IS deploys in its expansion related propaganda," including the notion that the caliphate is a "pious, harmonious, and thriving Islamic state," and that "jihad" is "an opportunity for brotherhood and excitement."[22] In connection with the latter, videos released by the so-called Islamic State show fighters from Western countries drinking tea together and swimming in a large pool. The implication is clear: such intense camaraderie could never be experienced in the West.

It's worth restating that most young Muslims don't respond to such propaganda, and the vast majority of those who do refrain from joining extremist groups or perpetrating terrorist acts. Still, interviews and other material from extremists suggest that they crystalize terms of engagement. Nidal Hassan, the U.S. army psychiatrist who shot and killed thirteen people at Fort Hood, believed that the United States was waging a "war against Islam." As he related, "My complicity was on behalf of a government that openly acknowledges that it would hate for the law of Almighty Allah to be the supreme law of the land." Hassan begged forgiveness from his fellow Muslims for "participating in the illegal and immoral aggression against Muslims, their religion and their lands."[23] Such is the script learned from extremist propaganda.

A WINNING STRATEGY

As suspicious as many young Muslims have become of the United States, our government can still expand the boundaries of its CVE strategy and utilize traditional public diplomacy[24] to change attitudes and beliefs.* First and foremost, our government must devote more resources to countering misperceptions about America. This was the conclusion of the 2003 Djerejian Report,† which noted that we spent a little over half a billion dollars a year on all public diplomacy programs worldwide. Much of that money went to pay salaries, not fund communications programs at scale. "Because of a lack of funds," the report observed, "very little public diplomacy work is carried on outside national capitals—a mistake, in our view, because the impact is often greater in such areas. We found that funding for public diplomacy outreach programs comes to only $25 million for the entire Arab and Muslim world—a depressingly small amount. To say that financial resources are inadequate to the task is a gross understatement."[25]

Although the Djerejian Report suffered from well-documented flaws,[26] its critique on this point was valid, and the situation has hardly improved in the decade and a half since it was issued. The need for public diplomacy has increased significantly, and while dollar-wise funding has increased, it remains foolishly inadequate. In 2016, the United States spent $2.03 billion on public diplomacy, but this was nearly 3 percent less than its spending the prior fiscal year.[27] Instead of advancing the war on extremism, we are prematurely retreating.

The Djerejian Report identified a number of other obstacles to effective public diplomacy, noting that "the State Department lacks

---

* We should start by streamlining the way our government approaches and organizes public diplomacy. Traditionally, the State Department's office of the undersecretary for public diplomacy and public affairs was responsible for cultivating America's image and fostering its brand. When CVE began, it was a natural expectation that this division of labor would continue, and that the public diplomacy arm would undermine misperceptions about America and endeavor to "win hearts and minds" abroad. Throughout the twenty-first century, however, various agencies have competed for control over American branding and CVE, resulting in a lack of integration and uniformity in approach.

† At the behest of Secretary of State Colin Powell, distinguished American diplomat Ambassador Djerejian chaired the congressionally mandated bipartisan Advisory Group on Public Diplomacy for the Arab and Muslim World. They released their findings in a 2003 report called "Changing Minds, Winning Peace."

the human resources for such crucial efforts. More than half the public affairs officers responding to the September 2003 GAO survey on public diplomacy said that the number of foreign service officers available for public diplomacy is insufficient." According to the report, the department needed "well trained staff with an in-depth knowledge of the culture in target countries and fluency in local languages" in order to execute successful public diplomacy campaigns. "Since 9/11, especially, it has become clear that training, knowledge, and fluency are all sorely inadequate."

And an inability to spend or read the necessary languages is just part of the personnel disaster. Over a decade later, we still don't have enough people with the particular skill sets we need to conduct effective public diplomacy. In a 2017 interview Katherine Brown, former executive director of the U.S. Advisory Commission on Public Diplomacy, told me "when it comes to doing countering violent extremism projects . . . in a robust and meaningful way, you can't just give that to the traditional public diplomacy officers," as their time is occupied with other work. You need dedicated staff who can "get out into the community and develop relationships" in a strategic way that "tracks with our foreign policy goals and isn't just one-off or ad-hoc." These folks must have deep expertise, not just the general training that foreign service officers receive.[28] Where are these kinds of people in the State Department and elsewhere in our government? We simply don't have them—and we have no coherent program to find and develop them.

The United States mustn't simply focus on the reach of CVE programs. It must devise tools to measure and evaluate their efficacy in different places around the world.[29] Because the State Department lacks rigorous, quantitative, and longitudinal studies to track the efficacy of public diplomacy programs, we are forced to rely on qualitative data and anecdotes. As Brown pointed out, the State Department public diplomacy operations spend less than 2 percent on their audience research, impact evaluation, and digital analytics operations. And it gets worse. "Under the Trump administration," she notes, "our ability to conduct such research has diminished, as many top positions have been left unfilled and hiring freezes have been put in place in a deliberate attempt to starve the agency. We need to reverse this trend if we are to have any hope of challenging notions that America is at war with Islam."[30]

We also need to streamline the lengthy process of obtaining clearances, so that we can respond more quickly when public relations crises emerge. And instead of letting each department's press team react independently, we should develop a standard set of actions for all government departments, including the White House, for discussing our nation's diversity and our welcoming of all faiths, ethnicities, and other forms of difference. For example, we should mandate that officials draw on historic facts about our nation and Islam and that they distribute data on diversity of religions within our nation. The standard set of highlights must be embedded, and all departments should have facts on hand about the respect American presidents have shown for Islam, the demographics of our American Muslim population, the appointment and election of Muslim officials over our nation's history, and related topics.

In laying down standards, we should mandate that no language coming out of government in written or verbal form ever imply a logic of "us" versus "them." To ensure clear incorporation of accurate American history with relation to Islam and diversity of faiths, the federal government might partner with the Smithsonian Institution to develop an appropriate set of talking points and learning centers within relevant U.S.-funded museums. Few people realize that nearly all large agencies have on-staff historians. To further improve our communication, we should connect them with one another so as to better coordinate how we recount the history of our own diverse citizens. We should require that not just diplomats, but other officials across the interagency pass basic training about how we communicate our history and why. These officials should further demonstrate knowledge about religious faiths in America, and a specific awareness of Islam in America. Right now, any training is ad hoc, as is the communication itself.

We should also mandate the use of standardized American English translations in all communications, so that our officials don't misunderstand the meanings of foreign terms like "jihad," "Allah," and "madrassa."[31] At present, we do not have a standardized way of speaking to domestic or international audiences, and spokespersons at each department and agency choose terminology as they see fit. This leads to all kinds of errors. Americans now keep hearing the word "madrassa" and incorrectly think that means "a school that teaches extremist thinking." In truth, a madrassa is simply a school. Likewise, the term "jihad" has been repurposed by extremists, and we are unknowingly reinforcing their meaning. When we misuse language we betray our cultural ignorance. In the already sensitive world of diplomacy and public outreach, words and phrases matter.

More diversity within department agencies, starting at the ground level and extending up through the senior leadership ranks, will further enable us to frame communications in ways that global audiences find authentic and respectful. This diversity shouldn't just entail welcoming in people of different heritages and ethnicity, but also people who possess different kinds of expertise. We also need an official U.S. "concierge service"—a place people around the world can go to obtain answers to questions about America.

As the Djerejian Report noted, "few scholars in the Muslim world are real specialists in American culture and society"—a situation that hasn't changed appreciably since 2003.[32] Organizing and funding "centers" all over the world dedicated to teaching local scholars about the United States—including "significant library collections, dedicated instructors, and electronic means of making available accurate and high-quality information about U.S. history, culture, and government"—can help puncture stereotypes and lead to greater understanding of America among Muslims.[33] America needs to reboot the system, regarding this for what it is: an opportunity to build meaningful partnerships for a new generation of Muslims. We need to go big and go wide, touching as many kids as possible by playing an active role in their daily lives.

Beyond changes in how we communicate, we must take steps to render our own society more inclusive and welcoming to others. Our communications tactics have so often failed because Muslims around the world see us as hypocritical. And they have reason to. Who "owns" U.S. culture and narratives about our country? Right now, the entertainment industry and those who scream the loudest control the narrative, perpetrating many stereotypes and biases. Overall, American opinions about Islam have continued to decline since 9/11.[34] How we speak about "the other"—not just Muslims, but anyone we perceive as different from ourselves—matters. President Trump stunned and angered the world when he referred to poor and predominantly black nations as "shithole countries."[35] Not only do some of the countries he had in mind contain substantial Muslim populations, but it was an easy step for the millions of people in Muslim-majority nations to assume he felt the same way about their homelands. If we want the world to take us seriously, we have to do a better job conducting ourselves as citizens according to the values enshrined in our own constitution and other founding documents.

We should also enlist the private sector to help us shift how others see our country. During the Bush administration, the U.S. Department of State partnered with Howcast.org, Google, YouTube, and MTV to host the "Alliance of Youth Movements Summit," which created a network of youth eager to build movements for good.* And

* After creating an online how-to manual to help galvanize kids, they wisely suggested that if Al Qaeda had a manual for doing evil, they would have one devoted to doing good as well. Today the organization is called movements.org. Following a White House roundtable aimed to inspire the private sector to apply its expertise to counterterrorism efforts, a group of American companies (including eBay and Pepsi) invited a handful of U.S. civil servants to visit eBay's campus and learn about marketing.

in August 2008, Kip Knight, who was the chief marketing officer of eBay, founded a "US Marketing Communications College" concept whereby a few dozen U.S. public servants learned from the marketing experts (and those company executives were also briefed about the complicated threat environment we faced). For a while, these marketing experts worked closely with the Foreign Service Institute in Virginia. Today the program is still active.

I would like to see us "reposition" our nation in the eyes of the world by launching an extensive, professionally curated five-year global awareness movement and campaign focused on young people (Generation Z and millennials). With support from philanthropists and corporate charities, we would create a dynamic series of media touch points to tell America's story, drawing on Hollywood, Madison Avenue, academia, and Silicon Valley to spotlight our commitment to diversity, respect, and inclusion. As part of this program, we could mobilize presidential libraries and former presidents to help publicize America's history as a force for good around the world. We could focus our communications around "regional hubs," helping residents in certain geographical areas around the world understand how they've contributed to America's national story. Enlisting the help of film stars, musicians, and gamers in this global campaign would help us reach younger Muslims turned off by more traditional appeals, as well as show non-Muslims a side of Islam far distant from stereotypes.

American Muslim youth stand to play an important role and could be especially effective as change agents overseas. All Muslims are required to give alms at the rate of 2.8 percent of their earnings (a practice known as *Zakat).* Young Muslims, like all global youth, are often short on money, but they have lots of time. What if instead of giving money, they could fulfill their religious obligations by donating their time in the "Zakat Corps," an entity modeled on the Peace Corps, which would enable American Muslims to travel overseas and help communities through teaching, training, or volunteering?

American Muslim acts of philanthropy could be captured in YouTube videos, advertisements, comedy, and other online platforms, projecting a more complex understanding of America and American Islam. The Zakat Corps, or other ventures like it, would serve to disrupt the notion that American Muslims are uniformly oppressed, while helping to portray America as a source of good in the world.

The tactics described so far are only the beginning of how government might partner with the private sector to disrupt extremist us-versus-them narratives. Other ideas worth pursuing include:

- Building local outreach centers dedicated to pushing back against us-versus-them narratives of all kinds. Corporations and local philanthropists could help fund these centers and provide talent and expertise to help run them and develop programming. Such soft power interventions have been effectively used in the past. In Iceland, an evidence-based approach brought parents, schools, and government together to prevent kids from trying drugs. Parents were trained on the importance of spending time with their kids, recreational opportunities were created to give kids an alternative to trying drugs, mandatory curfews for kids were instituted, and laws were passed to restrict access to tobacco and alcohol, among other measures. The results were impressive. As a profile in *The Atlantic* reported: "Between 1997 and 2012, the percentage of kids aged 15 and 16 who reported often or almost always spending time with their parents on weekdays doubled—from 23 percent to 46 percent—and the percentage who participated in organized sports at least four times a week increased from 24 percent to 42 percent. Meanwhile, cigarette smoking, drinking and cannabis use in this age group plummeted."[36]
- Creating a MacArthur Prize–type award, supported by philanthropists, companies, or others in the private sector,

to reward innovative thinking in the area of diversity and inclusion.

- Creating an initiative in partnership with several communication schools, media companies, and NGOs to publicly assess and rank media coverage of Muslims. We need a national discussion on the role of media in CVE, including the impact of tone, coverage decisions, awareness of Islamic history, and the choice of experts consulted. The media collectively has a role to play in helping us stop the flow of stereotypes about Islam and Muslims. This kind of effort has happened on a small scale—we just need to broaden and scale it.
- Producing a series of free books for younger readers that teach an inclusive American history. The publishing industry could come together behind this project, drawing on its impressive roster of writing talent.
- Creating a national CVE clearinghouse. Government should create an organization akin to the Center for Exploited Children that serves as a clearinghouse for information on extremist exploitation of youth. Among other tasks, this clearinghouse would generate an authoritative ranking of social media platforms and the risks they pose to kids, as the organization Transparency International currently does.

In sum, we must push back against widespread mistrust and misunderstanding among Muslim youth with a coordinated and cohesive effort that encompasses both communications and ethics, and that is aimed at audiences globally and ourselves. Some of this effort must come from the private sector. We should also encourage the creation of an American Muslim Museum spotlighting America's Muslim populations, the most diverse in the world. Privately funded, such a museum would send a strong signal around the world that Muslims are a significant part of the American story. It would also present a valuable opportunity for non-Muslims to educate themselves about American Muslims and their significant contributions to American culture and life.

As important as the private sector is when it comes to shifting Muslim perspectives on America, the most important initiatives will take place inside our government. Again, we need standard ways of communicating that Muslims will find respectful and honest. CVE includes reaffirming standards of decorum that make for a civilized society. And it's about individual as well as organizational action. Each one of us can, in our own daily speech and conduct, affirm our commitment to the values enshrined in our constitution, negating the vilification of the "other" that undergirds all extremist ideology.

A GENERATION OF AMERICA HATERS?

When President Obama took office in early 2009, I wondered if the anti-Americanism I had seen up to that point in European cities would ebb. Like many, I hoped that his historic 2009 speech in Cairo would help win friends among Muslims of all ages. I was cheered when he unveiled a number of initiatives after the Cairo speech designed to engage with Muslims, and when he used the power of his office to signify respect for Islamic history (for example, referencing Islamic philosophy in his public statements as well as Muslim contributions to science, art, technology, and other fields). At first, it seemed that such efforts were bearing fruit. As Marc Lynch, professor of political science at George Washington University, noted, "Early in Obama's first term, opinion surveys in the Arab world recorded a surge of more positive attitudes toward the United States, mostly in response to the popular new president."[37] Yet afterward, as the Arab Spring fell apart, religiously aligned political parties took power in several countries, fomenting anti-Americanism. As American policies further inflamed sentiment among Muslims in the Middle East, extremism gained an increasing foothold there. Lynch remarked that Muslims were angry at the United States "when its military intervenes in the region (in Libya) and when it does not (in Syria), and they are outraged when Washington supports democratic elections (in Egypt, where Islamists won) and when it does not (in Bahrain, for example)."[38] To that list, I might add any number of other issues, including the United States' failure to take in many Syrian refugees, its failure to prevent the rise of the so-called Islamic State, its failure to nurture peace efforts between Israel and the Palestinians, and in general, its perceived retreat from humanitarian engagement with the Middle East.

Since his election as President, Donald Trump has seemingly gone out of his way to alienate Muslims, lumping together in his words and actions all of the world's 1.6 billion Muslims with members of terrorist groups like the so-called Islamic State. A number of his closest advisors have done the same. As Professor Stephen Walt at Harvard University's Kennedy School of Government has written, Trump makes "no real distinction between jihadi terrorists and the entire Muslim religion. In this view, a hardened Islamic State killer is no different from that nice Muslim family who lives downstairs, next door, or across the street."[39] On a number of occasions, Trump has stated that the United States is fighting against "radical Islamic terrorism," language that Muslims around the world read as implicating them simply because of their religion. As Trump lurches between terms like "Islamic" and "Islamist," Muslims conclude once again that he is speaking about all of Islam. To them, Trump's ban on travel and his decision in 2017 to break with previous U.S. presidents and decline to host an official White House Ramadan celebration only confirm his hostility toward all of Islam, not just the extremists who advocate or foment violence in Islam's name.

Trump's rhetoric isn't just a display of breathtaking ignorance.*

* Trump's tendency to regard all Muslims as a singular threat seemed to reflect a monolithic understanding of Muslims and Islam. As discussed in chapter 3, this understanding is false. Beyond partaking of a common history, global Islam and Muslims couldn't be more diverse.

It's an unmitigated catastrophe for the United States and our struggle against extremist ideology. As Walt has explained: "Perhaps the most important task for any strategist is to figure out what the main threats and opportunities are, and then to devise policies that can defuse the former and exploit the latter. Making all of Islam our enemy and viewing the world through the lens of a vast 'civilizational clash' fails on both criteria."[40] Walt is assuredly right. Trump's rhetoric amounts to a perverse infusion of new blood into the body of extremist ideology. When an American president demonizes all of Islam, the extremists point this out to their supporters and potential recruits as confirmation that they were right all along about America. As General David Petraeus has remarked, "those who flirt with hate speech against Muslims should realize they are playing directly into the hands of al-Qaeda and Islamic State."[41]

In addition, Trump's rhetoric has emboldened far-right, anti-Muslim extremists in the United States and abroad, with some going on to commit acts of violence against Muslims. Acts of violence or hate toward Muslims surged in the wake of 9/11, and it soared again in 2015 in the wake of extremist attacks in the United States, and more recently after Donald Trump's election.[42] In office, Trump enacted immigration reform disproportionately targeting Muslim-majority states, and retweeted anti-Muslim videos.[43] In one incident in Minnesota, two Muslims were shot as the gunman yelled out "Fuck Muslims." In New York, a man threatened an imam and his entire mosque, saying, "You fucking Muslims. I heard you're here to conquer us."[44] And in Texas, a man attempted to run over a Muslim man, saying, "Take your rag ass back to your country. I'm gonna fucking kill you."[45]

Muslim youth don't necessarily hear of every such incident, but accounts of such episodes do spread via social and traditional media. Muslim youth also hear about the general climate of anti-Muslim bigotry from friends or family members who live in or visit the United States. Each new act of violence on either side, coupled with new, harshly anti-Muslim rhetoric from the president, causes a hardening of ideological loyalties, making it easier to recruit new followers to each extremist cause. As author and extremism analyst J. M. Berger has pointed out, "the growing resonance between ISIS extremism and its anti-Muslim extremist counterparts . . . is creating new risks for escalation. This means not just the possibility that each movement can attract new recruits, but also that their virulent ideologies could seize an ever-larger portion of the public discourse."[46]

If we don't change direction and mobilize different tactics now, it could take decades to undo the damage that Trump and other high-profile politicians and public servants have done with their anti-Muslim rhetoric, and that other American cultural icons before them have done unwittingly and out of ignorance. If nothing changes, an entire generation of Muslim youth—both around the world, and in the United States itself—will reach maturity believing that the United States regards them suspiciously, doesn't accept them, and is out to get them. That generation will become tragically susceptible to the rallying cries of extremists who proffer an "us versus them" view of the world and who proclaim their determination to wage a long-term war against America and the West.*

It is not too late. We can break the logic of "us versus them." We just have to commit ourselves to the task. In the next chapter, I'll describe how government might reorganize itself and reorient its CVE policies to put us in a winning position.

---

* If we continue to "[make] all of Islam our enemy," reasons Walt, this will "bog us down in more interminable conflicts in places that are not vital U.S. interests, distract us from other foreign-policy issues, and sap the wealth and strength that we may need to deal with more serious challenges, including long-neglected problems here at home." Walt, "Five Ways Donald Trump Is Wrong About Islam."

CHAPTER SEVEN

#STARTUPGOVERNMENT

As I described in chapter 1, I first understood the limitations of a traditional approach to fighting extremist ideology shortly after 9/11. I was working on the National Security Council, and my colleagues and I noted with concern how much leverage Al Qaeda seemed to have with young Muslims. The group was speaking to Muslims directly via long, videotaped sermons, on YouTube, and on channels like Al Jazeera. Their rhetoric was outrageous: paeans to Islam, to the glories of martyrdom, and to the wonders that awaited valiant martyrs in heaven. Muslims around the world were appalled, and we policy makers were frustrated. Why weren't mainstream Muslim voices more prominent? Why did young Muslims have to encounter all of this crazy talk when venturing online?

In 2004 and 2005, my colleagues and I held many conversations with Muslims from across America, engaging with advocacy groups, professional organizations, scholars, religious leaders, independent thinkers, and entrepreneurs. Very often, these groups didn't agree with Bush administration policies, but that didn't matter: we wanted authentic perspectives from across the political spectrum, and we also wanted to include minority groups from within the Islamic community. The media and general public kept clamoring for a single, authoritative Islam akin to the pope in Christianity to denounce extremism, but we understood that liberal and conservative Muslim voices from around the world were both essential, as were those of gay, straight, Arab, African, European, South Asian, East Asian, Central Asian, and American Muslims, to name a few. *Everyone* had to have equal play and attention.

We asked these individuals and groups why they thought Al Qaeda's ideology appealed to youth, and how they thought we might push back. They kept telling us: Al Qaeda did not represent Islam, and mainstream Muslims like them needed more exposure. But they felt powerless. As they explained, the media never covered the "real Islam" that they practiced, yet it allowed Osama bin Laden countless hours of airtime to sell his horrible ideas for free.

I was not the only one who emerged from these conversations convinced that the U.S. government needed to actively promote alternative voices, creating a flood of "counter-content." We couldn't take extremist voices off the air without violating our traditions of free speech.* But we could add an array of vibrant, new voices from across the political spectrum to reject violence and "drown out the crazies," as a well-known American imam once told me.

Government tends to reward cautious, steady people who don't stick out their necks, and it punishes risk takers who question the status quo. Also, you can't move anything forward in government without receiving buy-in from other colleagues. In our case, we

---

* The recent proliferation of hate speech has led to increased scrutiny about how government should balance free speech with protection from harm. Many people now, moreover, have less exposure to a diversity of ideas, thanks in part to the tendency of social media to create personalized information bubbles in which people only receive news stories and topics that confirm their preexisting ideological inclinations, opinions, and prejudices.

needed public diplomacy officers, political officers, and ambassadors in our embassies around the world to buy in, not just Washington officials. We also didn't know whether our grassroots efforts would work over the long term, or if they would backfire in some fashion. How could we determine that a local entrepreneur who claimed to be eager to fight extremism was legitimate? How could we guarantee that he or she wouldn't do anything in the future to embarrass the U.S. government?

We tried to play it as safe as we could. As I've discussed in earlier chapters, we encouraged religious scholars or imams when they spoke out, and helped governments in Muslim-majority countries that were openly condemning extremist violence. We also lent our support to independent NGOs that were issuing statements disavowing extremism—a local organization in Senegal, for instance, or a German Islamic group. We took care not to promote one "kind" of Islamic practice (for example, Sufism or Salafism) but rather to help lift voices representing all ethnicities, heritages, and varieties of Islam. But as noted, funding was less than minuscule and coordination between agencies slight at best.

Still, we did what we could to improvise solutions. Seeking to spark an international movement among youth, we worked with pop artists popular among young Muslims and athletes in specific localities or regions, encouraging them to take public stances against extremism. We toyed with the notion of inviting youth in local communities to talk with us, listening to these youths very closely, and when possible arranging to fund their bespoke initiatives. The more conversations I had with Muslims during my time at the NSC, the more I saw the value of spawning a global grassroots counter-extremist movement among youth themselves—what I later came to call a "youthquake." But as a member of the National Security Council, I couldn't focus on "operationalizing" our ideas. When I moved to the State Department, however, I had the clearance (and, again, a microscopically small budget) to build engagement with Muslim communities in Europe.*

What I discovered speaking to Muslims in Europe was that we were failing in our efforts to understand them. As many Muslims perceived it, we were guilty in our communications efforts of "trying to tell them how to be Muslim." They were right, and it went beyond the United States. In some cases, federal and local governments in countries like Belgium, the United Kingdom, Germany, and Spain had been indirectly or directly touting the more peaceful, Sufi "form" of Islam as preferable over other varieties. As my conversations revealed, such heavy-handed attempts were only stirring up more resentment. Millennials believed that America and their governments both had a particular kind of "approved" Islam they were pushing, and were unable to talk about Islam in a sophisticated way. In their eyes, we seemed to treat Arabs as the only Muslims who counted, and we were also publicly discussing extremism in terms of the Sunni-Shia divide—another problematic "us" versus "them" framework.

To take but one example, at some point during the first few years after 9/11, the State Department's Bureau of International Information Programs (IIP) released a magazine called *Being Muslim in America.*[1] Obviously, our government was taking other steps to shift public perceptions of America, but American diplomats abroad, and specifically public diplomacy officers, were asking for concrete tools they could use to help tell our story, and they appreciated having this pamphlet on hand. By the Obama administration's first term, embassies were asking for more magazines to disseminate, and more were eagerly supplied.

A number of American Muslims had loudly criticized the mag-

* After Dan Fried, Elliott Abrams, and Juan Zarate briefed Steve Hadley and Secretary Rice about this experimental approach, I received support. Still, money for CVE had not been allocated for the coming year, so it was hard to get unrestricted funds to do CVE.

azine. Some didn't mind it,[2] but many others (myself included) perceived it as a blatant caricature of Muslims by non-Muslims. The magazine's photographs depicted American Muslim women as headscarf-wearing Arabs and the men as constantly kneeling in prayer. Although Muslims had resided in America for generations (in fact since the colonists began to import slaves), the magazine's images showed primarily recent immigrants. Also, IIP published no comparable magazines that year about members of other traditions. There was no "Being Christian in America" or "Being Hindu in America." As a result, it felt to many Muslims as if the government was singling them out as the "other." The government evidently felt so nervous about Muslims, so uncomfortable around them, that it needed to try to "appeal" to them in a bizarrely ham-handed way.

Upon seeing this magazine, I did everything I could to convince IIP either to fix the images it contained, stop printing it, or revise it to cover all faiths in America, their origins, and varieties of current practice. As I pointed out, the United States not only has the world's most diverse Muslim community but also affords Muslims the most freedom to practice of any country. To influence Muslims around the world to see America as it really was, we didn't need to showcase an artificial, non-Muslim interpretation of Muslims. We would be far better off designing a "Faiths in America" resource that talked about all faiths in America and stressed what we Americans see every day around us. We are a country that values "faith,"[3] and in which all people enjoy the constitutional right to practice as they see fit. Why not simply show this?

I had seen many other great initiatives come out of IIP, like the American Spaces programs, which provide opportunities to learn about our democracy and our nation's history and to connect with students in America. I had also worked with IIP on several Muslim engagement programs over the years. I recall asking IIP why we would reprint something that not only dated from the previous administration (President Bush still appeared in the pamphlet, not

President Obama) but failed to address some of the key problems from the first printing. To its great credit, IIP did try to change some aspects of its original magazine, but the leadership team wasn't ready to stop producing it. Senior staff claimed that our embassies and consulates around the world loved the magazines. After all, the bureau had dispensed 400,000 copies of the first printing, and public diplomacy officers had told them of the magazines' impact on extremist recruitment. But those officers were clearly wrong. Reading a magazine written by the U.S. government was about as credible to a young Muslim as the State Department's social media efforts against the so-called Islamic State later would be. The messenger matters, and frankly, the U.S. government is the wrong messenger for this message, in this context.*

Muslims in America is just one example among many flawed approaches to fighting the war of ideas that I encountered. Repeatedly, the U.S. government trotted out stereotypical Muslims as if they were zoo creatures,† attempting to persuade Muslims that "America did not hate Muslims," but mostly only succeeding in betraying ignorance and a lack of respect for them. Quite often, for instance, our embassies sponsored interfaith meetings that attempted to bring local faith leaders together in dialogue. Set aside the fact that these events tended to be "one-off," not part of any integrated program or strategy. They also selected the "safest," least controversial Muslims to participate. Men with long beards, turbans, robes, headscarves—that's the "authentic" look U.S. government sought.‡ Where were

---

* According to cultural expert Camilo La Cruz, pamphlets are not an effective means for reaching young audiences. As he says, communication is no longer one-way in the age of social media, but rather a continuous, two-way dialogue. We can't simply, "'throw pamphlets out of an airplane and tell people a story.' That doesn't work anymore. It's a very dated view of the world." Camilo La Cruz, interview with the author, New York City, December 19, 2016.

† A well-regarded senior diplomat made this remark to me.

‡ During the Obama administration, many colleagues at State and at Homeland Security were alarmed to see the White House positioning of mostly headscarf-wearing Muslim women around the president rather than men and women of various practices. To them, this distorted the image of Islam in America, conveying

the many other, legitimate Muslim figures who happened to dress (and perhaps think) differently? Where were female scholars and theologians?

Our initial efforts to coordinate Muslim engagement had also been woefully insufficient. In 2006, for instance, Heidi Fincken, senior advisor to Undersecretary of Public Diplomacy and Public Affairs Karen Hughes, and I coauthored a list of basic needs for the undersecretary as to how we might help stem extremist recruiting. We recommended several steps to enable us to better reach out to local Muslim community groups: a calendar of outreach events (including conferences and idea summits organized inside and outside government) and opportunities for engagement with American Muslims; a state-by-state list of specialty media catering to Muslim communities; a master list of Muslim influencers across the world and a list of key influencers in the U.S.; contact information for Muslim organizations such as schools and mosques; and so on. We lacked all of these tools, and they were so obvious! Mind you, other countries were even further behind. Few foreign governments were even doing "engagement," much less pushing back hard against extremist ideology. We would ask our embassies to share how their countries were listening to local Muslims and supporting initiatives to fight extremist ideas, and we received back nothing of substance—they told us, for instance, that a minister had given a talk and invited some Muslims to attend. The national and local law enforcement and counterterrorism teams in these countries were working on stopping violence, but doing little if anything to stop recruitment or radicalization.

We also hadn't figured out that Muslim youth weren't listening to established authorities in their home communities. We believed

---

the notion that *all* American Muslim women wore headscarves. Cultural diplomacy from the White House can make a big difference to our nation and the world. In this instance, more sensitivity to Islamic diversity vis-à-vis ethnicity, practice, and sartorial custom would have sent an important message.

it would help to convince prominent Muslim scholars to publicly disavow violence in the name of Islam. We turned first to the Middle East, hoping that rejection of Al Qaeda by scholars there would carry symbolic weight, prompting Muslims elsewhere to reject the appeal of extremist ideology. The approach seemed to make sense, but while these measures helped us line up a coalition of countries and institutions within those counties that were determined to fight extremist groups—an important and worthy accomplishment—they did nothing to win over Muslim youth. As we discovered, these youth didn't care what a prominent imam or sheikh said, or that the UN was making declarations, or that America was talking about the coalition of countries fighting Al Qaeda. Press releases, speeches, proclamations—these meant nothing, and the very forms of communication they took were outdated.

ACTIVATING CREDIBLE VOICES AGAINST VIOLENT EXTREMISM

As I've mentioned, my first real CVE efforts, undertaken again in the wake of the Danish cartoon crisis, focused on European Muslims and their ideological and cultural experiences. As I made my way through those communities across the continent, I had the idea of creating a network specifically for young Muslim professionals in Europe. I felt that by helping Western young Muslims support and encourage one another, we could amplify their distaste for the foreign ideologies that were populating in Europe. Furthermore, the network was not defined by nation or theology, so supporting and promoting young Muslim professionals could help the broader, non-Muslim populace see Muslims as "normal" citizens. In a world before Facebook (in its present incarnation), Twitter, Snapchat, WhatsApp, and other social networks had caught fire, the creation of such a network seemed an experiment well worth trying.

In 2008, working with the Institute for Strategic Dialogue (ISD) in Great Britain and the Salzburg Global Seminar, an Austrian NGO originally founded in 1947 to "encourage the revival of intellectual dialogue in post-war Europe," we handpicked fifty young, accomplished Muslim professionals from across Europe to participate in discussions and brainstorming sessions. We spent months planning this particular gathering, thinking through whom we should invite, how we should organize the event, and what we might reasonably hope to accomplish.*

Each of the Muslim professionals we asked to attend had previously helped lead teams of other Muslims in some capacity, and each recognized the urgent need to organize credible voices within Muslim communities to stem the extremist tide. Ahmed Larouz, a young Muslim entrepreneur residing in the Netherlands, remembered that although his expectations of the event weren't terribly high, he "didn't want to miss [it] because [he] thought, there's something new happening [. . . that . . .] we [didn't] have in Europe," an effort to connect "the leaders of Europe from [the] diaspora or from a Muslim background."[4] Another participant, Zahed Amanullah, remembered feeling skeptical at first when I reached out to him. "The idea that government would actually play a positive role in helping Muslims find their place and engage with the rest of society was really an alien concept," he said. That the American government would be bringing young Muslims together seemed especially suspicious, for "if Muslims were engaged from the State Department, they had a tinge of PR to it." Still, Zahed and his peers realized that they "had to do something" to fight back against extremist ideology, and they didn't know what—they felt isolated in their respective countries. "It was very difficult for us to coordinate," Zahed said. "This was before social media. It was still difficult to even realize that there were leaders in other countries and other regions that

* I have had a close working relationship with ISD since 2007. As of this writing, the relationship is ongoing.

had the same backgrounds but were otherwise isolated and couldn't leverage their faith background in a positive way."[5] They agreed to set aside their feelings about the U.S. government and attend our event with open minds.

The gathering was an unqualified success. Held in Salzburg's beautiful Schloss Leopoldskron, the event included robust conversations about identity and belonging, foreign ideology and influence, the role of literature and the media in fighting back against extremism, and the role that women could play. Participants discussed their governments' failures to reach out to Muslims, the increasing sense of alienation Muslims felt, and participants' own fears of external and internal extremist ideologies within their communities. I distinctly remember one session, held in the palace's Chinese Room, decorated with water-blue walls, ancient porcelain, and elegant couches, in which we brainstormed how we might use innovative technologies to enhance identity in Muslim communities. In other sessions, we discussed strategies that European professionals might deploy to publicize their own stories and send positive messages about Muslim identity in Europe.

These conversations were not always easy—some personalities didn't jive, the participants sometimes held conflicting opinions, and language barriers sometimes impeded dialogue (we spoke in English, a second language to most of these Europeans). Still, locked away from the world for four days, this group had a chance to develop a cohesive identity and access funds that could help seed their CVE ideas. Attendees opened up to one another, and a sense of excitement took hold. Recalls Zahed: "It only took a little while when we were able to get to know each other that we realized that there were the seeds of a really ambitious and dynamic network of people that could do great things." As he explained, "It's one of those rare things, I know from my generation, to find people who think outside the box, who have multiple identities, aren't ashamed of their Muslim identity, but they also aren't ashamed to be Western, and that they managed to navigate the social economic cultural landscape and had this confidence from that."[6]

Although the U.S. government funded these sessions and I helped organize them, we kept a low profile, hiring neutral, third-party professional facilitators to run the workshops and conversations. Of course, participants knew that the American government had organized the event—where else would the money have come from? Always present and listening in the background, I was fascinated to see that so many of these leaders had never before come together. In 2008, European governments were not yet performing this kind of engagement across Europe. One day as we broke for tea, a German Muslim approached me and said, "This is really amazing. I would not have believed that the country that went to war in Iraq was interested in helping us."

Before the meeting concluded, we created a new platform called Connecting European Dynamic Achievers and Role Models, or CEDAR, the first ever pan-European-Muslim professional network. Rooful Ali, a British Muslim, came up with the name, which he thought would work well across Europe. Some participants pushed back, believing that "CEDAR" evoked Lebanon, known for its cedar trees, and thus suggested a bias toward Arab Muslims. In the end, the presence of the words "connecting," "dynamic," and "achievers" seemed compelling enough to most participants, so CEDAR it was. The objective of the new organization was to "foster a culture of achievement amongst Europe's diverse communities," promoting "positive perceptions of European Muslims' contributions to society." ISD agreed to house and incubate CEDAR, raising funds from its own donors to supplement the small funds I was able to obtain for the seeding and launch event in Salzburg. The State Department had no mechanism for CVE funding, nor were officials willing to share their budgets to ensure that we could grow it and develop it further. But working together, we managed.

ISD interacted closely with members of the network, helping to keep the conversations going, attract more members, and explore new opportunities for collaboration, like partnerships with previous ISD-partnered youth organizations across Europe or private companies working with ISD to do leadership training for youth. As the network grew, CEDAR members delivered an array of exciting initiatives, including the very first mosque-based professional mentoring programs to inspire young Muslims, professional development opportunities across Europe for CEDAR members, a program showcasing the accomplishments of Muslim women, and creation of the first database of Muslim elected officials in Europe. CEDAR members presented themselves as role models in opposition to the extremists, shifting perspectives on what it meant to be modern and Muslim in Europe. As a participant from the United Kingdom remarked, "I think the reason why so many of us have taken time out of our very busy professional lives for CEDAR is because this possibility of working together with like-minded people from a variety of national contexts and variety of experiences is absolutely critical to the future of Islam in Europe."[7] As of 2018, CEDAR remained in existence and had spawned a number of offshoots, from small, community-led initiatives dedicated to pluralism training to larger efforts like community activism and anti-hate campaigns.

It might not seem as if a network such as CEDAR can make a significant impact, but when you look more deeply, you find that it can. As Zahed saw it, grassroots, peer-to-peer networks like CEDAR were a prototype for what would "create progress and ownership" among would-be activists. "We're all used to our communities dictating structure from above, and it's so stifling," he explains. The peer-to-peer quality of CEDAR, by contrast, was energizing and liberating. Zahed notes that fueled by CEDAR, he spent the next decade cultivating a network of activists, including some in the United States, and learned how much he could accomplish by working transatlantically. It made a difference, too, that the participants controlled CEDAR and determined its scope of activities.

Thanks to CEDAR, Zahed met Muddassar Ahmed, a British entrepreneur and communication specialist, who tapped him to help run another organization he had founded, Concordia Forum, which convened elected officials, journalists, technology professionals, corporate CEOs, and others with a Muslim background at an annual retreat loosely modeled after the Salzburg experience.* This group in turn helped spawn a range of CVE programs and initiatives and to support individuals like Rachid Benzine, who holds conferences around CVE themes, and Hisham Abdel Gawad, an educator who helps show Muslim kids how to answer questions about their religious identity. Journalists and producers have met through Concordia Forum, learning to coordinate on social media to project counter-extremist messages. Philanthropists have also connected through this network to set up social justice funds such as the Pillars Fund and the El Hibri Foundation and crowdsourcing platforms like LaunchGood that are taking action against extremism.[8] Keep in mind, all of this reflects the organizing activities of just two of CEDAR's members.

All told, CEDAR has had an important ripple effect through Muslim communities globally, leading to dozens of programs that have touched thousands of lives. With some four hundred members, the group has inspired a generation of young Muslims to take on leadership roles in their communities. As Ahmed Larouz observes, the goal is "to inspire the coming generations. You don't have to do the same work all the time, but if we can attract [members of] other generations [and pass on the vision . . .], that's a big achievement."[9]

CEDAR was one of many networks I helped create in Europe during the second Bush administration. Another came out of our brain trust meetings at the NSC. Juan Zarate and others wanted to create networks that specifically engaged Muslim women, recognizing how critical mothers could be in pushing back against extremist

* Concordia Forum is the name of both the conference and an associated global network.

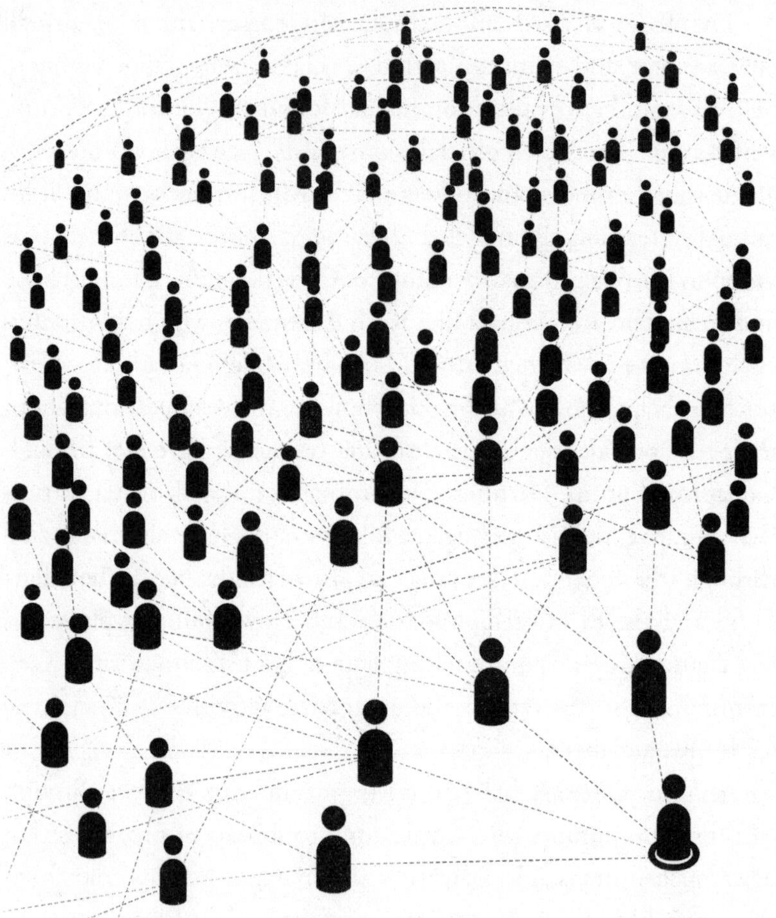

Connecting like-minded individuals can have an important ripple effect, leading to dozens of programs and inspired actors.

Illustrated by Nafisa Nandini Crishna

ideology. Mothers are often the first to see ideological changes in their kids. Also, we knew from organizations like Mothers Against Drunk Driving (MADD) that mothers spoke with particular authority and urgency on topics dealing with youth protection. They had been particularly successful at galvanizing communities around important issues, such as bullying, school nutrition, safe sex, and Internet safety.

The more we talked and researched the subject, the more we recognized that no groups of Muslim mothers out there were condemning Al Qaeda attacks. We spoke with programing staff at MADD's main office as well as some national chapter leaders and school principles to learn about what had contributed to that organization's success. As they told us, it was important that MADD was grassroots, an organic outgrowth of their local communities. Local chapters were organized differently; sometimes the local parent-teacher association had taken the lead in establishing a chapter, other times it was a prominent family in the community that had stepped in to bring mothers together. Ultimately, close connections between mothers and local student groups helped MADD to have an impact. We also spoke with local chapters of a number of other grassroots organizations, including the YMCA and the Boys and Girls Clubs to understand how they operated. Combining this information with other data from government experts on the role of women in communities, we vetted our idea for a MADD-like organization for Muslim women with officials at both the National Security Council and the State Department. Since this would be a European initiative, I also had to solicit the approval of my boss at the time, Dan Fried.

We wound up receiving the approvals we needed, and got to work setting up the organization.* Zarate suggested we call it Sisters Against Violent Extremism (SAVE). Again, we didn't want the U.S. government to launch the organization directly, given its credibility issues with Muslims and the need to have a local organization's understanding and know-how. I eventually connected with Edit Schlaffer, a Viennese social scientist who founded and ran an NGO called Women Without Borders. She loved the idea of SAVE and had the grassroots connections required to build a network of

* We initially called it Women Against Violent Extremism (WAVE), but after working closely with senior State colleague Karen Volker and several NSC colleagues, we began to brainstorm alternative names.

mothers across European Muslim communities. The start-up funds required were modest—about $30,000. Schlaffer agreed with us: SAVE couldn't succeed if it was publicly associated with the United States government, but since we were using taxpayer money, the State Department would have to be transparent in reporting that it was funding SAVE. We agreed that the United States would not be listed publicly as a sponsor, but that if anybody approached Dr. Schlaffer and asked where the idea and money for SAVE originated, she would disclose its origins.

These concerns out of the way, another issue arose: the National Security Council was totally behind the project, but my bureau at the State Department didn't have the $30,000 in its budget, and we could not convince the seasoned foreign service officer who was in charge of public diplomacy grants at State to experiment with the idea. Public diplomacy funds were needed elsewhere, and many focused career staff at State worried about the idea of "wasting money" on European Muslims, when they knew that these efforts would not be reflected in the larger highlights of State Department activity presented to Congress. Worse, such unusual pilot projects were just the sort to be criticized on Capitol Hill, which controlled the State Department's funding. From the point of view of these officials, SAVE was little more than a pet project that would hopefully soon fade away.

Desperate, I went to the State Department's Near Eastern Affairs Bureau and spoke with a woman there who had come from Goldman Sachs and was not interested in the department's bureaucratic battles. I told her that the NSC supported the creation of SAVE, and that I really believed the idea was a good one. Although it was unusual for regional bureaus to share funds, she gave me the money we needed to launch the project.

Working closely with Schlaffer through our European embassies, we focused at first on raising consciousness about extremism, giving Muslim women whose children had been radicalized a forum for talking about extremism in a safe, confidential manner through carefully executed sessions all across Europe that Schlaffer ran. As more women began to trust one another via Schlaffer's expert and sensitive process of engagement, these local groups began to form chapters across Europe. Collectively, these chapters gave rise to a coalition of women of different experiences, cultures, ethnicities, and heritages, serving as a forum in which they could discuss how they might fight back against extremism.

With SAVE chapters popping up in cities across Europe, and with Schlaffer successfully raising money from her own government and private donors, we asked her to take the program global. We still wanted the program to maintain its independence from the U.S. government but imagined her running a much larger organization with an international advisory board composed of Muslim and non-Muslim experts, and support from both government and the private sector. Schlaffer had wonderful ideas about how to galvanize mothers, including through film, school curricula, and even a pan-African radio program featuring mothers speaking out about their kids' recruitment into extremist groups. We wanted to see these ideas come to fruition, and by and large they have. As of this writing, SAVE has trained women around the world to spot signs of radicalization, educating them on specific actions they can take to prevent extremists from corrupting their kids. SAVE also helps local communities in countries like India, Zanzibar, Pakistan, Egypt, France, Northern Ireland, Afghanistan, and Nigeria create safety nets for kids, places where they can go to learn the truth about extremist ideology and explore their own cultural identities. The U.S. government has spun off SAVE, and today it subsists largely thanks to Schlaffer's vision, determination, and fund-raising prowess.

Another network we launched in 2008 was called the European Media and Technology Entrepreneurs Network (EMTEN). Al Jazeera was widely watched in Muslim communities at the time, and I kept hearing that European youth needed to hear more European

Muslim voices and perspectives in the media. Individual entrepreneurs in a number of countries were entering this space but they were not connected with one another. In a conversation with a Spanish Muslim, I asked, "Do you know about the others like you in France, Italy, or Belgium?" He had not. Using our convening power, our embassies across Europe decided to create another networked community.

Seeking out major TV and radio networks that at the time served Muslim audiences, we brought Muslim media professionals together to explore how they might get the message out to local communities. Some of those gathered told us they wanted help from the U.S. government in finding mainstream television networks like the BBC or CNN and film studios like Sony and Paramount that might wish to develop and air programs about young European Muslims. Others wanted to create talk-show programing that featured Muslim youth interacting with their European peers. In their view, such shows would build greater self-awareness and integration among European Muslims, as well as transmit knowledge about Muslim experiences to non-Muslim Europeans. The group developed protocols and best practices dealing with the sharing of stories about Muslims, the vetting of experts featured on the media, audience analysis and the interpretation of demographic trends, the tackling of stereotypes, and much more. Group members also shared knowledge about how to create partnerships with mainstream news organizations, and how to solicit universities and NGOs to provide training in journalistic methods. With blogging then becoming more important, we created a network of European Muslim bloggers, influencers who could write about extremism in ways that would capture the attention of young Muslims and counter the stories and ideas that extremists disseminated.

All of this was a radical strategy at the time, but Dan Fried, Elliott Abrams, and Juan Zarate kept reminding me that even though others within the interagency might not have bought in yet, Hadley,

Secretary Rice, and the president wanted us to see what we might accomplish if we served as supporters and conveners of "credible voices" inside Muslim communities. Thus was born a prototype for the discipline later dubbed "CVE."

At around this time, I also experimented with a number of other innovative programs that specifically dealt with youth and identity. For instance, to help younger Muslims with a critical question I kept hearing—"how do we know if what our imam is saying is right?"—we decided to put more content online to expose youth to the vast differences that existed in how imams were educated and thinking about theology. Until meeting with John Palfrey and Urs Gasser, authors of the 2008 book *Born Digital: Understanding the First Generation of Digital Natives,* I had struggled to understand how precisely millennials interacted with technology—back then, that knowledge didn't seem to exist within government. Drawing on the insights of these two experts, I asked fellow officials at the State Department and the National Counterterrorism Center why we weren't mobilizing technology to speak specifically to millennials. Jared Cohen, then in the Strategic Planning Office at the Department of State, and I put together memos and concept notes on what was called the "War of Ideas" for Zarate, Abrams, Fried, Karen Hughes (and then her successor James Glassman), and others. These memos, on subjects like Muslim entrepreneurship and technology, Scaling Up New Voices, and Muslims in Public Office, circulated around the State Department and the interagency.

With the help of Harvard University's Berkman Center for Internet and Society (now called the Berkman Klein Center), I gathered a group of creative young people together for what could be called a pre-hackathon. I asked Shahed and Zahed Amanullah, two brothers who were also entrepreneurs living in Austin and London, respectively,* to attend. One provocative idea that surfaced was to

* Shahed founded online magazine altmuslim.com.

create a website that provided information about local imams and showed users where they existed on the ideological spectrum. We called this proposed platform E-mams and envisioned it as an interactive site where Muslim youth could go to learn about Islam in a modern, moderate, interactive environment. Users could rate their own imams, learn where they went to school, and explore their positions on issues ranging from prayer to lifestyle choices. The site would focus on educating youth about global Muslim diversity, and on broadening users' exposure to theology from both European and Eastern sources. We wanted to expose youth to the great breadth of theological interpretations that existed on everyday issues that concerned them so they would develop a more critical perspective on the religious teachings they encountered. With that exposure, young Muslims would see that many so-called Islamic scholars with extremist views actually possessed very little training, and they would discover that other imams existed who shared their own perspectives. E-mams did eventually come to fruition though a grant from the Pentagon, although under a different name: wiki-imams. But as it goes with government, the project was eventually shelved when a new team at the Department of Defense came in.

While making new connections, we also were trying to use traditional channels through the State Department's Public Diplomacy and Public Affairs Bureau to open up new dialogue. We expanded the Citizen Dialogue Program that Karen Hughes had begun in 2006, sending teams of four American Muslims—an imam, a businessperson, a student, and another professional—across the globe in 2007 to interact with local Muslim communities and religious leaders. Holding discussions on topics like Islam in America and the compatibility of Islam and democracy, the program sought to give Muslim community members a venue for talking about identity-related issues and for puncturing myths perpetrated by extremists in their messaging. It also sought to help us uncover new areas of interest, such as blogging training, library science, and the organization of youth centers, in which we could create programs.

Some other regional bureaus and elements within the Public Diplomacy Bureau and Counterterrorism Bureau within the State Department pushed back at Citizen Dialogue, accusing us of "pandering" to European Muslims and spending too much money and attention on building bonds between American Muslims and European Muslims. "The war is in Iraq and Afghanistan," they would say, "not Europe," or, "This is a problem for European governments to tackle," or, "Al Qaeda is not going to become powerful in Europe, and so we don't need to focus much on Muslim youth there." Congressional staff also cast doubt on Citizen Dialogue, contending that America didn't have a problem with extremist ideology the way Europe did, and that we never would, on account of our history of assimilating immigration.

Ignoring the critics, and utilizing the European Bureau's funds, we persevered with Citizen Dialogue and an array of other innovative programs and networks in Europe. As before, these programs engaged with individuals and groups that the U.S. government had never before consulted in this way, such as American Muslim entrepreneurs, academic researchers, technologists—anyone with a fresh perspective on identity. In building these programs, we also cut across geographies and administrative silos, a step that State Department officials and others at our embassies just weren't taking. On a number of levels, we were "opening up" the problem of extremist ideology, attempting to wield government power in a way that was far more collaborative and inclusive than ever before, and that drew on systems thinking.

NEW NETWORKS CONCEIVED CIRCA 2007

- **SAVE (Sisters Against Violent Extremism):** Using the Mothers Against Drunk Driving (MADD) grassroots model of social change, this global group raises awareness about the dangers of violent extremist ideology.

- **Network of Formers:** These former members of extremist groups work to counter narratives and tactics used by violent extremists.
- **European Media and Technology Entrepreneurs Network:** A network of Muslim media entrepreneurs building online platforms to engage mainstream Muslim participation in countering online extremism.
- **Women and Public Service Network:** A partnership between the U.S. Department of State, three of America's "Seven Sister" colleges (that is, Smith, Mount Holyoke, and Wellesley), and European Muslim communities, promoting female leadership, public service, excellence, and related values.
- **Al Qaeda Victims Network:** A global network of Al Qaeda victims with international media exposure.
- **Action Incubator:** Forty of Europe's "best and brightest" young Muslims put their minds together, devising innovative CVE approaches that bear on technology, media, women's empowerment, and related issues.
- **European Muslim Professionals Network:** An action-oriented network promoting the European Muslim professional class.
- **Pan-European Politics and Policy Network:** A network aimed at increasing Muslim participation in European communities, policy, and politics.
- **Pan-European Muslim Media Network:** A network of European Muslim professionals aimed at fostering greater inclusion of Muslims in European journalism and media.
- **Pan-European Muslim Women's Network:** A network aimed at empowering professional Muslim women in Europe by promoting diversity, inclusiveness, and leadership.
- **Pan-European Muslim Information and Communications**

Technology Network: A network of leading Muslim technology entrepreneurs aimed at advancing understanding and cooperation between Muslims and non-Muslims.
- **Network of European Muslim Elected Officials:** A network of elected Muslim officials that promotes the compatibility of Islam and democracy by fostering community involvement and mentorship.

Beginning in 2009, as the U.S. government's first-ever special representative to Muslim communities, I began to create similar programs globally based on the work we did in Europe. Working out of our temporary office on the first floor of the State Department, with a sign reading "Obama Transition Team" on our door, my new team and I explored various ideas for structuring and building a giant global millennial network. Should we host a grand summit in partnership with a large media company, inviting a VIP keynote to draw attention? How could we involve embassies, since they lacked funding for CVE in their budgets? As a friend and social entrepreneur in London suggested, what about promoting this network on the sidelines of the Hajj, the largest meeting place of Muslims anywhere on earth? Or what about asking TED to work with us to curate a branded event that showcased Muslim millennial speakers who were designing ways to fight extremism? We determined that we had to use a platform like Facebook and organize the network so that our embassies would find interaction with it easy, and so that youth would find it welcoming and easy to access. As the idea of the network took shape, I asked my team what we should call it. Yasmine Hafiz, coauthor of *The American Muslim Teenager's Handbook* and an intern in my office, said, "Let's call it Generation Change!"

To further flesh out the Generation Change concept, my team and I spoke with numerous American Muslims with whom I'd interacted over the past four years, as well as contacts at the State Department's regional bureaus and friends at Democratic, Republican, and nonpartisan think tanks like the Brookings Institution, the Washington Institute for Near East Policy, the Council on Foreign Relations, the International Republican Institute, the National Democratic Institute, the Hudson Institute, the Atlantic Council, RAND, and the New America Foundation. I also talked in great length with CEDAR members about what features of their network were working well, and how a larger group might mobilize them. Many NGOs told me that a network like Generation Change would be quite welcome in conjunction with the "new beginning" that Obama was launching vis-à-vis Muslims worldwide. They also felt that Generation Change could serve as a powerful symbol of agency to galvanize youth. My increasingly positive colleagues at State even hoped we could connect the network with other programs within the department, like the International Visitor Leadership Programs* or newer working groups dedicated to public-private partnerships.

Once we had conducted our research and analysis, we consulted with diplomats, from U.S. former ambassadors and undersecretaries to current foreign ambassadors to the United States, about how we might best launch the Generation Change effort in a way that would gain support from the State Department's regional and functional bureaus and from nations themselves. I wrote a memo to Secretary Clinton describing what I wanted to do and why, proposing that we launch the network with a special event that brought American Muslims to the State Department. She agreed, and in September 2010 we brought together seventy-five American Muslim filmmakers, entrepreneurs, musicians, and other innovators to discuss the identity crisis and how to mobilize against extremism. Speakers included a diverse array of prominent Muslims, including a current foreign service officer, a comedian, poets, and a comic book cre-

* IVLP, a program housed in the Bureau for Educational and Cultural Affairs at the U.S. Department of State, facilitates a professional exchange program in which international leaders come to America for short visits.

ator. That evening, the secretary offered remarks about Generation Change at an elegant feast in the department's Ben Franklin Room marking the Holy Month of Ramadan.

During the months and years after this launch, we partnered with our embassies around the world, asking them to find local change makers within their communities to become part of the Generation Change network. By the time I left the State Department in early 2014, we had seeded thirty chapters of Generation Change, bringing together more than five hundred handpicked influencers. As part of the program, these young men and women had the opportunity to receive small grants of a few thousand dollars each to make a difference in their communities, with these grants going to fund training in leadership and entrepreneurialism as well as workshops focused on peace-building skills and conflict resolution.

We planned to grow Generation Change inside of government and then find a nongovernment partner to take it over and run it.* We feared that if left inside of government, this and similar programs would wither and die, as such programs rarely survive when their founders leave. Bureaucratic turf wars are rampant at State, and an idea's external provenance constitutes reason enough for it to die in the minds of many officials. But as of this writing, Generation Change is still going strong, maintained under the auspices of the U.S. Institute of Peace, which has strengthened programming to enhance local community efforts through a "train the trainer" model.[10] Generation Change members have had significant impacts on their communities, helping wage the war of ideas against the extremists. A member in Belgium created a comic book called *The Muslim Rangers* that presented a generation of Muslim kids with new superhero role models to look up to, and another member in Trinidad created a telephone hot line that local youth could call to receive answers to religious questions. Other projects have included:

---

* We eventually transferred every single program that we designed to outside entities.

- A portal "that helped to organize and guide the online Belgian Muslim community."
- A program in Ghana that connects young, budding technologists with local mentors at small businesses.
- "Muslim Frank Talk," an online forum originating in South Africa that encourages "frank discussion about sensitive issues within Muslim communities."
- A "Youth Leadership Summit" in Mogadishu that convenes "successful and motivated young Somali leaders to amplify their ability to create positive change in their country."
- A "Video Contest Against Tribalism & Racism" in Sudan.

These projects were all very small and grassroots, but when you add them together, dozens of programs across the world moving in unison, they have the potential to have a significant impact on the global battle against extremist recruiting. As a participant in a 2015 training in Kenya said, "this is the generation that is unstoppable . . . a generation that can change the world." Who knows how many more youth might have been recruited by extremists in local communities if these programs hadn't existed?

It was not enough to build a platform that allowed youth to communicate with one another, share ideas, and facilitate change. I had stayed in close touch with the Berkman Center, and had been learning from former extremists, technology experts, and intelligence analysts about extremists' increasing efforts to recruit youth using Google, Facebook, and Twitter (chapter 5). I wondered what more we could do to mobilize the young Muslims I had been meeting to create appealing counter-content online, and specifically to train them to use social media to counter specific extremist narratives. During my travels, many youth had told me that they yearned to craft their own, anti-extremist messaging online, but just weren't sure how to go about doing so.

In researching the idea of an online skills training program, my team spoke with Muslims outside government to see if anything like this existed in the private sector. As far as we could tell, it didn't. Having received encouraging feedback from other members of Secretary Clinton's senior team, we began pondering the logistics of building such a program from scratch. At around this time, my friend Imam Magid of the All Dulles Area Muslim Society asked to meet with me, introducing me to Humera Khan, an engineer and theologian unknown to the State Department. Humera and I shared a common vision, and after some due diligence, I suggested to Shahed that he might enlist her to help us build out this education program. The two wound up working closely together, alongside colleagues at State and the National Counterterrorism Center. We also reached out to members of Generation Change to help us craft and launch the program in ways that would gain maximum traction in their communities. Launched in 2011, Viral Peace, as the program was called, started in the Philippines and helped Muslim youth understand what extremists were doing online to target them, how to build strategies for transmitting CVE ideas to their peers online, and how to fashion greater resilience and leadership skills within their communities. By 2013, Viral Peace was conducting dozens of trainings across South Asia, the Middle East, North Africa, and Africa. As of this writing, Humera is still conducting these trainings, and her hard work helping to develop curriculums and training modules has been recognized across the interagency.

In creating all these programs, my method merged ethnography with entrepreneurialism. I spent time on the ground speaking to thousands of youth as well as local leaders in Muslim communities, tracking not merely the trends I've discussed earlier in this book, but also looking for gaps in our efforts against extremism. What portions of the war of ideas were we not waging? What support did Muslim youth require so as to become immune to extremist messaging, and what *weren't* they receiving? Visiting these communities firsthand and learning about them from the inside was vital to understanding new or emerging needs that the U.S. government and other actors weren't yet addressing.

All of these programs were first-of-their kind pilots, embodying a degree of experimentation atypical in policy circles. Once a pilot had proved successful, I didn't have the resources at my disposal to scale up the initiative across the world, or to run it over the long term. (My total budget while serving as the special representative to Muslim communities was around $2 million—a paltry sum by Washington standards.) In many cases, we managed to hand over the administration of successful programs to NGOs, universities, or think-do tanks that would keep them running and hopefully expand and build on them. One organization developed in my office, a network of young elected leaders from the United States and Europe called the Transatlantic Inclusion Leadership Network (TILN), has reached new heights under the auspices of the German Marshall Fund.* SAVE continues under the aegis of Dr. Schlaffer's Women Without Borders organization. Harvard University's Berkman Klein Center for Internet & Society oversees Viral Peace and has expanded it to address the broader problem of online hate. Initially, the Institute for Strategic Dialogue ran CEDAR, but now the organization operates under an independent board.

Quite often, however, we couldn't find private donors to subsidize it, nor could we find government money, and then as now,

* Spearheaded by my colleague Lora Berg in 2011, TILN brings young leaders together for skills-building and networking workshops, helping them gain fluency in transatlantic leadership so that they can create more inclusive, equitable societies. Program alumni have provided mutual support and solidarity, campaigning on behalf of their colleagues and providing expertise on specific policy issues. As Berg told me, "alumni in the Netherlands have founded the Dutch Inclusion Leaders Network, an alumnus in Greece has carried out [national] inclusive leadership training, and . . . alumni in Finland and in Italy [are planning] inclusive leadership events." TILN alumni also "consult together on how to respond to events and issues that require a public stand. This includes public responses to terrorism, and to political changes such as Brexit and the [2016] U.S. election. The goal is to find a positive path forward as leaders in their respective countries." Since the German Marshall Fund took over TILN's administration, the network has continued to grow, with alumni from Europe addressing U.S. political caucuses, and American alumni meeting with politicians in Europe to help devise strategies for rendering the political system there more inclusive. Lora Berg, interview with the author, September 9, 2016.

nobody in the U.S. government was charged with overseeing the waging of the ideological war in all its dimensions. The U.S. government didn't even track other CVE programs under way elsewhere in the world, so we didn't know how or where to invest financially so as to achieve larger goals. We needed—and still desperately need—someone whose job it is to wake up each day, understand the ideological battlefield, review the assets at our disposal (for example, program ideas, technologies, and partnerships with local groups), and deploy them accordingly.

As the Bush administration drew to a close in 2008, we recommended to the Obama team that they charge an assistant to the president or an official of equal stature with overseeing the war of ideas. As I've recounted, it wasn't until the very end of the Obama administration that the rise of the so-called Islamic State caused officials to pay serious attention to extremist ideology. Even then, the administration did so in a very limited way. Officials remained uncertain about whether ideology constituted a "real" threat to the homeland, or whether its scourge extended only to Europe and other areas. Officials also didn't want to repeat mistakes made by European governments, like promoting a particular NGO only to find out later that some of its membership or key leaders were in fact speaking out against their country's values.* CVE continued to exist, but as a mere shadow of what it might have been.

A NEW APPROACH TO FIGHTING EXTREMISM

Imagine what might happen if all these programs I've mentioned were scaled up dramatically, along with newer efforts developed over

* Despite lack of coordination and a paucity of funding, some of our early CVE efforts continue to function to this day.

the last couple of years specifically to deal with recruitment, so that they could reach mass audiences of Muslim youth. Among these newer efforts are ISD's Counter-Conversation direct online interventions program, which uses former extremists to interact with vulnerable youth interested in extremist ideas; initiatives like the Strong Cities Network, the Internet Citizens Program, and the YouthCAN Initiative, which scale and optimize grassroots CVE efforts of all kinds; Extreme Dialogue, which provides tools for teachers to help facilitate safe classroom discussions around extremism and radicalization; and the Digital Resilience program, which equips young people with critical thinking skills and an increased awareness of extremist propaganda techniques; to name but a few.

Imagine if we had a constant stream of these programs emerging, in line with shifting trends in local Muslim communities, and mobilizing the latest research into relevant topics like behavioral change, the adolescent mind, and neo-Nazi narratives. We would still need strong military and law enforcement actions to curtail violent extremist activity, especially in the short term. We would also still need conventional forms of outreach to build support for America and its policies. But we would finally have a viable means of getting *inside* Muslim communities and connecting with Muslim youth to inoculate them against extremism.

To connect with youth, you have to be embedded in their world, understanding their ever-shifting norms and contexts. You have to know, say, if Generation Z kids are living in more multigenerational households, or if more of their parents are pressuring them to get real-world work experiences—features of their lives that might seem disconnected from extremism, but that in fact might shape how they perceive reality and their identities. And you have to glean and process information like this in real time because, as Camilo La Cruz of sparks & honey (a consultancy specializing in culture) notes, "the changes might be happening at [such] a speed [that] by the time you decide to put a message out in market, the messenger is not right, or the message has shifted, or there is [something that] you're not taking into consideration."[11]

Sparks & honey CEO and founder Terry Young regards this gleaning and processing of information as cultural listening. He conceives of it as a combination of social media monitoring and analysis, secondary research into popular culture, and "on-the-ground, primary research combined together to truly understand humans holistically." As I've suggested, government has no capacity like this specifically dedicated to youth in local communities around the world. At best, an embassy's public diplomacy officer might occasionally pen a cable about a new cultural behavior he or she has happened to notice. Meanwhile, a thousand other cultural behaviors, of which government has been completely unaware, have come and gone.

Even if we had a raw listening capacity on the ground, nobody in government is charged with the function of what we might call *connective interpretation*—that is, methodically compiling raw cultural data from around the world, analyzing it synthetically to identify trends, and making actionable recommendations to drive interventions. Like the initial gathering of empirical data, connective interpretation requires the specialized skills of cultural researchers and analysts rooted in disciplines like communications, psychology, sociology, ethnography, marketing, history, theology, media technology, and futurism. As Young reflects, it requires people who are "highly curious," who "love exploration . . . people that dwell at the edge to find the little small nuances that may seem fringe today but that become something big tomorrow." But there is another layer, too: "We need the analytical talent that can quantify this type of work. We [need] data scientists that are going in and running models or [doing] quantification for something that has typically been more social-science oriented, that has not been as quantified."[12] At present, very few people with the skills and mentality of "edge dwellers" work in government, nor have we applied quantitative analysis to their insights.

Other kinds of tactics are necessary, too, to reduce the amount of extremist messaging available. As I discussed in chapter 3, for instance, government must clamp down on the Saudis and other allies and buttress local Muslim cultures and traditions. That isn't easy, of course. Our Gulf allies support extremist ideology and a monolithic interpretation of Islam, but they also provide intelligence, access to military facilities, and other resources in the fight against terrorist groups. Qatar, for instance, has maintained ties to groups such as the Muslim Brotherhood, Hamas, and most disturbingly, Al Qaeda.[13] At the same time, Qatar serves as home to Al Udeid Air Base, "the largest, most important U.S. military facility in the Middle East."* And for all the billions the Saudis have given to fund the spread of Wahhabi ideology, the kingdom has also provided intelligence about Al Qaeda plots against the United States, has helped the United States bomb the so-called Islamic State, and has helped spur a "Muslim coalition against what it called the 'disease' of Islamic extremism." We must push our allies to clamp down on Wahhabi ideology, but we must do so in ways that don't compromise those strategic alliances.

All of this tactical focus on our allies and partners should not stop us from also looking inward and appreciating how we ourselves unwittingly affirm extremist ideas of a monolithic Islam. Rejecting the idea of the "Muslim world," for example, is an important start, but as I discussed in chapter 6, we must thoroughly review the entire lexicon we use when talking about Muslims and Islam. The point here is not to be politically correct. Rather, it's to act in our *own* interests to support Islamic diversity and counteract extremist narratives. Other steps we can take include funding the conservation

---

* Daniel Byman and William McCants, "The Danger of Picking Sides in the Qatar Crisis," *The Atlantic*, June 16, 2017, https://www.theatlantic.com/international/archive/2017/06/qatar-saudi-arabia-trump-isis-terrorism/530640/. As Byman and McCants write: "The United States has even benefited from the ambiguous ties between Qatar's Gulf partners and terrorist groups: When America sought the release of a hostage held by al-Qaeda's affiliate in Syria, it turned to Qatar to broker the deal."

of local traditions and sacred spaces around the world—not just for Muslims but also for Jews, Hindus, Christians, and other groups within Muslim-majority countries; and changing the way we interface with Muslims to include multiple voices. If we don't undertake a larger effort to preserve Islamic heritage, a generation of Muslims risks falling under the sway of an especially intolerant, divisive, and violent brand of ideology that is marketed incorrectly as "Islam."

If government is to make use of all the insight about youth that it gleans from a cultural listening capacity, it must also develop a capacity to experiment, move quickly, embrace technology, partner with others, and take a certain amount of risk. Groups like the so-called Islamic State are extremely entrepreneurial in virtually every aspect of their operations. They are, in truth, the quintessential start-ups. Government can learn to become genuinely entrepreneurial as well—while still deploying the massive resources that it alone possesses.

I can't emphasize enough how important listening and quick-response execution is in CVE.* It can make a profound difference. To take but one example, in 2010, in my travels around the world, I began to detect a change in how women were thinking about identity. More of them were embracing extremist views, following a recruitment path that until now had been mainly followed by young men. Alarmed, I approached a senior counterterrorism official and explained that we needed to invest in research and intelligence gathering to understand why this trend had materialized, and what its impact might be. "Oh, yes," he said, "absolutely, that's a fine idea." Did he provide me with a single penny to pursue this research, much less design and implement CVE programs targeting potential female recruits? Not at all. This trend continued to grow, and several years

* Such efforts require governments to begin tracking and understanding cultural and demographic trends around the world in many different domains. We need to understand social, economic, political, cultural, and religious developments inside communities in order to understand fully how and why youth are embracing rigid "us versus them" mind-sets about the expression of Islamic identity.

later, women and girls emerged as a visible presence in the ranks of the so-called Islamic State, who aggressively recruited them. What might have happened had we moved quickly to implement CVE programs specially targeted at women, inundating them with positive and alternative messaging? We would have preempted extremist recruiting. Instead, we're left to respond once the ideological "damage" has already been done.

A more aggressive, entrepreneurial approach to CVE executed at scale might sound costly and difficult to enact, but individual governments don't have to do it all. Our government and those of our allies and partners might share responsibility on CVE-related tasks, allowing for greater focus, responsiveness, and speed. Perhaps the United Kingdom would concentrate on going deep into local communities and collecting relevant, ethnographic data, while the United States would create messaging and media via film, and partners in the Middle East would focus on Arab content. Working together, we can address the problem of extremist recruitment holistically and proactively, while minimizing the burden on any one government and maximizing the expertise brought to bear.

When it comes to making CVE processes more entrepreneurial, we still have far to go. When I served under both the Bush and Obama administrations, I operated like a start-up, gauging early successes and failures and adjusting accordingly. Yet my entrepreneurial efforts engendered massive institutional resistance. Government talks all the time of becoming more entrepreneurial, but when it comes to extremism, the federal government remains a lumbering bureaucracy. It isn't set up to handle an approach that is fast-moving, dynamic, experimental, grassroots, cross-disciplinary, and collaborative. The barriers are many: slow and inflexible budgeting processes; an ingrained resistance to risk taking, creativity, and novelty; a tendency to revert to the same outside partners and experts; political competition and infighting between departments and teams; and a siloed structure that precludes us from understanding and reacting to extremism in a holistic, comprehensive way. Lately, agencies have given out innovation prizes and held "hackathons" and TED-like events, but don't let that fool you—even amid the supposed disruptions of President Trump, the entire system of Washington remains engineered to resist quick change.

If we are to wage the war of ideas at scale, we have to overcome these barriers to the extent possible. I am not saying we need to "change" Washington—that simply won't happen. Government can't run the way private businesses do: it has a public purpose, as well as different needs, stakeholders, and "owners." Its traditions have value. But that doesn't mean government can't run *better* than it currently does. With respect to extremism, we must take the current system and supplement it, making government more expansive, holistic, forward-looking, and strategic.

To produce an anti-recruitment strategy, we must again draw on experts from a broad range of disciplines. We must create a central authority—an organizational "home" for our counter-extremism efforts—and charge it with crafting this strategy. This authority would also oversee execution of the strategy, coordinating our anti-recruitment efforts across government bureaucracies, including the Departments of Homeland Security, Health and Human Services, Defense, Education, State, and the Treasury, as well as organizations, networks, and groups within those departments. Government already has many resources and capacities necessary for the fight against extremist ideology. We don't need to "reinvent the wheel." But we do need to coordinate efforts much more fluidly and efficiently than we currently do. We must think bigger.

We should also engage more profoundly with state and local governments. America has yet to develop a truly national effort across all fifty states that links mayors and governors in the fight against extremism. Though we have seen devastating attacks in places like Orlando and San Bernardino, we lack the resources to significantly expand CVE efforts at the local level. Mayors and governors need to solicit grassroots ideas, but they must also have the financial resources and teams in place to implement those ideas. As of 2018, the rise of hate crimes in communities across the United States makes this effort that much more urgent. With the most diverse group of Muslims anywhere on the planet, we Americans have an opportunity to think differently about who we are and to craft narratives that welcome in American Muslim youth.* We need a national plan that allows the Department of Homeland Security to give every state the resources necessary to build educational, health, and peer-to-peer programs.

In addition to these proposals, I could recommend dozens, even hundreds of changes large and small as to how our branches of government organize, manage, and execute CVE. Some examples of these recommendations:

- *We should redesign the State department for CVE.* Each regional bureau should have a deputy assistant secretary in a nonpublic diplomacy role whose sole responsibility is CVE oversight and programming. That person needs a small staff in Washington to work with him or her alongside senior staff in the counterterrorism bureau, as well as a full-time, dedicated counterpart on the ground in every embassy around the world focused on programming and engagement.
- *We should develop new ways of engaging embassies in the fight against extremist ideas.* First, we should assign a staff member at each embassy to bear specific responsibility for cultural listening and to coordinate in this function with colleagues

* During 2015 and 2016, I had the opportunity to serve on the Homeland Security Advisory Council, where I advocated for more local action to combat extremist ideology. In June 2016, the CVE task force formulated a plan to help mayors and governors in all fifty states deal with the extremist threat. For more information, please consult Homeland Security's "Counter Violent Extremism (CVE) Subcommittee Final Interim Report," https://www.dhs.gov/publication/hsac-cve-subcommittee-final-interim-report.

at other embassies. Second, we should give embassies more freedom to experiment with new programs and to build partnerships with local businesses and NGOs, fostering more collaboration across our embassies and rewarding regional embassies when they work together, share information, and avoid duplication of efforts.

- *We should rebuild consequential diplomatic senior-level channels with Muslim multilateral organizations,* including the Organization of Islamic Cooperation and the Arab League. We should reinstate the envoy to the OIC to represent American Muslims, and insist that minority Muslim countries play a greater role in CVE.
- *We should adopt common definitions for extremism and CVE.* Just as public health officials can define the stages of a disease and dedicate particular programs to the reduction of specific risks, so we should do the same here.
- *We should create a CVE measurement index* that allows us to compare CVE programs across states and nations for their efficacy, allowing private funders and government to feel comfortable supporting specific efforts. Metrics for the index could include measurements of programs' sizes, frequencies, and impacts on their intended audiences.
- *We should create globally vetted lists of experts who work on different elements of CVE.*
- *We should apply financial and legal pressure on tech companies* to destroy opportunities to spread hate. As we saw in chapter 5, this means levying consequences like financial fines or taxing them.
- *We should relieve the Global Engagement Center of responsibility for producing counter-content,* shifting that responsibility to outside professionals in communications, advertising, and marketing firms.

- *We should boost the National Security Language Initiative's efforts* to bring more language speakers into the State Department, the Department of Defense, and our intelligence agencies.
- *We should help local governments assess their existing programming,* helping them determine which programs could also be used to combat violent extremism. If vital programming doesn't exist, we should give localities easy access to rapid response funding so that they can launch it.
- *We should be proactive and creative in collaborating with businesses.* Washington must be bolder in creating public-private partnerships that help us translate valuable, on-the-ground embassy knowledge into innovative programs.
- *We should implement more rewards for nontraditional problem solving within government.* A senior British official recently told me, "When we see a problem, we solve it in the traditional ways." Let's incent bureaucrats to take more risks, following the lead of companies like Google, 3M, Xerox, Volkswagen, and Yum brands. Likewise, we should implement a U.S. government prize for individuals inside and outside government who have made the greatest CVE contributions.
- *We should develop a multisector analysis strategy to plan for future changes in extremist recruitment and radicalization.* At present, we have no programs aimed at anticipating what will happen five, ten, or twenty years from now on the ideological battlefield. Certain research arms inside and outside of government might provide some analysis, but these insights aren't operationalized.
- *Government officials, up to and including the president, must speak and behave in ways that respect all faiths, including Islam.*
- *Congress should pass stricter legal or financial consequences for social media companies, media outlets, schools, and individuals that promote hate speech.* Our nation must rethink how we

can uphold the First Amendment while still protecting our communities from extremist threats.

- *Congress should require foreign financiers of religious schools, centers, and houses of worship to undergo a vetting process by our state governments, ensuring that none of these donors are financing hate speech.*
- *We should build an American Youth Protection Center* that serves as a clearinghouse for knowledge about youth radicalization. This center should allow academic experts in a number of relevant fields to work together to further our knowledge of youth behavior, the risks extremists pose, and potential interventions.

Beyond a wide-ranging reorganization and reconceptualization of how we wage the war of ideas, government must increase its intellectual and financial commitment to fighting extremist ideology. Policy makers and other experts have talked endlessly about countering extremism, and yet as we've seen, the interest in and funding for programs that truly could make a difference just isn't there. That must change. We must now dramatically "scale up" innovative, entrepreneurial CVE programs if we are to prevail. Ultimately, we need to monopolize the marketplace of ideas on- and offline, inspiring credible voices that give new agency and purpose to this generation.*

We remain locked into thinking that we can deal with the extremist threat primarily through military means alone. Our soft power approach to date has been ad hoc, disrespected, uncoordinated, and unimaginative. The remedy is, first, adoption of the grand strategy mentioned above, and second, leveraging of all of our diplomatic tools to execute that strategy. We can't create an ideological

* I've taken language in this paragraph and the next directly from a statement I gave in a hearing before the Committee on Homeland Security on July 15, 2015. For a transcript of the hearing, see https://www.gpo.gov/fdsys/pkg/CHRG-114hhrg97916/pdf/CHRG-114hhrg97916.pdf.

countermovement on the backs of a few isolated government-funded programs. It requires much broader commitment and focus. Our strategy must be a cohesive, integrated, coherent, and comprehensive approach to the threat we face. We must wage a battle on all fronts with money, accountability, and experienced personnel. We have yet to unleash the full power of our skills in the soft power space. When we truly go "all in," we'll see how vulnerable the extremists really are. We might never rid the world entirely of extremism, but by reducing extremism's appeal and dramatically depleting the supply of new recruits, we can certainly remove it as a significant threat.

Congress should allocate resources across government to deal with the extremist threat as needed, increasing the funds available domestically and internationally through the Department of Homeland Security as well as the U.S. Department of State. This money can flow in many different forms, including grants for research on radicalization and extremism, grants for CVE innovation laboratories, grants for embassies to build and grow new CVE programs, unrestricted grants for rapid deployment of projects that do not fit neatly into the yearly fiscal planning cycles, and so on. But let me be clear. Going "all in" doesn't mean creating some huge, new government bureaucracy or investing billions of dollars. Combating extremist ideology and recruitment isn't costly compared with conventional military interventions.[14] Right now we spend about $100–150 million on countering extremist ideology, about *one-tenth* of 1 percent of the defense budget. That's all! If we devoted $1 billion per year, we could significantly impede extremist recruiting within a generation.[15] We do also have to pay attention to restructuring government so that it can respond more nimbly and effectively to extremist threats. And we have to fully commit ourselves intellectually to waging the war of ideas.

To power the comprehensive policy reorientation described above, we need one additional, critically important element: leadership. The bold, innovative strategy and tactics I'm advocating won't congeal unless leaders at the highest levels provide sufficient cover. When Hillary Clinton appointed me special representative to Muslim communities, she took a significant reputational risk. She had recently begun her tenure as secretary of state. Although she and her staff had vetted me, my approach was unorthodox, and I had come up in a Republican administration. Rather than proceed with more traditional options, Secretary Clinton had the vision to seek out new directions in our outreach to Muslims.

We need leaders at her level and below to show similar boldness and courage. We need leaders to talk about what we *can* do, not what we can't. We need leaders to stop thinking only about the credit they may or may not receive for particular policies, devoting resources to projects that might fail or that won't be "branded" with the U.S. government's imprimatur. We need leaders dedicated to authentic programs that work rather than the glitzy photo op. We need leaders across government who are making decisions every day about optics, engagement, and inclusion to think about the signals the United States is sending and the importance of diverse voices. In this regard, officials like Capricia Marshall, former chief of protocol of the United States; Julianna Smoot, former White House social secretary; George Selim, former Department of Homeland Security Director of the Office of Community Partnerships; and Paul Monteiro, a former White House public engagement advisor, were vitally important players during the Obama administration. And we need a Congress that takes the ideological war seriously, assuring that the U.S. government has the funds necessary to wage this war appropriately, and holds countries accountable for spreading violent extremist ideology. Only then will a fresher, more dynamic, more entrepreneurial mind-set begin to take hold in government bureaucracies around the issue of extremism. Ultimately, we need leadership from the White House that compels people in each department and agency within our government to think differently about extremist ideology and what they are doing to stop its appeal. The president needs to think about building a new kind of army of people who are doing the work of CVE, hiring the *right* kind of people—those with real skills and expertise—to get the job done, and rallying our government to deliver on this critical priority.

CHAPTER EIGHT

GLOBAL BUSINESS ON THE FRONT LINES

In a speech at the 2008 World Economic Forum in Davos, Switzerland, Microsoft cofounder Bill Gates made an impassioned plea for capitalism's renewal. The world needed "another level of innovation," Gates claimed, "not just technology innovation," but "system innovation." He laid out a notion of what he termed "creative capitalism," describing it as "an approach where governments, businesses, and non-profits work together to stretch the reach of market forces so that more people can make a profit, or gain recognition, doing work that eases the world's inequities." The point of creative capitalism was to use market forces to achieve sustainable solutions to pressing issues that would otherwise be impossible. "As we refine and improve this approach," Gates claimed, "there is every reason to believe [that the] engines of change will become larger, stronger, and more efficient."[1]

Since Gates's speech, numerous forward-leaning global business leaders have advocated that the world's most prominent multinational companies focus not merely on turning a profit, but on addressing larger human challenges. This doesn't mean the profit motive is completely absent. At firms like Unilever, the multinational consumer products giant, executives now see "doing good" not merely as a nice thing to do, but as part of their business models, integral to their firm's strategies, growth, profitability, and competitiveness. The agribusiness giant Olam has begun to take action to aid in the effort to realize the United Nations' seventeen Sustainable Development Goals by 2030.[2] For example, they addressed Goal 2 (to "end hunger, achieve food security and improved nutrition and promote sustainable agriculture") by advocating for food security through increasing productivity, supporting smallholder nutrition, and improving water and irrigation usage, among other initiatives aiming to invest in rural development.[3] And they worked on Goal 17 ("Strengthen the means of implementation and revitalize the global partnership for sustainable development") by partnering with customers, donors, and governments focused on sustainable development.[4] Olam also convened a coalition of industry players to identify and seek sustainable solutions to issues related to the agricultural value chain. In the process, the organization has mobilized its 56,000-strong workforce by raising awareness of SDG's.[5]

Companies like Olam understand that government alone cannot solve humanity's problems—we must mobilize the resources of global business as well. And when we do, individual companies benefit, becoming more competitive, innovative, and stable. Describing his firm's pursuit of the sustainable development goals, Unilever CEO Paul Polman has said: "We are creating a much stronger ecosystem that takes our risk away, but it also creates enormous opportunities to broaden our products. Because once you work in partnerships often with governments or with civil society, it creates other opportunities to grow your business."[6]

The UN's Sustainable Development Goals cover big challenges like poverty, inequality, climate change, hunger, and affordable and clean energy. What might a more enlightened brand of capitalism look like when applied to extremism? For one possibility, we might look to Against Violent Extremism (AVE), the world's first and only network of former extremists. The organization was launched in 2011 by Google Ideas, a "think-do" tank funded by Google and devoted to exploring how "technology can enable people to confront threats in the face of conflict, instability, and repression." Four other organizations helped with the launch: the Gen Next Foundation, the Institute for Strategic Dialogue, the Council on Foreign Relations, and the Tribeca Film Institute. AVE grew out of thinking in the NSC brain trust meetings held in Juan Zarate's office; beginning in 2006, we (Juan Zarate, Elliott Abrams, Dan Fried, Karen Volker, Jared Cohen, and others) had speculated how useful it might be to convene former members of the Irish Republican Army, former Al Qaeda members, former gang members, as well as survivors of extremist attacks to serve as perhaps the most credible voices speaking on this issue.

The network of more than 470 members, which today is run by ISD and the Gen Next Foundation, seeks to empower former extremists and survivors to contest and help inoculate youth from extremist ideology. Members have a chance to meet one another, gain access to investment funds, compare ideas, and promote their messages about constructive dialogue and nonviolence. Their voices are especially relevant, since they're grounded in firsthand experiences with extremism. At present, AVE is supporting a number of promising projects, such as "Own Your Brain," a clearinghouse of firsthand stories that reveal how extremists prey on young people's vulnerabilities, and Project Communitas, a program that galvanizes youth across Canada to reject extremism and instead help build their communities.

Against Violent Extremism is an excellent but rare example of the kind of contributions that large multinationals can make in the ideological battle against violent extremism. Although technology firms have lately begun to act against extremism, many other of the largest companies in the United States and elsewhere still haven't stepped up. As a matter of fact, historian Nancy Koehn, a professor at Harvard Business School, told me in early 2017 that she was "hard-pressed" to think of any large multinational that had "taken some action" against extremism.[7]

The reality is that many multinationals have an overriding, economic stake in demolishing the recruitment capabilities of groups like the so-called Islamic State. To win against extremism, we need to mobilize the vast financial resources and expertise of private companies. A number of large companies, including but not limited to those with youth-focused business models, can help themselves and our society by creating and spreading messages that encourage young Muslims—indeed anyone compelled by extremist ideologies—to think about their identities in healthier ways.

Beyond the direct reach they might enjoy with millennials, many large multinationals can also help because they understand this audience and the cutting-edge marketing techniques involved with reaching them better than anyone and, critically, because they possess abundant data about both youth and human behavior generally. Data today is the backbone of business, and it might well also be the most important resource large companies have for CVE, as we can potentially use it to block pernicious content on the global and local levels and track sources of mischief.[8] In addition, large companies possess considerable traditional resources—branch offices, distribution centers, factories, and so on—within local communities. Virtually every part of the fight against extremism affords an important opportunity for these companies, and especially youth-focused ones, to contribute. Just as companies have acted to solve problems ranging from hunger to cancer to education, so now we must inspire them to act against extremism.

As the Unilever example suggests, the fundamental reason that multinationals generally haven't yet stepped up is that they have not perceived it in their economic interests to do so. From a practical standpoint, we probably shouldn't fault them for this. Despite rhetoric about public-spiritedness, most companies won't engage in any social cause if it somehow doesn't serve their interests. For-profit companies are precisely that—for profit. As a *Forbes* article has argued, companies generally derive four important benefits from social good campaigns: they imbue their organizations with purpose, motivate employees, build stronger brands, and connect more closely with the communities they serve. Per the article's title, these benefits are primary reasons "Why More and More Companies Are Doing Social Good."[9]

Even some of our favorite companies that seem to be acting in public-spirited ways will find ways to turn these actions to their benefit. Patagonia, the outdoor lifestyle brand, for instance, drew attention when it mobilized its website to challenge the Trump administration's decision to shrink the size of protected national monuments. Yet Patagonia's action, public-spirited as it was, boosted the company's marketing efforts by affirming its authenticity in the eyes of its core customers.[10]

When it comes to CVE, companies fear wading into issues that they perceive to be "political" or security related. As they see it, they risk sparking controversy or even becoming a target of extremists. And for what? What could the upside possibly be for their businesses?

In fact, there very much *is* an upside. First, as we'll see a bit later in more detail, companies stand to benefit financially from the more favorable risk environment that better security will create. Do you want your supply chain disrupted or your production facility or retail locations attacked? Do you want the local economies in which you do business to stall or contract? When an attack occurs in a city like Barcelona or Boston, the community sustains a financial hit—as do businesses connected with the community. Businesses thrive when the larger economies of which they are a part are thriving. As evidence shows, terrorist acts exact a terrible toll on local and national economies. Further, they polarize and destabilize societies.

By failing to rise up against extremist recruitment, businesses are leaving themselves and their larger economies vulnerable to dislocation, instability, and loss. If you add to that the potentially catastrophic disruptions that could occur when extremist groups steal data and seize control or shut down websites, you realize all that large companies stand to gain by fighting back against extremist recruiting.

But large companies that engaged around CVE would see other potential benefits. Engagement with CVE would make companies stronger, more relevant, and more resilient, even as it allows them to help solve a pressing global problem. Government can use its expertise to lay out an agenda for fighting extremism, but businesses can leverage their resources to transform the environment in local communities, so that kids no longer find extremist ideology so appealing. Extremism *is* a "normal" or "safe" issue for large companies to address, like public health, education, or the environment currently are. If you lead, manage, or work in a large corporation, rest assured that your organization *can* make a difference. And your organization will have much to gain in the process.

TOO HOT TO HANDLE

I first understood the potential that existed for large private and public companies to help in 2004, before I had formed my full theory of extremism as a cultural and ideological system. I was at the National Security Council and working on the State Department's Broader Middle East and North Africa Initiative. As part of my work, I spoke with representatives of the World Bank and other global business leaders about how to move ahead on BMENA priorities. I had several conversations with colleagues on the NSC, including Peter Feaver, Mike Doran, Elliott Abrams, Will Inboden, Steve Slick, and Heidi Avery, about how we needed to get American business leaders to understand that they shared the U.S. government's devotion to democracy and the rule of law, and that we all needed to work together to inculcate these values in the Middle East and North Africa.

Those discussions in turn led my colleagues in the National Security Council's Office of Combating Terrorism and me to another idea: What if we could find global, U.S.-based companies that could help us stop Al Qaeda's ideology? In a series of conversations at the White House and a nearby café, we brainstormed companies that we felt might be interested in taking up this mission as part of their community or "corporate social responsibility" activities. We generated a long list of brands that served millennials, including giants like McDonald's, Coca-Cola, and Microsoft, as well as others like Ben & Jerry's, Nike, Hershey, and Dunkin' Donuts. Perhaps, we thought, some of these companies might want to use a portion of their profits to help fund youth protection programs. But that was just the beginning. In one memorable conversation, I joined Todd Hinnen and Maren Brooks of Juan Zarate's team to conceive recommendations for bringing the corporate sector on board. Crammed into Todd's tiny office in the Old Executive Office Building in Washington, D.C., with the door open to catch Juan as he came back from a meeting, we fantasized about getting companies on our list to band together and work with us on a wide array of programs related to Muslim youth, including mentorship programs built along the lines of the Big Brother Big Sister model; television advertisements featuring diverse American voices; an "emergency" hot line for youth and parents; public service announcements for feature films, with a number to text to learn more about radicalization; and a *Shark Tank*–like show that allowed youth to share their ideas for stopping violent ideology's appeal. We envisioned galvanizing these companies by inviting their CEOs to the White House to meet with President Bush.

This wasn't pie-in-the-sky thinking. Immediately after 9/11, the

American private sector had participated broadly in helping the country recover from the terrorist attacks. Patriotic sentiment was coursing through the country, and business executives and employees joined everyone else in wanting to affirm American strength. According to numbers compiled by the Foundation Center, corporations, foundations, and private philanthropists donated at least $2.8 billion to relief efforts during the two years after 9/11, with 38 percent of that coming from foundations and corporations.[11] The largest corporate donor of those tracked by the Foundation Center, ExxonMobil, gave over $16 million, while Citibank, the second largest donor, contributed $15 million. Other large donors included Deutsche Bank Americas Foundation, the GE Foundation, JPMorgan Chase, the Verizon Foundation, and the Coca-Cola Company. Overall, 9/11 was a defining moment in American individual and corporate giving, despite a challenging economy. As Michael Solomon, spokesman for the *Chronicle of Philanthropy*, told CNN Money, "September 11 was the first time there was such an outpouring for an event like that. When [Hurricane] Katrina came along, charities and donors were ready for that moment."[12]

The U.S. government also turned to business, and particularly the entertainment industry, to see if it could help thwart Al Qaeda's recruiting efforts. In November 2001, more than four dozen Hollywood executives representing ABC, NBC, Fox, WB, and other major networks met with top administration officials in a closed-door session to discuss how the entertainment industry could help. The Bush administration didn't seek to dictate content choices to the industry. Rather, it hoped that entertainment companies could simply highlight key themes helpful to the War on Terror.[13] As the *Chicago Tribune* reported, "Among the ideas was the administration's insistence that this conflict is not a war against Islam, but rather a war on terrorism."[14]

The U.S. government also asked video game and digital entertainment companies to consider how they might enhance their model of play so that youth could bolster their identities or learn about extremist efforts to lure them in. Although many companies in other industries, such as children's toys, food and beverage, and financial service expressed interest, my colleagues and I found it surprisingly difficult to get them to involve themselves with the War on Terror's ideological aspects. Some companies, particularly advertising or communications firms, sought payment for their efforts. Although they often did pro bono work in their communities, helping homeless shelters or raising funds to fight cancer, they regarded fighting recruitment as a government prerogative, not a charitable cause. Although they might have been correct, the State Department had no money to contract with private companies on anti-recruitment efforts.

At Fortune 500 companies, executives were willing to aid the hard power component of the war on terrorism, with UPS "flying pallets in to airfields in Iraq and Afghanistan" and Honeywell "conducting repairs and managing supply-chains for the Army and Navy."[15] But when it came to the ideological fight, large multinationals feared that their boards would reject any charitable efforts that seemed to touch foreign policy or religion. President Bush wasn't popular in many Muslim-majority countries where these companies operated, and executives and boards worried that their brand would become tarnished if it became too closely aligned with the Bush administration. They certainly didn't want popular anger with the Bush administration to prompt terrorist attacks against their own facilities abroad. Building an after-school lunch program for kids or contributing funds toward a soccer field in a local community was fine in their minds. So were larger programs to further causes like women's entrepreneurship or earthquake relief in Pakistan.[16] But giving money to an NGO, say, that was setting up an anti-extremist hotline in a local community or making videos urging Muslim kids not to become extremists seemed dangerously "political."

These attitudes persisted for years after 9/11, and they prevail as of this writing. Even as the threat posed by terrorism has intensified, we haven't managed to persuade most multinational corporations to engage in large-scale CVE collaborations with government. In the wake of the 2008 Mumbai hotel bombings, I invited representatives of well-known global hotel chains to discuss investing in prevention programs, including a series of television and print advertising campaigns that targeted local influencers, and a program that encouraged young Muslims to build local chapters in schools to push back against hateful ideology. But the hotel representatives all declined.* In 2010, I met with the CEO of one of India's largest companies and asked if the company could fund advertisements featuring Bollywood stars that would educate kids about extremist ideology. I noted that Richard Gere had launched the Heroes Project in India to create humorous PSAs about using condoms, and that despite the subject's sensitivity, that campaign was highly regarded and had contributed to public awareness and activism. Initially, the CEO expressed interest, but company officials later demurred. In 2012, I inquired whether a major U.S. publisher might donate books on the diversity of Islam so that the State Department, partnering with an Ivy League university, could create a virtual library. The idea was to make it easy for kids to consult these texts online and, through a Harry Potter–inspired interface, to "magically" connect to other, similar writings. We had already lined up a designer to create this space, but we did not have the books. The publisher responded that it "didn't want to be connected with terrorism," and that in its view, there were "bigger" issues around which they wanted to engage.†

---

* Though I should note that there were several exceptions, like the Taj Group, which placed several ads in India, the United States, and elsewhere, implicitly defying violence and terror.

† Later, during the Obama administration, the Department of State went even further. Knowing how vital it was to increase collaboration, it created the Public-Private Partnerships Office, hoping to enlist the corporate sector to assist in solving a variety of problems, including education, women's empowerment, and human trafficking. For more, see the Office of Global Partnerships, U.S. State Department, https://www.state.gov/s/partnerships/mission/.

Since leaving government, I've approached businesses of all kinds as well as private philanthropists and foundations to help fund an NGO dedicated to fighting extremism. Consistently, business leaders and philanthropists opted not to get involved. As Christopher Graves, chairman of Ogilvy Public Relations Worldwide, explained to me, these businesses may simply have overlooked the connection between their brand and fighting extremism. If a corporation is smart, Graves observes, it prioritizes the causes with which it chooses to become associated so that it aligns with brand values.[17]

Brands that serve millennials (and Generation Z)—Starbucks, H&M, Adidas, Apple, to name a few—might seem to possess a strong rationale for funding the fight against extremism. Other large companies might not understand how counter-extremist initiatives correspond to their brand identity or mission. But even for these companies, diversifying their giving portfolios to include support for CVE initiatives might still have value as a public relations move. Millennials, just like the public at large, appreciate and admire companies giving to good causes, for no other reason than it's the right thing to do. And when companies seem too "on strategy," they can seem too calculating and lose their credibility with skeptical customers.[18] Authenticity is not just sought after by young people seeking theological counsel, but by consumers generally.

THE BUSINESS CASE FOR PRIVATE SECTOR ACTION

Bhaskar Chakravorti, a dean at Tufts University's Fletcher School of Law and Diplomacy, has researched corporate motivations for contributing to business sustainability initiatives such as the UN's Sustainable Development Goals. As he and his colleagues have found, "The most frequently cited motivation was the mitigation of business risk from potential disruption of operations, supplies, or reputational damage."[19] Risk mitigation is likewise at the core of the business case for corporate participation and investment in CVE.

The direct costs of terrorist attacks are undeniably high. Following the 9/11 attacks, the *New York Times* tabulated a range of costs accruing from the tragedy. Their analysis found some $55 billion in physical damages to structures, a figure dwarfed by the $123 billion sustained in approximate economic damages. But by the *Times'* estimation, these costs were only the beginning. Setting up the Department of Homeland Security, fighting wars against terror, paying veterans' benefits—together these massive projects cost the country some *$3 trillion* and counting.[20] Such damage wasn't spread equally across the economy. Some sectors, like transportation and tourism, bore a heavier burden. Following the 9/11 attacks, American air travel decreased by about a third, and the increased security hassles lowered demand for air travel by more than 7 percent.[21]

As the Brookings Institution has concluded, "violent extremism poses a clear threat to companies, employees, and customers." In 2016, after attacks in Egypt, Lebanon, Mali, and France, American travel bookings declined by 10 percent, affecting "more than $7.8 billion in travel spending." In the aftermath of the Paris attacks in November 2016, a single airline, Air France–KLM, "lost an estimated $73.5 million." Companies now must bear the costs of terrorism insurance—well over half of American companies carry it. As the report notes, "Companies are becoming increasingly aware of the potential direct and indirect losses they can suffer from violent extremist attacks."[22]

As large as they are, direct costs, including infrastructure damages, disturbances in stock markets, and increased insurance premiums don't capture terrorism's full economic impact. Most costs incurred from terrorism—including losses sustained from decreases in foreign direct investment (FDI), international trade, capital flows, and tourism—are indirect and far more difficult to measure.[23] Since the November 13, 2015, terrorist attacks on Paris, open-border policies and immigrant flows have come under siege across Europe. The protectionist upsurge prompted Britain's departure from the European Union, which in turn has left the larger Eurozone economy in peril. Beyond the tremendous human costs of closed borders, the European Commission estimated that the bill to reinstate border checks and passport controls could run as high as 18 billion euros ($20 billion) per year. Reinstatement of passport checks will cost between 2.5–4.5 billion euros in administrative time, and increased police and other staff would reach a price tag of nearly 1.1 billion euros. Even more, the French government estimates "that the return of border checks and passport controls could cost Europe as much as 100 billion euros ($110 billion) over a decade, knocking 0.8% of Europe's GDP by 2025 in the worst case."[24]

When the United States closed its borders after 9/11, the automaker Ford couldn't import components from Canada and Mexico. The company had to shut down assembly lines, leading the company to miss its fourth-quarter 2001 output targets by 13 percent.[25] Increases in security and surveillance across the Schengen Zone* also result in waning productivity—again, difficult to measure. Furthermore, a staggering 70–80 percent of the European economy is based on consumer consumption. In the wake of the Paris attack, with Europeans tightening their belts and tourists staying home, at least some portion of the tremendous decrease of revenues at cinemas, restaurants, hotels, museums, and small boutiques undoubtedly owed to terrorism.[26]

It goes on: the Chartered Institute of Procurement and Supply noted in 2015 that European supply chains have grown increasingly unstable in recent years due to the rise of terrorism and the influx of refugees.[27] While in 2003 the risk for disruption in the flow of supplies stood at around 40 percent, by 2015 it hovered at around

---

* The Schengen Zone denotes the region in which twenty-six European countries have officially abolished their internal borders, functioning as a single region for travel purposes.

80 percent.[28] The institute also found that European supply chains were quite possibly accruing billions in extra costs, as the influx of refugees from war-torn Middle Eastern countries was prompting the closure of internal borders. One expert, John Glen, of the Cranfield School of Management, remarked that "the European migrant crisis and conflicts in the Middle East mean that the risks are getting closer and feeling more acute," even though they have traditionally seemed minimal.[29] In the Middle East, by contrast, terrorism from the so-called Islamic State comprised the chief cause of supply chain disturbances in Tunisia, Bahrain, Kuwait, and Turkey, as these countries have been forced to use more expensive oceanic routes to move products.

When terrorism continues unchecked over a long period, the impact on economic growth can mount. As one commentator has noted, government spending on "drones, cruise missiles and surveillance technology . . . [leaves] less available for private investment in productivity-enhancing plants and equipment. Insurance premiums (and losses) also rise, as do regulations that inhibit the freewheeling entrepreneurship that underpins healthy long-term growth."[30] A 2017 report by the Institute for Economics and Peace quantifies peace and its benefits, asserting that "the notion that war is good for the economy has been disproved, and the economic benefits of peace are being recognized globally." The cost of preventing violence globally stands at $9.46 trillion per year, "almost double the size of the world's agriculture sector."[31]

As bad as the economic threat posed by terrorism is around the world, it's getting worse. The Institute for Economics and Peace estimated the global costs from terrorism in 2011 at about $12 billion, a conservative number that represented primarily direct costs. That rose steadily in the years that followed, reaching $89.6 billion in 2015, a number that significantly surpassed the 2001 figure.[32] In the years to come, I expect the potential costs to be greater still, assuming no concerted action against recruitment is taken. The possibilities are frightening. So far, terrorists have not unleashed a radiological attack on a major city. What if they do? What kinds of economic dislocations will result? So far, they have not targeted a major logistics hub. What would happen to national and local economies and to individual corporations if terrorists attacked the Strait of Hormuz, conduit for about a fifth of global oil traffic? What would happen if terrorists hit major ports, or an electrical grid?

Such scenarios are not alarmist. A 2016 study by the Center for Strategic and International Studies found that a majority of people in the eight countries it surveyed believed that "it is likely that violent extremist groups will acquire and use weapons of mass destruction in their lifetime."[33] As one observer has remarked, private companies should "accept the likelihood of such attacks" to supply chains and take action to mitigate risk.[34] More generally, leaders in the private sector should recognize that terrorism will only worsen if nothing is done about extremist ideology and recruitment. No matter where in the world their business is located, they will have a much more difficult time operating five or ten years from now.

Skeptics might counter that extremism constitutes a simple security risk, and hence falls under government's purview.* It's true that countering extremism entails assuring our society's basic safety—a unifying, nonpolitical cause if there ever was one. But extremism isn't just an ordinary security risk. It's a vast and systemic threat. Between 2014 and 2016, the so-called Islamic State alone "conducted or inspired more than 140 terrorist attacks in 29 countries *other* than Iraq and Syria."[35]

Extremists don't simply want to win control over a certain geographic area. They're not trying to defeat a single state or army.

---

* But as Bhaskar Chakravorti reminded me, the matter is more complex: "Countering violent extremism is a classic 'public good.' Private parties, individuals and companies, collectively benefit from investments made in it but have an incentive to free-ride because they get the benefits of CVE whether or not they pay. In other words, there is market failure. This is why governments are considered the natural 'owners' of this 'good.'" Bhaskar Chakravorti, e-mail with the author, April 15, 2018.

They're seeking to undermine and destroy the entire intellectual, political, legal, and cultural order that has underpinned capitalism's rise since the mid-eighteenth century. They're taking on Western civilization. And guess what? They're succeeding. The more extremism expands, the more the legitimacy of our system is contested and corroded. The very fact that countries affected by terrorism can't tarnish the appeal of groups like the so-called Islamic State establishes, in the extremists' eyes and those of potential recruits, the weakness of Western civilization.

A small-scale attack by the so-called Islamic State in the United States or Europe might do limited economic damage, but it does just a little bit more to undermine faith in our governing principles and institutions. When governments are forced to clamp down in their efforts to fight terror, our system of individual freedoms, free markets, limited government, scientific rationality, and so on takes a hit.

Private sector organizations benefit from the liberal order that sprang up in the West and that still largely governs global exchange. Thus, these organizations must regard extremist ideology as a mortal threat to the economic system in which they thrive. By joining the fight out of self-interest, they serve the public good. They must affirm that Western civilization is strong, valuable, and intact.

My second response to the contention that fighting extremist recruiting falls under the government's exclusive purview is that the public sector simply doesn't have the means to fight recruiting on its own. This isn't a Cold War "battle of ideas" we're waging, but twenty-first-century ideological warfare. To win, we need to surround kids with positive ideas, extending our influence to all areas of their lives, online and off, at school and at home. That's a monumental task, and the private sector—and specifically large, global firms—simply must be part of the equation.

The UN Sustainable Development Goals recognize the importance of business and government working *together* to address pressing global problems. In fact, Goal 17, "revitalize the global partnerships for sustainable development," articulates precisely what this book has been arguing vis-à-vis extremism: That "[a] successful sustainable development agenda requires partnerships between governments, the private sector and civil society."[36] To address issues like supply chain inefficiencies, food waste, and the welfare of small local suppliers, Unilever partnered with a large number of NGOs and governmental organizations. As the Fletcher School of Law and Diplomacy's Chakravorti has acknowledged, not all firms have the resources to work with dozens or (even hundreds) of diverse partners. And yet companies with "more limited resources" might still focus on building a smaller number of "strategic relationships, establishing trust and building bridges across natural organizational chasms."[37]

The benefits of doing so extend far beyond risk mitigation. As scholars like Chakravorti and Harvard Business School's Michael Porter have observed, adversity often is a boon for innovation, entrepreneurship, and competitive advantage.[38] In an interview with me, Chakravorti further explained that partnering strategically to address pressing social issues can help companies gain expertise and build partnerships at the local level, allowing them to execute better. Starbucks's partnership with an NGO called YouthBuild USA, which trains at-risk youth and gives them access to education, mentorship, and development resources, has helped it to address its staffing needs as it has opened retail locations in underprivileged areas. Of course, Starbucks has experienced setbacks when it comes to diversity and inclusion. Notably, in April 2018, Starbucks sparked international controversy after one of its employees had two black men arrested for loitering in a Philadelphia store. The following month, Starbucks took bold action, announcing it would close eight thousand of its national stores to provide diversity and sensitivity training.[39] This was an important step in affirming the brand's values and determining whether such training can reduce future such incidents. Global firms like Starbucks that take decisive action in addressing systemic issues within a community, whether it's inclusion, diversity, or extremist narratives, will not only embed themselves more firmly in the local market but gain more insight into customer needs and perspectives. By cementing their relationships with local partners, they'll have the "boots on the ground" they need to execute better as employers and marketers. This will in turn expose them to new ideas, mind-sets, knowledge, and business opportunities.

Companies will also likely find all kinds of "unmet needs," to adopt Chakravorti's terminology, to which they might apply their own "unneeded resources." A case in point: the abundance of corporate data mentioned earlier. Companies like, Coca-Cola, Twitter, and many others possess vast amounts of information about consumers—much more than government agencies do. Using these vast sums of data and metadata analysis can help a local NGO understand how to best create youth-specific interventions. Coke already has information about the kinds of ads to which kids respond in, say, Boston's South End or Cairo's Heliopolis, and NGOs creating videos or school programs that help educate youth about extremist messaging can benefit from that information. Deploying this data, we'll be in a much better position to develop messages that help youth resolve identity crises in healthier ways.

Beyond innovation, taking action on CVE would prove a boon to companies' brand reputations. Many Americans now expect businesses to stake out positions on public issues,* and corporate leaders are increasingly perceiving social activism as a core business imperative, driven in many cases by pressure from employees, custom-

---

* In one recent study, 43 percent of respondents agreed that "CEOs have responsibility to speak up about issues that are important to society." Millennials were more likely than other generational cohorts to be "favorable toward CEOs taking public positions on hotly debated current issues." "The Dawn of CEO Activism," Weber Shandwick and KRC Research, June 2016, http://www.webershandwick.com/uploads/news/files/the-dawn-of-ceo-activism.pdf. "Nearly nine in 10 global consumers (86%) believe they are a powerful force in influencing companies today. Even more global executives (91%) agree. Such power has expanded dramatically in recent years, as nearly seven in 10 consumers (68%) report that companies are influenced more today by consumer opinions than five years ago. Six in 10 executives (59%) have observed the same phenomenon." "The Company Behind the Brand II: In Goodness We Trust," Weber Shandwick, February 2017, http://webershandwick.scot/wp-content/uploads/2017/02/CBB-report-FINAL.pdf.

ers, and social media. Tim Cook, CEO of Apple, spoke out against the state of Indiana's "Religious Freedom Restoration Act" on the grounds that it discriminated against gays and lesbians.[40] When the state of North Carolina passed a bill restricting the rights of transgender people, PayPal and Deutsche Bank pulled back from business investments they had planned in the state, and executives at other firms publicly wrote to express their opposition.

Following the election of Donald Trump as president, companies such as Anheuser-Busch and Airbnb broadcast Super Bowl ads celebrating immigrants and diversity, respectively. Likewise, in the wake of President Trump's initial executive order temporarily banning people from seven Muslim-majority nations from entering the United States, corporate activism exploded. Executives at many large companies became vocal critics, with 160 biotech leaders signing a letter condemning the measure. Starbucks's CEO, Howard Schultz, announced that "he planned to hire 10,000 refugees in 75 countries over five years."[41] As Professor Aaron Chatterji from Duke University's Fuqua School of Business was quoted as saying, "Silence used to be the default posture," but thanks to political polarization, it's now "a choose-a-side mentality. The middle is harder to occupy. And with the proliferation of social media, it's kind of like a microphone that's always on. If you're not speaking out, it's more conspicuous."[42]

Salesforce's CEO Marc Benioff has spoken of a "third [political] party emerging in this country, which is the party of CEOs."[43] Whether or not that's true, Nancy Koehn sees such corporate activism as more than just a passing fad. Pointing to CEOs like Schultz, Unilever's Paul Polman (who likes to say, rightly, that he represents one of the world's biggest NGOs), and John Mackey of Whole Foods, she observes that more CEOs are practicing values-based leadership, basing their brands and their value propositions on their beliefs. This is "not because they woke up altruistic," Koehn notes, but because "they believe it's good business, and that it's the future."[44] As she further explains, a combination of structural forces prod large corporations to go beyond conventional thinking about "corporate social responsibility" and to take a stronger "activist" stance on issues. These forces include shrinking governmental budgets, corporations' increasingly global nature, and the rise of millennials who may feel "disenfranchised at the ballot box but don't feel disenfranchised as consumers."

Other experts make similar points. In a 2018 *Harvard Business Review* cover story, Chatterji and Michael W. Toffel argue that "CEO activism is part of a societal shift that some have called 'the politicization of everything.' The ideological polarization in our political system—fueled by social media—has created a highly-charged environment in which business leaders are increasingly on the spot to offer their views on complex issues with which they might have little experience." It goes beyond offering views: leaders must also take action. For example, in the wake of the devastating Parkland attack, Edward Stack, the CEO of sporting goods giant Dick's, announced that his company would take a stand by no longer carrying assault weapons or selling firearms to people younger than twenty-one. Even after a backlash by his own employees, Stack held firm, stating "we suspected that speaking out would have a negative impact on our business. But this was about our values and standing up for what we think is right."[45] Similarly, Nordstrom pulled Ivanka Trump's clothing line from its stores after deciding that Trump had become a controversial brand.

With corporate activism and social awareness becoming the "new normal," corporate leaders should regard waging the battle against extremist ideology as a reputational opportunity on par with causes like fighting poverty, illiteracy, environmental degradation, or AIDS/HIV. A new international study by Unilever reveals that a third of all consumers are now choosing to buy from brands they believe are doing social or environmental good, based on their social and environmental impact, and that an estimated 966-billion-euro opportunity exists for brands that make their sustainability credentials clear.[46] As companies gravitate toward causes that relate directly to their businesses, why wouldn't a firm like Chevron, whose facilities are subject to attack by terrorist groups,* step up against extremism? Wouldn't it make sense for an insurance company like Aetna to fund a national program dedicated to building out CVE programs? After all, the company already insures customers against terrorist attacks and helps customers understand security risks,[47] so it would benefit financially and reputationally from helping to prevent them. Why wouldn't Sony, PepsiCo, Frito-Lay, and other international brands that market to youth want to be perceived as courageously standing up for kids' well-being? Conversely, what brand wants to see its advertising budgets funding campaigns that appear next to extremist content online?

In fact, hundreds of popular brands ceased advertising on YouTube and Google when they discovered that their products and services appeared alongside hate-promoting, extremist groups. As a 2017 *Business Insider* profile detailed, "more than 250 brands—from L'Oréal, to McDonald's, Audi, and HSBC—had suspended their campaigns from YouTube (and in some cases, Google's display ad platform that serves ads to third-party websites) until Google could give them assurances that their ads would not appear next to videos containing hate speech, promoting terror organizations, or other obviously unsafe content for their brands to be associated with."[48] Companies are clearly fearful of being linked in any way with hate groups (including white supremacist as well as other extremist groups), and it is not hard to imagine that they would, in the future, take steps beyond a simple boycott. In fact, such an aggressive response

* Chevron's facilities in Nigeria were attacked multiple times in 2016, including an attack on May 4, 2016, that affected "approximately 35,000 barrels per day (bpd) of Chevron's net crude oil production," and another on May 26, 2016, that caused Chevron to temporarily shut down all of its onshore activities. James Burgess, "Shell Evacuates Oil Personnel After Chevron Platform Bombing," *Oil Price,* May 9, 2016, https://oilprice.com/Latest-Energy-News/World-News/Shell-Evacuates-Oil-Personnel-After-Chevron-Platform-Bombing.html; Ruth Maclean, "Niger Delta Avengers Militants Shut Down Chevron Oil Facility," *Guardian,* May 26, 2016, https://www.theguardian.com/world/2016/may/26/niger-delta-avengers-militants-shut-down-chevron-oil-facility.

to contentious "hot-button issues" like extremism may soon become standard practice—a welcome development, to say the least.[49]

In sum, supporting CVE is both a necessity in today's risk environment and a huge, untapped opportunity. But there's a final point to consider: engagement with CVE doesn't have to bust the budgets of individual companies. Many firms already have data. They already have marketing expertise. They already have logistical capacities. It would cost potentially very little to leverage these assets in new ways relevant to CVE. Companies just need to understand the opportunities that exist in the markets they serve, and then commit to do what it takes to realize them.

GETTING DOWN TO BUSINESS

So, what precisely should *your* business do? The answer will vary depending on the kind of company you are, your industry, your size, and so on. As a general rule, five categories of companies have the most to offer—and to gain—from engagement with CVE. Technology companies (like Facebook or Apple), international youth-oriented brands (like Xbox and H&M), and global or regional brands catering to Muslims (players in the growing "halal" market discussed in chapter 4) should all engage with CVE, as they all directly impact how Muslim kids form their identities. The core businesses of these companies either relate to consumers most directly targeted for recruitment by extremists or the technological means extremists use to target youth. What might happen if other large organizations launched a global CVE campaign that integrated voices from local communities, and that extended for a period of years? It's nice when companies sponsor large benefit concerts in support of a cause, but imagine the impact of a campaign that appealed directly to youth, that incorporated celebrities, that mobilized the deep marketing insights that companies have about youth, and that didn't quickly vanish? The effect would be a much-needed *normalization* of conversation about extremism in the social world of youth.

Some youth-oriented brands are uniquely positioned to influence youth: those belonging to professional sporting teams and leagues. For soccer, the British Premier League has unparalleled global reach, and boasts star Muslim athletes like Paul Pogba, Mesut Özil, and Mohamed Salah. In the United States, the NFL traditionally has been active in youth initiatives, investing "more than $325 million to grants, health and fitness programming for youth and media time for public service announcements."[50] The NFL also has many Muslim athletes who might serve as credible peer role models for Muslim youth, including Aqib Talib and Mohamed Sanu. Imagine how powerful it might be if these figures began making public statements about identity and religious diversity, or if the NFL unveiled a program to teach diversity in the schools.

A fourth class of companies that should engage are multinationals whose products probably don't bear on identity formation among Muslim youth directly, but who nevertheless exert a strong presence in their daily lives: companies like Gannett (which, in addition to newspapers in most American states, has a major presence in the United Kingdom), Viacom, and Starbucks. A final, much broader category of company that should engage are those whose supply chains, sales, or other key aspects of operations are directly jeopardized by terrorist attacks. Firms like Amazon, FedEx, and UPS, for instance, have a clear stake in fighting back against extremist recruitment, as do, arguably, entire industries such as hospitality, commodities, and air travel.

The many companies that fall into these five categories can contribute in four basic ways. First, as I've said, companies can contribute their *data*. We desperately need deeper insights into youth that go beyond generic demographics. Think of the vast troves of consumer data that global giants like Amazon or Mars Inc. have about changing desires and obsessions, and also questions such as how people in general change their minds, how they turn ideas into action, or how they resist some ideas but not others. Or think of the data that Comcast, Verizon, Google, Samsung, or YouTube have about the media habits of youth. As of this writing, little of this corporate data has been used to support CVE efforts. Imagine if we had a global clearinghouse of CVE data contributed by private companies across an array of industries like utilities, retail, consumer packaged goods, and so on. Imagine if experts in a variety of academic fields could come together to interpret that data and collaborate with a grassroots coalition of CVE organizations leading to creating new CVE initiatives. Imagine if multiple companies within industries banded together to share their data, eliminating legitimate concerns about competitors "free-riding" to their own bottom line advantage. All of this would give us a monumental advantage over extremist groups, who possess little if any data. And compared with the price of military responses, the cost would be negligible. If grassroots actors create a coalition and companies and government work with them to execute on needs, concerns about a "big brother" government using data to watch and control us would be mitigated, because NGOs and others from civil society would be the ones driving it.

Second, private sector organizations must contribute financial support either to sponsor anti-extremist programming and initiatives directly or to fund NGOs that are executing these initiatives. Large corporations and corporate foundations already have significant resources at their disposal. According to the Conference Board, the average large company participating in its survey dispensed more than $21 million in 2015 to NGOs or direct initiatives.[51] And companies routinely make meaningful commitments over many years to specific causes. Starbucks has partnered with Bono and Bobby Shriver's NGO (RED) for eight years, and also contributed more than $14 million to the Geneva-based financing institution Global Fund, to help finance HIV/AIDS prevention, education, and treatment programs.[52] The company has also invested more than $70 million in collaborative farmer programs and activities, including C.A.F.E. (Coffee and Farmer Equity) practices, farmer support centers, farmer loans, and forest carbon projects.[53] To scale up the grassroots programs I described in the previous chapter, we need this kind of funding—not just from Starbucks, but from dozens of large companies.

You might wonder why government shouldn't at least pay for CVE initiatives by itself. Doesn't it have the biggest pockets of all? It does, but almost all of that funding is designated for traditional military and law enforcement interventions against terrorist groups. Even if more government funding were available, corporate spending would still hold significant advantages. Governmental budgeting processes are slow and cumbersome. Every dollar has to be allocated months, if not years, in advance and justified transparently in keeping with government's fiduciary responsibility to taxpayers. The real world—and certainly the world of millennials—doesn't move according to the rhythms of government bureaucracy. When something happens in the world relevant to Muslim millennials, we need to respond swiftly. That's what the bad guys are doing—they're reacting instantaneously, within hours, to exploit news events. Private sector money can help us seed and scale up CVE programs so that we're not always reacting and playing catch-up.

Private sector money can also help us become more entrepreneurial in developing CVE programs, in ways and to an extent that are as yet unknown. When I served as special representative, I had a budget and the license to take risks, but such an arrangement was extremely rare. Inside government bureaucracies, officials are subject to intense political scrutiny regarding allocation of funds, and they get more credit for avoiding risks and doing what is already known to work. We'll never develop strong, grassroots CVE programs with a mentality steeped in politics and risk aversion. Private sector money allows for far more flexibility and responsiveness.

PROVIDING THE KNOWLEDGE TO COUNTER EXTREMISM

A third, critically important way that private sector organizations can join the fight is by lending unconventional skills and expertise. I've already discussed the need for experts in communications, religious studies, psychology, anthropology, marketing, consumer culture, social media, mobile technology, and so on when it comes to government programs. But we also need artists, writers, comedians, filmmakers, and other creative people who understand millennials and can help us reach them. Some of these people work inside government, but by and large, this talent resides in the private sector.

The same is true of technological expertise: Silicon Valley has vast expertise and resources that it could use to augment government efforts. But companies can contribute many other forms of expertise, too. When it comes to marketing, large U.S. corporations and the communications firms that work with them have the world's best data, talent, social listening tools, and behavior-change tools. Even if they are not communications companies per se, most large firms have marketing departments and extensive experience performing consumer research and executing promotional campaigns. To take but one example, why should government employees create a CVE mobile campaign on its own? In other areas, governments and NGOs are turning to private sector communications firms. In Turkey, Ogilvy Public Relations created an ingenious "flashlight" app to help women combat domestic violence. If the icon is tapped by a man, the phone's light turns on as he'd expect. The female user of the app, however, knows to shake the phone in a certain way. When she does so in an emergency situation, the app alerts a preset group of people that she is or is about to become a domestic violence victim. Pretty cool, right? As Ogilvy Public Relations chairman Chris Graves related, this app and programs like it didn't come out of thin air. They required considerable knowledge about the app's consumers, the cultural context, technology, and so on. Government can't afford to build up such expertise from scratch when it already exists in the private sector.[54]

One example of a promising project that could benefit from corporate expertise is an app under development by the group Against Violent Extremism. As the Institute for Strategic Dialogue's CEO Sasha Havlicek has told me, this app would connect former extremists from across the globe so that they could support one another with expertise, tools, and ideas. More than that, the app would build on ISD's pioneering direct online interventions program—Counter-Conversations—matching former extremists, survivors of extremist attacks, and trained counselors with individuals publicly posting support for violent extremist action and ideologies online. ISD has already run a scaled pilot of this scheme with financial support from Facebook, building a unique, semiautomated methodology to identify people harboring extremist and violent sentiment at scale, and training formers, survivors, and social workers to engage with these individuals directly through Facebook Messenger. But with more industry expertise and funding, the project might have been even more ambitious and executed for longer than the six months that resources allowed.

Larger companies possess other kinds of expertise that in many cases equals or exceeds what government can mobilize. In her book *I Believe in Zero,* U.S. Fund for UNICEF CEO Caryl Stern tells of how in the wake of the 2010 Haiti earthquake, her organization needed to supply fifty thousand emergency survival kits containing toiletries and other items to children who had been separated from their families. And here's the catch: the packets needed to be organized and shipped within seventy-two hours. Stern's organization raised money for kids. It wasn't set up to solicit and ship physical goods. Stern didn't have expertise in logistics. But she knew an organization that did.

She called executives at UPS, the global shipping company, telling them, "'You guys are the logistics experts. What do I do?'" Hours later, a UPS executive arrived in Stern's office to help her tackle the problem. The company made available one of its warehouses in New Jersey where the kits could be assembled as well as a plane to take them down to Miami, where they would be loaded on a ship. The kits were packaged and shipped on time.[55] This is precisely the kind of partnership that government and private sector actors need to maintain when it comes to CVE, with one difference: We need such partnerships to exist at scale and to persist over extended periods.

Beyond specific expertise, we need the entrepreneurial energy that the private sector brings to problems. Even if government actors could dispense money more freely and fluidly than they traditionally have, they still aren't used to thinking in fresh ways about issues. They tend toward stasis, using conventional practices, concepts, talent, and vendors, and seldom veering outside them. Government officials remain in their narrow silos and don't know what they don't know. Private sector people, by contrast, tend as a group to be more results oriented, since their career advancement and bonuses typically hinge on whether they make their numbers. I acknowledge these statements are broad and may seem unfair, but while neither sector is perfect, government alone does not have what it will take to respond in the moment to extremist recruitment efforts. The private sector's dynamism can help.

MORE CREDIBLE CVE MESSAGES

Critically, private sector businesses can contribute by helping to create credible CVE content. NGOs active in the CVE space *crave* private support for content. That's because interventions of any kind feel different when they come from private actors as opposed to government. Brands like Target or McDonald's are already embedded in kids' lives, thanks to billions of dollars spent on marketing. These brands are known and trusted. If they were to build a community center for the purpose, say, of taking kids off the street, its meaning would be different than if a municipal or federal government built the same building. Members of the public would perceive the government-sponsored community center as less welcoming, less personal, and possibly less trusted than the corporate-sponsored facility. Brands have personality. They have color. They trigger emotions. Governments generally don't (or at least, they don't trigger positive emotions). When it comes to CVE interventions, private sector gestures are thus by definition better able to connect with their intended audiences than those overtly associated with government.

One unique asset that many brands have are high-profile spokespeople who possess credible brands in their own right. The private sector has scarcely begun to mobilize entertainment celebrities, sports figures, recording artists, and others to counter violent extremism. Beyond celebrity appeals, companies often have wide latitude in how they deliver credible messages in brand-sensitive ways. Gap, for instance, might wish to partner with Muslim fashion mavens to help change ideas about the compatibility of Muslim and modern identities throughout the year, not just during Ramadan. LEGO might send affirmative messages about diversity by developing an entire focus area around religious architecture, allowing kids the opportunity to build not just churches or mosques but temples, stupas, synagogues, and so on. Disney, Netflix, and HBO might wish to deploy story lines and merchandise for children that promote messages of inclusion and religious respect, presenting more heroes that are either non-Western or Muslim or both. For a good example of what is possible in the entertainment industry, see Disney's *Zootopia,* a film that in the words of one observer not only promoted "values of tolerance, inclusion and equality," as many children's films do, but "highlights how and why that equality is challenged."* If efforts like this abounded, we would witness a much-needed *normalization* of conversation about extremism in the social world of youth.

Companies can also turn to advertising to deliver powerful CVE messages. During the 2016 presidential election, Fiat Chrysler came out with a striking TV spot for its 2017 Jeep Cherokee model. In a political campaign season marred by xenophobia and implicit and blatant anti-Muslim sentiment, the ad showed images of America's ethnic, lifestyle, and religious diversity while conveying the message, "What Unites us is stronger than what divides us." Notably, it featured Muslim convert Yusuf Islam (formerly Cat Stevens) singing his classic song, "If You Want to Sing Out, Sing Out." Beyond its direct political meaning in the context of an election, this ad's twin messages of diversity and unification helped in the war of ideas by taking issue with the extremist narrative of an inevitable "clash of civilizations." The ad normalized for a mainstream audience the notion that diversity and America go hand in hand. If the U.S. government had put out this ad, the message would have fallen flat with young people. But the ad seemed more authentic coming from a brand like Chrysler. As Fiat Chrysler's global chief marketing officer, Olivier François, explained, the idea of "Free to Be" "embraces two important core tenants [*sic*] of the brand, freedom and adventure, that any Jeep brand marketing campaign is intended to deliver."[56]

Was the ad risky for the company? Not necessarily. Fiat Chrysler's defense of our system against the forces that would question it was done in a way that could help it sell products. As a marketing executive at Dannon recently observed, "We're in an environment where, wherever you stand on the political spectrum, I think it's clear to all of us right now that we're looking to actors outside of our government to help drive the social justice agenda."[57] In such an envi-

* This research was conducted with assistance from students at the Fletcher School of Law and Diplomacy, Tufts University, December 2017.

ronment, it might arguably be riskier for some companies *not* to take a political stand. Their brands might come across as less engaged or relevant as compared with their more activist peers. In the event of a miscue, these companies would lack a history of activism and clearly defined brand allegiances that might cause customers to give them the benefit of the doubt.

We need private companies to help change the conversation and articulate our civilization's ethos, values, and way of life. Imagine if a hundred times each day Muslim youth heard trusted brands telling them that they *are* welcomed, that many kinds of identity are accepted in our society, that there *is* room in the modern world for them as Muslims. Imagine, too, how powerful it would be if dozens or hundreds of companies found creative, brand-appropriate ways to mainstream religious diversity, not just within Islam but all religions. The extremists would have a far harder time gaining a foothold in the minds of young Muslims. Remember: extremist groups are brands competing not only with voices of mutual respect but also frequently with each other. A deluge of appealing CVE messages would leave them outnumbered and outgunned, their voices paling in comparison to those of so many other trusted, influential brands. Muslim youth (and non-Muslims as well) would come away not necessarily with more clarity about their identities, but with more understanding of which solutions to their internal struggles are correct, righteous, and healthy, and which decidedly are not.

PARTNERING ON CVE

Many companies are already working on social action projects that in some way come close to CVE. It would take relatively little for them to advance those efforts a bit further to make a difference in Muslim communities. Sephora has publicly supported diversity in the modeling profession. Why not extend that to talk specifically about religious diversity?[58] KIND snacks has undertaken a storytelling program to promote the virtue of kindness and encourage people to "rediscover our shared humanity." Why not extend this program into the CVE domain, looking at the demographic of Muslim youth and applying the ethic of kindness in specifically religious contexts?[59] What if MasterCard, which has partnered with aid organizations to develop digital vouchers, prepaid debit cards, and other instruments to help refugees, layered on CVE messaging and related educational opportunities, helping inoculate these same refugees to extremist narratives? What if Airbnb, which has helped refugees find housing through its Open Homes platform, did the same?[60]

Although some might disparage public-private partnerships, associating them with outsourcing practices that cheapen the quality of public services, in fact public-private partnerships have often served the public interest well while simultaneously generating profits for companies. During the Cold War, the federal government "partnered with the necessary private sector organizations" to help America land men on the moon, and it outsourced scientific research for the war on cancer to private sector groups.[61] Since 9/11, the government has relied on partnerships with logistics companies, military contractors, and food service companies to supply our armed services and wage the War on Terror.[62] It's unrealistic to think that government will possess all the knowledge it needs to pursue public objectives. Given the weight of government bureaucracies, as well as their political loyalties, it's also unrealistic to think that governments will always move first to serve evolving public needs. When it came to food safety or regulation of tobacco, for instance, the medical industry pushed for much-needed change. And with the coming of the Internet, citizens, businesses, and business leaders feel empowered as never before to pursue the public good, even if they're not always successful in the end (witness Mark Zuckerberg's pledge of $100 million to Newark, New Jersey's public schools).

As regards CVE, public-private partnerships could accomplish a great deal. What if the U.S. government and a network of radio stations worldwide partnered to roll out large numbers of podcasts that targeted youth and informed them about extremism and radicalization? In fact, what if government partnered with entertainment companies of all kinds to mainstream CVE content?

Government can and should facilitate public-private partnerships that provide economic benefits to the private sector. For instance, it should consider providing tax incentives to companies that agree to assist it with CVE programs and initiatives, and it should consider paying technology companies directly to take down bad content faster, more accurately, and more comprehensively. Governments might also provide security (via subsidies for local law enforcement within the United States and overseas, as well as grants) for people outside government who are working on CVE. Right now, individuals must take personal risks to do this work, and for some, the danger proves too great.

As much as government might do to make public-private partnerships easier and more attractive, these arrangements are not the only ones that private companies might consider. They should also explore how they might partner with one another (private-private partnerships) to fight back against extremist ideology. What if entire industries came together behind CVE? What if hospitality companies partnered with an NGO like the YMCA to build community resilience programs in local communities? What if news companies collectively launched initiatives to spotlight Muslim role models who are strong, diverse, and public-spirited? Companies like Accenture, Coca-Cola, Chevron, Total, BP, Gucci, Halliburton, and Bayer are already coming together in coalitions and partnerships to make progress on other issues, like poverty, malaria, girls' education, child marriage, clean water, HIV, and tuberculosis. They can do the same with CVE.

TACKLING A NEW MISSION

Earlier I mentioned H&M, one of the most beloved millennial-friendly brands routinely mentioned on "top 10" lists next to Apple, Sony, Samsung, and Starbucks.[63] One reason may be H&M's consistent, long-term engagement with causes dear to millennials' hearts. In 2008, H&M teamed up with local NGOs in Bangladesh to develop a series of short films to teach workers about their rights. In 2015, they expanded this program to India.[64] In 2013, a few weeks after the collapse of a factory in Bangladesh, H&M was one of the first brands to sign an agreement to work toward fire and building safety for its workers.[65] In 2013 and again in 2015 and 2016, H&M ran its "Comeback Clothes" campaign aimed at collecting unwanted clothing and textiles to recycle them and bring them new life. H&M aimed to use only sustainably sourced cotton by 2020, and for all of its strategic suppliers to pay their employees a living wage by 2018.[66] Other H&M corporate social responsibility initiatives have focused on water usage and stewardship (in partnership with the World Wildlife Fund), early childhood education (in partnership with UNICEF), and women's economic empowerment (in partnership with CARE).

Sustainability, economic inequality, workers' rights, water uses, and early childhood education are all critically important issues that appeal to millennials and potentially relate to H&M's brand. But what about extremism? Wouldn't this cause be a logical fit for a brand like H&M? Extremist recruiting impacts its customer base directly. It's a global issue affecting all of the markets in which H&M operates. And by taking a stand against extremism and hate, H&M might be able to further build its brand among millennials, forge strong grassroots partnerships, gain new insights into youth, and trigger more innovation inside the company. So why hasn't H&M as of this writing made extremism part of its "creative capitalism"–inspired efforts? It's an opportunity ripe for the taking!

As I have suggested, there's no one model for how companies might engage with CVE. The point is to step up and play some role in galvanizing public sentiment and Muslim youth specifically against extremist narratives. Doing so would lend a whole new force to our CVE efforts. No longer would CVE seem to be the preoccupation of nameless, faceless government bureaucrats. The issue would become *normalized,* seen as a cause behind which our entire society can mount a response. The full engagement of business would also bring new perspectives, creativity, and energy to the fight. We'd move much faster, and at far greater scale. We'd mount a far more integrated response, hitting many more "touch points" in the lives of young Muslims. All of this would allow us to drown out extremist messages far more effectively. And when we achieved a critical mass of involvement by large multinationals, we'd start to see more small- and mid-sized businesses follow their lead and become involved, too. The more resources we can bring to the ideological battle on the national, regional, and local levels, the more we'll saturate Muslim teens with positive messaging, stopping extremist recruiting in its tracks.

Corporate involvement in CVE may still feel like a stretch to you. If so, consider this: Companies were once loath to become involved with HIV/AIDS advocacy. But today, doing so poses no particular problem. Should the swell of activist CEOs continue, fueled by customer expectations and demands, and should the extremist threat deepen, we might see a similar shift take place with CVE. Nancy Koehn thinks so. She told me that she was "fairly confident that as the threat of terrorism grows, companies will become more involved [in fighting back]." CEO activism is "an evolutionary phenomenon and it is growing at an accelerated pace." She further notes that "if there's a global conflict—and lots of historians like myself view that likelihood as much greater than it was before [the 2016 presidential election], then all bets are off. Then it's entirely possible we'll see business' footprint [in CVE]."[67] But we cannot just wait around for a great CEO awakening—we must catalyze the shift.

As powerful as a new collaboration between business, nonprofits, and government around CVE could prove, it still would not entirely solve the problem of extremist recruiting. There are players within local communities that have even more exposure to and credibility with Muslim youth than brands like H&M. I'm talking about prominent individuals and groups within local communities. Brands might enjoy access to young people, but there are places in their lives where they can't penetrate. Within these more personal, intimate places, anti-extremist messages can become even more critical. In the next chapter, I'll describe what local civil society, the third and final plank in the fight against extremism, might accomplish when fully mobilized.

CHAPTER NINE

BUILDING DUMBLEDORE'S ARMY

In November 2016, a Somali refugee named Abdul Razak Ali Artan drove his car onto the campus at Ohio State University, jumped a curb, and plowed into a group of pedestrians. Jumping out of the vehicle, he ran around with a butcher knife in his hand, plunging it into people at random. "He was completely silent" during the attack, a witness was quoted as saying, describing it as "very creepy."[1] Two minutes later, Artan was dead, brought down by three shots from a quick-thinking police officer on the scene. Eleven of Artan's victims were injured, and the Columbus community—including some fifty thousand residents of Somali descent—was on edge.[2]

Was this a terrorist attack? Authorities were unsure, but the evidence seemed to point to that conclusion. Minutes before the attack, Artan had posted a message on Facebook lauding the Al Qaeda cleric Anwar al-Awlaki and expressing his own, deeply felt frustrations. "I can't take it anymore," he said. "America! Stop interfering with other countries, especially the Muslim Ummah [the global Muslim community]. We are not weak, remember that."[3]

Local Somali Americans were stunned and appalled by Artan's

violence. "I'm just shocked that people do stupid stuff," a young Somali American said.[4] Yet sadly, the incident was not the first involving a member of Columbus's Somali population. In 2015, a twenty-three-year-old Somali immigrant was charged with "traveling to Syria to support an al Qaeda affiliate and returning to the U.S. with plans to launch a terrorist attack."[5] In 2010, a former Columbus resident of Somali descent was killed in Mogadishu while fighting for the Al-Shabaab terrorist group. As media reported, the combatant had "attended a mosque in Columbus where several Al-Shabaab figures [had] appeared for fundraising and recruitment."[6] And in 2007, a Somali immigrant received ten years in prison for having plotted an attack on a local shopping mall five years earlier.[7]

Somalis in Columbus have not stood idle in the face of extremism. They've fought back, and they've made the fight personal. During the 2000s, Mohamed A. Ali, a young American Somali community activist with roots in Columbus, didn't like what he was seeing in his city. After graduating from Boston College Law School, he had moved back to Columbus to work at an immigration law firm, serving Somali immigrants and refugees. Thanks to this work, he thought he understood some of the factors that made youth more vulnerable to extremist messages. Tens of thousands of Somali refugees had settled in Columbus in recent years, having been moved from refugee camps in Kenya and Ethiopia. Upon arriving in the United States, they were experiencing culture shock, feeling alienated and disconnected from mainstream America. "The community was very isolated," Ali told me, "and they wouldn't really engage with people outside of their community. Most people would spend their days speaking to other Somalis and wouldn't even try with other people outside of the community."[8] While it would have been easier for Ali to simply focus on his own education and career, he decided to take action, creating and running programs designed to help local Somalis become more integrated with the wider Columbus community.

In 2010, Ali took his efforts to a new level. He joined Generation Change, the change-maker platform I mentioned in chapter 7. Generation Change built both local networks of young Muslim scholars, bloggers, scientists, artists, musicians, journalists, entrepreneurs, teachers, student group leaders, and cultural activists, as well as a global network of individuals working to effect positive change. As Ali remembers, the experience of interacting with like-minded peers was invigorating. "It changed my perspective on some of the causes of radicalization," he says, and it also gave him a language to describe what he was doing. "I had never heard of 'countering violent extremism,' or 'counter-extremism,' or 'counter-radicalization' before I joined Generation Change. We were seeing some of these kids become radicalized, and we were . . . engaging them, but we weren't really using that language." Ali also gained leadership training and insight into what people in other parts of the world were doing to combat extremism in their communities.

During a 2010 trip to the Somali capital of Mogadishu, Ali's new perspective led him to an epiphany. "One of the things that really struck me was this huge youth population that was essentially doing nothing. . . . Some of them were really disheartened, facing injustice."[9] To remedy this situation, Ali resolved to move to Mogadishu and start a local chapter of Generation Change. Due to the unstable security situation on the ground, the U.S. government could not seed a chapter there, nor could we find the young social entrepreneurs needed to build action locally. So, in 2012, Ali created his own chapter of Generation Change as well as of the Iftiin Foundation,* "an organization that incubates social entrepreneurs, young leaders, and their groundbreaking projects to encourage a culture of change and innovation in Somalia."[10] As Ali explains, Generation Change helped him understand the potential that social entrepreneurship had in "preventing youth from becoming radicalized." If youth felt

---

* Iftiin means "light" in Somali.

engaged, if they were building something positive and given agency and discrete identities in their communities, they would reject extremist messages.[11]

Mohamed A. Ali is from the precise demographic whom extremists routinely target. Not only did he not fall prey to their ideology, but he has dedicated his life to keeping others in his community safe. In 2013, he trained fifty young people in Mogadishu to become peer leaders in countering extremist narratives. They worked on "peace enterprises" such as offering microenterprise grants for female entrepreneurs and building old fashioned people-to-people digital and social networks for Somali youth. One participant organized soccer matches between former members of the Al-Shabaab terrorist group and youth at local universities, helping the former build friendships and reintegrate peacefully into the community. In 2017, Ali's organization helped provide cognitive behavioral therapy and psychosocial counseling to war-affected youth (including ex-combatants), as well as entrepreneurship training and social integration skills-building. Over the course of a year, his organization has worked with nearly 700 vulnerable and at-risk youth and more than 300 ex-combatants to help them forgo extremism and live productive lives. Many of these graduates of his organization's programming now serve as ambassadors for peace and progress within their communities.[12]

Ali's success shows that fighting extremism isn't primarily a job for government or multinational corporations—it's a job for individuals, networks of individuals, and community organizations acting at the local level. It's a job for all of us in our capacity as activists, teachers, parents, neighbors, and friends.

Not long ago, I held a discussion with a group of Harvard undergraduates, who were typically diverse in ethnicity, religion, class, perspective, and gender. The geometric, redbrick building in which we met stood less than two miles from where the Tsarnaev brothers killed police officer Sean Collier right after the 2013 Boston Marathon bombings. As we tackled the question of how kids become radicalized, we began brainstorming on how societies could better insulate their citizens from the so-called Islamic State's recruiters. None of the students disputed my contention that governments lack credibility with youth and hence cannot convince vulnerable young people to reject extremist ideas. Yet as some of the students pointed out, there is a group in our society that possesses far more credibility: young people themselves. A class of 2015 undergraduate named Inesha conveyed this idea in a way any millennial would understand, chiming in with a reference from the Harry Potter franchise. She said, "If you want this generation to understand what you really mean, you have to say we have to build Dumbledore's Army." Even with his formidable magic powers, Harry Potter still needed help from friends and peers in his battle again evil. He needed an army. And so do we in our fight against extremist ideology.*

If you're a young person, then you and your peers can make a difference by applying your unique talents to the challenge of countering extremism. You don't have to create a new NGO, like Ali did. You can speak out, write a blog, create videos, form a club, write poetry, produce music, or simply model ideas in your everyday life that counter extremist thinking, such as openness toward and acceptance of others different from you. If you're not a young person, you, too, can contribute by amplifying messages of inclusivity and diversity within your local community, social circle, and family, and by helping to lift up the voices of concerned youth.

Whatever our age or station in life, the direct and indirect actions we take to help young people resolve their identity crises and to counter hateful rhetoric in our communities represent important interventions. These interventions might be small, directly impacting just a few people. But small actions are immeasurably important.

---

* This analysis first appeared in an op-ed I wrote for the *Boston Globe:* Farah Pandith, "Building Dumbledore's Army to Beat ISIS," *Boston Globe,* December 16, 2015, https://www.bostonglobe.com/opinion/2015/12/16/building-dumbledore-army-fight-isis/Atam9w40VgGcuPaDcDoW6M/story.html.

Support from government and business can give such actions more reach, dramatically enhancing their impact. But even without such support, an innumerable number of small actions have the potential to mesh together and grow over time into a mega-narrative more powerful than that of hate and destruction.

Some youth are already inspiring their peers to resist hate, to contest stereotypes, and to resolve issues of identity in healthy ways. The conversations are happening all around us, in many cases independently of government. There just needs to be many more of them, and our communities need to celebrate and promote them. We need to galvanize local individuals, and young people especially, unleashing the power of what I call the "youthquake."[13] When we do, we'll vanquish the appeal of extremist ideology.

UNDERSTANDING OUR OWN "MAGIC" POWERS

My talk of local action and a youthquake might strike some people as overly optimistic. Can grassroots individuals and groups really make headway against a problem so large, frightening, and entrenched as extremism? They can. One open-mic night in a local neighborhood* or one young woman blogging about her identity as a Norwegian Afghan won't solve the problem of extremist ideology in a particular city or town, much less around the world. But thousands of kids taking a whole range of positive actions, lauded by their peers, publicized through social media platforms, and sup-

* Open-mic nights are popular in many communities around the world. In 2017, for instance, *The Economist* ran a piece about the popularity of personal storytelling and open-mic nights in Lebanon. At one such event, the Hakaya Storytelling Night, a young Palestinian refugee shared her experiences of marginalization and stigmatization throughout her childhood in Lebanon. The article goes on to report that in Beirut, "gatherings devoted to sharing true stories are promoting tolerance and social cohesion, breaking taboos and allowing marginalised voices to be heard." "Autobiographical Storytelling Is Bridging Divides in Beirut," *Economist*, June 28, 2017, https://www.economist.com/blogs/prospero/2017/06/listen-and-learn.

ported by business and government, will have a tremendous impact over time.

In some ways, the notion of a youthquake seems fairly obvious. It has lately become clear that individuals armed with technology now possess dramatic new powers. Citizen activism has flourished online,* and young people acting at the grassroots level have accomplished monumental tasks that once would have seemed impossible. They've taken down repressive dictators whose regimes have wielded power for decades. They've forced leadership at large companies to adjust their policies. They've brought about dramatic shifts in attitudes and social mores, most recently as they've marched by the millions to demand gun control in America. And they've also served as gatekeepers for communities.†

Homophobia has existed for generations in the United States, but in just a few years, public opinion in the United States has shifted dramatically in favor of LGBT rights. In 2013, in fact, one national poll found that "81% of 18–29 year olds" supported marriage equality.[14] That didn't happen because government mandated it from above. It happened because after decades of grassroots activism, a generation of young people popularized enthusiasm for such rights from below. As Eliza Byard, executive director of the Gay, Lesbian and Straight Education Network (GLSEN) told me, "anti-LGBT

* Consider, for instance, the digital civil rights movement. WeTheProtesters (WTP) is a multipronged initiative attempting to combat police brutality, systemic racism, and lack of transparency in the government and law enforcement communities. According to its Open Letter, WTP aims to promote "the fundamental humanity of blackness," pave a road to justice, create a community rooted in honesty, and establish a "new political and social reality that respects and affirms blackness and the humanity therein." Founded in January 2015, the group tracks instances of police brutality through its "Mapping Police Violence" platform. "We the Protestors," Scribd, January 15, 2015, https://www.scribd.com/doc/252760366/WTP-Open-Letter-1-15-15.

† In his book *The Seventh Sense,* Joshua Cooper Ramo observes that "today, no position is more important, formidable, influential or profitable than that of gatekeeper." This is because "gatekeepers choose what we see. They determine the rules we follow, what we can and can't change. They reward us too—once we're inside—with benefits of speed, knowledge, and safety." Joshua Cooper Ramo, *The Seventh Sense: Power, Fortune, and Survival in the Age of Networks* (Boston: Little, Brown, 2016), 236–37.

speech and anti LGBT attitudes were totally intractable" back in 1990, when her organization was founded. It was "tilting at windmills to think that you could get students to not use anti-LGBT language." Since then, thousands of student-led gay-straight alliances (GSAs) cropped up at schools around the country, organizing themselves in connection with GLSEN's regional chapters. These groups "[signal] to the entire community that LGBT people are a present and organized and accepted daily part of their school," Byard says. In fact, research has shown a "direct correlation between the presence of a GSA at a school and . . . improvement in individual LGBT student experience," as well as a "shift in overall student experience at that school."[15] The roots of systemic change in favor of LGBT rights occurred at the "nano-level," through student and faculty involvement in GSAs as well as other acts of student grassroots engagement, such as participation in GLSEN's national day of silence, "one of the largest youth-led days of action for any issue." As Byard wrote in 2013, it was "young people" taking action at the local level who were collectively "reshaping the marriage equality debate."[16]

Local action has also played a pivotal role in ridding the world of the scourge of polio. Soliciting small donations, the 35,000 local Rotary clubs around the world have "reduced polio cases by 99.9 percent worldwide" since 1979.[17] By wisely channeling those modest funds, members of Rotary clubs—individuals like you and me—"have helped immunize more than 2.5 billion children against polio in 122 countries."[18] Rotary members have also made a difference by taking a number of grassroots actions to raise public awareness about the disease, such as posting messages on Facebook, signing petitions, and writing letters to local politicians. Polio isn't yet vanquished, but it's well on its way, partly thanks to grassroots engagement.

Extremist ideology is more vulnerable than some of the cultural conventions, institutions, and diseases already vanquished by grassroots movements. Extremist groups are far less stable than states, for instance. They possess much more limited economic and military assets, and their membership is vague and shifting. At times, these groups thrive, while at other moments they go dormant. It is also worth noting that they don't need much money to cause a lot of damage. Their power ultimately derives from the appeal of their ideology—that's what allows them to build armies. But ideology can be disrupted, its effects nullified. Civil resistance, organization, and passion have on many occasions removed entrenched governments from power, even when those governments have had access to police and military force. Certainly "the power of the people" can prevail against extremist groups.

Abdul Razak Ali's 2016 attack at Ohio State is not evidence that efforts like that of Mohamed A. Ali are failures; it's entirely possible that without such outreach there would have been scores of Columbus attacks committed by multiple young extremists.* Thus we should be clear what we mean by "solving the problem" of extremism. No strategy can promise to deliver a world entirely free of terrorism. Extremists will continue to set off bombs, shoot people, and commit other acts of violence no matter how engaged citizens, business, and government become. What we *can* accomplish is to dramatically reduce the threat terrorism poses and the damage it does.

HIV used to kill almost everyone who contracted it within a matter of months or, at best, a few years. Today advances in treatment have transformed HIV into a disease many people can live with for years, symptom-free, the virus barely detectable in their bloodstreams. Absolutely crucial was the "people power" push by activists to force the government and drug companies to change their policies. And while government provided some money for the research and development of new therapies, these therapies have comprised only

* Erik Brynjolfsson, coauthor of *The Second Machine Age,* told me that it would be a mistake to underestimate the power of individuals today to achieve good in the world. Digital technologies, he said, "are more powerful tools than we ever had before, which means we have more ability to shape our outcomes than we ever had before."

part of the solution. Communities have also engaged, with teachers, social workers, and business all coming together to help change sexual behavior at the grassroots level. HIV was a *systemic* threat and a systemic approach has largely beaten it back. That's what we can achieve with extremism. If we muster a grassroots movement at scale, we can transform it from a dire and costly security threat into a malady that, while still present, doesn't significantly disrupt society's functioning.

A WORLD OF CHANGE MAKERS

I know that individual actors hold the key to a solution because I've personally witnessed their impact. During my travels, I've encountered hundreds of individuals who have taken up the fight against extremist ideology in their local communities. My job, after all, was to serve as a talent scout, seeking out young people who could influence their peers not merely to reject extremist ideology per se, but to think more constructively about the foundational issues of identity, social awareness, and diversity. When I began this work during the second term of George W. Bush's administration, I suspected that these people were out there in significant numbers, but I wasn't sure. Happily, my trips and other research consistently turned up many inspiring examples of individuals who were rising up to help turn their communities against extremism.

The sheer diversity of these entrepreneurial efforts was astounding. I had the pleasure on several occasions of meeting Daniyal Noorani, whose 2010 short animated video *Find Heaven* critiqued social injustices in Pakistan and showed how extremism had "taken the country by the throat." Noorani grew up in the Pakistani city of Lahore, where he says he had "an idyllic childhood."[19] In 2002, he began attending college in the United States, and enjoyed "the space to kind of explore my own identity and what being Muslim meant to me." But he found himself "in a position where I was defending my religion and a part of my identity—explaining the fact that not all Muslims are extremists."

Noorani sought to cast light on those "who use religion to manipulate people," especially the "impoverished and confused."[20] He was specifically motivated when detecting "an apathy regarding suicide bombings" unfolding in Pakistan. Living in Boston, he had recently learned how to play the guitar. "People didn't know whether they condemned it or whether they supported it," he told me. "So I wanted to write a song on the subject and made people actually think about it." The accompanying video attracted an online following—"not necessarily Gangnam-style viral," Noorani says, "but it got coverage in the press and went into some film festivals. It was something that was positive and that generated a healthy conversation about the issues."[21] It was not shown widely in Pakistan, however, as broadcasters deemed it too provocative.[22] Still, Noorani received positive responses from strangers, including a Pakistani teacher who wrote to say that she had shown the video to her students, who had "decided to perform it for their annual school day."[23]

Other young social entrepreneurs I encountered didn't focus on extremism directly, but spread ideas that implicitly contested extremist narratives or that explored general issues of identity. In 2008, I met an entrepreneur in Paris who manufactured and sold exquisite, high-end candles. The packaging and scents of his products were breathtakingly beautiful, but I noticed that one of his candles was imprinted with the name of a rural village about an hour outside central Paris. The village had been the scene of some very public riots and car burnings, and the media had reported that gang members and a large number of ethnic minorities now lived there. I wondered about this: why had this entrepreneur given such a name to a product that was so divine? "Ah," he told me, "that's on purpose. I'm pairing a name that people associate with something so horrible with a product that is so beautiful and luxurious. When you smell the candle and see what it's called, you understand that there is beauty even in this place." In his own, unique way, this entrepreneur was contesting the harsh dichotomies upon which extremists thrive. If our standard concepts of "beauty" and "squalor" didn't fully describe reality, what other prevailing concepts also needed softening?

Theatrical productions can make such points every bit as effectively as consumer goods. Luqman Ali runs the Khayaal Theater Company in the British city of Luton. Home to a large population of Muslims, Luton is a tough industrial town that tops lists of the worst places to live in Great Britain. A survey found participants lamenting its "dreary architecture and lack of leisure and entertainment facilities," with one "[describing] the town as 'the brick and iron temple to global pollution.' " One Luton property owner described it as "an ugly, hard-drinking place with absolutely nothing to see and nothing to do."[24] But Luton does have something to see: the Khayaal Theater Company. As Luqman told me, the group does the "cultural work of diffusing a discourse of humanitarian story and dream [as an antidote to] the fixation on exclusive religious dogma and doctrine."[25] More specifically, the company's productions, funded almost exclusively by private donations, aim to "promote inter-cultural dialogue, engagement and understanding by demonstrating reconciliation between East and West, the traditional and the modern, and Muslims and people of other faiths and traditions."[26]

When I first met Ali in 2007 at an event hosted by the U.S. embassy, I was taken by his ideas about identity and the ability of the arts to serve as a bridge to greater understanding. Ali was bent on exposing kids to the true diversity of Muslim experience, arousing their curiosity about Muslim heroes and heroines, like those in medieval Spain's great centers of learning, who helped transmit classical antiquity to posterity. His vision seemed even more powerful some months later when I visited Luton, which has been the target of extremist recruiting.[27] I spoke to young people there who seemed alienated from British society, and who told me they didn't really know what it meant to be Muslim. If a parent or teacher lectured them about how to think about their lives, they would ignore it. But when Muslim characters in a play brought identity issues alive, the messages of inclusivity and reconciliation seemed authentic, compelling—and fun. Youth could relate not only with curiosity but also with enthusiasm.

Other individuals I met fought back against extremism by giving young Muslims opportunities to explore identity creatively and to connect with one another. In Khartoum, Sudan, enterprising millennials organized open-mic nights in which they could express their struggles and resentments.[28] I'll never forget how, in a gathering of young people in our embassy in Khartoum, a young woman said defiantly, "Why should we let [the extremists] tell us how to live our lives? We want to talk and take part! We have open-mic nights here in Khartoum even though it may be unwise. But I don't care. What will they do? If they put us in jail we will still not be silent." In Oslo, Norway, a Norwegian of African descent named Elvis Nwosu organized a program in which immigrant youth explored their struggles through the creation of personal videos. In a lunch organized by the U.S. embassy with him and a few of the young Muslims he had worked with, I was struck by how much stronger they had felt as a result of sharing their experiences. No longer did they feel marginalized. All of a sudden, they appreciated their own worth. Nwosu has since continued his advocacy work and been elected to the Oslo city council.

In London, Asim Siddiqui helped found the City Circle, "a safe space for communities to self-critically discuss and debate issues that concern them." The group sponsors events that "challenge the belief that there is a conflict between a Muslim and British identity."[29] In Beirut, Ziad Fahed ran the Lebanese Interreligious Academy, an organization designed "to foster and facilitate the interaction and the communication among University students from different cultural and religious communities."[30] Meeting with Fahed and his students in Beirut in 2012, I was struck by his passion. "We are a country with many confessions," he said, "and we have had a complicated history. But we are an ancient civilization and this generation needs to be inspired to be who we have been." In his work as a professor and lecturer, Fahed emphasized the importance of diversity and communicating outside one's own religious group. One of his students pulled me aside after our conversation and asked, "Can you please connect us to other students like us?"

Many other individuals have contributed to the war of ideas by creating positive role models for youth, or by convincing them of their own power to become role models and effect change. Shocked by the events of 9/11, Dr. Naif al-Mutawa, a Kuwaiti clinical psychiatrist and father of five boys who lives in Kuwait, created "The 99," Muslim comic book heroes that "reinforce positive messages of Islam and cross cultures to create a new moral framework for confronting evil."[31] As al-Mutawa has explained, his vision was "based on the belief that the only way to beat extremism is through arts and culture."[32] A first-of-its-kind project, The 99 went global to great acclaim, including a "shout-out" by President Barack Obama in the presidential Entrepreneurship Summit in Washington, D.C.* (Upon learning that in recent issues characters had met up with Batman, Superman, and other long-standing superheroes, Obama said, "I hear they are making progress.") Vali Nasr, dean of the School of Advanced International Studies at Johns Hopkins University, has called for Muslims in the United States and elsewhere to "become

* At a White House meeting early in the first term of the Obama administration, Ben Rhodes, former deputy national security advisor for strategic communications, and Denis McDonough, former White House chief of staff, asked colleagues to brainstorm new ideas for how the president could engage with Muslims. Drawing on my firsthand experience in Muslim communities, I proposed a series of entrepreneurship summits at the White House. I believed this would inspire more Muslims to serve as social entrepreneurs in their communities. My proposal was positive, suggesting the White House focus on global Muslim entrepreneurship. The summits became a fundamental CVE pillar in the Obama administration and continued into the Trump administration, ultimately giving rise to a large, global network of social and business entrepreneurs (both Muslim and non-Muslim). Summit participants have since told me of the summit's important impact on their work. Though many parts of the U.S. government helped in this effort, the White House's attention and dedication to enlisting private sector partners, universities, and foreign governments proved decisive. The importance of President Obama's team was especially pivotal in catalyzing and energizing a global cadre of actors. Hundreds of global entrepreneurs have since heeded the call and trusted in their ability to effect change.

comfortable with marrying tradition with a modern world."[33] With The 99, al-Mutawa has delivered on that nicely. Others have followed in his footsteps, using cartoons to inspire young Muslims and steer them away from extremism.[34]

It goes on: the Washington, D.C.–based Muslim hip-hop artists Native Deen created music with "street cred," proving to youth that Islam in the United States was diverse, and that people could integrate Muslim and American identities in positive ways. In Malaysia, an entrepreneur named Dash Dhakshinamoorthy established business idea bake-offs as well as a school called Startup School Asia, with the goal of getting "more young people to think about how they can change the world, how they can become problem solvers."[35] It's a goal that Dhakshinamoorthy tied in directly to keeping vulnerable kids safe: "What we have done is to channel their energy to [be more creative] . . . the global entrepreneurship movement . . . has basically shown that you as an individual can be a creator. You don't have to be a destroyer. And you can make things happen. What you need to do is connect with more like-minded people. What I've done is to serve as the glue that holds this together."[36]

I also encountered many individuals and groups around the world that were seeking to counter extremists' monopolization of Sheikh Google. Starting in 2008, the Muslim Voices podcast counteracted the black-and-white pseudo-certainties of extremist narratives by providing programming that "[tackled] the complexities of Islam and the often-complicated relations between Muslims and non-Muslims."[37] Listeners were confronted by a multiplicity of voices reflecting a range of Muslim viewpoints, backgrounds, and experiences. More recently, the BuzzFeed podcast *See Something Say Something* has challenged stereotypes of American Muslims, exposing listeners to the population's true diversity.[38] Ahmed Ali Akbar, the podcast's host, pitched the idea, which has received much acclaim and millions of downloads. As Akbar relates: "The podcast was started as an expansion of the work I was doing [as a staff writer at BuzzFeed] on the website and [as a] a central place for various Muslim voices to speak honestly and without judgement. The initial idea, which has since modified with the time, was that it would capture the kind of conversations young American Muslims have while drinking chai, and talking to Muslims of different backgrounds than themselves."[39]

An initiative called Imams Online has provided a forum for young, progressive Muslim religious leaders to share "positive Islamic content," helping to support Muslim parents and provide non-Muslims with a way into Islam that they can trust.[40] Other organizations in the United States, Great Britain, and elsewhere have helped local mosques open their doors to their surrounding communities, so that they can build relationships with non-Muslims. NGOs like the London-based Faith Associates have also created materials to help mosques become more transparent, so that extremist preachers have a harder time establishing themselves.[41] And the University of California, Berkeley, has created a course for its young engineering students called "Designing Technology to Counter Violent Extremism."[42] This one-of-a-kind class was assembled from scratch by two uniquely qualified instructors, Björn Hartmann and Zvika Krieger. Hartmann is an associate professor of electrical engineering and computer sciences and faculty director of the Jacobs Institute for Design Innovation, which hosts the course. Krieger, a specialist in design thinking and foreign policy, is a former State Department representative to Silicon Valley and senior advisor for technology and innovation.[43]

FROM MICRO TO MEGA

To help convey the vast potential that such entrepreneurialism represents, let me share a loose typology of grassroots CVE interventions. Some interventions, what I call "micro-solutions," have the potential to touch an entire group—a neighborhood, for instance, or a local faith community. In Denmark, mothers banded together to create a hotline for other parents to call if they thought their children may be becoming radicalized.[44] In Trinidad and Tobago, youth created a hotline of their own where their peers could safely talk about issues like identity and religion. In 2008, when the right-wing Dutch politician Geert Wilders released the inflammatory, anti-Islam film *Fitna,* local Muslims of Moroccan descent responded with a humorous campaign[*] to give Wilders a hug virtually because "his mother did not love him enough." The gesture sent a normalizing message about the religion: that contrary to the film's own assertions, Muslims weren't violent, they had a sense of humor, and they could and decidedly would rise above the hatred of others.[45] Other examples have included the practice in many communities of holding interfaith celebrations at Christmas, Diwali, or Eid.

A second class of CVE interventions—what I call "macro-solutions"—can touch still more people, making waves that ripple outward to reach people in a number of possibly far-flung communities. Young Muslim bloggers, cartoonists, and hip-hop artists can reach thousands of people or more across national boundaries. Ambassadors Charles H. Rivkin and Matthew Barzun exercised leadership in outreach efforts abroad, spearheading initiatives that made a difference in the areas of film, music, entrepreneurship, and cultural exchange.[†] Likewise, the Paris-based organization La Ruche ("The Beehive") has opened a second collective workspace in Kuala Lumpur, Malaysia, to advance immigrant and minority entrepreneurship, giving young Muslims tools they need to get connected, get busy, become productive members of society, and help other youth explore their identities in healthy ways.[‡]

* The virtual campaign was called "Hug Wilders."

† Charles H. Rivkin was ambassador to France during the Obama administration (2009–2013), and Matthew Barzun served as ambassador to Sweden (2009–11), and to the Court of St. James's (2013–17).

‡ La Ruche worked with my office to globalize their platform. In 2013, Secretary of State John Kerry announced its launch at the Malaysian Global Entrepreneurship Summit.

As La Ruche's founder, Charlotte Hochman, told me in an interview, she'd been inspired in 2008 after seeing "a lot of local communities getting organized" and taking action in innovative ways "when the government or private sector were not providing sufficient answers."[46] Hochman realized that many immigrants wanted to create new programs and initiatives in their communities, but that "there was no common means of action for these people to have a conversation or be visible." She resolved to bring these people together, "even though they [were] in different sectors and didn't necessarily [share a common identity]," and named her initiative La Ruche (the Beehive) as a nod to the French tradition of collective action.[47] As she remembers, in 2008 the U.S. government was quick to lend its support. "The team at the U.S. embassy in France was really engaged with the suburbs and on the lookout for community organizing," she said. "They're really the only ones that were doing this at the time."[48]

La Ruche not only successfully filled a need but found that they were overwhelmed with interest and activity, leaving Hochman "amazed at the transformation of people who were involved over a year with us," as well as at the creation of a "thriving community of people who were burning to innovate and to create."[49] Further, La Ruche helped to normalize the concept of diversity at a time when it was difficult to discuss in France, bringing together other entrepreneurs who were challenging norms in different fields such as supply chain and human resources. While I visited La Ruche in 2007, I met Saïd Hammouche, a forerunner on diversity, whose firm, Mozaïk RH, specialized in making the workplace more diverse by bringing together recruiters and young graduates from minority backgrounds and working-class neighborhoods. The firm helped with creating CVs, interview preparation, and individualized mentoring, including specialized programs for women.[50] I felt inspired by Hammouche's idea of helping French companies to create new role models for Muslim youth while also tackling a challenging social issue. At La Ruche, Hammouche worked closely with a wide group of innovators to understand how diversity training he provided could build inroads into a very traditional work model in France.

Macro-solutions like La Ruche are powerful, but still other interventions can resonate even more widely, making their mark within entire countries and internationally. I mentioned the efforts of Dash Dhakshinamoorthy to galvanize entrepreneurship in Malaysia and beyond. Another instance of such "mega solutions" is the interfaith Ramadan Festival created by the Dutch social entrepreneur and politician Ahmed Larouz. Inspired by the warm hospitality he had experienced when visiting with an American Christian family, Larouz designed a program whereby individual Muslim families opened up their homes to non-Muslims. The idea was to break down barriers between Muslims and non-Muslims and affirm the spirit of generosity and respect.

As Ahmed remembers, European governments in the mid-2000s were "not really dealing" with integrating immigrant populations.[51] Terrorist attacks like the ones on the Madrid and London mass transit systems were taking place. After his eye-opening experience in America, he resolved to start hospitality dinners in the context of a "Ramadan festival." His first efforts were a success, with an initial rollout of more than two hundred events in nine cities across the Netherlands. The Dutch prime minister offered Ramadan wishes to the country's one million Muslims "for the first time in history." "We had hundreds of families open their doors," Ahmed says, "but also hundreds of families came to visit Muslims in their houses. And we [even] inspired people from Norway. . . . Ministers took part [in] it, mayors went out to the houses." The program spread within a few years to more than forty cities, in a number of countries.[52] Even more, the Ramadan Festival was copied in nations and cities across Europe, garnering Ahmed an award from the United Nations. "We are just normal citizens trying to do things which other citizens could do," he says. Fighting extremism means providing kids with "the right tools." Over time, Ahmed believes, the forces of moderation will win.*

Other immensely influential and important "mega" initiatives are geared specifically toward giving female Muslims more of a voice in their religion. In many cultures, Muslim women were forced to accept at face value what others told them about their faith, their role, and their culture. They were not going to the source itself, the Qur'an, so as to understand its words in context. Though a wealth of scholarship was available to anyone with Internet connection, it wasn't easy for women to obtain neutral translations of the Qur'an, or to understand the many nuances of specific translations. Through regular columns in the newspapers and in women's magazines, as well as through civic organizations and schools, the Malaysian group Sisters in Islam published numerous materials on the subject of women's rights, took public stands on court, and sent memoranda to the Malaysian government on subjects like criminal justice and domestic violence. The group also built an international network "to share scholarship, strategies, and best practices on work related to family laws in Muslim contexts,"[53] in 2009 launching Musawah,[54] a "global movement for equality and justice in the Muslim family."[55] Highly controversial in Malaysia, Sisters in Islam has inspired Muslim women across the world seeking alternatives to conservative, patriarchal interpretations of Islamic doctrine.

To bring the full weight of civil society's collective action to bear against extremist ideology, we obviously want and need as many "mega" interventions as possible. But micro- and macro-interventions are important as well because they are far more numerous, and be-

* As Ahmed told me, "you don't need like only the government positions, you need different, different levels of the community, different sectors of the community involved to tackle our challenges. And not only our progressive leaders or the government leaders . . . you need everybody." Interview with the author, December 2016.

cause they can balloon in number, size, and scope if provided with the right kind of support. Here we arrive at the crux of both my frustration and my optimism: to date, grassroots interventions of all types have barely received any support from government, large corporations, or the media.

I've described my own efforts within the U.S. government to find and nurture local change makers. My small team and I did everything we could to push forward exciting ventures as we discovered them, but we didn't have the resources to help social entrepreneurs scale up their projects, to find hundreds of other start-up ventures that might have existed in local communities, or to inspire and help countless other people to hatch exciting new ventures of their own.* During the latter part of the Obama administration, other parts of our government began investing in such initiatives. In particular, Jeh Johnson, the secretary for homeland security, was focused on learning about and investing in American civil society action in the CVE space. He fought to obtain funds and built a team dedicated to extend support to these efforts. Yet such "one-off" programs supported by government without a design strategy couldn't yield long-term, quantifiable results. We simply weren't building the "mega" machine that we needed, and still need. In addition, corporations weren't investing at scale, and philanthropists and foundations investing in "big bet" ideas were also not touching the issue of protecting youth from extremism. As a result, there remains to this day a vast potential that remains untapped. Daniyal Noorani put it well:

* Through my experience in the State Department's European and Eurasian Affairs Bureau, I knew that there was far more that society and government could be doing to build momentum around CVE and learn from past mistakes. At an event in Doha, Qatar, in late 2008, prior to Barack Obama's election as president, I met Susan Rice, who would become his national security advisor. She asked me for information about what the Obama administration should do around CVE should he emerge victorious in the election. I addressed two memos to her in January 2009, detailing all that I had learned while undertaking Muslim engagement work at the National Security Council and while pioneering CVE for the U.S. government and making recommendations for what Obama should do within his first hundred days in office. To her credit, National Security Advisor Rice supported the White House CVE Summit initially proposed by George Selim.

"If my short video could have such an impact on the youth of Pakistan, consider what the results of a well-funded and concerted media effort against the extremist ideology would be."[56]

The potential for change would be vastly greater if we could spur far more people to follow the example of the social entrepreneurs I've mentioned and to take action. But that would require that the media take more responsibility than it has. Journalists exult in the latest innovative tech solutions for fighting extremism,* but that interest is of recent vintage. The kinds of projects I'm describing here have existed for a decade.† A profile piece in a publication like the *New York Times, Newsweek,* or *Wall Street Journal* would have boosted the work of these social entrepreneurs, giving them access to money and connections, and in general legitimizing their efforts in the eyes of the public. Yet despite my best efforts to call on journalists and urge them to check out what individuals and nonprofits were doing in cities across the world, most weren't interested. Instead, they wanted stories that had more sex appeal. "Do you know someone who got radicalized and then left?" they asked me. "Can you connect me to a woman who is married to a terrorist?" "Are there programs that you can *prove* stopped youth from going to fight?"‡

* Witness a 2016 piece touting students who are using "lean startup principles" to develop CVE projects: Blaise Zerega, "Stanford Students Are Using Lean Startup Principles to Help Fight ISIS," *VentureBeat,* December 27, 2016, http://venturebeat.com/2016/12/26/stanford-students-are-using-lean-startup-principles-to-help-fight-isis/.

† In 2007, we held the first hackathon-like event for CVE at Harvard University's Berkman Klein Center for Internet & Society. That event resulted in the idea of a platform called "E-mams," which rated these religious leaders and helped youth understand their local imam's ideological predilections and values. Few people were exposed to E-mams or many comparable grassroots initiatives because journalists largely declined to cover them.

‡ Media coverage of Muslims remains skewed. According to a 2017 report, "Since 2004, there has not been a single year in which television coverage of Muslims has been positive on balance." Muslims rarely speak for themselves in the media. Instead, they are spoken about, primarily in negative terms. "What journalists underplay are positive developments in the Muslim community and the efforts of that community to forge a place in America, which includes combating those in their community who hold extremist ideologies that do not reflect their values or faith."Meighan Stone, "Snake and Stranger: Media Coverage of Muslims and Refugee Policy," Shorenstein Center, July 18, 2017, https://shorensteincenter.org/media-coverage-muslims

If the media had paid more attention to the efforts of local individuals and put pressure on companies and philanthropists to help them, these initiatives themselves might have mushroomed in size and reach. The notion that government can fight extremist ideology in a different way—with a light touch, and in partnership with grassroots actors—would have taken root. Tens of thousands of additional concerned citizens potentially would have taken up the cause.

We can't wait for media coverage to change. If you're a young person of any religion or ethnic background, think about your own skills, talents, and resources. How might you apply them to fight back against extremist ideas, both online and off? This is a battle that *you* can wage. Despite ongoing terrorist activity and the rancorous dialogue about Muslims and immigrants that has flared up in many countries, positive change is happening. Millennials are natural entrepreneurs and activists, and they're making a difference, one neighborhood at a time. But we need many more of them—in Muslim communities and beyond. And we need individuals from other generations to take action as well and to encourage and support millennials in their efforts.

FIGHTING EXTREMISM WHERE YOU ARE

Even if you're not a young entrepreneur inclined to launch a new NGO, you can still take action against extremist ideology inside your local community. Muslim parents, teachers, and scholars might engage by launching conversations, classes, and projects that contest extremist notions of a "pure," monolithic way of being Muslim. If you're a scholar, translate the Qur'an into your local language with

-refugee-policy/?utm_medium=social&utm_campaign=hks-twitter&utm_source=twitter. Katie Couric's 2018 series, *The Muslim Next Door* (National Geographic Channel), is a rare exception.

explanatory footnotes, invoking your own local understandings and traditions, or use translations of the Qur'an that are carefully vetted. If you're an educator of any kind or a parent, ensure that foreign ideologies are not creeping into schoolbooks, after-school programs, and peer networks by taking a hands-on approach, as you would with anything else that put your child at risk.* Explore Islamic diversity using music, painting, dance, or other arts. Whether you're Muslim or non-Muslim, if you work in a school or social agency, create or replicate programs and support systems that help kids from all backgrounds communicate with one another, work out issues of religious identity, and obtain additional help if they need it. Spotlight the importance of diversity through history, and include Muslim role models in discussions of philosophers, leaders, artists, and scientists. Create programs that build awareness about extremism among young people and parents. Bring in speakers or create volunteer opportunities that expose kids to different faith traditions and ethnicities.

If you run a local business or manage a team inside a local organization, there is likewise a lot you can do. Be more mindful about how you speak about Islam and Muslims. Don't assume that all Muslims are from the Middle East, or that their religion is monolithic. Educate yourself and your employees about the diversity that might exist in your local community. Be sure to make *all* of your employees and customers feel welcome, no matter what their religion or level of observance. Hold holiday celebrations and other events to celebrate different faiths, heritages, and cultures. Introduce your retail customers (if you sell at retail) to purchase options that

---

* A Tanzanian imam once said that it was only when he began researching the origin of the textbooks he was using in the mosque schools and comparing them to others that he appreciated how dramatically different they were. He then designed his own books which emphasized compassion rather than hate. This recalls Ziad Asali's (founder and president of the American Task Force on Palestine) statement following an event I attended at the Council on Foreign Relations in Washington: "Extremist ideology is like a pandemic. People need to prevent its spread like we do with a virus. Each person must take action and there must be collective action in partnership with local, national and international governments."

reflect a variety of customs and cultures. Do your part to support local youth, partnering with schools and other organizations on programs that deal with issues of diversity, inclusion, identity, equity, and mutual respect. Fight hate wherever and however it appears.

If you're a local political leader, you're especially well positioned to mobilize your community against extremist ideology. Support other local community groups in their efforts to engage and educate local youth about the extremist threat. Set the tone by speaking of Muslims in ways that recognize their historic diversity. Use Ramadan and other religious and cultural observances to expose non-Muslims to Islam, and to forge new relationships between members of different faith communities. When orchestrating interfaith events, be careful about how you choose Muslims to highlight. Don't make the mistake that governments often make and pick people who you believe "look" Muslim, as that will only perpetuate harmful stereotypes. Send a message to kids that they can be Muslim in many ways, not just the rigid, supposedly "authentic" ways that extremist ideology extolls.

During my travels, I've witnessed firsthand the power of local officials—and mayors in particular—to fight back against extremist ideology. While visiting with young people in Istanbul in 2011, I was impressed at how many of them seemed determined to explain the historic diversity of Ottoman culture, how it wove together Islamic, Christian, and Jewish traditions. I wondered how these youths had become so passionate and well informed about the subject. Later in the trip, when I had an opportunity to meet with Ahmet Misbah Demircan, the charismatic mayor of Beyoglu municipality and president of the Istanbul Boğazı Municipalities Union, I understood why. In addition to a summer camp program his office ran that taught diversity and inclusion to local kids, Demircan had created an innovative new treasure-hunt-style program in partnership with local schools. Kids received "passports," and they collected passport stamps by visiting local churches, synagogues, and mosques. At each stop, they learned about local faith traditions and their history. No religion was presented as better than any of the others—as the kids learned, all had helped make Istanbul what it was. The last stamp children received came from the mayor's office, where they had a chance to meet the mayor personally.* This was his way of underscoring the principle of cohesion and inclusivity in his community. As he told me, he was really proud of his efforts in this area. Every adult had to do his or her part to raise kids so that they would not marginalize some portion of the community as "the other."

Other mayors have also helped to fight back against extremism in their local communities. In Louisville, Kentucky, mayor Greg Fischer has committed his city to becoming internationally recognized as a "compassionate city." One focus of that initiative has been interfaith relations: the city supports organizations like the Center for Interfaith Relations, which hosts an annual "Festival of Faiths" celebration, and Interfaith Paths to Peace, which promotes "interfaith understanding and peacemaking."[57] In Anaheim, California, Mayor Tom Tait created a "City of Kindness," drawing the attention of His Holiness the Dalai Lama.[58] And London mayor Sadiq Khan has taken on extremist ideology by contesting the underlying notion of a "clash of civilizations." Speaking of his own mayoral election, he noted that "I am the West, I am a Londoner, I'm British, I'm of Islamic faith, Asian origin, Pakistan heritage, so whether it's [ISIS] or these others who want to destroy our way of life and talk about the West, they're talking about me. What better antidote to the hatred they spew than someone like me being in this position?"[59] As Khan has suggested, community members in London had a responsibility to show kids that they could be "British, Muslim and successful," and to point to British Muslim role models like the Olympic athlete Mohamed Farah. "We're not simply tolerating each other," he has

* By some estimates, some ten thousand students participated in the 2015–16 school year.

said. "You tolerate a toothache, I don't want to be tolerated. We respect, we embrace, and we celebrate, which is fantastic."[60]

THE ROLE OF PHILANTHROPY

Another, critically important way in which individual citizens can mobilize against extremist ideology is through philanthropy. I've described how immensely difficult it has been to convince large corporate, private, and family foundations to step up and support NGOs running entrepreneurial grassroots initiatives. But it isn't just large charities that must step forward. Private individuals have a huge role to play on the global, national, and local stage. So far, private philanthropists at all levels have steered clear of funding CVE projects, providing only token and scattered assistance. Like charitable foundations and corporations, they think of CVE as political or security related, something for government to support, not individuals. They don't see CVE programs for what they are: youth protection initiatives.

In recent years, philanthropists have become more interested in making "big bets," concentrating huge sums on a specific area of need. They're also focused on driving systemic change rather than on merely delivering local interventions.[61] As a 2016 *Forbes* article explained, "modern philanthropists, who have used disruptive thinking to create fortunes at ever younger ages, are more inclined to use their money to try to actually solve problems rather than salve wounds."[62] Where, I wonder, is the "Bill Gates" of CVE—the pioneer philanthropist who looks at this issue and says, "Yes, I'm betting that going all in and building a capacity outside of government to counter extremist ideas will help us solve this issue"? I've spoken with dozens of wealthy donors, and so far, nobody has been brave enough to step forward. In June 2017, Amazon founder Jeff Bezos tweeted asking for ideas as to how his philanthropy can help the world in the near term, as he put it, "at the intersection of urgent need and lasting impact."[63] My message to Jeff and others: this is your issue!

An eight-figure, "big bet" donation such as prominent philanthropists are now making in areas like clean energy or education would have a major impact on youth both nationally and globally, and it would indirectly better both the economy and society at large. Just as Google Fiber is providing its superfast gigabit broadband technology in certain cities and towns across America, so philanthropists can decide to reboot the status quo in their localities. In local cities and towns, making smaller-scale "big bets" could change the environment in which kids grow up, inoculating entire communities against extremism. Philanthropists can also contribute their innovative thinking and business acumen, and their participation can lend legitimacy to CVE, galvanizing other philanthropists to get involved.

Whether philanthropists wish to make "big bets" or smaller investments in protecting communities, there are many ways that they can make a difference in CVE over both the short and long term. Givers can support local NGOs working on CVE issues, providing money, access to networks of locally influential people, and access to volunteers. Of course, the most salient interventions—the ones that deliver profound, comprehensive, systemic change—are those that shape the way youth form their identities, thereby interrupting the radicalization process. Philanthropists could reinforce good behavior on the part of youth and discourage bad behavior by collaborating with and supporting influencers. They could, for instance, support academic researchers studying the child and adolescent mind; social entrepreneurs developing local youth resilience programs; NGOs performing anti-hate work and fighting extremism online; local teachers and schools that want to incorporate new lessons about inclusivity, anti-hate, empathy, and identity into the standard curriculum; artists and musicians working with these themes; hospitals offering mental health expertise to local families; organizations offering interfaith initiatives and family counseling; and many others. Citizens have already begun taking action in these areas. What we're missing is the engine—both financial and social—that will allow us to scale these programs up in and across local communities. The more "touch points" with youth that philanthropists help us create, the more we can disrupt the larger system underlying extremism.

Some philanthropists might acknowledge the value of CVE, yet feel uncertain about giving money to little-known social entrepreneurs or activists. In fact, there are many ways that philanthropists can partner with well-known, reputable individuals or organizations to pursue CVE initiatives. Philanthropists could donate to a university or "think-do" tank working on CVE. They could support the United Nations–backed Strong Cities Network.* They could work directly with mayors' offices to build resilience programs in communities. They could donate to large foundations, specifically bequeathing funds for CVE purposes. And of course, they could give to proven NGOs that are already partnering with governments. The Institute of Strategic Dialogue, for instance, has a ten-year track record, and has been carefully vetted. These organizations are out there, if you know where to look.

Recall Luqman Ali's Khayaal Theater Company. Ali told me in 2017 that his organization had "half a dozen potentially world-class stage productions with global appeal" in preparation, each of which would cost hundreds of thousands of dollars to develop into international touring productions. Yet Luqman wouldn't be able to produce those plays without significant investment.†

---

* The Strong Cities Network also has a Mayoral Public-Private Partnership Task Force, a partnership with the Anti-Defamation League, German Marshall Fund, and the Institute for Strategic Dialogue.

† "With a million pounds we'd scale up the processes involved . . . to put in place the soft and hard infrastructure necessary for the proliferation of cultural creativity and production in specifically the storytelling and theatre art forms. We'd demonstrate a story of positive attitudinal change by sharing the many individual,

When I pitch CVE projects to philanthropists, they often cite their skepticism about measurement as a reason not to give. They ask whether I have any quantitative evidence suggesting that funding small NGOs and credible voices truly works. These are challenging questions. To some extent, a chicken-and-egg problem exists here: metrics don't exist because philanthropists haven't funded individual programs long enough for their organizers to collect data proving their efficacy. Sasha Havlicek of the Institute for Strategic Dialogue told me that her organization not only had potent CVE tools but also methodologies to measure their impact. Still, she said, "none of these programs has received investment at scale over a long enough time-frame to give us statistically significant data, and without such investment [in the data], it will be impossible to measure whether they have resulted in any longer term attitudinal or behavioral change." To mount a CVE response proportional to what the extremists are mounting, Havlicek estimates that her organization would need a five-million-pound investment (for data analysis) in one midsize city over three years. That funding "would result in the most comprehensive data to date on longitudinal, systemic impact, answering the question 'does this work?' once and for all."[64]

Havlicek's programs aside, many CVE projects simply are not susceptible to "hard" measurement in the way that other interventions might be. We can track how many kids a given intervention is reaching, and we can also track attitudinal and behavioral changes in youth, but it's difficult if not impossible to establish that a given intervention "caused" specific changes in behavior or attitude.* A large body of aca-

communal, and social case studies that we have accrued over the past two decades." Luqman Ali, director of Khayaal Theater Company, e-mail to the author, July 4, 2017.

* Take, for instance, online programs that nudge youth toward CVE messaging when they are searching for certain content (for example, travel logistics to Syria or Iraq to fight with so-called ISIS). We can track how many users were redirected, but we can't know if a given youth actually joined so-called ISIS's ranks. We therefore can't establish clear causality and measure the impact of an intervention with quantitative precision.

demic research has yet to identify a single "factor" that causes a kid to become an extremist, nor has it indicated a single, clear, "silver bullet" solution. Such failure doesn't mean that a practical solution doesn't exist, or that we shouldn't experiment with possible solutions.

Modern societies thrive on data and science, but we also have to recognize the limitations of our knowledge when it comes to humanistic pursuits like CVE. You can't quantify the intrinsic value of a work of art, yet that doesn't stop us from finding novels and paintings compelling and worthy of our time. Similarly, we won't "solve" the problem of extremism unless philanthropists are willing to part at least somewhat with their need for quantitative metrics. "Big bet" philanthropy is inherently about taking risks—betting on a potential solution to a social problem that we think will work, but aren't sure. When Dave and Dana Dornsife committed $75 million over five years to bring clean water and sanitation to millions of Africans, they had no guarantee that their money would achieve its intended objective. They gave anyway, gathering information and experience and taking what Dave termed "a calculated risk."[65] Younger philanthropists, who tend to see themselves as social activists or change leaders as opposed to passive donors, are increasingly showing a similar predilection for bold, systemic giving.* As we've seen, CVE allows for precisely that degree of change (and young donors have in fact funded anti-hate NGOs).

* "The successful entrepreneur types, tend to look for technology, for enabling platforms, they tend to look at data . . . innovation and entrepreneurship as the sine qua non of social change. . . . So, their happy place in between there is when philanthropy can fund innovation that proves that it has impact and can scale and then through coordination of the stakeholders in the space—the bilaterals, the multilaterals, governments, the local governments . . . the local entrepreneurs . . . all the different stakeholders. Then they can say, we have proven a relatively profitable business model for an intervention that works, which can be shared with a more diverse set of players, including private sector and market-based actors. We will now hand this over to the more logical players. . . . It's about using philanthropic capital to derive innovations that have the potential to change the system, to bring in innovation that can go beyond a single organization. A true social entrepreneur wants the innovation to be used beyond his or her own organization. Such people want to scale the innovation, scale the impact." J. Alexander Sloan, vice president of strategic partnerships and communications at Tide, interview with the author, March 17, 2017.

COMING TOGETHER AGAINST EXTREMISM

However local individuals and groups choose to engage around CVE, they will gain more traction if they can also come together to mobilize the community's own unique strengths, assets, and attributes. In Houston, two leaders in a Muslim community, Tameez and Wardah Khalid, created a comprehensive plan to counter violent extremism in consultation with the local sheriff's department that brought together many actors in the community, including mental health providers, prison personnel, local mosques, and educational experts.[66] In New South Wales, Australia, a wide-ranging community partnership to counter extremism formed in 2016 engaged fourteen organizations across the community, including cultural centers and local Muslim associations.[67]

How might you bring a range of actors together to create an innovative CVE program or solution? My hometown of Boston is known for its strength in industries like higher education, medicine, and technology. It boasts dozens of colleges and universities and hundreds of companies. It was also directly impacted by the so-called Islamic State when the Tsarnaev brothers set off bombs at the Boston Marathon on Patriot's Day 2013. In the hours and days that followed, Boston bravely, resiliently, and fiercely reacted with the motto of "Boston Strong." Again mobilizing such focus and unifying energy, why couldn't the city create a "Countering Extremism Laboratory" that would empower kids to fight extremist ideology, with help from experts from local universities, mental health institutions, technology labs, and companies? Mimicking other kinds of entrepreneurial "labs," this one could have the subject matter expertise, technological assistance, and entrepreneurial expertise to facilitate the creation by kids of a range of media-related projects, including apps and online platforms geared toward younger audiences. Such a hive for creative ideas could be fashioned along the lines of the Broad Institute in Cambridge, Massachusetts, for example, where ethnographers, anthropologists, engineers, medical doctors, data analysts, advertisers, and others would collaborate on projects and share information. This is a fairly obvious solution that would mobilize Boston's existing strengths. Yet so far, it hasn't happened.[68]

Within local communities, Muslims have a special responsibility to participate in and lead CVE initiatives. Whether Muslims like it or not, many non-Muslim philanthropists want to see the community most affected by terrorist recruiting (and most victimized by it)[69] stand up to protect their kids. When I speak publicly, the single most common question posed to me is why Muslims aren't doing more to stop extremism, including by donating to initiatives dedicated to CVE. It's a good question. Obviously, Muslims have taken numerous steps to dissuade their youth from embracing extremist ideas, including some of the projects covered in this chapter, but they haven't done nearly enough on the funding side. In the United States, for instance, Muslims have barely given to CVE causes, even though they are among the wealthiest of minority groups.[70] In 2008, while serving in the Bush administration, I worked with Juan Zarate, Adnan Kifayat, George Selim, and others on an idea for building a nongovernmental fund to bring money from key American Muslim donors into CVE.* Nobody whom we approached would contribute. American Muslims simply were not interested.

It's not that American Muslims are parsimonious—far from it. As mentioned in an earlier chapter, almsgiving is central to Islam, one of the religion's five pillars, and Muslims richly support worthy causes such as alleviating poverty or building schools.† By some

* Together with a D.C.-based philanthropy and impact investing consultancy founded by a former government administration official, an award-winning global expert in social impact bonds and philanthropic investing, and the Gen Next Foundation, we designed a formal giving structure and prepared to launch it with money from key American Muslim donors.

† American Muslims give an estimated $10 billion or more, much of it going to "building mosques and schools and funding non-religious organizations" in the United States. Saima Zaman, "A New Era of Muslim-American Philanthropy Requires Fewer Obstacles to Giving," *Philanthropy News Digest*, June 23, 2009, http://philanthropynewsdigest.org/commentary-and-opinion/new-era-of-muslim-american-philanthropy.

estimates, global charitable giving by Muslims amounted to between $200 billion and $1 trillion in 2012. Even the smaller number is "15 times more than global humanitarian aid contributions in 2011."[71] In the minds of Muslims, CVE doesn't rank with traditional charitable causes. Why? As many American Muslims have told me, terrorists are not "real Muslims." Why, some Muslims argue, do they have a special obligation to deal with the problem? Like members of other minority groups, Muslims resist the idea that the sins of a few define their entire population. They feel stigmatized already and want to get on with their lives. They want extremism to go away, and with it, the unwanted attention extremism brings from the outside world. To connect themselves with the problem can seem like a confession to a crime they didn't commit.*

Whether Muslims want to or not, they must step up and lead and help fund CVE initiatives in their local communities. Among youth, no support is more "authentic" than Muslim support. Imagine what would happen if American Muslims supported CVE programs (social service hot lines, mental health interventions, research grants, open dialogue forums, youth programs, innovation labs, media campaigns, AI interventions, genius grants, and so on) at scale, both through volunteer efforts and philanthropic giving? They would revolutionize the landscape. Small NGOs would no longer have to accept money from the wealthy Gulf states—they would have other options. Non-Muslims would feel far more comfortable getting behind CVE. Rightly or wrongly, it's harder to convince non-Muslims to fight the war of ideas when Muslims themselves aren't stepping up

---

* As I detail in chapter 6, in 2006, after trying and failing to obtain financial support for CVE from American Muslim philanthropists, I conceived the following idea: convert time into money. I thought that I might perhaps engage a new team of actors—Muslim millennials themselves—through a project I called the Zakat Corps. Like the Peace Corps, the Zakat Corps would send young American Muslims overseas, where they would donate their time (instead of money they didn't have) to work on local projects. The project would expose global Muslim communities to American Muslims and their model of cultural integration, correcting misconceptions about American Islam. Unfortunately, I wasn't able to secure funding for this project, and it never materialized.

financially. As Iranian American intellectual and celebrated author Reza Aslan remarked in 2011 at a gathering of the Islamic Scholarship Fund, American Muslims were worth $160 billion a year.[72] As a group, they wield immense financial clout. They just need to "put their money where their mouth is." Extremism may impact all of us, but it is in the first instance a direct threat to Muslim kids. All of us—including Muslims—must work together on the solutions.

NANO-INTERVENTIONS

In 2009, my mother moved from the Boston area to a city in the southern United States. After decades of practicing medicine up north, she wanted to escape the cold winters during her retirement and spend as much time as possible on one of her great passions, gardening. She was out one day in her new, rose-filled yard when a Christian neighbor named Hilda stopped by. Mom had noticed that many cars were parked outside Hilda's house on Wednesdays, and so she asked why. Hilda replied that this was her weekly Bible study meeting, and they were studying "women of the Old Testament." "Oh, how wonderful," Mom responded. "Can I come?"

Mom is a devout Muslim and extremely erudite about her religion. She memorized the Qur'an at the age of five and continued to educate herself throughout her life, reading many scholarly texts and translations of the Qur'an, comparing versions, analyzing sources, and researching commentary from academics in the East and West. But she also knew a lot about the other Abrahamic faiths and was well versed in the Christian Bible (it is a holy book for Muslims, too). Still, she realized that her question had put Hilda in an awkward position. Mom's new community was culturally conservative and quite homogeneous demographically. Would her neighbors find it appropriate for a Muslim to attend a Christian Bible study group? Hilda said she would check with the church and let Mom know.

The next day, Hilda informed Mom that the group would love to have her. At her first meeting, Mom thanked the group for including her and offered to answer any questions they might have. "You might not have any Muslim friends or know much about the religion," she said. "Let me be the face of Islam for you." The women took her up on it, and ever since, Mom has participated actively in the group. On dozens of occasions, she has answered questions about the Qur'an and about confusing items the women heard about on the news. Once, when the local church was welcoming a new deacon, Mom helped organize the event and cook for it. As a result of her efforts, a community of Christians knows a bit more about Muslims and Islam. Mom, meanwhile, has had a chance to forge relationships with other people of faith who love, respect, and care for her as she does them. Both Mom and her neighbors have come to believe more than ever in the virtues of a respectful, inclusive society.

My mom's experience points to another, extremely important way in which individuals must join the fight against extremism: through direct, personal interactions with others around them. Building on the typology I described earlier, we can think of our everyday behavior as "nano-interventions" that help change the attitudes, beliefs, and behaviors of people in our families, workplaces, and social circles. In the aftermath of horrible attacks on Jewish cemeteries in Missouri in February 2017, Muslims raised money to help.[73] That's a powerfully symbolic nano-intervention, but there are a multitude of others. Nano-interventions can be as simple as a gesture of kindness or respect rendered to a person in a different religion, a statement confirming that everybody in the community belongs, or an act of engagement across religious or ethnic boundaries. If our goal is to help shift individual youths' thinking about identity and ultimately their behavior, then we need everyone around these youths to help make that happen. Mass media communications, social media messaging, and local programming can all shape the mental environment in which kids live. But for CVE to really hit home, kids need to encounter it all the time. And that means those around them must constantly articulate and affirm these messages and values in their own actions.

I'm particularly attuned to the importance of personal, one-on-one interactions because of my years spent engaging directly with young people. The very fact that I, a Muslim, was connecting with Muslim youth contested their preconceived notions of America, the American government, and the government's intentions toward Muslims. By speaking about Islam's rich history in America and offering my firsthand experiences growing up Muslim, I debunked many elements of extremist narratives in ways that youth found authentic. In every country I visited, people expressed to me how powerful it was to see a Muslim in a senior U.S. government position taking time to *listen* to Muslims. At a school in Guyana, kids told me that I was showing them "what America is really about." In Thailand, kids told me, "You don't realize it, but because you are you, you make us see America differently." In Iraq, they said, "We need to see people like you here. It makes us see America differently."

Individuals have the power to help others see themselves and others differently. We have the power to explode stereotypes; to affirm the importance of inclusion, equity, diversity, and respect; to alert kids to the dangers of extremist thinking; and to let kids know that there are many ways to be a member of any group or religion. Muslims again have a special responsibility. If you're parenting a Muslim teen, impress these ideas upon him or her and live them yourselves. If you're an educator or a community leader, make inclusivity and diversity a key message. If you're a millennial, serve as a role model for your peers. One local imam I met counseled confused youth, helping them "go deep" into Muslim identity and how to square it with modern life. A librarian I met made a point of being even more careful about selecting which books about Islam interested students should read. So many people out there are taking action to contest extremist narratives and assumptions in their daily lives. They don't necessarily receive a lot of attention, and sometimes they're not even aware of the impact they're having. Yet that impact is real. Take up the cause and realize that *you* have a responsibility and an opportunity to fight bigotry and hate.

When it comes to identity, the character of our everyday environments matter—how immediate friends and relatives behave, how they make us feel. During my years in government, many young Muslims asked me why I felt so confident being both American and Muslim. The answer, as I've suggested, is that it was never an issue for me growing up. For my classmates and teachers, I was just another member of the class. I was not defined by my heritage or religion. My environment gave me that comfort and confidence, and I was very lucky to grow up without intellectual borders and in a pretty open-minded community. But every community has minds that can be opened. Each of us can behave in ways that help others feel like they belong, so that they can explore and express their identities in healthy, productive ways. The simple act of listening goes a long way. As special representative, I often made headway by listening with an open mind to young Muslims, and accepting their perspectives as true for *them*. Listening to those around us implicitly conveys acceptance and respect, sometimes even more powerfully than the words "I accept you" do.

In addition to my mother, my uncle Dr. Mian Ashraf served as an important role model for me. A heart surgeon, he would tell me, "I operate on hearts. I have held human hearts in my hand. Remember, there is no difference between the heart of a Muslim, Jew, Hindu, or Christian." He was the one who took me to Sunday school and mosque, making sure that my brother, cousins, and I were learning about Islam and the many local traditions that fed into it. He never, ever spoke about the "right" or "wrong" way to be a Muslim (sects and practices of all kinds were equal in his mind), and he brought all guests from many ethnic backgrounds to my mom's house after prayers for our traditional Sunday meal. Because I was exposed to all this diversity, it became "normal" for me. I knew in *my* heart—as I do today—that Islam looked very different depending on your ethnicity and traditions, and that far from posing a problem, such diversity was a source of richness and beauty.

In the wake of the 2016 attack at Ohio State, a professor at the university, Mohammed Omer, reflected on his own personal role as a member of the Somali community: "I feel that I have now a huge responsibility on my shoulder right now. That I have to double my efforts. That's my job, is to make sure that I teach the people how beautiful our values and culture [are]."[74] All of us should feel this kind of urgency, no matter what our station in society. And we should feel it at all times. If we've waited until an attack has already taken place, we've waited too long. Just as Omer has the power to impact how the kids he teaches view themselves, their traditions, and the world, we all have a similar power—as parents, teachers, neighbors, and friends.

Non-Muslims can help win the war of ideas. When my uncle was president of the Islamic Center of New England (one of America's oldest mosques), the congregation sought out land to build a new, larger mosque in the town of Milton, Massachusetts.[75] The congregation found a perfect property—a former Catholic monastery was up for sale—but Milton residents were so fearful of Muslims that some of them paid more than a million in cash for the land before the congregation could, preventing us from building the mosque there. The *Boston Globe* ran a story about this episode, and afterward, a man in the nearby town of Sharon called my uncle and told him that he owned some land in Sharon that would be suitable for a mosque.[76] He also told my uncle that the town, which was predominantly Jewish, would welcome the mosque.[77]

Our congregation built the mosque there, and the town did welcome it. At the groundbreaking ceremony, my uncle made sure that all members of the community were invited. We had rabbis, a Greek Orthodox bishop, Catholic priests, and others in attendance, and the first person to put a spade in the ground was a local rabbi. It was an incredible day, a moving experience of generosity and openness of spirit.[78] All of us learned something, including our Muslim community. We learned to move beyond stereotypes about Jews and Christians and easy and incorrect notions of "us" and "them." In this instance, non-Muslims—the man who sold the land, the rabbis who worked with the imam, the members of Jewish congregations that reached out to build trust, the local government leaders who welcomed in Muslims from outside—helped sow the seeds of collaboration among our communities.*

Extremism isn't just a "Muslim issue." It's an issue for all humanity. How do we treat people in a way that respects their dignity? With bigotry and hatred roiling the world around us, all of us must do everything we can to push back. If we treat someone who is different from us well, if we listen and get to know him, her, she, he, or they, we send the message that ours is an inclusive society. Youth watch us, and over time many of them come to see themselves and their world differently. In 2010, Hannah Rosenthal, the State Department's special envoy to combat and monitor anti-Semitism, and I attended a conference in Kazakhstan, and felt inspired to do more than just give speeches about mutual respect. We created an initiative called Hours Against Hate, asking young people to devote just one hour of their time to doing something for another person who is different than they are.† Thousands of young people around the world took us up on the challenge, learning about others around them and developing their powers of empathy. They appreciated that

---

* Secretary John Kerry spoke about this event in a 2013 speech at a U.S. State Department dinner in the Ben Franklin Room. Congressman Bill Keating, an important partner in this effort, spoke with me privately, following the speech, about that day and its continued relevance to the country. For John Kerry's speech, see, "Remarks at the Ramadan Iftar Dinner," Washington, D.C., July 24, 2013, https://2009-2017.state.gov/secretary/remarks/2013/07/212390.htm.

† An early partner in this global effort was Alan Solomont, the U.S. ambassador to Spain, who embraced the program and launched a series of related activities across Spain, beginning in Córdoba.

they could go beyond mere words, taking *action* that would bridge differences and build understanding. The 2012 London Olympic and Paralympic games became an official partner of Hours Against Hate, and we featured the program at a number of Olympic related events.[79] In 2017, the Muhammad Ali Center, based in Louisville, Kentucky, announced plans to partner with the Institute for Strategic Dialogue and the Gen Next Foundation to rekindle the effort through a new online campaign and partnerships. Now it's your turn. Reach out and connect with someone who doesn't look like you, pray like you, love like you, live like you. By doing so, you will contribute in a small way toward solving the problem of extremism. As more people everywhere take this and other actions, we'll make slow but steady strides toward a world of mutual respect and security.[80]

REASON FOR HOPE

If government would take CVE seriously in the way I've outlined, and were business and civil society to join forces, we'd see an ideological sea change in communities around the world. We'd have millions of "foot soldiers" fighting the ideological war in every conceivable capacity—a true Dumbledore's army. We'd flood the market with credible voices urging youth to forgo hatred and mistrust. We'd cut off the steady flow of new recruits that are the lifeblood of extremist movements. Even if leaders at the top might be behaving and speaking in ways that confirm extremist narratives, their examples would pale beside the outpouring of other voices that contest these narratives. In the years to come, nation-states will continue to face significant threats from nonstate actors empowered by digital technologies. Isn't it time to take one of these threats off the table?

In 2006, at a White House Iftar event convened by President Bush, I had a chance to meet an impressive young Muslim woman who had served as a first responder during 9/11. Our conversation drifted to the emerging problem of extremism in Muslim communities. "It's so scary," this woman said, a glint of determination in her eyes, "but we can't let them win. We can't let them destroy who we are as Americans. We need to do more to bring our communities together. When we defend our country, putting our lives at risk, we don't care about what someone's name or faith is. We know they have our back. This is who we are!" Let's look to this woman and the many other thoughtful, dedicated people described in this chapter—including Luqman, Dash, Charlotte, Naif, Said, Sasha, Elvis, Zahed, Asim, Mohamed, Ziad, Daniyal, Hilda, and Ahmed—and help them to realize their dreams of inclusiveness, openness, and understanding. Our world will become a safer, more secure, more humane place. I believe in these individuals. Do you?

EPILOGUE

THE PROMISE OF OPEN POWER

Some problems facing mankind, such as global warming or disease, seem so massive and complex as to be intractable. The appeal of extremist ideology, happily, is not one of these. The threat posed to global security by violent extremist groups is extremely serious and growing worse, but if my experiences have taught me anything, it is that sustainable and effective solutions to this problem do exist. We are not powerless against a group like the so-called Islamic State or Al Qaeda—although it might often seem that way.

Military force is no doubt vitally important to defeating terrorist organizations on the battlefield, but its limited scope and short-term payoff do not ultimately make us safer. That recognition begs a number of questions. Does the United States government, and other governments around the world, believe this is a solvable problem? Does the public believe it has a role to play? Has the global conversation since 9/11 allowed societies to expand their thinking to allow for new tools and mobilization? Can government itself even imagine a new reality?

Further, we might ask: During George W. Bush's second term, why were some officials inside the State Department and in other agencies so resistant to programs that engaged with Muslims to counter extremist ideology? Why was the Obama administration so slow to invest in the expansion of existing CVE strategies and programs? Why isn't the Trump administration building a massive operation to stop recruitment? Why didn't Congress take up this nonlethal avenue, devoting resources to protecting America's youth and preventing the need for troops overseas? And why today do so many government officials, politicians, and commentators across the political spectrum continue to emphasize military solutions, failing to broaden their understanding and take seriously efforts that might prevent extremists from replenishing their ranks?

In the preceding chapters I have answered these questions by recourse to political and professional concerns, as well as to the stultifying nature of government bureaucracy. Over time, however, I've become convinced that neglect of the ideological dimension has another, more profound cause: governments have been deploying the very concepts of power in anachronistic ways. Dating from the twentieth century, prevailing modes of wielding power simply do not acknowledge certain salient features of the extremist threat, nor do they encourage us to act in ways that might effectively confront extremism and defeat it as both a military and ideological force. We are stuck using tools set up for a different reality—a world of much different demographics and technology. As a result, we have not addressed extremism imaginatively and in ways that are relevant, fitting, and impactful. When we do try to address extremist ideology in a "modern" way, we wind up just skimming the surface. We concern ourselves with how many "likes" a piece of content gets on a given social platform, not realizing that we can't exercise power unless we mobilize these and related tactics smartly, cohesively, and strategically.

Traditionally, as I explained earlier in this book, governments have pursued objectives through hard power solutions—military, physical, or economic coercion. Since Joseph Nye's initial articulation of the soft power concept during the 1990s, he clarified that "soft power was only one component of power, and rarely sufficient by itself."[1] Nye then set forth the term "smart power" to encompass the combination of "hard and soft power into a winning strategy." Writing specifically about the fight against extremism, he noted that America needed to deploy hard power against actors like Al Qaeda who are immune to persuasion, and soft power to appeal to mainstream Muslims.[2] Hillary Clinton invoked the "smart power" concept in 2009 during her confirmation hearing for the post of secretary of state, arguing that the United States should deploy "the full range of tools at our disposal—-diplomatic, economic, military, political, legal, and cultural—-picking the right tool, or combination of tools, for each situation. With smart power, diplomacy will be the vanguard of foreign policy."*

Like others in the foreign policy space after 9/11, I had become accustomed to thinking about strategies and tactics in light of hard and soft power. But extremism was spreading, despite the deployment of military force and efforts at coercion and persuasion. By 2005–6, when I was serving on the National Security Council, I began to realize that the prevailing ways that government officials were thinking about hard and soft power weren't adequate to the particular challenges posed by extremist ideology. Former national security advisor Stephen Hadley has remarked that our military "needs an effective civilian partner if victories on the battlefields are going to be converted into a sustainable peace."[3] Yet under the existing mantle of soft power as government officials were applying it, I didn't see us cultivating an effective civilian partner on the field in the fight against extremist recruiting.

---

* Secretary of Defense Robert Gates also endorsed the need for smart power, stating: "I am here to make the case for strengthening our capacity to use soft power and for better integrating it with hard power," as quoted in Eric Etheridge, "How Soft Power Got Smart," *New York Times,* January 14, 2009, https://opinionator.blogs.nytimes.com/2009/01/14/how-soft-power-got-smart/.

First, government officials were using soft power to influence beliefs and change impressions, but they weren't conceiving of the kind of intensive, all-encompassing influence required to shift one's self-concept, and consequently, one's behavior. Second, government officials were using soft and hard power as a way to wield influence over a limited number of nation-states and their populations. As nonstate actors, extremist groups were far more amorphous, agile, and opportunistic. Third, government officials were typically using hard and soft power to address limited geopolitical or security challenges. Extremism was a global phenomenon, crossing cultures and geographies. Fourth, officials seeking to apply hard and soft power were relying on the weight brought to bear by government itself—military force, or the impact of ideological legitimacy or credibility. Yet the U.S. government possessed limited credibility with youth vulnerable to extremist ideology. Officials couldn't simply deploy conventional soft power tools of persuasion and hope to succeed.

I also felt that the hard power versus soft power dichotomy was counterproductive because it seemed to marginalize soft power. Washington was built around hard power. The entire mental framework within the interagency was attuned to tangible, hard power goals and accomplishments, like military treaties, trade deals, and financial wins. Perceiving soft power as "soft," many policy makers outside of the State Department failed to give it any real attention. In their minds, soft power wasn't real power, but rather that "gushy" thing that others did to try to "win hearts and minds." Policy makers spent far less money on tools in the soft power domain (as the congressional budgets for the State Department attest), and their eyes glazed over when you began to speak to them about what soft power tactics could accomplish.

As I traveled around Europe in 2007–8 and began to understand what methods would prove successful, I found myself consistently frustrated by the inadequacy of the tools available to us given conventional ways of thinking about soft power. Looking at the array of existing soft power tactics left over from the Cold War, I realized that they left little room for innovative programs that I was encountering in other spaces, and that I wanted to apply to CVE. Governments seemed to be falling into something resembling the Kindleberger Trap (named after Charles Kindleberger, one of the intellectual architects of the Marshall Plan),[4] a situation in which countries lost power because they turned inward and didn't project it.[5] In pursuing their own, parochial interests, local constituencies within bureaucracies were preventing government from using its power to take on the issue of extremist recruiting. A dangerous power vacuum had emerged, and NGOs were scrambling to fill it, although they lacked both the resources and broad platforms to operate at scale.

I kept meeting social entrepreneurs who were taking conventional soft power tactics and concepts, synthesizing them together, and using them in innovative ways—evidence enough that big government hadn't remotely exhausted the ways that it might apply soft power. I found myself wanting to join these mavericks, venturing beyond the confines of existing bureaucracies to develop and execute CVE programs. I wanted to "disrupt" conventional government practices, "mess them up" by collaborating with a whole new range of actors, including social entrepreneurs, design theorists, behavior economists, artists, anthropologists, historians, musicians, athletes, architects, scientists, and technologists. I wanted to help expand and perhaps even redefine what soft power could be for government (recognizing that companies, nonprofits, and regular citizens also deploy hard and soft power every day in a variety of ways).* The traditional ways of applying hard and soft power simply didn't allow for such collaborations or the needed systematic, multidimensional thinking. Officials treated power as something that government wielded

* On the use of soft power in a business context, see Arlene S. Hirsch, "How to 'Soft Power' Your Way to a Senior Leadership Role," *SHRM* (April 14, 2017), downloaded May 15, 2018, https://www.shrm.org/resourcesandtools/hr-topics/behavioral-competencies/relationship-management/pages/how-to-soft-power-your-way-to-a-senior-leadership-role.aspx.

on others (and specifically, other state actors), not something that government and civil society collaborated on and wielded *together.* Under prevailing modes of applying hard and soft power, government didn't relinquish control over policy and its execution enough to allow for true creativity and experimentation. Government could not let go because it was government.

During my work in the Obama administration, as I took my experimental CVE programs global, I became convinced that CVE didn't just represent a new strategic approach to the problem. It embodied an entirely new way of applying soft power, a variant of it that I call "open power." As illustrated by the policy approach described in chapters 7 through 9, it entails a more fluid, nonhierarchical, and creative relationship between government and private actors. Rather than executing specific policies itself, government "opens up" the challenge, soliciting potential solutions from diverse actors. Government serves primarily as facilitator, intellectual partner, convener, and at times funder of nongovernment actors who might enjoy more credibility with local populations than government itself. A founding assumption of open power is that the global community can come together on a peer-to-peer basis to address a pressing public issue, given adequate respect, resources, and support from government. By acting to empower other actors rather than to monopolize the use of power, government can tackle global issues, giving rise to an almost limitless array of specific programs and interventions.

I am hardly the only one calling for a more collaborative, entrepreneurial approach to addressing social issues,* and looking across contemporary politics, we can actually observe aspects of open power taking shape and becoming mainstream. In 2017, newly elected French president Emmanuel Macron went outside the traditional political parties, convening a diverse group of political novices to

* See Jeremy Heimans and Henry Timms, *New Power: How Power Works in Our Hyperconnected World—and How to Make It Work for You* (New York: Doubleday, 2018).

run for legislative office under his banner. It seems that the philosophy entailed more than just building a diverse team. As Harvard Business School's Laura Morgan Roberts noted, "the power of differences transforms"—by introducing the collective experiences and knowledge of new sets of problem solvers, we open the way for innovative solutions.[6] Open power is not a call per se for more diversity in government (although research has long pointed to a strong correlation between diverse leadership and business performance).[7] Rather, it's simply a call for government to take responsibility for injecting new perspectives and ideas into what it does, so as to update and breathe new life into our older models of soft power.

Reflecting again on the CVE approach that I've outlined, we can say that open power entails a more flexible, experimental, and entrepreneurial approach to securing government objectives. Government relinquishes its sole focus on "intelligence" and strict channels of operation and instead "open-sources" ideas and solutions, using a variety of scientific and humanistic tools. It escapes siloed thinking, "opening the aperture" to see problems holistically, organically, and systemically, in their full complexity. It considers and includes local community points of view and insights, turning to companies, scholars, researchers, and activists, rather than attempting to impose solutions, harnessing the credibility that comes with peer-to-peer engagement. Open power is open-ended. It keeps changing and moving as global issues evolve and as new ideas come to light. Finally, open power "opens up" considerations of time. Whereas hard power has immediate effects and soft power as officials have traditionally deployed it can take decades, open power can work in both ways at once. You can mobilize open power quickly and strategically, but also in a continuous, ongoing fashion as conditions evolve.

Open power is in essence an effort to transform and improve government by rendering it more progressive, dynamic, and responsive to today's challenges. Other areas of society are evolving in similar ways, moving away from traditional constructs and categories, and lowering boundaries to foster collaboration and innovation. In business, leaders like Unilever's Paul Polman and Chobani's Hamdi Ulukaya have boldly redefined what a business enterprise can be in the course of tackling problems like global warming and refugee migration. Large corporations have also undertaken initiatives to spur innovation and collaboration across boundaries, crowdsourcing solutions from customers, employees, and other stakeholders. Firms like IDEO are even beginning to quantify traditionally "soft" concepts like innovation and develop frameworks for optimizing them.[8] While such initiatives have by no means all succeeded, and while business must do far more to prepare themselves for social, political, and environmental changes that bear on markets, the dynamism in business dwarfs what we see in government. That needs to change. Government needs to "open up" the way elements of the business community have, developing both methodologies and strategies. By becoming more innovative, government will be able to move faster, achieve better results, and operate in ways that citizens and other stakeholders find much more appealing. Most important, they'll be able to keep pace with existing challenges and anticipate new ones as they emerge.

Investment approaches such as venture philanthropy also entail taking open power risks for the sake of making truly transformative, systemic changes.* In a June 2017 speech at the Council on Foreign Relations, Michael Davidson, CEO of the Gen Next Foundation, recalled that it was the "adventurous approach" of venture investing that had inspired him to get involved with CVE. "Gen Next was the first to the fire," he said. "There's a leadership deficit in this area, and there needs to be a disruption in the philanthropy sector"—one toward "purpose-driven action" and toward "open versus closed models."[9]

---

* According to one source, venture philanthropy "was first used to describe 'an adventurous approach to funding unpopular social causes.'" Today is seeks "transformative social change." "Venture Philanthropy," Pecaut Center for Social Impact, https://leap-pecautcentre.ca/venture-philanthropy/.

Writing this book, I came to see that we could apply the open power concept not merely to extremism, but to a class of problems facing the world that tended to defy conventional hard and soft power solutions, and that share a number of common characteristics. Challenges such as certain diseases, poverty, sex trafficking, climate change, and drug addiction seem structurally similar in key respects to extremism, and hence susceptible to an open power approach. Like extremism, these issues:

- are all truly global and systemic.
- extend well beyond a simple conflict between traditional nation-states.
- hinge in part on individuals' behavior and self-concept.
- are all fast-moving like extremism, evolving in "real time."
- persist in part because of credibility gaps of various kinds on the part of government.
- have both short- and long-term consequences that must be dealt with simultaneously.

In sum, these issues are twenty-first-century issues, and they require a new, more nuanced, more fluid, more flexible, and more entrepreneurial application of soft power on the part of government if we are to make progress. They require that government officials exercise power *with* other actors rather than power *over* them.

As I've suggested with respect to CVE, government simply doesn't have the ability to implement durable solutions on its own to these problems. But that doesn't mean that solutions don't exist. They do—and executing them will depend on all of us taking responsibility and working together. Government doesn't "own" an issue like extremism. All of us do. We must therefore free ourselves from the conventions and silos that have formerly constrained society's responses. We must collaborate across disciplinary boundaries, recognizing that our way is not the only way, and that others have needs, perspectives, and insights that matter, too. And we must commit ourselves to constantly changing our mind-sets and approaches as the problems we're addressing change.

Sharing power across society and exercising it collaboratively doesn't result in government's "loss" of power or control over an issue, as more traditionally minded officials might believe. Power isn't zero-sum. In sharing it and exercising it collaboratively, government officials continue to wield influence, even if they operate in ways that deviate from government's traditional soft power tactics. Open power does require that officials place more trust in outside actors, sharing information far more readily than they have in the past, and admitting more transparently when they lack required knowledge and expertise or when experiments they've tried fail to bear fruit. Government will have to develop new mechanisms for sharing information with outside actors, as well as bureaucratic systems that recognize and allow for both experimentation and failure. This is a quite realistic task: government organizations like DARPA already have confidential methods that allow for the exploration of ideas with different kinds of outside partners while assuring that competitors or enemies don't obtain vital information.

The populist movements sweeping the West would have us believe that we can somehow make progress by closing ourselves off, locking ourselves down, retreating to the local. The truth is the exact opposite. To make progress on extremism and so much else, we need to open up even more than we have up to this point. The young people I've met around the world today are demanding it, and for good reason: Their future, and that of all the humans on planet Earth, depend on it.

ACKNOWLEDGMENTS

First, for the chance to experience the honor and privilege of serving my nation, I wish to thank Presidents George H. W. Bush, George W. Bush, and Barack Obama. I am grateful as well to First Ladies Barbara Pierce Bush and Hillary Rodham Clinton, without whose care and exceptional kindness the path of public service would not have been open to me. I describe my encounter with Hillary Clinton in the introduction, but the personal interest that Barbara Bush took in me after our initial interaction at Smith College in the fall of 1989 also changed my life's trajectory. As President George W. Bush once commented, "Aren't you lucky, you have your mother and my mother looking out for you!" Indeed.

There is no greater honor than working with intelligent, purposeful, and caring public servants who strive to protect and defend our constitution, and to serve a democratic nation of diverse Americans. To those who made it possible for me to serve again after our country was attacked on September 11, 2001, thank you—especially Andrew Card, Stephen P. Tocco, Condoleezza Rice, Stephen Hadley, and John Kerry. I also wish to thank my former colleagues at the White House and the National Security Council, the U.S. Department of State, the U.S. Agency for International Development, the U.S. Department of Homeland Security, the U.S. Department of Justice, the U.S. Department of the Treasury, the U.S. Department of Defense, the Central Intelligence Agency, and the National Counterterrorism Center. Though some of these colleagues, departments, and agencies (and bureaus, offices, and directorates) are mentioned in *How We Win,* dozens of others are not. Civil servants, foreign service officers, and political appointees of both parties at all levels have dedicated themselves to working on behalf of our nation, and their friendship, collaboration, and compassion over multiple administrations have supported my efforts and enhanced my understanding. From the bottom of my heart, thank you.

A special thank you also goes out to Elliott Abrams, Dan Fried, and Juan Zarate for their counsel, wisdom, support, and friendship over the years, and while writing this book. Thank you to the team in EUR circa 2007, especially Nerissa Cook. I wish to express my profound gratitude to Team S/SRMC, which turned our ideas into action across the globe. Dear friends and former colleagues to whom I already owe so much, thank you for helping me reconstruct my journey during the writing of *How We Win,* especially Adnan Kifayat, Sarah King Heck, Kate Berglund Fernandez, Karen Chandler, George Selim, Shahed Amanullah, Heather Tsavaris, and Lora Berg. For his immediate interest in making S/SRMC work, I wish to thank Michael Leiter. And, for providing accurate, helpful, and insightful knowledge during the book-writing process, several former colleagues deserve my thanks, including Ali Soufan, Will McCants, Matthew Levitt, Seamus Hughes, Shannon Green, and Katherine Brown.

Even with the help of these individuals and many others, I know that with the passage of time some details might not be exact. I have tried to be as honest and accurate as possible, and I apologize in advance for any flaws in the factual accounts presented in this book. Please know that all errors are my own.

I have benefited from the confidence and vision of my editor, Geoff Shandler, and the team at HarperCollins. My agent, Jud

Laghi, has been a true partner at every stage of this book, and I am profoundly grateful for his efforts. My dear friend and counsel, Tom Herman, quite literally made this book possible and offered me his wise judgment, insights, and friendship in numerous ways.

I began to think about writing *How We Win* in 2014 while serving as a spring fellow at the Institute of Politics at Harvard University's Kennedy School of Government. I wish to thank my fellow 2014 Spring Fellows and Study Group members, who enthusiastically supported my interest in writing a book on CVE, and several members of the IOP staff who provided assistance in making this happen: Eric Andersen, Cathy McLaughlin, Kerri Collins, Margaret Williams, and Teresa Verbic. Nicco Mele helped me understand the book publication process and was kind enough to introduce me to Carolyn Monaco, who provided helpful insights. I am lucky to have shared my ideas with the team at Harvard's National Preparedness Leadership Initiative, especially Eric McNulty. Harvard University (through its wide array of schools and centers) was an important source of partnership and support. In particular, I wish to thank Nicholas Burns, Joseph Nye, Graham Allison, Gary Samore, Cathryn Clüver, Hilary Rantisi, Alison Hillegeist, Urs Gasser, Martha Minow, Ali Asani, and former student researchers Dinesh Lingamaneni, Rana Abdelhamid, Nada Zohdy, Abhishek Raman, and Aaron Mukerjee. I am deeply grateful to James Stavridis, Gerard Sheehan, Richard Shultz, and Bhaskar Chakravorti at Tufts University's Fletcher School of Law and Diplomacy for their extraordinary care and helpful advice, and to Alysha Tierney, Marina Shalabi, and Carter Banker for their exceptional research efforts. I wish to thank my colleagues at the Council on Foreign Relations, in particular Richard Haass, James Lindsay, Andrew Palladino, and my spectacular research assistants Zachary Shapiro, Ella Lipin, Ari Heistein, Alexander Archuleta, and Ariella Rotenberg.

Dozens of people have read versions of the manuscript and offered adjustments and new ideas. Some went further, helping me to edit, polish, and refine the text. My deep appreciation goes out to you, as I know my requests were frequent and my timelines often inconvenient. Without the guidance, intellectual partnership, and kindness of Seth Schulman, this book would not exist. Thank you for your careful and imaginative thinking. I also owe a great debt to many people who sat for interviews (including some who do not appear in the text), and who otherwise shared their valuable knowledge and perspectives. These individuals include David Weinberg, Erik Brynjolfsson, Kurt Volker, Amartya Sen, Christopher Graves, Matthew Bryza, Shelina Janmohamed, Zahed Amanullah, Charlotte Hochman, Ahmed Larouz, Terry Young, Camilo La Cruz, Randy Kluver, Dash Dhakshinamoorthy, Daniyal Noorani, Joanna Shields, Mohamed Ali, Peter W. Singer, Luqman Ali, Shaukat Warraich, Eliza Byard, Nancy Koehn, Mark Bergman, Zia Sardar, Alex Sloan, Michael Janofsky, Bruce Hoffman, John Bellinger, Rachel Gostenhofer, Michael White, Nafisa Crishna, Rob Satloff, and Nick Springer. I am grateful to the members and staff of the DHS Advisory Council and its CVE Task Force, and the Center for Strategic and International Studies Commission on Countering Violent Extremism for insights and perspectives that helped shape the narrative.

How We Win describes programs that were built through the hard work of many American public servants at home and abroad, but they could not have happened without the collaboration of civil society—both individuals and organizations. My profound thanks for the trust these entities placed in me. And to the youth who shared their experiences, often in a very public way—thank you for your honesty. I learned from you, and I hope that this book reflects your experiences in a way that others can understand.

I am particularly grateful for a professional partnership that changed my life. Over breakfast at the Einstein Café in Berlin in 2007, I was lucky enough to meet the remarkable Sasha Havlicek. I must thank Karen Volker for that introduction, for it set in place a close collaboration and deep friendship that continues to this day. It has been a privilege to work with Sasha and the dynamic team at the Institute for Strategic Dialogue. Their feedback, insights, support, and reflections helped me greatly as *How We Win* came together. Thank you, too, to the always energetic members of Gen Next, especially Michael Davidson and Jared Cohen, who have cheered me on since I began writing this book. And, I must thank members of the IFFC, including Therese Raphael, Kate Collins, BH, and Elif Shafak, who kept me laughing even during the most challenging of times. A very special thank-you to dear friends John Marshall, Charles Cheever, Leocadia Zak, Kenneth Hansen, Dale DeLetis, Michael Gitlitz, Enoh Ebong, Abhishek Poddar, Hannah Rosenthal, DJS, Katherine Collins, Tracy Palandjian, Kerry Healey, Vivek Gupta, and Lisa Silva for encouragement and care. I am so grateful to the Gross family (Stewart, Lois, Hannah, Sarah, and Ben) and the Zafar family (Kashif, Sujatha, Rehan, and Amaan) for their incredible hospitality, love, and generosity in New York and London—truly my homes away from home.

I would like to thank my family members for their guidance, understanding, compassion, comfort, and love. I relied heavily on my wondrous mother, Mehbooba Anwar, while writing *How We Win*. I could not have completed this journey without her prayers and love, as well as her humor, especially when the challenges seemed unsurmountable. My patient, wise, loving brother Adeel remained dedicated and interested in my book journey from start to finish. I am so grateful for his uplifting words, reflections, and encouragement. I often thought about our Nanny, the late Helen Pike, as I wrote this book. After hearing "Irish need not apply" many times during her life, she would have been so happy to know that I was sharing my experience about the ideology of hate and extremism. My late uncle, Mian Ashraf, was also with me in spirit throughout, specifically his belief in humanity and the power of personal interactions. I want to thank my amazing aunt, Marian Klepser Ashraf, who made sure that I always had what I needed to make this book a reality, including at a number of crucial junctures.

Lastly, I would like to thank those who read this book and who, like me, know that there is more we can do together to confront extremist ideologies. I look forward to learning about your contributions to this effort. Visit me on www.farahpandith.com and share your stories.

The reference map was created in 2018 by U.S.-based cartographer Nick Springer. Its design reflects some of the diversity of Islamic art and iconography throughout the world. The border was inspired by Fatehpur Sikri, the Mughal Emperor Akbar's sixteenth-century imperial "City of Victory," which was a center of religious pluralism and cultural diversity. The stylized waves representing the ocean is a Timurid Period (c. 1370–1507) design, the decorative motif in the four corners references the African and Middle Eastern geometric traditions of Islamic art, and Ottoman and Persian traditions are reflected in the floral motif. In using the Winkel tripel projection, the map conveys a more realistic representation of our shared planet.

APPENDIX 1

FROM NATIONAL SECURITY STRATEGY, PRESIDENT GEORGE W. BUSH, 2006[1]

From the beginning, the War on Terror has been both a battle of arms and a battle of ideas—a fight against the terrorists and against their murderous ideology. In the short run, the fight involves using military force and other instruments of national power to kill or capture the terrorists, deny them safe haven or control of any nation; prevent them from gaining access to WMD; and cut off their sources of support. In the long run, winning the war on terror means winning the battle of ideas, for it is ideas that can turn the disenchanted into murderers willing to kill innocent victims. While the War on Terror is a battle of ideas, it is not a battle of religions. The transnational terrorists confronting us today exploit the proud religion of Islam to serve a violent political vision: the establishment, by terrorism and subversion, of a totalitarian empire that denies all political and religious freedom. These terrorists distort the idea of jihad into a call for murder against those they regard as apostates or unbelievers—including Christians, Jews, Hindus, other religious traditions, and all Muslims who disagree with them. Indeed, most of the terrorist attacks since September 11 have occurred in Muslim countries—and most of the victims have been Muslims. To wage this battle of ideas effectively, we must be clear-eyed about what does and does not give rise to terrorism.

APPENDIX 2

PRESIDENT OBAMA'S "A NEW BEGINNING" SPEECH

The following is a text of President Obama's prepared remarks to Muslims around the world, delivered on June 4, 2009, at Cairo University in Egypt, as released by the White House.[1]

I am honored to be in the timeless city of Cairo, and to be hosted by two remarkable institutions. For over a thousand years, Al-Azhar has stood as a beacon of Islamic learning, and for over a century, Cairo University has been a source of Egypt's advancement. Together, you represent the harmony between tradition and progress. I am grateful for your hospitality, and the hospitality of the people of Egypt. I am also proud to carry with me the goodwill of the American people, and a greeting of peace from Muslim communities in my country: assalaamu alaykum.

We meet at a time of tension between the United States and Muslims around the world—tension rooted in historical forces that go beyond any current policy debate. The relationship between Islam and the West includes centuries of coexistence and cooperation, but also conflict and religious wars. More recently, tension has been fed by colonialism that denied rights and opportunities to many Muslims, and a Cold War in which Muslim-majority countries were too often treated as proxies without regard to their own aspirations. Moreover, the sweeping change brought by modernity and globalization led many Muslims to view the West as hostile to the traditions of Islam.

Violent extremists have exploited these tensions in a small but potent minority of Muslims. The attacks of September 11th, 2001 and the continued efforts of these extremists to engage in violence against civilians has led some in my country to view Islam as inevitably hostile not only to America and Western countries but also to human rights. This has bred more fear and mistrust.

So long as our relationship is defined by our differences, we will empower those who sow hatred rather than peace, and who promote conflict rather than the cooperation that can help all of our people achieve justice and prosperity. This cycle of suspicion and discord must end.

I have come here to seek a new beginning between the United States and Muslims around the world; one based upon mutual interest and mutual respect; and one based upon the truth that America and Islam are not exclusive, and need not be in competition. Instead, they overlap, and share common principles—principles of justice and progress; tolerance and the dignity of all human beings.

I do so recognizing that change cannot happen overnight. No single speech can eradicate years of mistrust, nor can I answer in the time that I have all the complex questions that brought us to this point. But I am convinced that in order to move forward, we must say openly the things we hold in our hearts, and that too often are said only behind closed doors. There must be a sustained effort to listen to each other; to learn from each other; to respect one another; and to seek common ground. As the Holy Koran tells us, "Be conscious of God and speak always the truth." That is what I will try to do—to speak the truth as best I can, humbled by the task before us, and firm in my belief that the interests we share as human beings are far more powerful than the forces that drive us apart.

Part of this conviction is rooted in my own experience. I am a Christian, but my father came from a Kenyan family that includes generations of Muslims. As a boy, I spent several years in Indonesia and heard the call of the azaan at the break of dawn and the fall of dusk. As a young man, I worked in Chicago communities where many found dignity and peace in their Muslim faith.

As a student of history, I also know civilization's debt to Islam. It was Islam—at places like Al-Azhar University—that carried the light of learning through so many centuries, paving the way for Europe's Renaissance and Enlightenment. It was innovation in Muslim communities that developed the order of algebra; our magnetic compass and tools of navigation; our mastery of pens and printing; our understanding of how disease spreads and how it can be healed. Islamic culture has given us majestic arches and soaring spires; timeless poetry and cherished music; elegant calligraphy and places of peaceful contemplation. And throughout history, Islam has demonstrated through words and deeds the possibilities of religious tolerance and racial equality.

I know, too, that Islam has always been a part of America's story. The first nation to recognize my country was Morocco. In signing the Treaty of Tripoli in 1796, our second president, John Adams, wrote, "The United States has in itself no character of enmity against the laws, religion or tranquility of Muslims." And since our founding, American Muslims have enriched the United States. They have fought in our wars, served in government, stood for civil rights, started businesses, taught at our universities, excelled in our sports arenas, won Nobel Prizes, built our tallest building, and lit the Olympic torch. And when the first Muslim American was recently elected to Congress, he took the oath to defend our Constitution using the same Holy Koran that one of our Founding Fathers—Thomas Jefferson—kept in his personal library.

So I have known Islam on three continents before coming to the region where it was first revealed. That experience guides my conviction that partnership between America and Islam must be based on what Islam is, not what it isn't. And I consider it part of my responsibility as president of the United States to fight against negative stereotypes of Islam wherever they appear.

But that same principle must apply to Muslim perceptions of America. Just as Muslims do not fit a crude stereotype, America is not the crude stereotype of a self-interested empire. The United States has been one of the greatest sources of progress that the world has ever known. We were born out of revolution against an empire. We were founded upon the ideal that all are created equal, and we have shed blood and struggled for centuries to give meaning to those words—within our borders, and around the world. We are shaped by every culture, drawn from every end of the Earth, and dedicated to a simple concept: E pluribus unum: "Out of many, one."

Much has been made of the fact that an African American with the name Barack Hussein Obama could be elected president. But my personal story is not so unique. The dream of opportunity for all people has not come true for everyone in America, but its promise exists for all who come to our shores—that includes nearly seven million American Muslims in our country today who enjoy incomes and education that are higher than average.

Moreover, freedom in America is indivisible from the freedom to practice one's religion. That is why there is a mosque in every state of our union, and over 1,200 mosques within our borders. That is why the U.S. government has gone to court to protect the right of women and girls to wear the hijab, and to punish those who would deny it.

So let there be no doubt: Islam is a part of America. And I believe that America holds within her the truth that regardless of race, religion, or station in life, all of us share common aspirations—to live in peace and security; to get an education and to work with dignity; to love our families, our communities, and our God. These things we share. This is the hope of all humanity.

Of course, recognizing our common humanity is only the beginning of our task. Words alone cannot meet the needs of our people. These needs will be met only if we act boldly in the years ahead; and if we understand that the challenges we face are shared, and our failure to meet them will hurt us all.

For we have learned from recent experience that when a financial system weakens in one country, prosperity is hurt everywhere. When a new flu infects one human being, all are at risk. When one nation pursues a nuclear weapon, the risk of nuclear attack rises for all nations. When violent extremists operate in one stretch of mountains, people are endangered across an ocean. And when innocents in Bosnia and Darfur are slaughtered, that is a stain on our collective conscience. That is what it means to share this world in the twenty-first century. That is the responsibility we have to one another as human beings.

This is a difficult responsibility to embrace. For human history has often been a record of nations and tribes subjugating one another to serve their own interests. Yet in this new age, such attitudes are self-defeating. Given our interdependence, any world order that elevates one nation or group of people over another will inevitably fail. So whatever we think of the past, we must not be prisoners of it. Our problems must be dealt with through partnership; progress must be shared.

That does not mean we should ignore sources of tension. Indeed, it suggests the opposite: we must face these tensions squarely. And so in that spirit, let me speak as clearly and plainly as I can about some specific issues that I believe we must finally confront together.

The first issue that we have to confront is violent extremism in all of its forms.

In Ankara, I made clear that America is not—and never will be—at war with Islam. We will, however, relentlessly confront violent extremists who pose a grave threat to our security. Because we reject the same thing that people of all faiths reject: the killing of innocent men, women, and children. And it is my first duty as president to protect the American people.

The situation in Afghanistan demonstrates America's goals, and our need to work together. Over seven years ago, the United States pursued Al Qaeda and the Taliban with broad international support. We did not go by choice, we went because of necessity. I am aware that some question or justify the events of 9/11. But let us be clear: Al Qaeda killed nearly 3,000 people on that day. The victims were innocent men, women, and children from America and many other nations who had done nothing to harm anybody. And yet Al Qaeda chose to ruthlessly murder these people, claimed credit for the attack, and even now states their determination to kill on a massive scale. They have affiliates in many countries and are trying to expand their reach. These are not opinions to be debated; these are facts to be dealt with.

Make no mistake: we do not want to keep our troops in Afghanistan. We seek no military bases there. It is agonizing for America to lose our young men and women. It is costly and politically difficult to continue this conflict. We would gladly bring every single one of our troops home if we could be confident that there were not violent extremists in Afghanistan and Pakistan determined to kill as many Americans as they possibly can. But that is not yet the case.

That's why we're partnering with a coalition of forty-six countries. And despite the costs involved, America's commitment will not weaken. Indeed, none of us should tolerate these extremists. They have killed in many countries. They have killed people of different faiths—more than any other, they have killed Muslims. Their actions are irreconcilable with the rights of human beings, the progress of nations, and with Islam. The Holy Koran teaches that whoever kills an innocent, it is as if he has killed all mankind; and whoever saves a person, it is as if he has saved all mankind. The enduring faith of over a billion people is so much bigger than the narrow hatred of a few. Islam is not part of the problem in combating violent extremism—it is an important part of promoting peace.

We also know that military power alone is not going to solve the problems in Afghanistan and Pakistan. That is why we plan to invest $1.5 billion each year over the next five years to partner with Pakistanis to build schools and hospitals, roads and businesses, and hundreds of millions to help those who have been displaced. And that is why we are providing more than $2.8 billion to help Afghans develop their economy and deliver services that people depend upon.

Let me also address the issue of Iraq. Unlike Afghanistan, Iraq was a war of choice that provoked strong differences in my country and around the world. Although I believe that the Iraqi people are ultimately better off without the tyranny of Saddam Hussein, I also believe that events in Iraq have reminded America of the need to use diplomacy and build international consensus to resolve our problems whenever possible. Indeed, we can recall the words of Thomas Jefferson, who said: "I hope that our wisdom will grow with our power, and teach us that the less we use our power the greater it will be."

Today, America has a dual responsibility: to help Iraq forge a better future—and to leave Iraq to Iraqis. I have made it clear to the Iraqi people that we pursue no bases, and no claim on their territory or resources. Iraq's sovereignty is its own. That is why I ordered the removal of our combat brigades by next August. That is why we will honor our agreement with Iraq's democratically elected government to remove combat troops from Iraqi cities by July, and to remove all our troops from Iraq by 2012. We will help Iraq train its Security Forces and develop its economy. But we will support a secure and united Iraq as a partner, and never as a patron.

And finally, just as America can never tolerate violence by extremists, we must never alter our principles. 9/11 was an enormous trauma to our country. The fear and anger that it provoked was understandable, but in some cases, it led us to act contrary to our ideals. We are taking concrete actions to change course. I have unequivocally prohibited the use of torture by the United States, and I have ordered the prison at Guantanamo Bay closed by early next year.

So America will defend itself respectful of the sovereignty of nations and the rule of law. And we will do so in partnership with Muslim communities which are also threatened. The sooner the extremists are isolated and unwelcome in Muslim communities, the sooner we will all be safer.

The second major source of tension that we need to discuss is the situation between Israelis, Palestinians, and the Arab world.

America's strong bonds with Israel are well known. This bond is unbreakable. It is based upon cultural and historical ties, and the recognition that the aspiration for a Jewish homeland is rooted in a tragic history that cannot be denied.

Around the world, the Jewish people were persecuted for centuries, and anti-Semitism in Europe culminated in an unprecedented Holocaust. Tomorrow, I will visit Buchenwald, which was part of a network of camps where Jews were enslaved, tortured, shot, and gassed to death by the Third Reich. Six million Jews were killed—more than the entire Jewish population of Israel today. Denying that fact is baseless, ignorant, and hateful. Threatening Israel with destruction—or repeating vile stereotypes about Jews—is deeply wrong, and only serves to evoke in the minds of Israelis this most painful of memories while preventing the peace that the people of this region deserve.

On the other hand, it is also undeniable that the Palestinian people—Muslims and Christians—have suffered in pursuit of a homeland. For more than sixty years they have endured the pain of dislocation. Many wait in refugee camps in the West Bank, Gaza, and neighboring lands for a life of peace and security that they have never been able to lead. They endure the daily humiliations—large and small—that come with occupation. So let there be no doubt: the situation for the Palestinian people is intolerable. America will not turn our backs on the legitimate Palestinian aspiration for dignity, opportunity, and a state of their own.

For decades, there has been a stalemate: two peoples with legitimate aspirations, each with a painful history that makes compromise elusive. It is easy to point fingers—for Palestinians to point to the displacement brought by Israel's founding, and for Israelis to point to the constant hostility and attacks throughout its history from within its borders as well as beyond. But if we see this conflict only from one side or the other, then we will be blind to the truth: the only resolution is for the aspirations of both sides to be met through two states, where Israelis and Palestinians each live in peace and security.

That is in Israel's interest, Palestine's interest, America's interest, and the world's interest. That is why I intend to personally pursue this outcome with all the patience that the task requires. The obligations that the parties have agreed to under the Road Map are clear. For peace to come, it is time for them—and all of us—to live up to our responsibilities.

Palestinians must abandon violence. Resistance through violence and killing is wrong and does not succeed. For centuries, black people in America suffered the lash of the whip as slaves and the humiliation of segregation. But it was not violence that won full and equal rights. It was a peaceful and determined insistence upon the ideals at the center of America's founding. This same story can be told by people from South Africa to South Asia; from Eastern Europe to Indonesia. It's a story with a simple truth: that violence is a dead end. It is a sign of neither courage nor power to shoot rockets at sleeping children, or to blow up old women on a bus. That is not how moral authority is claimed; that is how it is surrendered.

Now is the time for Palestinians to focus on what they can build.

The Palestinian Authority must develop its capacity to govern, with institutions that serve the needs of its people. Hamas does have support among some Palestinians, but they also have responsibilities. To play a role in fulfilling Palestinian aspirations, and to unify the Palestinian people, Hamas must put an end to violence, recognize past agreements, and recognize Israel's right to exist.

At the same time, Israelis must acknowledge that just as Israel's right to exist cannot be denied, neither can Palestine's. The United States does not accept the legitimacy of continued Israeli settlements. This construction violates previous agreements and undermines efforts to achieve peace. It is time for these settlements to stop.

Israel must also live up to its obligations to ensure that Palestinians can live, and work, and develop their society. And just as it devastates Palestinian families, the continuing humanitarian crisis in Gaza does not serve Israel's security; neither does the continuing lack of opportunity in the West Bank. Progress in the daily lives of the Palestinian people must be part of a road to peace, and Israel must take concrete steps to enable such progress.

Finally, the Arab States must recognize that the Arab Peace Initiative was an important beginning, but not the end of their responsibilities. The Arab-Israeli conflict should no longer be used to distract the people of Arab nations from other problems. Instead, it must be a cause for action to help the Palestinian people develop the institutions that will sustain their state; to recognize Israel's legitimacy; and to choose progress over a self-defeating focus on the past.

America will align our policies with those who pursue peace, and say in public what we say in private to Israelis and Palestinians and Arabs. We cannot impose peace. But privately, many Muslims recognize that Israel will not go away. Likewise, many Israelis recognize the need for a Palestinian state. It is time for us to act on what everyone knows to be true.

Too many tears have flowed. Too much blood has been shed. All of us have a responsibility to work for the day when the mothers of Israelis and Palestinians can see their children grow up without fear; when the Holy Land of three great faiths is the place of peace that God intended it to be; when Jerusalem is a secure and lasting home for Jews and Christians and Muslims, and a place for all of the children of Abraham to mingle peacefully together as in the story of Isra, when Moses, Jesus, and Mohammed (peace be upon them) joined in prayer.

The third source of tension is our shared interest in the rights and responsibilities of nations on nuclear weapons.

This issue has been a source of tension between the United States and the Islamic Republic of Iran. For many years, Iran has defined itself in part by its opposition to my country, and there is indeed a tumultuous history between us. In the middle of the Cold War, the United States played a role in the overthrow of a democratically-elected Iranian government. Since the Islamic Revolution, Iran has played a role in acts of hostage-taking and violence against U.S. troops and civilians. This history is well known. Rather than remain trapped in the past, I have made it clear to Iran's leaders and people that my country is prepared to move forward. The question, now, is not what Iran is against, but rather what future it wants to build.

It will be hard to overcome decades of mistrust, but we will proceed with courage, rectitude and resolve. There will be many issues to discuss between our two countries, and we are willing to move forward without preconditions on the basis of mutual respect. But it is clear to all concerned that when it comes to nuclear weapons, we have reached a decisive point. This is not simply about America's interests. It is about preventing a nuclear arms race in the Middle East that could lead this region and the world down a hugely dangerous path.

I understand those who protest that some countries have weapons that others do not. No single nation should pick and choose which nations hold nuclear weapons. That is why I strongly reaffirmed America's commitment to seek a world in which no nations hold nuclear weapons. And any nation—including Iran—should have the right to access peaceful nuclear power if it complies with its responsibilities under the Nuclear Non-Proliferation Treaty. That commitment is at the core of the treaty, and it must be kept for all who fully abide by it. And I am hopeful that all countries in the region can share in this goal.

The fourth issue that I will address is democracy.

I know there has been controversy about the promotion of democracy in recent years, and much of this controversy is connected to the war in Iraq. So let me be clear: no system of government can or should be imposed upon one nation by any other.

That does not lessen my commitment, however, to governments that reflect the will of the people. Each nation gives life to this principle in its own way, grounded in the traditions of its own people. America does not presume to know what is best for everyone, just as we would not presume to pick the outcome of a peaceful election. But I do have an unyielding belief that all people yearn for certain things: the ability to speak your mind and have a say in how you are governed; confidence in the rule of law and the equal administration of justice; government that is transparent and doesn't steal from the people; the freedom to live as you choose. Those are not just American ideas, they are human rights, and that is why we will support them everywhere.

There is no straight line to realize this promise. But this much is clear: governments that protect these rights are ultimately more stable, successful, and secure. Suppressing ideas never succeeds in making them go away. America respects the right of all peaceful and law-abiding voices to be heard around the world, even if we disagree with them. And we will welcome all elected, peaceful governments—provided they govern with respect for all their people.

This last point is important because there are some who advocate for democracy only when they are out of power; once in power, they are ruthless in suppressing the rights of others. No matter where it takes hold, government of the people and by the people sets a single standard for all who hold power: you must maintain your power through consent, not coercion; you must respect the rights of minorities, and participate with a spirit of tolerance and compromise; you must place the interests of your people and the legitimate workings of the political process above your party. Without these ingredients, elections alone do not make true democracy.

The fifth issue that we must address together is religious freedom.

Islam has a proud tradition of tolerance. We see it in the history of Andalusia and Cordoba during the Inquisition. I saw it firsthand as a child in Indonesia, where devout Christians worshipped freely in an overwhelmingly Muslim country. That is the spirit we need today. People in every country should be free to choose and live their faith based upon the persuasion of the mind, heart, and soul. This tolerance is essential for religion to thrive, but it is being challenged in many different ways.

Among some Muslims, there is a disturbing tendency to measure one's own faith by the rejection of another's. The richness of religious diversity must be upheld—whether it is for Maronites in Lebanon or the Copts in Egypt. And fault lines must be closed among Muslims as well, as the divisions between Sunni and Shia have led to tragic violence, particularly in Iraq.

Freedom of religion is central to the ability of peoples to live together. We must always examine the ways in which we protect it. For instance, in the United States, rules on charitable giving have made it harder for Muslims to fulfill their religious obligation. That is why I am committed to working with American Muslims to ensure that they can fulfill zakat.

Likewise, it is important for Western countries to avoid impeding Muslim citizens from practicing religion as they see fit—for instance, by dictating what clothes a Muslim woman should wear. We cannot disguise hostility towards any religion behind the pretense of liberalism.

Indeed, faith should bring us together. That is why we are forging service projects in America that bring together Christians, Muslims, and Jews. That is why we welcome efforts like Saudi Arabian king Abdullah's interfaith dialogue and Turkey's leadership in the Alliance of Civilizations. Around the world, we can turn dialogue into interfaith service, so bridges between peoples lead to action—whether it is combating malaria in Africa, or providing relief after a natural disaster.

The sixth issue that I want to address is women's rights.

I know there is debate about this issue. I reject the view of some in the West that a woman who chooses to cover her hair is somehow less equal, but I do believe that a woman who is denied an education is denied equality. And it is no coincidence that countries where women are well educated are far more likely to be prosperous.

Now let me be clear: issues of women's equality are by no means simply an issue for Islam. In Turkey, Pakistan, Bangladesh, and Indonesia, we have seen Muslim-majority countries elect a woman to lead. Meanwhile, the struggle for women's equality continues in many aspects of American life, and in countries around the world.

Our daughters can contribute just as much to society as our sons, and our common prosperity will be advanced by allowing all humanity—men and women—to reach their full potential. I do not believe that women must make the same choices as men in order to be equal, and I respect those women who choose to live their lives in traditional roles. But it should be their choice. That is why the United States will partner with any Muslim-majority country to support expanded literacy for girls, and to help young women pursue employment through micro-financing that helps people live their dreams.

Finally, I want to discuss economic development and opportunity.

I know that for many, the face of globalization is contradictory. The Internet and television can bring knowledge and information, but also offensive sexuality and mindless violence. Trade can bring new wealth and opportunities, but also huge disruptions and changing communities. In all nations—including my own—this change can bring fear. Fear that because of modernity we will lose of control over our economic choices, our politics, and most importantly our identities—those things we most cherish about our communities, our families, our traditions, and our faith.

But I also know that human progress cannot be denied. There need not be contradiction between development and tradition. Countries like Japan and South Korea grew their economies while maintaining distinct cultures. The same is true for the astonishing progress within Muslim-majority countries from Kuala Lumpur to Dubai. In ancient times and in our times, Muslim communities have been at the forefront of innovation and education.

This is important because no development strategy can be based only upon what comes out of the ground, nor can it be sustained while young people are out of work. Many Gulf states have enjoyed great wealth as a consequence of oil, and some are beginning to focus it on broader development. But all of us must recognize that education and innovation will be the currency of the twenty-first century, and in too many Muslim communities there remains underinvestment in these areas. I am emphasizing such investments within my country. And while America in the past has focused on oil and gas in this part of the world, we now seek a broader engagement.

On education, we will expand exchange programs, and increase scholarships, like the one that brought my father to America, while encouraging more Americans to study in Muslim communities. And we will match promising Muslim students with internships in America; invest in online learning for teachers and children around the world; and create a new online network, so a teenager in Kansas can communicate instantly with a teenager in Cairo.

On economic development, we will create a new corps of business volunteers to partner with counterparts in Muslim-majority countries. And I will host a Summit on Entrepreneurship this year to identify how we can deepen ties between business leaders, foundations, and social entrepreneurs in the United States and Muslim communities around the world.

On science and technology, we will launch a new fund to support technological development in Muslim-majority countries, and to help transfer ideas to the marketplace so they can create jobs. We will open centers of scientific excellence in Africa, the Middle East, and Southeast Asia, and appoint new Science Envoys to collaborate on programs that develop new sources of energy, create green jobs, digitize records, clean water, and grow new crops. And today I am announcing a new global effort with the Organization of the Islamic Conference to eradicate polio. And we will also expand partnerships with Muslim communities to promote child and maternal health.

All these things must be done in partnership. Americans are ready to join with citizens and governments, community organizations, religious leaders, and businesses in Muslim communities around the world to help our people pursue a better life.

The issues that I have described will not be easy to address. But we have a responsibility to join together on behalf of the world we seek—a world where extremists no longer threaten our people, and American troops have come home; a world where Israelis and Palestinians are each secure in a state of their own, and nuclear energy is used for peaceful purposes; a world where governments serve their citizens, and the rights of all God's children are respected. Those are mutual interests. That is the world we seek. But we can only achieve it together.

I know there are many—Muslim and non-Muslim—who question whether we can forge this new beginning. Some are eager to stoke the flames of division, and to stand in the way of progress. Some suggest that it isn't worth the effort—that we are fated to disagree, and civilizations are doomed to clash. Many more are simply skeptical that real change can occur. There is so much fear, so much mistrust. But if we choose to be bound by the past, we will never move forward. And I want to particularly say this to young people of every faith, in every country—you, more than anyone, have the ability to remake this world.

All of us share this world for but a brief moment in time. The question is whether we spend that time focused on what pushes us apart, or whether we commit ourselves to an effort—a sustained effort—to find common ground, to focus on the future we seek for our children, and to respect the dignity of all human beings.

It is easier to start wars than to end them. It is easier to blame others than to look inward; to see what is different about someone than to find the things we share. But we should choose the right path, not just the easy path. There is also one rule that lies at the heart of every religion—that we do unto others as we would have them do unto us. This truth transcends nations and peoples—a belief that isn't new; that isn't black or white or brown; that isn't Christian, or Muslim or Jew. It's a belief that pulsed in the cradle of civilization, and that still beats in the heart of billions. It's a faith in other people, and it's what brought me here today.

We have the power to make the world we seek, but only if we have the courage to make a new beginning, keeping in mind what has been written.

The Holy Koran tells us, "O mankind! We have created you male and a female; and we have made you into nations and tribes so that you may know one another."

The Talmud tells us: "The whole of the Torah is for the purpose of promoting peace."

The Holy Bible tells us, "Blessed are the peacemakers, for they shall be called sons of God."

The people of the world can live together in peace. We know that is God's vision. Now, that must be our work here on Earth. Thank you. And may God's peace be upon you.

GLOSSARY

AHMADDIYA: a follower of the Ahmadi movement, founded in the nineteenth century

ALLAH: the Arabic word for the God of Abraham

BOHRA: follower of a sect of Islam within the Shia practice of Islam

CALIPH: a successor to the prophet Muhammad; a ruler of a Muslim-majority state

CALIPHATE: an area governed by a caliph; a region that is governed through Islamic teachings and practice

HADITH: a saying of the prophet Muhammad

HALAL: a specific way of preparing meat for consumption according to Islamic law

HIJAB: an Arabic term for a head covering (in a twenty-first century context)

IMAM: a person who leads Muslims in prayer; a person who is a religious community leader; a person who is well educated in Islamic theology (meanings vary)

ISLAM: a monotheistic religion; one of the three Abrahamic faiths, revealed through the prophet Muhammad

ISMAILI: a follower of a sect of Islam within the Shia practice of Islam

JIHAD: a spiritual struggle within oneself against sin; a fight against injustice

MUSLIM: a follower of the religion of Islam

NIQAB: an Arabic term for a face covering that leaves the eyes exposed

QUR'AN: the holy book of Islam, believed to be revealed by God to the prophet Muhammad through Angel Gabriel

RAMADAN: the ninth month of the Islamic (lunar) calendar where Muslims fast from sunrise to sunset

SHARIA LAW: Islamic system of law that governs communities of believers; interpretation across cultures and communities vary dramatically; rulings can be determined through judgment from Islamic scholars and jurists

SHIA: the second-largest branch of Islam; followers reject the first three caliphs and accept a fourth caliph, Ali, as the legitimate successor of the prophet Muhammad

SUFI: a follower of Sufism

SUFISM: a belief system in which believers search for the divine truth

SUNNI: the largest of the two main Islamic branches; followers accept the first three caliphs as successors of the prophet Muhammad

UMMA: the community of Muslims

ZAKAT: one of the five pillars of Islam; an obligatory religious charity

NOTES

INTRODUCTION

1. United Nations Development Program, "Arab Human Development Report 2002: Creating Opportunities for Future Generations," 2002, http://hdr.undp.org/sites/default/files/rbas_ahdr2002_en.pdf.
2. Shannon N. Green and Keith Proctor, "Turning Point: A New Comprehensive Strategy for Countering Violent Extremism," Center for Strategic and International Studies, November 2016, https://csis-ilab.github.io/cve/report/Turning_Point.pdf.
3. Richard Fry, "Millennials Projected to Overtake Baby Boomers as America's Largest Generation," Pew Research Center, March 1, 2018, http://www.pewresearch.org/fact-tank/2016/04/25/millennials-overtake-baby-boomers/.
4. "ADL Audit: U.S. Anti-Semitic Incidents Surged in 2016–17," *Anti-Defamation League,* accessed August 11, 2017, http://www.adl.org/sites/default/files/documents/Anti-Semitic%20Audit%20Print_vf2.pdf; "The Year in Hate: Trump Buoyed White Supremacists in 2017, Sparking Backlash Among Black Nationalist Groups," Southern Poverty Law Center, February 21, 2018, https://www.splcenter.org/news/2018/02/21/year-hate-trump-buoyed-white-supremacists-2017-sparking-backlash-among-black-nationalist; Aaron Williams, "Hate Crimes Rose the Day After Trump Was Elected, FBI Data Show," *Washington Post,* March 23, 2018, https://www.washingtonpost.com/news/post-nation/wp/2018/03/23/hate-crimes-rose-the-day-after-trump-was-elected-fbi-data-show/?utm_term=.ea08b84185a6.
5. Jenna Johnson, "Trump Calls for 'Total and Complete Shutdown of Muslims Entering the United States,'" *Washington Post,* December 7, 2015, https://www.washingtonpost.com/news/post-politics/wp/2015/12/07/donald-trump-calls

-for-total-and-complete-shutdown-of-muslims-entering-the-united-states/?noredirect=on&utm_term=.df561fae17fb.

6. Joseph S. Nye, *Soft Power: The Means to Success in World Politics* (New York: PublicAffairs, 2004).
7. Joseph Liu, "The Future of the Global Muslim Population," Pew Research Center Religion & Public Life Project, January 26, 2011, http://www.pewforum.org/2011/01/27/the-future-of-the-global-muslim-population/; "The Future of World Religions: Population Growth Projections, 2010–2050," Pew Research Center, April 2, 2015, http://assets.pewresearch.org/wp-content/uploads/sites/11/2015/03/PF_15.04.02_ProjectionsFullReport.pdf.

CHAPTER ONE: A FIGHT WE'RE LOSING

1. Daniel L. Byman, "Comparing Al Qaeda and ISIS: Different Goals, Different Targets," Brookings, April 29, 2015, https://www.brookings.edu/testimonies/comparing-al-qaeda-and-isis-different-goals-different-targets/.
2. Ibid.
3. Zachary Laub, "The Islamic State," Council on Foreign Relations, updated August 10, 2016, https://www.cfr.org/backgrounder/islamic-state.
4. Byman, "Comparing Al Qaeda and ISIS."
5. Laub, "The Islamic State."
6. Byman, "Comparing Al Qaeda and ISIS."
7. Laub, "The Islamic State."
8. Ibid.
9. Ibid.
10. Byman, "Comparing Al Qaeda and ISIS."
11. Ibid.
12. Ibid.
13. Ibid.
14. Ibid.
15. "Pitfalls and Promises: Security Implications of a Post-revolutionary Middle East," Canadian Security Intelligence Service, September 2014, https://www.csis.gc.ca/pblctns/wrldwtch/2014/Pitfalls_Promises_E_web.pdf.
16. Bruce Hoffman, "A Growing Terrorist Threat on Another 9/11," *Wall Street Journal,* September 8, 2017, https://www.wsj.com/articles/a-growing-terrorist-threat-on-another-9-11-1504888986.
17. Richard Shultz, *Strategic Culture and Strategic Studies: An Alternative Framework for Assessing al-Qaeda and the Global Jihad Movement* (MacDill Air Force Base, FL: Joint Special Operations University Press, 2012), 22.
18. Hoffman, "A Growing Terrorist Threat."
19. Laub, "The Islamic State."
20. Shultz, "Strategic Culture," 27–28 passim.
21. Rukmini Callimachi, "U.S. Seeks to Avoid Ground War Welcomed by Islamic State," *New York Times,* December 7, 2015, https://www.nytimes

.com/2015/12/08/world/middleeast/us-strategy-seeks-to-avoid-isis-prophecy .html.

22. Brian Michael Jenkins, Bruce Hoffman, and Martha Crenshaw, "How Much Really Changed About Terrorism on 9/11?" *The Atlantic,* September 11, 2016, https://www.theatlantic.com/international/archive/2016/09/jenkins-hoffman -crenshaw-september-11-al-qaeda/499334/.
23. Nye, *Soft Power,* 5.
24. "We Must Secure the Border and Build the Wall to Make America Safe Again," Department of Homeland Security, February 15, 2018, https://www .dhs.gov/news/2018/02/15/we-must-secure-border-and-build-wall-make -america-safe-again.
25. Joseph S. Nye, *The Future of Power* (New York: PublicAffairs, 2011), 84.
26. Ibid., 8, 17.
27. Ibid., 17.
28. Nicholas Burns, professor of the practice of diplomacy and international relations at the Harvard Kennedy School of Government, interview with the author, March 6, 2018.
29. Ibid.
30. Ibid.
31. Ibid.
32. Max Roser, Mohamed Nadgy, and Hannah Ritchie, "Terrorism," Our World in Data, updated January 2018, https://ourworldindata.org/terrorism.
33. Green and Proctor, "Turning Point," 2.
34. Ibid., 3.
35. Denise Lavoie, "Dzokhar Tsarnaev Gets Death Penalty for Boston Marathon Bombing," *Washington Times,* May 15, 2015, http://www.washingtontimes .com/news/2015/may/15/dzhokhar-tsarnaev-sentenced-boston-marathon -attack/.
36. Holly Yan, Pamela Brown, and Evan Perez, "Orlando Shooter Texted Wife During Attack, Source Says," CNN, June 17, 2016, http://www.cnn.com /2016/06/16/us/orlando-shooter-omar-mateen/.
37. "Survey Findings—Global Perceptions of Violent Extremism," Center for Strategic and International Studies, October 18, 2016, https://www.csis.org /analysis/survey-findings-global-perceptions-violent-extremism.
38. John Allen, "Remarks at Brookings-Doha U.S. Islamic World Forum," U.S. Department of State, June 3, 2015, https://2009-2017.state.gov/s/seci /243115.htm.
39. "ISIS: What It Will Take to Beat Terror Group," CNN, August 22, 2014; "Battling ISIS: A Long Campaign Ahead," *Financial Times,* June 8, 2015.
40. OED Online, s.v., "terrorism," http://www.oed.com/view/Entry/199608.
41. David Rapoport, "The Four Waves of Modern Terrorism," in Audrey Kurth Cronin and James M. Ludes, eds., *Attacking Terrorism: Elements of a Grand Strategy* (Washington, D.C.: Georgetown University Press, 2004), 46.

42. Shultz, "Strategic Culture," 16.
43. Ibid., 20–21.
44. Bruce Hoffman, former director of Georgetown University's Center for Security Studies, e-mail to the author, October 14, 2017.
45. Alfredo Carrillo, "Q&A: Bruce Hoffman, Outgoing Security Studies Director, Talks IS and Counterterrorism," *Hoya,* November 29, 2017, http://www.thehoya.com/qa-bruce-hoffman-outgoing-security-studies-director-talks-isis-counterterrorism/; Jenkins, Hoffman, and Crenshaw, "How Much Really Changed."
46. Hoffman, "A Growing Terrorist Threat."
47. Byman, "Comparing Al Qaeda and ISIS."
48. Ibid.
49. Graeme Wood, "What Isis Really Wants," *The Atlantic,* March 2015, https://www.theatlantic.com/magazine/archive/2015/03/what-isis-really-wants/384980/.
50. David Remnick, "Going the Distance: On and off the Road with Barack Obama," *The New Yorker,* January 27, 2014.
51. Shreeya Sinha, "Obama's Evolution on ISIS," *New York Times,* June 9, 2015, https://www.nytimes.com/interactive/2015/06/09/world/middleeast/obama-isis-strategy.html.
52. Ibid.
53. Ibid.
54. Carillo, "Q&A: Bruce Hoffman."
55. Hoffman, "A Growing Terrorist Threat."
56. Ibid.
57. President George W. Bush, Address to a Joint Session of Congress and the American People, September 20, 2001, http://www.washingtonpost.com/wp-srv/nation/specials/attacked/transcripts/bushaddress_092001.html.
58. National Security Council, "The National Security Strategy of the United States of America: March 2006," George W. Bush Archives, March 16, 2006, https://georgewbush-whitehouse.archives.gov/nsc/nss/2006/.
59. Matt Bryza, former diplomat, interview with the author, February 3, 2016.
60. Juan C. Zarate, former deputy assistant to the president and former deputy national security advisor for combatting terrorism, interview with the author, Washington, D.C., January 22, 2016.
61. Dana Priest and William M. Arkin, "A Hidden World, Growing Beyond Control," *Washington Post,* July 19, 2010, http://projects.washingtonpost.com/top-secret-america/articles/a-hidden-world-growing-beyond-control/print/.
62. Zarate, interview with the author.
63. The Obama administration did the same thing.
64. "Charlotte Beers Steps Down from State Department Role," *Campaign,* March 4, 2003, http://www.campaignlive.co.uk/article/charlotte-beers-steps-down-state-department-role/172066.

65. Jane Perlez, "Muslim-as-Apple-Pie Videos Are Greeted with Skepticism," *New York Times,* October 29, 2002, http://www.nytimes.com/2002/10/30/world/muslim-as-apple-pie-videos-are-greeted-with-skepticism.html.
66. David E. Kaplan, Aamir Latif, Kevin Whitelaw, and Julian E. Barnes, "Hearts, Minds, and Dollars," *U.S. News & World Report,* April 25, 2005.
67. "Charlotte Beers Steps Down."
68. Kurt Volker, diplomat and former U.S. Ambassador to NATO, interview with the author, Washington, D.C., March 7, 2016.
69. Charlotte Beers, "Public Diplomacy After 9/11," U.S. Department of State, December 8, 2002, https://2001-2009.state.gov/r/us/16269.htm.
70. James Glassman, "Strategic Public Diplomacy," testimony before the Senate Foreign Relations Committee, March 10, 2010.
71. "Chapter 5: Terrorist Safe Havens (Update to 7120 Report) 5.1a-5.1b. Strategies, Tactics, and Tools for Disrupting or Eliminating Safe Havens," U.S. Department of State, July 31, 2012, https://www.state.gov/j/ct/rls/crt/2011/195549.htm.
72. Greg Miller and Scott Higham, "In a Propaganda War Against Isis, the U.S. Tried to Play by the Enemy's Rules," *Washington Post,* May 8, 2015, https://www.washingtonpost.com/world/national-security/in-a-propaganda-war-us-tried-to-play-by-the-enemys-rules/2015/05/08/6eb6b732-e52f-11e4-81ea-0649268f729e_story.html?utm_term=.fe8301b77dbb.
73. "A New Center for Global Engagement," U.S. Department of State, January 8, 2016, https://2009-2017.state.gov/r/pa/prs/ps/2016/01/251066.htm.
74. Nahal Toosi, "Tillerson Spurns $80 Million to Counter Isis, Russian Propaganda," *Politico,* August 2, 2017, https://www.politico.com/story/2017/08/02/tillerson-isis-russia-propaganda-241218.
75. Green and Proctor, "Turning Point."
76. Ibid.
77. Zarate, interview with the author.
78. Bryza, interview with the author.
79. Ibid.
80. Kaplan, Latif, Whitelaw, and Barnes, "Hearts, Minds, and Dollars."
81. Green and Proctor, "Turning Point."
82. Ibid.
83. Eric Schmitt, "U.S. Intensifies Effort to Blunt ISIS' Message," *New York Times,* February 16, 2015, https://www.nytimes.com/2015/02/17/world/middleeast/us-intensifies-effort-to-blunt-isis-message.html?_r=2.
84. NSC colleagues, personal conversation with the author, White House Summit on Countering Violent Extremism, 2015.
85. Richard Barrett, "Beyond the Caliphate: Foreign Fighters and the Threat of Returnees," Soufan Center, October 2017, http://thesoufancenter.org/wp-content/uploads/2017/11/Beyond-the-Caliphate-Foreign-Fighters-and-the-Threat-of-Returnees-TSC-Report-October-2017-v3.pdf.

86. "Changes in Modus Operandi of Islamic State (IS) Revisited," *Europol,* November 2016.
87. Stewart Bell, "Europe Warned of ISIL Attack," *Montreal Gazette,* December 3, 2016, https://www.pressreader.com/canada/montreal-gazette/20161203/281767038841819.
88. "George Washington Extremism Tracker: Islamic State in America," George Washington University Program on Extremism, November 2016, https://cchs.gwu.edu/sites/cchs.gwu.edu/files/downloads/Nov.%202016%20Snapshot.pdf.
89. Ibid.
90. Richard Thornton, "White House Summit Combating Terrorism International Law Enforcement Leaders," C-span, accessed April 25, 2018, https://www.c-span.org/video/?324398-2/white-house-summit-combating-terrorism-international-law-enforcement-leaders&start=519.
91. Sarah Gilkes, "Not Just the Caliphate: Non-Islamic State-Related Jihadist Terrorism in America," George Washington University Program on Extremism, December 6, 2016, https://abcnews.go.com/images/US/gwu-program-extremism-not-just-caliphate-20161206.pdf.
92. "Terrorism Most Immediate Threat to UK, Says MI6," BBC, December 8, 2016, http://www.bbc.com/news/uk-38250432.
93. Zarate, interview with the author.
94. Jane Onyaga-Omara, "Islamic State Celebrates Donald Trump Election Victory," *USA Today,* November 10, 2016, http://www.usatoday.com/story/news/world/2016/11/10/extremists-celebrate-donald-trump-election-win/93580822/.

CHAPTER TWO: MILLENNIALS ADRIFT

1. This is a pseudonym.
2. John G. Horgan as quoted in Ella Rhodes, "We Stand Together," *Psychologist* 30 (July 2017), https://thepsychologist.bps.org.uk/we-stand-together.
3. "Prophet Mohammed Cartoons Controversy: Timeline," *Telegraph,* May 4, 2015, http://www.telegraph.co.uk/news/worldnews/europe/france/11341599/Prophet-Muhammad-cartoons-controversy-timeline.html.
4. "Video from Osama Bin Laden Threatened the EU over Reprinting of the Cartoon, Which He Claimed Was Part of a 'New Crusade' Against Islam Led by the Pope."
5. Dan Bilefsky, "Death Toll Mounts in Rioting over Cartoons," *International Herald Tribune,* February 8, 2006, https://web.archive.org/web/20060209032716/http:/www.iht.com:80/articles/2006/02/07/news/islam.php.
6. "Getting It Right: Lessons of the 'Cartoons Crisis' and Beyond," Euro-Mediterranean Study Commission (EuroMesco), Annual Report 2006, May 2007, 45.
7. Pernille Ammitzbøll and Lorenzo Vidino, "After the Danish Cartoon

Controversy," *Middle East Quarterly* 14 (January 1, 2007), http://meforum.org/1437/after-the-danish-cartoon-controversy; "Cartoons Row Hits Danish Exports," BBC News, September 9, 2006, http://news.bbc.co.uk/2/hi/europe/5329642.stm.

8. "Zurich Gives Go-Ahead to Poster with 'Racist Image of Islam,' Ahead of Swiss Vote on Allowing Minarets at Mosques," *Daily Mail,* updated October 8, 2009, http://www.dailymail.co.uk/news/article-1219048/Zurich-approves-poster-racist-image-Islam-ahead-Swiss-vote-allowing-minarets-mosques.html.
9. Kai Schultz, "Maldives, Tourist Havens, Casts Wary Eye on Growing Islamic Radicalization," *New York Times,* June 18, 2017, https://www.nytimes.com/2017/06/18/world/asia/maldives-islamic-radicalism.html?emc=edit_th_20170619&nl=todaysheadlines&nlid=57789694.
10. Peek, "Reactions and Response," 274.
11. Ibid., 274–75.
12. Ibid., 276–77.
13. Ibid., 279.
14. Ibid., 280–81.
15. Cainkar, *Homeland Insecurity,* 4.
16. "Gallup Poll of the Islamic World," Gallup, February 26, 2002, http://www.gallup.com/poll/5380/gallup-poll-islamic-world.aspx?version=print.
17. Benjamin Wormald, "New Pew Research Center Survey Finds Moderate Attitudes Among Muslim Americans," Pew Research Center Religion & Public Life Project, August 29, 2011, http://www.pewforum.org/2011/08/30/new-pew-research-center-survey-finds-moderate-attitudes-among-muslim-americans/.
18. "U.S. Muslims Concerned About Their Place in Society, but Continue to Believe in the American Dream," Pew Research Center Religion & Public Life Project, July 25, 2017, http://www.pewforum.org/2017/07/26/findings-from-pew-research-centers-2017-survey-of-us-muslims/?utm_content=buffer8b97c&utm_medium=social&utm_source=twitter.com&utm_campaign=buffer.
19. García Coll and Amy K. Marks, "Missing Developmental and Sociocultural Perspectives: Comment on the 'Psychology of Terrorism,'" *American Psychologist* 72, no. 7 (2017): 701–2.
20. Alan Taylor, "9/11: The Day of the Attacks," *The Atlantic,* September 8, 2011, https://www.theatlantic.com/photo/2011/09/911-the-day-of-the-attacks/100143/.
21. Steven Strasser and Pamela Abramson, "Why People Join Cults," *Newsweek,* December 3, 1984, http://www.lexisnexis.com.ezproxy.library.tufts.edu/hottopics/lnacademic/?shr=t&csi=5774&sr=HLEAD(%22Why+People+Join+Cults%22)+and+date+is+1984.
22. Scott Atran, "Don't Just Denounce Radicalized Youth. Engage with Them," *Washington Post,* August 15, 2017, https://www.washingtonpost.com/opinions

/dont-denounce-radicalized-youth-engage-with-them/2017/08/15/2e514cfa-81d8-11e7-902a-2a9f2d808496_story.html?utm_term=.2299067389be.

23. Samuel Huntington, *The Clash of Civilizations and the Remaking of World Order* (New York: Simon & Schuster, 1996).
24. Matthew Levitt, "My Journey Through Brussels' Terrorist Safe Haven," Washington Institute for Near East Policy, March 27, 2016, http://www.washingtoninstitute.org/policy-analysis/view/my-journey-through-brussels-terrorist-safe-haven.
25. Jacob Feldman, "The Simplicity Principle in Perception and Cognition," *WIREs Cognitive Science* 7, no. 5 (2016): 330, http://onlinelibrary.wiley.com.ezproxy.library.tufts.edu/doi/10.1002/wcs.1406/abstract; Tania Lombrozo, "Simplicity and Probability in Causal Explanation," *Cognitive Psychology* 55, no. 3 (2007): 238, http://ac.els-cdn.com.ezproxy.library.tufts.edu/S0010028506000739/1-s2.0-S0010028506000739-main.pdf?_tid=b3f30bc4-417c-11e7-9330-00000aab0f6b&acdnat=1495739131_c7e4ad4bbaecea876d1ee0984abf3800.
26. Seth Schwartz, Curtis Dunkel, and Alan Waterman, "Terrorism: An Identity Theory Perspective," *Studies in Conflict and Terrorism* 32 (2009): 540, http://sethschwartz.info/wp-content/uploads/2010/08/Identity-and-Terrorism1.pdf.
27. Ibid.
28. Coll and Amy K. Marks, "Missing Developmental and Sociocultural Perspectives."

CHAPTER THREE: PLAGUE FROM THE GULF

1. Alice Wu, "Harmony and Martyrdom Among China's Hui Muslims," *The New Yorker,* June 6, 2016, https://www.newyorker.com/news/news-desk/harmony-and-martyrdom-among-chinas-hui-muslims.
2. Nicholas Kristof, "Obama in Saudi Arabia, Exporter of Oil and Bigotry," *New York Times,* April 20, 2016, https://www.nytimes.com/2016/04/21/opinion/obama-in-saudi-arabia-exporter-of-oil-and-bigotry.html.
3. For estimates see Daniel Pipes, "No Saudi Money for American Mosques," *Hill,* August 22, 2016, http://thehill.com/blogs/Congress-blog/foreign-policy/292188-no-saudi-money-for-american-mosques; Brian Viner, "Last Night's TV: The Qur'an, Channel 4; Banged Up, Five," *Independent,* July 14, 2008, https://www.independent.co.uk/arts-entertainment/tv/reviews/last-nights-tv-the-quran-channel-4-banged-up-five-867474.html; Carol E. B. Choksy and Jamsheed K. Choksy, "The Saudi Connection: Wahhabism and Global Jihad," *World Affairs,* May/June 2015, http://www.worldaffairsjournal.org/article/saudi-connection-wahhabism-and-global-jihad.
4. Will McCants, public policy manager at Google, interview with the author, December 14, 2016. Until 2015, so-called Islamic State used official Saudi textbooks in their so-called caliphate.
5. Ziauddin Sardar, "Viewpoint: The Global Voices Reclaiming Islam," BBC,

September 5, 2005, http://news.bbc.co.uk/2/hi/programmes/battle_for_islam/4203918.stm.

6. Please consult the glossary for a definition of this term.
7. Quintan Wiktorowicz, "A Genealogy of Radical Islam," *Studies in Conflict & Terrorism* 28, no. 2 (2005), http://insct.syr.edu/wp-content/uploads/2013/03/Wicktorovitcz.2005.Geneology-of-Radical-Islam.pdf.
8. Wiktorowicz, "Anatomy of the Salafi Movement," 207.
9. David Commins, *The Wahhabi Mission and Saudi Arabia* (London: Tauris, 2006), vi; Krithika Varagur, "Saudi Arabia Is Redefining Islam for the World's Largest Muslim Nation," *The Atlantic,* March 2, 2017, https://www.theatlantic.com/international/archive/2017/03/saudi-arabia-salman-visit-indonesia/518310/.
10. Commins, *The Wahhabi Mission,* vi.
11. Wael Mahdi, "There Is No Such Thing as Wahabism, Saudi Prince Says," *National,* March 17, 2010, http://www.thenational.ae/news/world/middle-east/there-is-no-such-thing-as-wahabism-saudi-prince-says; Jeffrey Goldberg, "Saudi Crown Prince: Iran's Supreme Leader 'Makes Hitler Look Good,'" *The Atlantic,* April 2, 2018, https://www.theatlantic.com/international/archive/2018/04/mohammed-bin-salman-iran-israel/557036/.
12. David Weinberg, former senior fellow for the Foundation for Defense of Democracies, interview with the author, Washington, D.C., June 8, 2016.
13. Nicholas Pelham, "The People Who Shaped Islamic Civilisation," *1843 Magazine,* December 5, 2016, https://www.1843magazine.com/culture/the-daily/the-people-who-shaped-islamic-civilisation.
14. Ibid.
15. McCants, interview with the author.
16. Off-the-record briefing during the Commission on Countering Violent Extremism at the Center for Strategic and International Studies, Washington, D.C., February 23, 2016, https://www.csis.org/events/csis-commission-countering-violent-extremism.
17. Michaela Prokop, "Saudi Arabia: The Politics of Education," *International Affairs* 79, no. 1 (2003): 77–89, http://www.jstor.org/stable/3095542.
18. *Saudi Arabia's Curriculum of Intolerance* (Washington, DC: Center for Religious Freedom 2006), https://freedomhouse.org/sites/default/files/CurriculumOfIntolerance.pdf; Nina Shea, "Teaching Hate, Inspiring Terrorism: Saudi Arabia's Educational Curriculum," Hudson, July 19, 2017, https://www.hudson.org/research/13778-teaching-hate-inspiring-terrorism-saudi-arabia-s-educational-curriculum.
19. Justin Ling and Ben Makuch, "Cables Released by WikiLeaks Show Saudi Money Flowed to Newspapers in Canada," VICE News, June 23, 2015, https://news.vice.com/article/cables-released-by-wikileaks-show-saudi-money-flowed-to-newspapers-in-canada.
20. "Saudi Arabia," U.S. Department of State, July 30, 2012, https://www

.state.gov/documents/organization/193117.pdf; "State Dept. Study on Saudi Textbooks," *New York Times,* August 25, 2016, https://www.nytimes.com/interactive/2016/08/17/international-home/document-state-dept-study-on-saudi-textbooks.html.

21. Karen Armstrong, "Wahhabism to ISIS: How Saudi Arabia Exported the Main Source of Global Terrorism," *New Statesmen,* November 27, 2014, http://www.newstatesman.com/world-affairs/2014/11/wahhabism-isis-how-saudi-arabia-exported-main-source-global-terrorism.
22. Elliott Abrams, senior fellow for Middle Eastern Studies at the Council on Foreign Relations, interview with the author, Washington, D.C., April 11, 2016.
23. Franklin Foer, "Moral Hazard," *The New Republic,* November 18, 2002, https://newrepublic.com/article/66588/moral-hazard.
24. Simon Henderson, "Terrorism: Two Years after 9/11, Connecting the Dots: Hearing Before the Subcommittee on Terrorism, Technology, and Homeland Security of the Committee on the Judiciary, United States Senate, One Hundred Eighth Congress, First Session, September 10, 2003," U.S. Senate Judiciary Committee, September 2003, http://hdl.handle.net/2027/pst.000063524789. See also Scott Shane, "Saudis and Extremism: 'Both the Arsonists and the Firefighters,'" *New York Times,* August 25, 2016, http://www.nytimes.com/2016/08/26/world/middleeast/saudi-arabia-islam.html?_r=0.
25. Ahmed Ali Fayyaz, "Kashmir's Changing Colors, From pro-Pak Green to ISIS' Black," *Quint,* November 20, 2017, https://www.thequint.com/voices/opinion/kashmir-isis-flags-funeral-militancy.
26. Ziauddin Sardar, *Reading the Qur'an: The Contemporary Relevance of the Sacred Text of Islam* (Oxford: Oxford University Press, 2011), 39–49.
27. Ziauddin Sardar, "Limits of Translation," Interactive, November 24, 2013, http://interactive.net.in/limits-of-translations/.
28. Sardar, *Reading the Qur'an,* 39–49.
29. Ibid.
30. Karen Elliott House, *On Saudi Arabia: Its People, Past, Religion, Fault Lines—and Future* (New York: Vintage Books, 2013), 234; Armstrong, "Wahhabism to ISIS"; Daniel Burke, "Could This Quran Curb Extremism?" CNN, July 15, 2016, http://www.cnn.com/2015/11/25/living/study-quran-extremism/; "Holy Qur'an Copies Distributed for Free," *Saudi Gazette,* September 4, 2017, http://saudigazette.com.sa/article/516569/SAUDI-ARABIA/Holy-Quran.
31. Armstrong, "Wahhabism to ISIS."
32. Drew DeSilver and David Masci, "World's Muslim Population More Widespread than You Might Think," Pew Research Center, January 31, 2017, http://www.pewresearch.org/fact-tank/2017/01/31/worlds-muslim-population-more-widespread-than-you-might-think/.
33. "Culture and Religion: The Arabization of Islam," Altmuslim (blog), *Patheos,* January 9, 2008, http://www.patheos.com/blogs/altmuslim/2008/01/the_arabization_of_islam/.

34. Zainab Fattah, "Guide to $400 Billion in Saudi-U.S. Deals: Black Hawks to Oil," Bloomberg, May 22, 2017, https://www.bloomberg.com/news/articles/2017-05-22/guide-to-400-billion-in-saudi-u-s-deals-black-hawks-to-oil.
35. Abrams, interview with the author.
36. "Transcript: Saudi King Abdullah Talks to Barbara Walters," ABC News, October 14, 2005, http://abcnews.go.com/2020/International/story?id=1214706&page=1; Weinberg, "Congress Must Act."
37. "A Nation Challenged; U.S. Moves to Seize Saudi Charity Assets," *New York Times,* March 12, 2002, http://www.nytimes.com/2002/03/12/world/a-nation-challenged-us-moves-to-seize-saudi-charity-assets.html?rref=collection%2Ftimestopic%2FTerrorism&mtrref=www.nytimes.com&gwh=559A1679B2480E0737D10BA7103C06B8&gwt=pay.
38. Paul O'Neill, "Fact Sheet: Designations of Somalia and Bosnia-Herzegovina Branches of Al-Haramain Islamic Foundation," U.S. Department of the Treasury, March 11, 2002, https://fas.org/irp/news/2002/03/dot031102fact.html.
39. Abrams, interview with the author.
40. Ibid.
41. Weinberg, interview with the author.
42. Ibid.
43. McCants, interview with the author.
44. Weinberg, interview with the author (Washington, D.C.), June 28, 2016; Zoltan Pall, "Kuwaiti Salafism and Its Growing Influence in the Levant," Carnegie Endowment for International Peace, 2014, http://carnegieendowment.org/files/kuwaiti_salafists.pdf.
45. McCants, interview with the author.
46. Weinberg, "How to Build a More Sustainable and Mutually Beneficial Relationship," 6.
47. Ibid.
48. Nicholas Kristof, "The Terrorists the Saudis Cultivate in Peaceful Countries," *New York Times,* July 3, 2016, https://www.nytimes.com/2016/07/03/opinion/sunday/the-terrorists-the-saudis-cultivate-in-peaceful-countries.html?mcubz=3.
49. Eleanor Albert, "The Rohingya Crisis," Council of Foreign Relations, February 9, 2018, https://www.cfr.org/backgrounder/rohingya-crisis.
50. Gall, "How Kosovo Was Turned."
51. Ibid.
52. Ibid.
53. Ziauddin Sardar, "Ziauddin Sardar: Reform is Islam's Best Kept Secret," *Guardian,* August 31, 2005, https://www.theguardian.com/world/2005/sep/01/religion.uk1.
54. Gall, "How Kosovo Was Turned."

55. Ibid.
56. Ibid.
57. Please consult the Glossary.
58. Gall, "How Kosovo Was Turned."
59. Brian Ross, "U.S.: Saudis Still Filling Al Qaeda's Coffers," ABC News, December 17, 2007, http://www.imra.org.il/story.php3?id=36052.
60. Choksy and Choksy, "The Saudi Connection."
61. "Remarks of Under Secretary for Terrorism and Financial Intelligence David Cohen before the Center for a New American Security on 'Confronting New Threats in Terrorist Financing,'" U.S. Department of the Treasury, March 4, 2014, https://www.treasury.gov/press-center/press-releases/Pages/jl2308.aspx.
62. Choksy and Choksy, "The Saudi Connection."
63. Michael Georgy, "Saudi Arabia, UAE Funded Jihadi Networks," Reuters, May 22, 2011, http://www.reuters.com/article/us-pakistan-saudi-uae-idUSTRE74L0ER20110522.
64. Krithika Varagur, "Saudi Arabia Is Redefining Islam for the World's Largest Muslim Nation," *The Atlantic,* March 2, 2017, https://www.theatlantic.com/international/archive/2017/03/saudi-arabia-salman-visit-indonesia/518310/.
65. Ibid.; Pallavi Aiyar, "In Indonesia, Madrassas of Moderation," *New York Times,* February 10, 2015, https://www.nytimes.com/2015/02/11/opinion/in-indonesia-madrassas-of-moderation.html?_r=0.
66. Irfan Ahmed, "The Destruction of Holy Sites in Mecca and Medina," *Islamica Magazine* 1 (2006): 30, https://www.scribd.com/doc/6999574/Spirit.
67. Ibid.
68. Carla Power, "Saudi Arabia Bulldozes Over Its Heritage," *Time,* November 14, 2014, 2016, http://time.com/3584585/saudi-arabia-bulldozes-over-its-heritage/.
69. Nicolai Ouroussoff, "New Look for Mecca: Gargantuan and Gaudy," *New York Times,* December 29, 2010, http://www.nytimes.com/2010/12/30/arts/design/30mecca.html?pagewanted=1&ref=general&src=me&_r=0.
70. Andrew Johnson, "Mecca Under Threat," *Independent,* November 12, 2015, http://www.islamicpluralism.org/2425/mecca-under-threat.
71. Power, "Saudi Arabia Bulldozes Over Its Heritage."
72. Sardar, "The Destruction of Mecca."
73. Power, "Saudi Arabia Bulldozes Over Its Heritage."
74. Johnson, "Mecca Under Threat."
75. Power, "Saudi Arabia Bulldozes Over Its Heritage."
76. Ibid.
77. Sardar, "The Destruction of Mecca."
78. Barry Bearak, "Over World Protests, Taliban Are Destroying Ancient Buddhas," *New York Times,* March 4, 2001, https://www.nytimes.com/2001/03/04/world/over-world-protests-taliban-are-destroying-ancient-buddhas.html.
79. Sarah Donilon, "A Doctrine of Destruction: ISIS Attempts to Erase History,"

Politic, May 19, 2016, http://thepolitic.org/a-doctrine-of-destruction-isis-attempts-to-erase-history/.

80. "Buddha Attacked by Taliban Gets Facelift in Pakistan," *Dawn,* June 25, 2012, http://www.dawn.com/news/729361/buddha-attacked-by-taliban-gets-facelift-in-pakistan. See Osser, "Why Is Saudi Arabia Destroying the Cultural Heritage of Mecca and Medina?"
81. Charlie Sorrel, "Mapping How Terrorists Are Destroying the World's Cultural Sites," Co.Exist, May 27, 2016, http://www.fastcoexist.com/3060249/mapping-how-terrorists-are-destroying-the-worlds-cultural-sites?utm_source=mailchimp&utm_medium=email&utm_campaign=coexist-daily&position=4&partner=newsletter&campaign_date=05272016.
82. See their interactive website: https://theantiquitiescoalition.org.
83. Sorrel, "Mapping How Terrorists."
84. Loveday Morris, "Islamic State Isn't Just Destroying Ancient Artifacts—It's Selling Them," *Washington Post,* June 8, 2015, https://theantiquitiescoalition.org/ac-news/islamic-state-isnt-just-destroying-ancient-artifacts-its-selling-them-2/.
85. Ibid.
86. Dana Ford and Mohammed Tawfeeq, "Extremists Destroy Jonah's Tomb, Officials Say," CNN, July 25, 2014, http://www.cnn.com/2014/07/24/world/iraq-violence/.
87. Michael Martinez and Mohammed Tawfeeq, "ISIS Bulldozes Ruins of Ancient Assyrian City of Nimrud, Iraqi Ministry Says," CNN, March 6, 2016, http://www.cnn.com/2015/03/05/world/iraq-isis-destroys-ancient-city-nimrud/index.html.
88. Morris, "Islamic State."
89. Morgan Winsor, "Isis Destroys Khorsabad: Third Archaeological Site in Iraq Wrecked by Islamic State, Report Says," *International Business Times,* March 10, 2015, http://www.ibtimes.com/isis-destroys-khorsabad-third-archaeological-site-iraq-wrecked-islamic-state-report-1842836.
90. Kareem Shaheen, "Isis Video Confirms Destruction at Unesco World Heritage Site in Hatra," *Guardian,* April 5, 2016, http://www.theguardian.com/world/2015/apr/05/isis-video-confirms-destruction-at-unesco-world-heritage-site-on-hatra.
91. Martinez and Tawfeeq, "ISIS Bulldozes Ruins."
92. Winsor, "Isis Destroys Khorsabad."
93. Andrew Curry, "Here Are the Ancient Sites ISIS Has Damaged and Destroyed," *National Geographic,* September 1, 2015, http://news.nationalgeographic.com/2015/09/150901-isis-destruction-looting-ancient-sites-iraq-syria-archaeology/.
94. Weinberg, interview with the author.
95. Shane, "Saudis and Extremism."
96. United States Commission on International Religious Freedom, "USCIRF

Annual Report 2016—Tier 1 CPCs Designated by the State Department and Recommended by USCIRF—Saudi Arabia," May 2, 2016, available at http://www.refworld.org/docid/57307cf6c.html.

97. Adnan Kifayat, former cochair of the Homeland Security Advisory Council's CVE task force, interview with the author, March 19, 2018.
98. Bashir Ahmad Ansar, "Islamic Scholars Go Head-to-Head with ISIS Propaganda Machine," *Cipher Brief,* October 26, 2017, https://www.thecipherbrief.com/column_article/islamic-scholars-go-head-head-isis-propaganda-machine#.WfKTMx9GanE.twitter.
99. Ibid.
100. "New Terror Laws 'Would Criminalise Thought,' Watchdog Warns," BBC, October 25, 2017, http://www.bbc.com/news/uk-41744815.
101. David Weinberg, "A Backlash Builds Against Saudi Salafism," *Real Clear World,* December 12, 2015, http://www.realclearworld.com/articles/2015/12/12/a_backlash_builds_against_saudi_salafism_111620.html.
102. "In Belgium, Arguments About Islam Grow Louder," *The Economist,* October 25, 2017, https://www.economist.com/blogs/erasmus/2017/10/islam-and-belgium-0; Alissa de Carbonnel, "Belgium Takes Back Brussels' Grand Mosque from Saudi Government," Reuters, March 16, 2018, https://www.reuters.com/article/us-europe-attacks-belgium/belgium-takes-back-brussels-grand-mosque-from-saudi-government-idUSKCN1GS2B3.
103. De Carbonnel, "Belgium Takes Back."
104. "Cultural Property, Art and Antiquities Investigations," U.S. Immigrations and Customs Enforcement, https://www.ice.gov/cultural-art-investigations.
105. Farah Pandith and Juan Zarate, "Winning the War of Ideas," Center for Strategic and International Studies, November 15, 2015, https://csis-prod.s3.amazonaws.com/s3fs public/legacy_files/files/publication/151116_Pandith_War_Ideas.pdf.
106. Jonathan Stemple, "Saudi Arabia Seeks to End U.S. Lawsuits over Sept. 11 Attacks," Reuters, August 1, 2017, https://www.reuters.com/article/usa-saudi-sept11/saudi-arabia-seeks-to-end-u-s-lawsuits-over-sept-11-attacks-idUSL1N1KN148.
107. Elliott McLaughlin, "Saudi Crown Prince Promises 'a More Moderate Islam,'" CNN, October 24, 2017, http://www.cnn.com/2017/10/24/middleeast/saudi-arabia-prince-more-moderate-islam/index.html.
108. Lulwa Shalhoub, "Global Center to Combat Extremism Launched in Riyadh," *Arab News,* May 22, 2017, http://www.arabnews.com/node/1103136/saudi-arabia.
109. Nasir Al-Biqami, secretary general of the Global Center for Combating Extremist Ideology, quoted in ibid.
110. Martin Chulov, "I Will Return Saudi Arabia to Moderate Islam, Says Crown Prince," *Guardian,* October 24, 2017, https://www.theguardian.com/world/2017/oct/24/i-will-return-saudi-arabia-moderate-islam-crown-prince.

111. Weinberg, "How to Build a More Sustainable and Mutually Beneficial Relationship," 2.

CHAPTER FOUR: HALALIZATION

1. *Oxford Living Dictionary,* s.v. "halal." https://en.oxforddictionaries.com/definition/halal.
2. Shelina Janmohamed, British author, interview with the author, June 14, 2016.
3. Ibid.
4. Timothy P. A. Cooper, "Why Is the Khaleeji Hijab So Controversial," Vice, September 18, 2013, https://www.vice.com/read/khaleeji-hijab.
5. Leila Ahmed and Joshua E. Keating, "Veil of Ignorance," *Foreign Policy* 186 (2011): 40, https://www.jstor.org/stable/i40055609.
6. Ibid., 40–42.
7. Ibid., 42.
8. Azeem Ibrahim, "Why We Need an Islamic Tartan," Huffington Post, September 16, 2012, http://www.huffingtonpost.com/azeem-ibrahim/why-we-need-an-islamic-ta_b_1677245.html.
9. "Tajikistan Shaves 13,000 Beards in 'Radicalism' Battle," Al Jazeera English, accessed September 13, 2017, http://www.aljazeera.com/news/2016/01/tajikistan-shaves-13000-men-beards-radicalism-160120133352747.html.
10. Shana Chandra and Hamza Chandra, "Interview: Speaking Dress," *Vestoj,* accessed September 13, 2017, http://vestoj.com/speaking-dress/.
11. Courtney Tenz, "Fashion's Marketing to Muslim Women Draws Ire in France," *Deutsche Welle,* April 29, 2016, http://www.dw.com/en/fashions-marketing-to-muslim-women-draws-ire-in-france/a-19222823.
12. Ibid.
13. Karin Wasteson, "The Rise of 'Islamic Chic' and Hijab Haute Couture," *Fair Observer,* July 16, 2015, http://www.fairobserver.com/region/europe/the-rise-of-islamic-chic-and-hijab-haute-couture-31097/.
14. "Halal Certification," Halal Industry Development Corporation, accessed May 25, 2016, http://www.hdcglobal.com/publisher/certification.
15. "Halal World Series," Halal Industry Development Corporation, http://www.hdcglobal.com/publisher/cu_halal_world_tv_series.
16. James Sivalingam, "Sleepless for Mamak in Seattle," New Straits Times Online, May 14, 2016, http://www.nst.com.my/news/2016/05/145624/sleepless-mamak-seattle.
17. May Warren, "Halal Food Fest a Fusion of Flavours," *Toronto Star,* May 22, 2016, https://www.thestar.com/news/gta/2016/05/22/halal-food-fest-a-fusion-of-flavours.html.
18. "San Jose Welcomes the Halal Guys with Its First Bay Area Location," RestaurantNews.com, May 17, 2016, http://www.restaurantnews.com/san-jose-welcomes-the-halal-guys-with-its-first-bay-area-location/.
19. Waquiddin Rajak Belait, "Kg Mumong MPK to Get Halal Seal for Chilli

Sauce," *Brunei Times,* accessed May 16, 2016, http://energy.gov.bn/Lists/LatestHeadlines/DispForm.aspx?ID=1843&Source=http%3A%2F%2Fenergy%2Egov%2Ebn%2Flists%2Flatestheadlines%2Fallitems%2Easpx%3FPaged%3DTRUE%26PagedPrev%3DTRUE%26p_Date%3D20160509%252016%253A00%253A00%26p_Created%3D20160510%252001%253A32%253A19%26p_ID%3D1816%26SortField%3Darticle%255Fx002d%255Fimage%26SortDir%3DAsc%26PageFirstRow%3D4021%26SortField%3Darticle%255Fx002d%255Fimage%26SortDir%3DAsc%26%26View%3D%7B1732BEE9-C75F-4045-A7A3-DF473848875C%7D&ContentTypeId=0x01001197DEBBB6416A44B5571C3C02FDFBD6.

20. Samantha Cooney, "Ignorance and Fear Are Big Obstacles for Muslim Startup Founders," Mashable, May 22, 2016, http://mashable.com/2016/05/22/muslim-entrepreneurs/#NMIxaa9g98qX.
21. "Opinion: Halal Makeup Becoming Popular in Industry," Halal Focus, May 21, 2016, http://halalfocus.net/opinion-halal-makeup-becoming-popular-in-industry/.
22. Jenn Mills, "You Can Now Buy 'Halal Dildos' and Toys at Sex Shop Targeted at Muslims," metro.co.uk, November 13, 2015, http://metro.co.uk/2015/11/13/you-can-now-buy-halal-dildos-and-toys-at-sex-shop-targeted-at-muslims-5498980/.
23. You can see the offerings on display at ibraheemtoyhouse.com.
24. Stephanie Busari, "The Hijab-Wearing Barbie Who's Become an Instagram Star," CNN, February 8, 2016, http://www.cnn.com/2016/02/08/fashion/hijarbie-nigeria-student/.
25. Ibid.
26. Lim Li Min, "Hijabs on the Catwalk: Modest Fashion Hits the Mainstream," TRT World, May 24, 2016, http://www.trtworld.com/art-culture/hijabs-on-the-catwalk-modest-fashion-hits-the-mainstream-112168.
27. Ibid.
28. For Halal tourism information, please see the brochures offered at "Global Muslim Travel Market Rankings and Indexes," Crescent Ratings, accessed May 25, 2016, https://www.crescentrating.com/travel-index-ranking.html.
29. Ibid.
30. Luiz Romero, "The Number of Muslim Travelers Should Grow to Almost 170 Million in 2020, Fueling the Halal Tourism Industry," Quartz, June 6, 2017, https://qz.com/index/999245/halal-hotels-tours-cruises-close-to-120-million-muslim-travelers-are-energizing-the-halal-tourism-industry/.
31. Lydia Green, "Why Millions of Muslims Are Signing Up for Online Dating," BBC News, December 10, 2014, http://www.bbc.com/news/magazine-30397272.
32. Ibid.
33. Ibid.

34. "Website Helps Users Find a Second Wife," *Pakistan Today,* June 1, 2016, http://www.pakistantoday.com.pk/2016/06/01/entertainment/website-helps-users-find-a-second-wife/.
35. Olivia Ward, "Love Your Wife? This Man Wants to Help You to Find Another," *Toronto Star,* May 29, 2016, https://www.thestar.com/news/world/2016/05/29/love-your-wife-this-man-wants-to-help-you-to-find-another.html.
36. Preeti Jha, "Superheroes and Hijabs: Malaysia's Muslim Cosplayers," Al Jazeera, June 2, 2017, http://www.aljazeera.com/indepth/features/2017/05/superheroes-hijabs-malaysia-muslim-cosplayers-170530075048287.html.
37. "Understanding and Avoiding Gangs," D.C. Metropolitan Police Department, https://mpdc.dc.gov/page/understanding-and-avoiding-gangs; Michael Carlie, "Determining if a Gang Is Present," Into the Abyss: A Personal Journey into the World of Street Gangs (blog) accessed April 7, 2018, https://people.missouristate.edu/michaelcarlie/SOLUTIONS/ISSUE/is_there_a_gang_situation.htm; "Gang Involvement," Mesa Police Department, accessed April 7, 2018, http://www.mesaaz.gov/home/showdocument?id=4758. See also Donnie Harris, *Gangland* (Spring Hill, TN: Holy Fire, 2004).
38. Rukmini Callimachi, "ISIS Enshrines a Theology of Rape," *New York Times,* August 13, 2015, http://www.nytimes.com/2015/08/14/world/middleeast/isis-enshrines-a-theology-of-rape.html?_r=0.
39. Ibid.
40. Shelina Janmohamed, British author, interview with the author, June 14, 2016.
41. F. Brinkley Bruton, "Turkey's President Erdogan Calls Women Who Work 'Half Persons,'" NBC News, June 8, 2016, http://www.nbcnews.com/news/world/turkey-s-president-erdogan-calls-women-who-work-half-persons-n586421.
42. Ibid.
43. Lizabeth Paulat, "Why Is Turkey's President Going After Women?" Care 2, June 12, 2016, http://www.care2.com/causes/why-is-turkeys-president-going-after-women.html.
44. See S. Craig Watkins, *Hip Hop Matters: Politics, Pop Culture, and the Struggle for the Soul of a Movement* (Boston: Beacon Press, 2005).
45. "ISIS Takes Jihadists on Honeymoon in Iraq and Syria," *Al Arabiya,* July 23, 2014, http://english.alarabiya.net/en/variety/2014/07/23/ISIS-takes-jihadists-on-honeymoon-in-Iraq-and-Syria.html; Erin Marie Saltman and Melanie Smith, "'Til Martyrdom Do Us Part: Gender and the ISIS Phenomenon,'" Institute for Strategic Dialogue, 2015, http://www.isdglobal.org/wp-content/uploads/2016/02/Till_Martyrdom_Do_Us_Part_Gender_and_the_ISIS_Phenomenon.pdf.
46. Simon Cottee, "What ISIS Women Want," *Foreign Policy,* May 17, 2016, http://foreignpolicy.com/2016/05/17/what-isis-women-want-gendered-jihad/.
47. Ibid.

48. David Ignatius, "The Islamic State Feeds Off Western Islamophobia," *Washington Post,* June 2, 2016, https://www.washingtonpost.com/opinions/the-islamic-state-is-fueled-by-islamophobia/2016/06/02/37109540-28ff-11e6-b989-4e5479715b54_story.html?utm_term=.2ff8b41db82b.
49. Caryle Murphey, "Behind the Veil: Why Islam's Most Visible Symbol Is Spreading," *Christian Science Monitor,* December 12, 2009, http://www.csmonitor.com/World/Middle-East/2009/1213/Behind-the-veil-Why-Islam-s-most-visible-symbol-is-spreading.
50. Ibid.
51. Shawn Hubler, "Redondo Beach Schools Ban Gang-Related Clothing," *Los Angeles Times,* September 6, 1990, http://articles.latimes.com/1990-09-06/local/me-806_1_redondo-beach-city-school.
52. Caroline Mimbs Nyce, "Can School Dress Codes Help Curb Gang Violence," *The Atlantic,* May 24, 2016, https://www.theatlantic.com/notes/2016/05/can-dress-codes-rules-help-curb-gang-violence/482976/.
53. Amber Jamieson, "Barbie's Big Makeover—A Welcome Change That's 'Ridiculously Late,'" *Guardian,* January 28, 2016, https://www.theguardian.com/lifeandstyle/2016/jan/28/barbie-curvy-makeover-mattel-sales-diversity.

CHAPTER FIVE: SHEIKH GOOGLE

1. Bodine-Baron, Elizabeth, Todd C. Helmus, Madeline Magnuson, and Zev Winkelman, "Examining ISIS Support and Opposition Networks on Twitter," RAND Corporation, 2016, https://www.rand.org/pubs/research_reports/RR1328.html.
2. Urs Gasser, executive director of the Berkman Klein Center for Internet & Society at Harvard University and a Professor of Practice at Harvard Law School, interview with the author, August 9, 2016.
3. Ibid.
4. Michael Leiter, "Ideology and Terror: Understanding the Tools, Tactics, and Techniques of Violent Extremism," U.S. Senate Committee on Homeland Security and Government Affairs, June 14, 2017, https://www.hsgac.senate.gov/hearings/ideology-and-terror-understanding-the-tools-tactics-and-techniques-of-violent-extremism.
5. Jacob Davey and Julia Ebner, "The Fringe Insurgency: Connectivity, Convergence, and Mainstreaming of the Extreme Right," Institute for Strategic Dialogue, October, 22, 2017, https://www.isdglobal.org/wp-content/uploads/2017/10/The-Fringe-Insurgency-221017_2.pdf.
6. Ibid.
7. Connell McCluskey and Manuele Santoprete, "A Bare Bones Mathematical Model of Radicalization," Cornell University Library, November 10, 2017, https://arxiv.org/pdf/1711.03227v1.pdf.
8. Shahed Amanullah, co-founder and CTO of Affinis Labs, phone interview with the author, July 5, 2016.

9. Eszter Hargittai and Amanda Hinnant, "Differences in Young Adults' Use of the Internet," *Sage Journals* 35, no. 5 (2008): 602–21.
10. S. Amanullah, interview with the author.
11. Joanna Shields, former first minister for internet safety and security for the United Kingdom and the founder of WePROTECT, interview with the author, April 18, 2016.
12. Thomas L. Friedman, *Thank You for Being Late: An Optimist's Guide to Thriving in the Age of Accelerations* (New York: Farrar, Straus and Giroux, 2016).
13. "In Tehran, You Can Choose a Marriage That Lasts for Three Minutes," Vocativ, April 15, 2014, http://www.vocativ.com/world/iran/tehran-can-choose-marriage-lasts-3-minutes/.
14. Zaina Salem, "The Religion of Social Media: When Islam Meets the Web," *Islamic Monthly,* May 16, 2016, https://www.theislamicmonthly.com/the-religion-of-social-media-when-islam-meets-the-web/.
15. "The Online Ummah," *The Economist,* August 18, 2012, http://www.economist.com/node/21560541.
16. Aqsa Mahmud, "How to Foster Safe Vulnerability in the Muslim Third Space—The Townhall Dialogue Series," Altmuslim (blog), *Patheos,* May 12, 2014, http://www.patheos.com/blogs/altmuslim/2014/05/how-to-foster-safe-vulnerability-in-the-muslim-third-space-the-townhall-dialogue-series/.
17. Ibid.
18. "Dialogue Series," Town Hall Dialogue, accessed May 6, 2018, http://www.townhalldialogue.com/dialogue-series.html.
19. Mahmud, "How to Foster Safe Vulnerability in the Muslim Third Space"; "The Townhall Dialogue Series" (http://www.townhalldialogue.com/).
20. Hadith of the Day, by Hadith of the Day Ltd, is available at the iTunes Store: https://itunes.apple.com/us/app/hadith-of-the-day/id480437544?mt=8.
21. Salem, "The Religion of Social Media."
22. Shelina Janmohamed, British author, interview with the author, June 14, 2016.
23. Samantha Guzman, "Millennials Are Not Keeping the Faith," *KERA News,* June 27, 2016, http://keranews.org/post/millennials-are-not-keeping-faith.
24. S. Amanullah, interview with the author.
25. Janmohamed, interview with the author.
26. Fox, "Technology Changing Way We Practice Religion."
27. S. Amanullah, interview with the author.
28. Ibid.
29. "Dr. Amr Khaled," The Muslim 500, accessed July 18, 2016, http://themuslim500.com/profile/dr-amr-khaled.
30. Samantha M. Shapiro, "Ministering to the Upwardly Mobile Muslim," *New York Times,* April 30, 2006, http://www.nytimes.com/2006/04/30/magazine/ministering-to-the-upwardly-mobile-muslim.html?mcubz=1.
31. "Saudi Arabia Gives Top Prize to Cleric Who Blames George Bush for 9/11,"

Guardian, March 1, 2015, https://www.theguardian.com/world/2015/mar/02/saudi-arabia-gives-top-prize-to-cleric-who-blames-george-bush-for-911.

32. Nushmia Khan, "The Snapchat Imam," Quartz, March 25, 2016, http://qz.com/646902/this-imam-delivers-eight-second-snapchat-sermons/.
33. Urs Gasser, executive director of the Berkman Klein Center for Internet & Society at Harvard University and a Professor of Practice at Harvard Law School, interview with the author, August 10, 2016.
34. Janmohamed, interview with the author.
35. Eli Pariser, *The Filter Bubble: What the Internet Is Hiding from You* (London: Penguin Books, 2012).
36. Peter W. Singer, strategist at New America and an editor at *Popular Science* magazine, interview with the author, November 17, 2017; Issie Lapowsky, "What Did Cambridge Analytica Really Do for Trump's Campaign?" *Wired,* October 26, 2017, https://www.wired.com/story/what-did-cambridge-analytica-really-do-for-trumps-campaign/.
37. Timothy Egan, "We're with Stupid," *New York Times,* November 17, 2017, https://www.nytimes.com/2017/11/17/opinion/were-with-stupid.html.
38. Shields, interview with the author.
39. Joel Stein, "Millennials: The Me Me Me Generation," *Time,* May 20, 2013, http://time.com/247/millennials-the-me-me-me-generation/.
40. Ibid.
41. Scott Shane and Ben Hubbard, "ISIS Displaying a Deft Command of Varied Media," *New York Times,* August 30, 2014, http://www.nytimes.com/2014/08/31/world/middleeast/isis-displaying-a-deft-command-of-varied-media.html?_r=0.
42. Eric Schmitt, "U.S. Intensifies Effort to Blunt ISIS' Message," *New York Times,* February 16, 2016, http://www.nytimes.com/2015/02/17/world/middleeast/us-intensifies-effort-to-blunt-isis-message.html?_r=0.
43. Josh Meyer, "ISIS Has Help Desk for Terrorists Staffed Around the Clock," NBC News, November 16, 2015, https://www.nbcnews.com/storyline/paris-terror-attacks/isis-has-help-desk-terrorists-staffed-around-clock-n464391.
44. Ruth Fogarty, "'You're a Dead Man': Undercover with an Islamic State Terror Cell," ABC News, July 11, 2016, http://www.abc.net.au/news/2016-07-11/undercover-with-an-islamic-state-terror-cell/7583246.
45. The reporter managed to sever the budding relationship, although she has since faced threats to her safety.
46. Anna Erelle, "Skyping with the Enemy: I Went Undercover as a Jihadi Girlfriend," *Guardian,* May 26, 2015, https://www.theguardian.com/world/2015/may/26/french-journalist-poses-muslim-convert-isis-anna-erelle.
47. Karen Yourish and Jasmine C. Lee, "What the Americans Drawn to ISIS Had in Common," *New York Times,* July 6, 2016, https://www.nytimes.com/interactive/2016/07/06/us/isis-in-america.html.
48. "Man Sentenced to 15 Years in Prison for Trying to Aid Islamic State," CBS

Local, July 25, 2016, http://losangeles.cbslocal.com/2016/07/25/man-sentenced-to-15-years-in-prison-for-trying-to-aid-islamic-state/; "California Man, 22, Given 15 Years Prison for Trying to Join ISIS," CBS News, July 25, 2016, https://www.cbsnews.com/news/california-adam-dandach-15-years-prison-trying-to-join-isis/; Katie Zavadski, "The United States of ISIS: More Popular Than Al Qaeda Ever Was," Daily Beast, September 11, 2015, http://www.thedailybeast.com/the-united-states-of-isis-more-popular-than-al-qaeda-ever-was.

49. "California Man."
50. Sasha Havlicek, CEO/director of Institute for Strategic Dialogue, interview with the author, London, February 2018; Mark Bridge, "YouTube Program Drives Viewers to Extreme Content," *Times,* February 9, 2018, https://www.thetimes.co.uk/article/youtube-programe-drives-viewers-to-extreme-content-02x8tscr5.
51. "Brussels Explosions: What We Know About Airport and Metro Attacks," BBC News, April 9, 2016, http://www.bbc.com/news/world-europe-35869985.
52. Adam Boult, "#YouAintNoMuslimBruv: A 'Very London' Response to Leytonstone Tube Terror Attack," *Telegraph,* December 6, 2015, http://www.telegraph.co.uk/news/uknews/12035744/YouAintNoMuslimBruv-A-very-London-response-to-Leytonstone-Tube-terror-attack.html.
53. Daniel Marans, "Thousands Use #MuslimsAreNotTerrorist to Combat Islamophobia," Huffington Post, November 14, 2015, http://www.huffingtonpost.com/entry/muslims-are-not-terrorist-hashtag_us_5647a7c6e4b045bf3def6992.
54. Christina Medici Scolaro, "Facebook Expands 'Safety Check' After Paris Attacks," CNBC, November 16, 2016, https://www.cnbc.com/2015/11/16/facebook-expands-safety-check-after-paris-attacks.html.
55. Al Baker and Marc Santora, "San Bernardino Attackers Discussed Jihad in Private Messages, F.B.I. Says," *New York Times,* December 16, 2015, http://www.nytimes.com/2015/12/17/us/san-bernardino-attackers-discussed-jihad-in-private-messages-fbi-says.html?_r=0.
56. Justin Sink, "Obama Wants Silicon Valley's Help to Fight Terror Online," Bloomberg, December 6, 2015, http://www.bloomberg.com/politics/articles/2015-12-07/obama-wants-silicon-valley-s-help-as-terrorists-embrace-social.
57. See chapter 1 of Nicco Mele, *The End of Big: How the Internet Makes David the New Goliath* (New York: St. Martin's, 2013).
58. Havlicek, interview with the author.
59. Melissa Eddy and Mark Scott, "Facebook and Twitter Could Face Fines in Germany Over Hate Speech Posts," *New York Times,* March 14, 2017, https://www.nytimes.com/2017/03/14/technology/germany-hate-speech-facebook-tech.html?mcubz=0&_r=0; Heidi Tworek, "How Germany is Tackling Hate

Speech," *Foreign Affairs,* May 16, 2017, https://www.foreignaffairs.com/articles/germany/2017-05-16/how-germany-tackling-hate-speech.

60. Official Medium channel of the Embassy of Italy in Washington, D.C., "G7 Statement on the Fight Against Terrorism and Violent Extremism," Medium, May 27, 2017, https://medium.com/g7inus/g7-statement-on-the-fight-against-terrorism-and-violent-extremism-de53d1da862b.
61. Mark Scott and Janosch Delcker, "Free Speech vs. Censorship in Germany," *Politico,* updated January 6, 2018, https://www.politico.eu/article/germany-hate-speech-netzdg-facebook-youtube-google-twitter-free-speech/.
62. Olivia Solon, "Counter-Terrorism Was Never Meant to Be Silicon Valley's Job: Is That Why It's Failing?" *Guardian,* June 29, 2017, https://www.theguardian.com/technology/2017/jun/29/silicon-valley-counter-terrorism-facebook-twitter-youtube-google.
63. Julia Fioretti, "Social Media Giants Step up Joint Fight Against Extremist Content," Reuters, June 26, 2017, https://www.reuters.com/article/us-internet-extremism-idUSKBN19H20A.
64. Amar Toor, "Facebook Launches Program to Combat Hate Speech and Terrorist Propaganda in the UK," The Verge, June 23, 2017, https://www.theverge.com/2017/6/23/15860868/facebook-hate-speech-terrorism-uk-online-civil-courage-initiative.
65. "Facebook Launches Messaging App for Kids as Young as Six," *Financial Times,* December 4, 2017, https://www.ft.com/content/5fb4ed0e-d6f8-11e7-8c9a-d9c0a5c8d5c9.
66. Zahed Amanullah, entrepreneur, interview with the author, November 22, 2016.
67. Steven Musil, "YouTube Plans More People, Better Algorithms Policing Content," CNET, December 4, 2017, https://www.cnet.com/news/youtube-to-beef-up-staff-algorithms-policing-content/?ftag=COS-05-10aaa0b&linkId=45516215.
68. Havlicek, interview with the author.
69. "Bin Laden: Al Qaeda Motivated to Strike U.S. Again," CNN, October 30, 2004, http://www.cnn.com/2004/WORLD/meast/10/29/binladen.tape/index.html.
70. Scott and Delcker, "Free Speech vs. Censorship in Germany."
71. Jen Fitzpatrick, "Sorry for Our Google Maps Search Mess Up," Google Maps (official blog), May 21, 2015, https://maps.googleblog.com/2015/05/sorry-for-our-google-maps-search-mess-up.html; Brian Fung, "If You Search Google Maps for the N-Word, It Gives You the White House," *Washington Post,* May 19, 2015, https://www.washingtonpost.com/news/the-switch/wp/2015/05/19/if-you-search-google-maps-for-the-n-word-it-gives-you-the-white-house/?utm_term=.eb229a6153f5.
72. Mike Isaac, "Facebook Offers Tools for Those Who Fear a Friend May Be Suicidal," *New York Times,* June 14, 2016, https://www.nytimes

.com/2016/06/15/technology/facebook-offers-tools-for-those-who-fear-a-friend-may-be-suicidal.html.

73. Nick Wingflied, Mike Isaac, and Katie Benner. "Google and Facebook Take Aim at Fake News Sites," *New York Times,* November 15, 2016, http://www.nytimes.com/2016/11/15/technology/google-will-ban-websites-that-host-fake-news-from-using-its-ad-service.html.
74. Havlicek, interview with the author.
75. Secret Life of Muslims team, "What Does It Mean to Be Muslim? There Are 1.7 Billion Answers," Vox, November 21, 2016, http://www.vox.com/videos/2016/11/21/13697910/what-is-a-muslim.
76. Don Reisinger, "Watch the Amazon Ad That Tries to Heal America," *Fortune,* November 18, 2016, http://fortune.com/2016/11/18/amazon-ad-priest-imam/.
77. Katherine Schwab, "Can a Chatbot Be a Good Therapist? This Scientist-Founded Startup Says Yes," Fast Code Design, June 6, 2017, https://www.fastcodesign.com/90128341/can-a-chatbot-be-a-good-therapist-this-scientist-founded-startup-says-yes.
78. Heather Mack, "Woebot Labs Debuts Fully AI Mental Health Chatbot via Facebook Messenger," *Mobi Health News,* June 6, 2017, http://www.mobihealthnews.com/content/woebot-labs-debuts-fully-ai-mental-health-chatbot-facebook-messenger.
79. Sean Captain, "This Chatbot Is Trying Hard to Look and Feel Like Us," *Fast Company,* November 15, 2017, https://www.fastcompany.com/40495681/this-chatbot-is-trying-hard-to-look-and-feel-like-us.
80. Amie Tsang, "Amazon 'Reviewing' Its Website After It Suggest Bomb-Making Items," *New York Times,* September 20, 2017, https://www.nytimes.com/2017/09/20/technology/uk-amazon-bomb.html?mcubz=0; Natasha Lomas, "Another AI Chatbot Shown Spouting Offensive Views," *Tech Crunch,* October 24, 2017, https://techcrunch.com/2017/10/24/another-ai-chatbot-shown-spouting-offensive-views/.
81. Singer, interview with the author.
82. Shields, interview with the author.
83. Jeff Seldin, "U.S. in 'Crisis Mode' in Fight Against IS Online Messaging," Voice of America, July 6, 2016, http://www.voanews.com/content/united-states-crisis-mode-fight-islamic-state-online-messaging/3407346.html.
84. Ibid.

CHAPTER SIX: AMERICA THE BOGEYMAN

1. Bija Knowles, "World's 10 Dangerous Roads," CNN, April 25, 2011, http://travel.cnn.com/explorations/life/worlds-deadliest-roads-098394/.
2. Jeffrey Goldberg, "In the Party of God," *The New Yorker,* October 28, 2002, https://www.newyorker.com/magazine/2002/10/28/in-the-party-of-god-2.
3. Samuel Huntington, *The Clash of Civilizations and the Remaking of World Order* (New York: Simon & Schuster, 1996), 217.

4. Declan Walsh, "The Mystery of Dr Aafia Siddiqui," *Guardian,* November 23, 2009, https://www.theguardian.com/world/2009/nov/24/aafia-siddiqui-al-qaida.
5. Azhar Hussain, Ahmad Salim, and Arif Naveed, "Connecting the Dots: Education and Religious Discrimination in Pakistan," United Stations Commission on International Religious Freedom, November 2011, https://www.uscirf.gov/sites/default/files/resources/Pakistan-ConnectingTheDots-Email(3).pdf.
6. Amartya Sen, professor of economics and philosophy, interview with the author, Cambridge, Massachusetts, April 19, 2016. See also Jibran Ahmad, "Pakistan Province Rewrites Text Books to Satisfy Islamic Conservatives," Reuters, October 30, 2014, https://www.reuters.com/article/us-pakistan-education/pakistan-province-rewrites-text-books-to-satisfy-islamic-conservatives-idUSKBN0IJ1G820141030.
7. Jibran Ahmad, "Pakistan Province Rewrites Text Books to Satisfy Islamic Conservatives," Reuters, October 30, 2014, https://www.reuters.com/article/us-pakistan-education/pakistan-province-rewrites-text-books-to-satisfy-islamic-conservatives-idUSKBN0IJ1G820141030.
8. Matthew Gray, *Conspiracy Theories in the Arab World: Sources and Politics* (London: Routledge, 2010).
9. Robert Tait, "Mahmoud Ahmadinejad Accuses the West of Destroying Iran's Rain Clouds," *Telegraph,* September 10, 2012, http://www.telegraph.co.uk/news/worldnews/middleeast/iran/9533842/Mahmoud-Ahmadinejad-accuses-the-West-of-destroying-Irans-rain-clouds.html.
10. "Egyptian Paper: Israel-India Nuke Test Caused Tsunami," *Jerusalem Post,* January 6, 2005, http://www.webcitation.org/query?url=http://www.prisonplanet.com/articles/january2005/060105nuketest.htm&date=2011-06-06.
11. Ibid.
12. Peter Beinart, "The GOP's Islamophobia Problem," *The Atlantic,* February 13, 2015, http://www.theatlantic.com/national/archive/2015/02/anti-islam/385463/.
13. "Herman Cain Says U.S. Communities 'Have the Right' to Ban Mosques," Fox News, July 17, 2011, http://www.foxnews.com/politics/2011/07/17/cain-says-communities-have-right-to-ban-mosques.html; Beinart, "The GOP's Islamophobia Problem."
14. Former Representative Allen West as quoted in George Zornick, "GOP Candidate Allen West: People with 'Coexist' Bumper Stickers Want to 'Give Away Our Country,'" ThinkProgress, August 10, 2010, https://thinkprogress.org/gop-candidate-allen-west-people-with-coexist-bumper-stickers-want-to-give-away-our-country-491732098b3f/; Matthew Engel, "Calls on Israel to Expel West Bank Arabs," *Guardian,* May 3, 2002, https://www.theguardian.com/world/2002/may/04/israel3; Eugene Scott, "Analysis: How Roy Moore's

Rhetoric on Gays, Muslims Harks Back to Alabama's Past," *Washington Post,* September 27, 2017, https://www.washingtonpost.com/news/the-fix/wp/2017/09/27/roy-moores-values-could-take-alabama-back-to-a-place-many-of-its-residents-have-tried-to-get-past/?utm_term=.33ca3fa376c7.

15. "Public Remains Conflicted over Islam," Pew Research Center, August 24, 2010, http://www.pewforum.org/2010/08/24/public-remains-conflicted-over-islam/.
16. For background information on al-Awlaki, see Scott Shane, "The Lessons of Anwar al-Awlaki," *The NewYork Times Magazine,* August 27, 2015, https://www.nytimes.com/2015/08/30/magazine/the-lessons-of-anwar-al-awlaki.html?mcubz=0.
17. Paula Newton, "Purported Al-Awlaki Message Calls for Jihad Against U.S.," CNN, March 17, 2010, http://www.cnn.com/2010/WORLD/europe/03/17/al.awlaki.message/index.html.
18. Al Jazeera, "Interview: Anwar al-Awlaki," Al Jazeera, February 7, 2010, http://www.aljazeera.com/focus/2010/02/2010271074776870.html.
19. Michael Slackman, "Bin Laden Says West Is Waging War Against Islam," *New York Times,* April 24, 2006, http://www.nytimes.com/2006/04/24/world/middleeast/bin-laden-says-west-is-waging-war-against-islam.html.
20. J. M. Berger, "The Myth of Anwar al-Awlaki," *Foreign Policy,* August 10, 2011, http://foreignpolicy.com/2011/08/10/the-myth-of-anwar-al-awlaki/.
21. "The Return of Khilafah," *Dabiq* 1 (2014): 10, https://clarionproject.org/docs/isis-isil-islamic-state-magazine-Issue-1-the-return-of-khilafah.pdf.
22. Daveed Gartenstein-Ross, Nathaniel Barr, and Bridget Moreng, "The Islamic State's Global Propaganda Strategy," International Centre for Counter-Terrorism, The Hague, May 2016, https://www.icct.nl/wp-content/uploads/2016/03/ICCT-Gartenstein-Ross-IS-Global-Propaganda-Strategy-March2016.pdf.
23. Greg McCune, "Accused Fort Hood Shooter Says He Participated in War on Islam," Reuters, July 27, 2013, https://www.reuters.com/article/us-usa-crime-forthood/accused-fort-hood-shooter-says-he-participated-in-war-on-islam-idUSBRE96Q0B120130727.
24. For a definition and history of public diplomacy, see "Defining Public Diplomacy," University of Southern California Center on Public Diplomacy, accessed April 8, 2018, https://uscpublicdiplomacy.org/page/what-pd.
25. Edward P. Djerejian, "Changing Minds, Winning Peace: A New Strategic Direction for U.S. Public Diplomacy in the Arab & Muslim World," Advisory Group on Public Diplomacy for the Arab and Muslim World, October 1, 2003, https://www.state.gov/documents/organization/24882.pdf.
26. Robert Satloff, "The Djerejian Report on Public Diplomacy: First Impressions," Washington Institute, October 1, 2003, http://www.washingtoninstitute.org/policy-analysis/view/the-djerejian-report-on-public-diplomacy-first-impressions.

27. "2017 Comprehensive Annual Report on Public Diplomacy and International Broadcasting," U.S. Department of State, October 6, 2017, https://www.state.gov/pdcommission/reports/274698.htm.
28. Katherine Brown, president and CEO of Global Ties U.S., interview with the author, September 15, 2017.
29. Ibid.
30. Ibid.
31. Homeland Security Advisory Council, "Countering Violent Extremism Subcommittee: Interim Report and Recommendations," Department of Homeland Security, June 2016, https://www.dhs.gov/sites/default/files/publications/HSAC/HSAC%20CVE%20Final%20Interim%20Report%20June%209%202016%20508%20compliant.pdf.
32. Satloff, "The Djerejian Report on Public Diplomacy."
33. Ibid.
34. "Public Remains Conflicted Over Islam," Pew Research Center, August 24, 2010, http://www.pewforum.org/2010/08/24/public-remains-conflicted-over-islam/.
35. Eli Watkins and Abby Phillip, "Trump Decries Immigrants from 'Shithole Countries' Coming to U.S.," CNN, updated January 12, 2018, https://www.cnn.com/2018/01/11/politics/immigrants-shithole-countries-trump/index.html.
36. Emma Young, "How Iceland Got Teens to Say No to Drugs," *The Atlantic,* January 19, 2017, https://www.theatlantic.com/health/archive/2017/01/teens-drugs-iceland/513668/.
37. Marc Lynch, "The Persistence of Arab Anti-Americanism," *Foreign Affairs,* May/June 2013, https://www.foreignaffairs.com/reviews/review-essay/persistence-arab-anti-americanism.
38. Ibid.
39. Stephen Walt, "Five Ways Donald Trump Is Wrong About Islam," *Foreign Policy,* February 17, 2017, http://foreignpolicy.com/2017/02/17/five-ways-donald-trump-is-wrong-about-islam/.
40. Ibid.
41. David Petraeus, "David Petraeus: Anti-Muslim Bigotry Aids Islamist Terrorists," *Washington Post,* May 13, 2016.
42. Katayoun Kishi, "Anti-Muslim Assaults Reach 9/11-Era Levels, FBI Data Show," Pew Research Center, November 21, 2016, http://www.pewresearch.org/fact-tank/2016/11/21/anti-muslim-assaults-reach-911-era-levels-fbi-data-show/.
43. Sabrina Siddiqui, "Trump's Anti-Muslim Retweets Prompt Backlash in Washington: 'The President Is Racist,'" *Guardian,* November 29, 2017, https://www.theguardian.com/us-news/2017/nov/29/trumps-anti-muslim-retweets-prompt-backlash-in-washington-the-president-is-racist.
44. Christopher Mathias, "There Were a Lot of Alleged Anti-Muslim

Crimes During This Year's Ramadan," Huffington Post, July 15, 2016, https://www.huffingtonpost.com/entry/anti-muslim-crimes-ramadan_us_5786a2c4e4b03fc3ee4f1d99.

45. Ibid.
46. J. M. Berger, "London and the Clash of the Extremists," *The Atlantic,* June 19, 2017, https://www.theatlantic.com/international/archive/2017/06/london-terror-isis-finsbury-park/530838/.

CHAPTER SEVEN: #STARTUPGOVERNMENT

1. "Being Muslim in America," U.S. State Department: Bureau of International Information Programs, March 2009, https://photos.state.gov/libraries/korea/49271/dwoa_122709/being-muslim-in-america.pdf.
2. "State Dept Issues Booklet on Being Muslim in America," *Arab American News,* June 9, 2009, http://www.arabamericannews.com/2009/06/09/State-Dept-issues-booklet-on-being-Muslim-in-America/.
3. Mohamed Younis, "Muslim Americans Exemplify Diversity, Potential," Gallup, March 2, 2009, http://news.gallup.com/poll/116260/muslim-americans-exemplify-diversity-potential.aspx.
4. Ahmed Larouz, speaker, nomad, social innovator, interview with the author, December 2016.
5. Zahed Amanullah, entrepreneur, interview with the author, November 22, 2016.
6. Ibid.
7. Abdul Rehman-Malik, "Report to the Open Society Foundations," Institute for Strategic Dialogue, January 2011.
8. Z. Amanullah, interview with the author.
9. Larouz, interview with the author.
10. United States Institute of Peace, "The Generation Change Program," YouTube video, 3.59, July 7, 2015, https://www.youtube.com/watch?v=si99PkctSCc&feature=youtu.be.
11. Camilo La Cruz, executive vice president and head of content at sparks & honey, interview with the author, New York City, December 19, 2016.
12. Terry Young, founder and CEO of sparks & honey, interview with the author, New York City, December 19, 2016.
13. Matthew Levitt and Katherine Bauer, "Qatar Doesn't Need a Blockade. It Needs an Audit," *Foreign Policy,* June 15, 2017, http://foreignpolicy.com/2017/06/15/qatar-doesnt-back-moderate-extremists-it-bankrolls-al-qaeda/.
14. Farah Pandith, "The Rise of Radicalization: Is the U.S. Government Failing to Counter International and Domestic Terrorism?" Council on Foreign Relations, July 15, 2015, https://www.cfr.org/sites/default/files/pdf/2015/07/Farah%20Pandith%207.15.15.pdf.
15. Green and Proctor, "Turning Point."

CHAPTER EIGHT: GLOBAL BUSINESS ON THE FRONT LINES

1. Bill Gates, "Creative Capitalism," speech, World Economic Forum, Davos, Switzerland, January 24, 2008.
2. "Olam Supports Sustainable Development Goals," Olam Group, January 3, 2016, http://olamgroup.com/news-bites/olam-supports-launch-sustainable-development-goals/#sthash.HRxFCnuQ.dpbs.
3. "#Envision2030 Goal 2: Zero Hunger," United Nations Department of Economic and Social Affairs Division for Inclusive Social Development, accessed May 25, 2018, https://www.un.org/development/desa/disabilities/envision2030-goal2.html.
4. "#Envision2030 Goal 17: Partnerships for the Goals," United Nations Department of Economic and Social Affairs Division for Inclusive Social Development, accessed May 29, 2018, https://www.un.org/development/desa/disabilities/envision2030-goal17.html.
5. Bhaskar Chakravorti, "What Businesses Need to Know About Sustainable Development Goals," *Harvard Business Review,* November 20, 2015, https://hbr.org/2015/11/what-businesses-need-to-know-about-sustainable-development-goals.
6. Bhaskar Chakravorti, "Why 'Partnerships for Sustainable Development' Counts as an Essential Sustainable Development Goal," *Forbes,* August 16, 2016, https://www.forbes.com/sites/bhaskarchakravorti/2016/08/16/why-partnerships-for-sustainable-development-counts-as-an-essential-sustainable-development-goal/#211d050e1b12.
7. Nancy Koehn, historian of business at Harvard Business School, interview with the author, September 20, 2017.
8. Bhaskar Chakravorti, Dean of Global Business at the Fletcher School of Law and Diplomacy, interview with the author, Medford, Massachusetts, July 20, 2017.
9. Brian Rashid, "Why More and More Companies Are Doing Social Good," *Forbes,* April 25, 2017, https://www.forbes.com/forbes/welcome/?toURL=https://www.forbes.com/sites/brianrashid/2017/04/25/why-more-and-more-companies-are-doing-social-good/&refURL=&referrer=#4644d1fadb07.
10. Christine Hauser, "Patagonia, REI and Other Outdoor Retailers Protest Trump's Decision to Shrink Utah Monuments," *New York Times,* December 5, 2017, https://www.nytimes.com/2017/12/05/business/patagonia-trump-utah.html?_r=0.
11. Loren Renz and Leslie Marino, "Giving in the Aftermath of 9/11: 2003 Update on the Foundation and Corporate Response," Foundation Center, December 2003.
12. Aaron Smith, "How Sept. 11 Changed Charity in America," CNN Money, September 6, 2011, http://money.cnn.com/2011/09/06/news/economy/katrina_donations_911/index.htm.

13. Vincent J. Schodolski, "Administration Drafts Hollywood in War Effort," *Chicago Tribune,* November 12, 2001, http://articles.chicagotribune.com/2001-11-12/news/0111120234_1_rove-patriotic-films-major-studios.
14. Ibid.
15. Merrick Carey, "Public-Private Partnerships: Presentation to the Elliott School of International Affairs, George Washington University," Lexington Institute, September 14, 2007, http://www.lexingtoninstitute.org/public-private-partnerships/.
16. Henry Crumpton, "The Role of Public and Private Partnerships in the Global War on Terrorism," remarks given to the 5th Annual International Counterterrorism Conference, Public and Private Partnerships, Washington, D.C., April 20, 2006.
17. Christopher Graves, founding president of the Ogilvy Center for Behavioral Science, interview with the author, Washington, D.C., August 23, 2016.
18. Steven Overly, "Why We Scoff When McDonald's Hands Out Fitness Trackers," *Washington Post,* August 20, 2016, https://www.washingtonpost.com/news/innovations/wp/2016/08/20/why-we-scoff-when-mcdonalds-hands-out-fitness-trackers/?utm_term=.97dc26d7e81b.
19. Chakravorti, "What Businesses Need to Know."
20. Andrew Ross Sorkin, "The Hidden Costs of Terrorism," *New York Times,* November 17, 2015, http://www.nytimes.com/2015/11/17/business/dealbook/the-fallout-from-attacks-is-measured-in-more-than-stock-markets.html?_r=1.
21. Walter Enders and Eric Olson, "Measuring the Economic Costs of Terrorism," Department of Economics Finance and Legal Studies, Culverhouse College of Commerce & Business administration, University of Tuscaloosa, accessed December 2, 2016, http://www.socsci.uci.edu/~mrgarfin/OUP/papers/Enders.pdf.
22. All quotes and data in this paragraph taken from Eric Rosand and Alistair Millar, "How the Private Sector Can Be Harnessed to Stop Violent Extremism," Brookings Institution, January 31, 2017, https://www.brookings.edu/blog/order-from-chaos/2017/01/31/how-the-private-sector-can-be-harnessed-to-stop-violent-extremism/.
23. Enders and Olson, "Measuring the Economic Costs of Terrorism."
24. Mark Thompson, "Borders Could Cost Europe $20 Billion a Year," CNN Money, March 4, 2016, http://money.cnn.com/2016/03/04/news/economy/europe-borders-schengen-cost-of-collapse/index.html.
25. Wolfgang Lehmacher, "How Safe Are Our Supply Chains from Terrorist Attack?" World Economic Forum, December 11, 2015, https://www.weforum.org/agenda/2015/12/how-safe-are-our-supply-chains-from-terrorist-attack/.
26. Frank Holmes, "The Global Cost of Terrorism Is at an All-Time High," *Business Insider,* March 28, 2016, http://www.businessinsider.com/global-cost-of-terrorism-at-all-time-high-2016-3.
27. Gill Plimmer, "Global Supply Chains Hit by Terror Threats and Flows

of Migrants," *Financial Times,* November 18, 2015, https://www.ft.com/content/05bfb10e-8de3-11e5-a549-b89a1dfede9b.

28. Ibid.
29. Ibid.
30. Tom Saler, "Calculating the Economic Cost of Terrorism," *Milwaukee Journal Sentinel,* November 21, 2015, http://archive.jsonline.com/business/calculating-the-economic-cost-of-terrorism-b99620389z1-352623021.html/.
31. "The Economic Cost of Violence Containment," Institute of for Economics and Peace, April 2017, http://visionofhumanity.org/app/uploads/2017/04/The-Economic-Cost-of-Violence-Containment.pdf.
32. "Global Terrorism Index 2016: Measuring and Understanding the Global Impact of Terrorism," Institute for Economics and Peace, 2016, http://visionofhumanity.org/app/uploads/2017/02/Global-Terrorism-Index-2016.pdf; Joe Myers, "What Is the Economic Impact of Terrorism?" World Economic Forum, November 19, 2015, https://www.weforum.org/agenda/2015/11/what-is-the-economic-impact-of-terrorism/.
33. "Views from Around the Globe: Countering Violent Extremism: A CSIS Commission on Countering Violent Extremism Survey," Center for Strategic and International Studies and the National Research Group, October 18, 2016, https://csis-prod.s3.amazonaws.com/s3fs-public/publication/161018_CVE_Full_Report_CSIS.pdf.
34. Wolfgang Lehmacher, "How Safe Are Our Supply Chains from Terrorist Attack?" World Economic Forum, December 11, 2015, https://www.weforum.org/agenda/2015/12/how-safe-are-our-supply-chains-from-terrorist-attack/.
35. Tim Lister et al., "ISIS: 143 Attacks in 29 Countries Have Killed 2,043," CNN, February 13, 2017, accessed November 1, 2017, http://www.cnn.com/2015/12/17/world/mapping-isis-attacks-around-the-world.
36. "Global Partnerships—United Nations Sustainable Development," United Nations, accessed November 2, 2017, http://www.un.org/sustainabledevelopment/globalpartnerships/.
37. Chakravorti, "Why 'Partnerships for Sustainable Development' Count."
38. Bhaskar Chakravorti, "Finding Competitive Advantage in Adversity," *Harvard Business Review,* July 31, 2014, https://hbr.org/2010/11/finding-competitive-advantage-in-adversity.
39. Dominic Rushe, "Starbucks to Close 8,000 U.S. Stores for Racial-Bias Training," *Guardian,* April 17, 2018, https://www.theguardian.com/business/2018/apr/17/starbucks-racism-training-close-stores-may-us.
40. "The Dawn of CEO Activism."
41. Jena McGregor and Elizabeth Dwoskin, "The Cost of Silence: Why More CEOs Are Speaking Out in the Trump Era," *Washington Post,* February 17, 2017, https://www.washingtonpost.com/news/on-leadership/wp/2017/02/17/the-cost-of-silence-why-more-ceos-are-speaking-out-in-the-trump-era/?postshare=7091487618405366&tid=ss_mail&utm_term=.b5598e9d3857.

42. Ibid.
43. "The Dawn of CEO Activism."
44. Koehn, interview with the author.
45. Kate Taylor, "Dick's Faced Boycott Threats When It Changed Its Gun Policies—but the Majority of America Agrees with the Retailer," *Business Insider,* March 26, 2018, http://www.businessinsider.com/dicks-boycott-threats-dont-mean-anything-2018-3.
46. "Report Shows a Third of Consumers Prefer Sustainable Brands," Unilever, May 1, 2017, https://www.unilever.com/news/press-releases/2017/report-shows-a-third-of-consumers-prefer-sustainable-brands.html.
47. "Terrorism: How Aetna International and Red24 Keep You Safe," Aetna, accessed April 8, 2018, https://www.aetnainternational.com/en/about-us/explore/living-abroad/travel/how-aetna-international-and-red24-keep-you-safe.html.
48. Lara O'Reilly, "The Real Motivations Behind the Growing YouTube Advertiser Boycott," *Business Insider,* March 22, 2017, http://www.businessinsider.com/why-advertisers-are-pulling-spend-from-youtube-2017-3.
49. Aaron K. Chatterji and Michael W. Toffel, "Divided We Lead: CEO Activism Has Entered the Mainstream," *Harvard Business Review,* March 2018, https://hbr.org/cover-story/2018/03/divided-we-lead.
50. "Beyond the Game: The NFL Social Responsibility Report," National Football League, March 24, 2017, http://www.nfl.com/static/content/public/photo/2017/03/24/0ap3000000795087.pdf.
51. "Giving in Numbers," CECP in association with the Conference Board, 2016, http://cecp.co/pdfs/giving_in_numbers/GIN2016_Finalweb.pdf.
52. "(STARBUCKS) RED," Starbucks, accessed November 30, 2016. https://www.starbucks.com/responsibility/community/starbucks-red.
53. "Farming Communities," Starbucks, accessed November 30, 2016, https://www.starbucks.com/responsibility/community/farmer-support.
54. Graves, interview with the author.
55. Caryl Stern, *I Believe in Zero: Learning from the World's Children* (New York: St. Martin's, 2013), 129–33.
56. E. J. Schultz, "Jeep Uses Cat Stevens Song in Unifying Debate Ad," *AdAge,* September 26, 2016, http://adage.com/article/cmo-strategy/jeep-cat-stevens-song-unifying-debate-ad/306025/.
57. Sapna Maheshwari, "Bowing to the Inevitable, Advertisers Embrace Advocate Role," *New York Times,* October 1, 2017, https://www.nytimes.com/2017/10/01/business/media/advertising-week-politics.html?smid=tw-nytimes&smtyp=cur.
58. Rachel Nussbaum, "Sephora Cast Its Own Employees for Its Most Diverse Campaign Yet," *Glamour,* October 30, 2017, https://www.glamour.com/story/sephora-holiday-ad-diversity.
59. "The World Needs More than Nice, the World Needs #moreKIND,"

Kind Snacks, accessed April 8, 2018, https://www.kindsnacks.com/morekind?utm_content=hero&utm_source=KIND+Community&utm_campaign=41c0dd5709-EMAIL_CAMPAIGN_2017_11_16&utm_medium=email&utm_term=0_0d4a4a47d6-41c0dd5709-37572589&mc_cid=41c0dd5709&mc_eid=ff1c15e4c5.

60. Grace Donnelly, "The World Faces a Growing Refugee Crisis: Here's What Some Companies Are Doing About It," *Fortune,* September 29, 2017, http://fortune.com/2017/09/29/how-companies-are-helping-refugees/.
61. Thomas Cellucci, "Innovative Public Private Partnerships: Pathway to Effectively Solving Problems," Department of Homeland Security, July 2010, https://www.dhs.gov/xlibrary/assets/st_innovative_public_private_partnerships_0710_version_2.pdf.
62. Carey, "Public-Private Partnerships."
63. For example, Ashley Lutz and Mallory Schlossberg, "The Top 100 Brands for Millennials," *Business Insider,* November 14, 2015, http://www.businessinsider.com/top-100- millennial-brands- 2015-5/#95-carters-6.
64. "H&M Conscious Actions Sustainability Report 2015," H&M, 2015, http://about.hm.com/content/dam/hmgroup/groupsite/documents/en/CSR/reports/2015%20Sustainability%20report/HM_SustainabilityReport_2015_final_FullReport_en.pdf; Juan Velasco and Paul Sullivan, "Where the Big Money Is," *New York Times,* February 19, 2017, https://www.nytimes.com/2017/02/19/your-money/where-the-big-money-is.html.
65. Steven Greenhouse, "Major Retailers Join Bangladesh Safety Plan," *New York Times,* May 13, 2013, http://www.nytimes.com/2013/05/14/business/global/hm-agrees-to-bangladesh-safety-plan.html.
66. "The Way to Sustainable Fashion," H&M Sustainability, accessed November 30, 2016, http://about.hm.com/en/sustainability/get-involved/the-way-to-sustainable-fashion.html.
67. Koehn, interview with the author.

CHAPTER NINE: BUILDING DUMBLEDORE'S ARMY

1. Emanuella Grinberg, Shimon Prokupecz, and Holly Yan, "Ohio State University: Attacker Killed, 11 Hospitalized After Campus Attack," CNN, November 28, 2016, http://www.cnn.com/2016/11/28/us/ohio-state-university-active-shooter/.
2. Aamer Madhani, "Accused Ohio State Attacker Reportedly Posted Rant Online," *USA Today,* November 29, 2016, http://www.usatoday.com/story/news/2016/11/28/somali-immigrant-identified-attacker-ohio-state/94563226/.
3. Pete Williams et al., "Suspect Identified in Ohio State Attack as Abdul Razak Ali Artan," NBC News, November 28, 2016, https://www.nbcnews.com/news/us-news/suspect-dead-after-ohio-state-university-car-knife-attack-n689076.
4. Mary Mogan Edward, Mark Ferenchik, and Encarnita Pyle, "Ohio State

Attack, Rhetoric Worry Young Somalis in Columbus," *Columbus Dispatch,* December 4, 2016, http://www.dispatch.com/content/stories/local/2016/12/04/attack-rhetoric-worry-young-somalis-in-columbus.html.

5. Andrew Grossman, "Ohio Man Indicted on Terror Charges," *Wall Street Journal,* April 16, 2015, http://www.wsj.com/articles/ohio-man-indicted-on-terror-charges-1429204856.
6. Patrick Poole, "Sources Confirm: Ohio Al-Shabaab Jihadist Killed in Somalia," *PJ Media,* September 21, 2010, https://pjmedia.com/blog/sources-confirm-ohio-al-shabaab-jihadist-killed-in-somalia/.
7. "Somali Gets 10 Years in Ohio Mall Terrorism Plot," NBC News, November 28, 2007, http://www.nbcnews.com/id/21998290/ns/us_news-security/t/somali-gets-years-ohio-mall-terrorism-plot/.
8. Mohamed A. Ali, American Somali community activist, interview with the author, September 7, 2016.
9. Ibid.
10. "Accelerating Peace Through Entrepreneurship," Iftiin Foundation, accessed November 17, 2017, http://www.iftiinfoundation.com/.
11. Ali, interview with the author.
12. Mohamed A. Ali, e-mail to the author, March 26, 2018.
13. "YouthQuake," TedxTeen, YouTube, 4.46, https://www.tedxteen.com/talks/youthquake-farah-pandith?rq=farah.
14. Eliza Byard, "The 81%: How Young Adults Are Reshaping the Marriage Equality Debate," MSNBC, March 26, 2013, http://www.msnbc.com/msnbc/the-81-how-young-adults-are-reshaping-the-m.
15. Eliza Byard, executive director of the Gay, Lesbian and Straight Education Network, interview with the author, November 17, 2017.
16. Eliza Byard, "How Young Adults."
17. "Fighting Disease," Rotary, accessed April 8, 2018, https://www.rotary.org/en/our-causes/fighting-disease.
18. Ibid.
19. Daniyal Noorani, movie producer, creator of Quaid Say Baatain, interview with the author, January 28, 2017.
20. Saddaf Fayyaz, "A Truly Divergent Message: Find Heaven by Daniyal Noorani (Interview)," Koolmuzone, January 29, 2010, http://www.koolmuzone.pk/2010/01/a-truly-divergent-message-find-heaven-by-daniyal-noorani-inteview/.
21. Noorani, interview with the author.
22. "Pakistani Animators Tackle Tough Social Issues," YouTube, 2.19, January 27, 2015, https://www.youtube.com/watch?v=VIl7SrGwNj4.
23. Daniyal Noorani, "Fighting Militancy with Music," *Foreign Policy,* June 4, 2010, http://foreignpolicy.com/2010/06/04/fighting-militancy-with-music/.
24. Roya Nikkah, "Ugly, Grey, Depressing: Why Luton Really Is the Worst Place in Britain," *Telegraph,* September 26, 2004, http://www.telegraph.co.uk/news

/uknews/1472650/Ugly-grey-depressing-why-Luton-really-is-the-worst-place-in-Britain.html.

25. Luqman Ali, director of Khayaal Theater Company, e-mail to the author, July 4, 2017.
26. For more on the Khayaal Theater Company, see their website: http://www.khayaal.co.uk/about.
27. "Two Guilty of Luton IS Terror Support Plot," BBC News, January 13, 2017, http://www.bbc.com/news/uk-england-beds-bucks-herts-38612219.
28. "Khartoum Open-Mic Night," White Ribbon Campaign, March 5, 2010, http://ourfuturehasnoviolenceagainstwomen.blogspot.com/2010/03/khartoum-open-mic-night-white-ribbon.html.
29. "Home," City Circle, accessed November 17, 2017, http://www.thecitycircle.com/about.
30. Taken from his curriculum vitae, http://www.ziadfahed.com/zf_content/15_cv/FILES/CV/pdf/ZF_CV_2016-11.pdf.
31. "TED Talks," Al-Mutawa, accessed November 17, 2017, http://www.al-mutawa.com/ted-talks/.
32. Christopher M. Schroeder, "Naif Al-Mutawa Fights to Bring 'THE 99' and Its Message to Wide U.S. Audience," *Washington Post,* October 11, 2011, https://www.washingtonpost.com/lifestyle/style/naif-al-mutawa-fights-to-bring-the-99-and-its-message-to-wide-us-audience/2011/10/07/gIQAmZdqdL_story.html?utm_term=.37a75140b428.
33. Ibid.
34. Lawrence Pintak, "Can Cartoons Save Pakistan's Children from Jihad?" *Foreign Policy,* August 22, 2016, http://foreignpolicy.com/2016/08/19/can-cartoons-save-pakistans-children-from-jihad/.
35. Dash Dhakshinamoorthy, Malaysian entrepreneur, interview with the author, January 24, 2017.
36. Ibid.
37. "Muslim Voices," Podtail (podcast), https://podtail.com/en/podcast/muslim-voices/.
38. "See Something Say Something: A New Podcast About Being Muslim in America," BuzzFeed, October 26, 2016, https://www.buzzfeed.com/seesomethingsaysomething/see-something-say-something-a-new-podcast-about-being-muslim?utm_term=.ib1rrbGrYR#.cnmNNeRN9.
39. Ahmed Akbar, podcast host, e-mail exchange with the author's research assistant, March 30, 2018.
40. "Imams Online: Digital Summit 2018," Imams Online, accessed April 8, 2018, http://imamsonline.com/about-us/.
41. See "Mosque Open Day," accessed November 17, 2017, http://www.mosqueopenday.com/; Shaukat Warraich and Feroze Kashaff, "Mosque Management Guide for Mosques & Islamic Centres," Issuu, 2007, https://issuu.com/faith.associates/docs/mmtk.

42. Björn Hartmann and Zvika Krieger, "DES INV 190-1/CS 194-131 Designing Technology to Counter Violent Extremism," University of California, Berkeley, course syllabus, 2017, accessed November 17, 2017, https://bcourses.berkeley.edu/courses/1456962/assignments/syllabus.
43. Nate Seltenrich, "Countering Extremism with Technology," Berkeley Engineering, March 13, 2017, https://engineering.berkeley.edu/2017/03/countering-extremism-technology.
44. "To Stop Kids from Radicalizing, Moms in Denmark Call Other Moms," NPR, May 8, 2016, http://www.npr.org/sections/parallels/2016/05/08/476890795/to-stop-kids-from-radicalizing-moms-in-denmark-call-other-moms.
45. Alissa J. Rubin, "Geert Wilders, Reclusive Provocateur, Rises Before Dutch Vote," *New York Times,* February 27, 2017, https://www.nytimes.com/2017/02/27/world/europe/geert-wilders-reclusive-provocateur-rises-before-dutch-vote.html.
46. Charlotte Hochman, founder of La Ruche, interview with the author, January 16, 2017.
47. La Ruche was an artist's collective in Paris, frequented by many of the greatest modernist artists of the twentieth century.
48. Hochman, interview with the author.
49. Ibid.
50. Nathalie Birchem, "Saïd Hammouche, DRH des banlieues," *La Croix,* May 15, 2015, https://www.la-croix.com/Solidarite/Dans-l-economie/Said-Hammouche-DRH-des-banlieues-2015-05-15-1312658.
51. Ahmed Larouz, speaker, nomad, social innovator, interview with the author, December 2016.
52. Ibid.
53. Zainah Anwar, "Muslim Sisterhood Sisters in Islam Empowers Feminist Muslims Zainah Anwar, Malaysia," Muslima, accessed January 7, 2017, http://muslima.globalfundforwomen.org/content/muslim-sisterhood.
54. "Our Journey," Musawah, accessed January 7, 2017, http://www.musawah.org/about-musawah/our-journey-0.
55. "About Musawah," Musawah, accessed January 7, 2017, http://www.musawah.org/about-musawah.
56. Daniyal Noorani, "Fighting Militancy with Music," *Foreign Policy,* June 4, 2010, http://foreignpolicy.com/2010/06/04/fighting-militancy-with-music/.
57. "Compassionate City," LouisvilleKy.gov, accessed November 18, 2017, https://louisvilleky.gov/government/compassionate-city.
58. Tom Tait, "Embracing Kindness to Build Stronger Communities," *Western City,* December 2017, http://www. westerncity.com/Western-City/December-2017/Embracing- Kindness-to-Build-Stronger- Communities.
59. Mark Leftly, "Exclusive: London Mayor Sadiq Khan on Islam, the E.U. and Donald Trump," *Time,* May 10, 2016, http://time.com/4322562/london-mayor-sadiq-khan-donald-trump/.

60. Ibid.
61. J. Alexander Sloan, vice president of strategic partnerships and communications at Tide, interview with the author, March 17, 2017.
62. Kerry A. Dolan, "Big Bet Philanthropy: How More Givers Are Spending Big and Taking Risks to Solve Society's Problems," *Forbes,* December 8, 2016, http://www.forbes.com/sites/kerryadolan/2016/11/30/big-bet-philanthropy-solving-social-problems/#4f35a23c3999.
63. Nick Wingfield, "Jeff Bezos Wants Ideas for Philanthropy, So He Asked Twitter," *New York Times,* June 15, 2017.
64. Sasha Havlicek, CEO/director of Institute for Strategic Dialogue, e-mail to the author, April 1, 2018.
65. Dolan, "Big Bet Philanthropy."
66. Mustafa Tameez and Wardah Khalid, "Building a Resilient Community to Counter Violent Extremism," Houston/Harrison County, 2014, https://assets.documentcloud.org/documents/2803541/Community-CVE-Plan-020415-v2.pdf; Fauzeya Rahman, "To Best Counter Extremism, Muslim Community Leaders Opt for Organic Approach," *Houston Chronicle,* June 26, 2016, http://www.houstonchronicle.com/news/houston-texas/houston/article/To-best-counter-extremism-Muslim-community-8321719.php.
67. Danuta Kozaki, "Community Partnerships Funded to Counter Rise of Violent Extremism in NSW," ABC News, March 24, 2016.
68. Pandith, "Building Dumbledore's Army."
69. Anthony Cordesman, "Tracking the Trends and Numbers: Islam, Terrorism, Stability, and Conflict in the Middle East," Center for Strategic and International Studies, February 15, 2017, https://csis-prod.s3.amazonaws.com/s3fs-public/publication/170215_MENA_Islam_Terrorism.pdf?UpPJuYw1I6XYXw1d14igmZrCeraXLyXj.
70. Joshua Holland, "The Truth About American Muslims," *The Nation,* December 8, 2015, https://www.thenation.com/article/heres-why-we-should-all-praise-allah-for-american-muslims/.
71. Fadi Itani, "The Muslim Zakat: A Vision of the 'Big Society'?" *New Statesman,* August 11, 2012, http://www.newstatesman.com/blogs/politics/2012/08/muslim-zakat-vision-big-society.
72. "Reza Aslan Hosted by the Islamic Scholarship Fund—Sep 2011," YouTube, 1:27:44, October 22, 2011, https://www.youtube.com/watch?v=V-44PTulBSU.
73. Colby Itkowitz, "'Every Person Deserves to Rest in Peace': American Muslims Raising Money to Repair Vandalized Jewish Cemetery," *Washington Post,* February 21, 2017, https://www.washingtonpost.com/news/inspired-life/wp/2017/02/21/every-person-deserves-to-rest-in-peace-american-muslims-raising-money-to-repair-vandalized-jewish-cemetery/?utm_term=.9009e3874d1f.
74. Kate Murphy, "Somali Professor After Ohio State Attack: 'We Need to Reach

Out,'" Cincinnati.com, December 1, 2016, http://www.cincinnati.com/story/news/2016/11/28/columbus-somali-leader-attack-timing-not-good/94561840/.

75. Sandy Coleman, "Islamic Center Finds Acceptance in Sharon," *Boston Globe,* August, 30 1992, https://secure.pqarchiver.com/boston/doc/294693405.html?FMT=ABS&FMTS=ABS:FT&type=current&date=Aug+30%2C+1992&author=Coleman%2C+Sandy&pub=Boston+Globe+%28pre-1997+Fulltext%29&edition=&startpage=1&desc=Islamic+center+finds+acceptance+in+Sharon.
76. Sandy Coleman, "Islamic Center Drops Suit Over Failed Purchase of Milton Land," *Boston Globe,* January 29, 1992, https://secure.pqarchiver.com/boston/doc/294649134.html?FMT=ABS&FMTS=ABS:FT&type=current&date=Jan+29%2C+1992&author=Coleman%2C+Sandy&pub=Boston+Globe+%28pre-1997+Fulltext%29&edition=&startpage=34&desc=Islamic+Center+drops+suit+over+failed+purchase+of+Milton+land.
77. Coleman, "Islamic Center Finds Acceptance in Sharon."
78. Diana L. Eck, *A New Religious America: How a "Christian Country" Has Become the World's Most Religiously Diverse Nation* (San Francisco: Harper San Francisco, 2002).
79. Farah Pandith, "Taking Global Action to Hate," Coca-Cola, March 21, 2013, http://www.coca-colacompany.com/stories/opinion-taking-global-action-to-fight-hate.
80. Some of these ideas echo points I made in "A New Narrative," Muslima, November 2012, http://muslima.globalfundforwomen.org/content/new-narrative.

EPILOGUE: THE PROMISE OF OPEN POWER

1. Joseph Nye, "Soft Power: The Origins and Political Progress of a Concept," Palgrave Communications, 2017, doi: 10.1057/palcomms.2017.8.
2. Joseph S. Nye Jr., "In Mideast, the Goal Is 'Smart Power,'" Harvard Kennedy School Belfer Center, August 19, 2006, https://www.belfercenter.org/publication/mideast-goal-smart-power.
3. Gardiner Harris, "A Shift From 'Soft Power' Diplomacy in Cuts to the State Dept.," *New York Times,* March 16, 2017, https://www.nytimes.com/2017/03/16/us/politics/trump-budget-cuts-state-department.html.
4. Joseph S. Nye, "The Kindleberger Trap by Joseph S. Nye," Project Syndicate, January 9, 2017, https://www.project-syndicate.org/commentary/trump-china-kindleberger-trap-by-joseph-s--nye-2017-01?barrier=accessreg.
5. Ibid.
6. The Partnership's 30th Anniversary Leadership Summit, Martha's Vineyard, Massachusetts, June 10, 2017.
7. Ibid.
8. Katharine Schwab, "Ideo Studied Innovation in 100 Companies—Here's What It Found," Co.Design, May 2, 2017, https://www.fastcodesign.com/3069069/ideo-studied-innovation-in-100-companies-heres-what-it-found.

9. Michael Davidson, "Remarks at the Council on Foreign Relations on-the-Record CVE Roundtable," Washington, D.C., June 26, 2017.

APPENDIX 1: FROM NATIONAL SECURITY STRATEGY, PRESIDENT GEORGE W. BUSH, 2006

1. "The National Security Strategy of the United States of America," White House, March 2006, https://www.state.gov/documents/organization/64884.pdf.

APPENDIX 2: PRESIDENT OBAMA'S "A NEW BEGINNING" SPEECH

1. Barack Obama, "Remarks by the President on a New Beginning," speech, Cairo University, June 4, 2009, White House Archives, https://obamawhitehouse.archives.gov/the-press-office/remarks-president-cairo-university-6-04-09.

BIBLIOGRAPHY

"Abbottabad Revisited," War on the Rocks, June 22, 2017. https://warontherocks.com/2017/06/abbottabad-revisited/.

"About." YouTube. Accessed February 9, 2018. https://www.youtube.com/yt/about/.

"Active Change Foundation." Accessed February 9, 2018. https://www.activechangefoundation.org/.

"Addressing the Muslim Market, Can You Afford Not To." http://imaratconsultants.com/wp-content/uploads/2012/10/Addressing-Muslim-Market.pdf.

"Adolescent Development," *New York Times Health Guide.* http://www.nytimes.com/health/guides/specialtopic/adolescent-development/overview.html.

"Announcing the Girls' Education Task Force." Global Coalition for Education (blog), March 6, 2015. http://gbc-education.org/girls-education-task-force/.

"Artificial Intelligence and the Rise of Extremism." Medium, October 20, 2017. https://medium.com/LazyNaarad/artificial-intelligence-and-the-rise-of-extremism-2efd3f1315e4.

"Beyond the Game: The NFL Social Responsibility Report—2016 Season." NFL, 2016. http://www.nfl.com/static/content/public/photo/2017/03/24/0ap3000000795087.pdf.

"Bin Laden Accuses West." Information Clearing House (blog), April 24, 2016. http://www.informationclearinghouse.info/article12830.htm.

"Bin Laden: Al Qaeda Motivated to Strike U.S. Again." CNN, October 20, 2004. http://www.cnn.com/2004/WORLD/meast/10/29/binladen.tape/.

"Biography." Beyoglu Municipality, n.d. en.beyoglu.bel.tr/mayors_office/default.aspx?SectionId=1661.

"Budget Amendment Justification Department of State, Foreign Operations, and Related Programs Fiscal Year 2015." U.S. Department of State, 2015. https://www.state.gov/documents/organization/234238.pdf.

"California School: U.S.-Flag Shirt 'Gang Related.'" WND. http://www.wnd.com/2015/10/california-school-u-s-flag-shirt-gang-related/.

"Can Britain Stop Terrorists While Defending Civil Liberties?" *National Interest Online,* June 5, 2017. https://nationalinterest.org/print/feature/can-britain-stop-terrorists-while-defending-civil-liberties-21012?page=show.

"Changing Minds Winning Peace: A New Strategic Direction for U.S. Public Diplomacy in the Arab & Muslim World." Advisory Group on Public Diplomacy for the Arab and Muslim World, October 1, 2003.

"City Council: Alexandria Is a 'City of Kindness and Compassion.'" WTOP, November 20, 2016. https://wtop.com/alexandria/2016/11/city-council-alexandria-city-kindness-compassion/.

"The Columbus Foundation." *The Big Table.* https://columbusfoundation.org/donors/types-of-funds/special-initiatives/the-big-table/.

———. *Gifts of Kindness.* https://columbusfoundation.org/donors/types-of-funds/special-initiatives/gifts-of-kindness/.

"The Coming ISIS–al Qaeda Merger." *Foreign Affairs Online,* March 29, 2016. https://www.foreignaffairs.com/articles/2016-03-29/coming-isis-al-qaeda-merger.

"Community Programs." NBA Bucks. Accessed February 25, 2018. http://www.nba.com/bucks/community/CR_Programs.html/.

"Compassionate City." LouisvilleKy.gov. Accessed February 28, 2018. https://louisvilleky.gov/government/compassionate-city.

"Confident. Connected. Open to Change." Millennials: A Portrait of Generation Next. Pew Research Center, February 2010.

"Congressional Dems, Republicans Agree Obama's Islamic State Strategy Is Now, at Best, Stuck in Neutral." Fox News, May 24, 2015. http://www.foxnews.com/politics/2015/05/24/congressional-dems-republicans-agree-ocongressional-dems-republicans-agree/.

"Corporate Alliance on Malaria in Africa (CAMA)." GBC Health, n.d. http://archive.gbchealth.org/our-work/collective-actions/cama/.

"Couture Creations by Kulthulm (_kulthulm_) Instagram Photos and Videos." Instagram. https://www.instagram.com/_kulthulm_/?hl=en.

"Digital Skills." Microsoft.com. Accessed February 24, 2018. https://www.microsoft.com/en-us/digital-skills.

"Digitally Connected: Global Perspectives on Youth and Digital Media." Research Publication. Berkman Center for Internet & Society at Harvard University, April 1, 2015.

"Divided We Lead." *Harvard Business Review,* March 23, 2018. https://hbr.org/cover-story/2018/03/divided-we-lead.

"Do Millennials Ever Put Down Their Mobiles?" EMarketer. March 16, 2015. https://www.emarketer.com/Article/Do-Millennials-Ever-Put-Down-Their-Mobiles/1012210.

"Donald Trump Addresses Radical Islamic Terrorism." *Hill,* August 15, 2016. http://thehill.com/blogs/pundits-blog/presidential-campaign/291498-full-transcript-donald-trump-addresses-radical.

"Education." NBA Cares, n.d. http://www.nba.com/nba_cares/mission/education.html.

"Fiscal Year 2015: Budget Amendment Justification: Department of State, Foreign Operations and Related Programs." http://www.state.gov/documents/organization/234238.pdf.

"Global Internet Forum to Counter Terrorism." Twitter Public Policy (blog), June 26, 2017. https://blog.twitter.com/official/en_us/topics/company/2017/Global-Internet-Forum-to-Counter-Terrorism.html.

"Global Terrorism Index 2015." Institute for Economics & Peace, 2015.

"Google's Vision Statement & Mission Statement." Panmore Institute, January 28, 2017. http://panmore.com/google-vision-statement-mission-statement.

"Graduate for Mas." Taco Bell Foundation. Accessed February 28, 2018. https://getschooled.com/graduate-for-mas.

"The Economic Cost of Violence Containment." ReliefWeb. https://reliefweb.int/report/world/economic-cost-violence-containment.

"Embracing Kindness to Build Stronger Communities." Western City. http://www.westerncity.com/Western-City/December-2017/Embracing-Kindness-to-Build-Stronger-Communities/.

"Fight Against ISIS Needs Troops to Be Effective, Michael Morell Says." CBS News, February 4, 2015. http://www.cbsnews.com/news/isis-threat-response-needs-troops-to-be-effective-michael-morell-says/.

"A Financial Profile of the Terrorism of Al-Qaeda and Its Affiliates." Perspectives on Terrorism. http://www.terrorismanalysts.com/pt/index.php/pot/article/view/113.

"The 411 on Inglot O2M: Is It Halal? Find Out What Jeddah Blog Thinks." Jeddah Blog, January 30, 2014. https://jeddah-blog.com/2014/01/30/inglot-o2m-the-halal-nail-polish/.

"#Fail." *The Economist,* March 20, 2015. https://www.economist.com/blogs/democracyinamerica/2015/03/starbucks-and-branding.

"#NotInMyName." Active Change Foundation, September 2014. http://isisnotinmyname.com/.

"HOME." Inner-City Muslim Action Network. http://www.imancentral.org/.

"Home." Between Arabs Project. http://www.betweenarabs.com/.

"How Much Really Changed About Terrorism on 9/11?" *The Atlantic,* September 11, 2016. http://www.theatlantic.com/international/archive/2016/09/jenkins-hoffman-crenshaw-september-11-al-qaeda/499334/.

"How Saudi Arabia Exports Radical Islam." *The Week,* August 8, 2015. http://theweek.com/articles/570297/how-saudi-arabia-exports-radical-islam.

"How Should Companies Navigate Polarized Politics in the Trump Era?" *PBS*

NewsHour, February 9, 2017. https://www.pbs.org/newshour/show/companies-navigate-polarized-politics-trump-era.

"ISIL Is Winning," *Politico,* September 10, 2015. http://www.politico.com/magazine/story/2015/09/isil-is-winning-213136.

"Islam and the West: Annual Report on the State of Dialogue." World Economic Forum Community of West and Islam Dialogue, 2008.

"Islamic Scholars Go Head-to-Head with ISIS Propaganda Machine." Cipher Brief. https://www.thecipherbrief.com/column_article/islamic-scholars-go-head-head-isis-propaganda-machine.

"Islamic State's (ISIS, ISIL) Horrific Magazine." Clarion Project (blog), September 10, 2014. https://clarionproject.org/islamic-state-isis-isil-propaganda-magazine-dabiq-50/#.

"KAU to Analyze Extremist Discourse on Social Media." *Arab News,* June 18, 2017. http://www.arabnews.com/node/1116801/saudi-arabia.

"Keeping Up With Today's Consumers." PowerPoint deck prepared for Macy's, July 2016.

"Key Statistics." University of Auckland. https://www.auckland.ac.nz/en/about-us/about-the-university/our-ranking-and-reputation/key-statistics.html.

"A Leap in the Dark: Muslims and the State in Twenty-first-Century Europe." *The Emancipation of Europe's Muslims* 1–29. doi:10.1515/9781400840373-005.

"Louisville Named 2015 Model City for Compassion." LouisvilleKy.gov, October 19, 2015. https://louisvilleky.gov/news/louisville-named-2015-model-city-compassion.

Mark Wahlberg & Taco Bell Foundation for Teens Team Up to Fight High School Dropout Crisis." PR Newswire. Accessed February 28, 2018. https://www.prnewswire.com/news-releases/mark-wahlberg--taco-bell-foundation-for-teens-team-up-to-fight-high-school-dropout-crisis-119392209.html.

"The Men, the Myths, the Legends: Why Millennial 'Dudes' Might Be More Receptive to Marketing Than We Thought." What People Watch, Listen to and Buy. http://www.nielsen.com/us/en/insights/news/2014/the-men-the-myths-the-legends-why-millennial-dudes-might-be-more-receptive-to-marketing.html.

"Microsoft's Approach to Terrorist Content Online." Microsoft Corporate Blogs, May 20, 2016. https://blogs.microsoft.com/on-the-issues/2016/05/20/microsofts-approach-terrorist-content-online/#lUQE38tZKQrTrFYZ.99.

"Muslim Lolita Fashion Is a New Trend Inspired by Japan." Bored Panda. https://www.boredpanda.com/muslim-lolita-hijab-japanese-fashion-anime/.

"Muslim Networks and Movements in Western Europe: Muslim World League and World Assembly of Muslim Youth," Pew Research Center, September 15, 2010. www.pewforum.org/2010/09/15/muslim-networks-and-movements-in-western-europe-muslim-world-league-and-world-assembly-of-muslim-youth/.

"Muslim Rangers." Facebook.com, December 24, 2012. https://www.facebook.com/events/561987350485350.

"Muslims Speak Out Against ISIS Following Paris Terror Attacks." ABC 7, November 16, 2015. http://abc7.com/society/muslims-speak-out-against-isis-following-paris-terror-attacks/1086310/.

"Nathan Heller—Contributors." *The New Yorker.* https://www.newyorker.com/contributors/nathan-heller.

"Obama Under Fire for Saying No 'Complete Strategy' Yet for Training Iraqis." Fox News, June 8, 2015. http://www.foxnews.com/politics/2015/06/08/obama-under-fire-for-saying-no-complete-strategy-yet-for-training-iraqis/.

"Occupational Pension Schemes Survey: UK, 2016." Office for National Statistics, United Kingdom, September 28, 2017. https://www.ons.gov.uk/peoplepopulationandcommunity/personalandhouseholdfinances/pensionssavingsandinvestments/bulletins/occupationalpensionschemessurvey/uk2016.

"The Online Ummah." *The Economist,* August 18, 2012. http://www.economist.com/node/21560541.

"Our DNA." Amazon.com. Accessed February 9, 2018. https://www.amazon.jobs/working/working-amazon/#our-dna.

"The Patterns in Global Terrorism: 1970–2016." Center for Strategic and International Studies, March 28, 2018. https://www.csis.org/analysis/patterns-global-terrorism-1970-2016.

"PD and Op Eds." Email to Rana Abdelhamid, January 8, 2016.

"The Pilot." Redirect Method. Accessed February 24, 2018. https://redirectmethod.org/pilot/.

"Private Sector Partners." USAID (blog), n.d. https://www.usaid.gov/powerafrica/privatesector.

"Quantum." Accessed February 24, 2018. http://www.quantum.com.lb/.

"Religion Information Data Explorer: GRF." Pew-Templeton Global Religious Futures Project. http://globalreligiousfutures.org/explorer.

"The Return of Kilafah." Dabiq, Ramadan 1435. https://clarionproject.org/docs/isis-isil-islamic-state-magazine-Issue-1-the-return-of-khilafah.pdf.

"S. Rept. 114-290—Department of State, Foreign Operations, and Related Programs Appropriations Bill, 2017." Congress.gov. https://www.Congress.gov/congressional-report/114th-Congress/senate-report/290.

"Saïd Hammouche, DRH Des Banlieues." *La Croix,* May 15, 2015. https://www.la-croix.com/Solidarite/Dans-l-economie/Said-Hammouche-DRH-des-banlieues-2015-05-15-1312658.

"The Saudi Connection: Wahhabism and Global Jihad." *World Affairs Journal.* http://www.worldaffairsjournal.org/article/saudi-connection-wahhabism-and-global-jihad.

"Scott Atran on Youth, Violent Extremism and Promoting Peace." *Neuroanthropology,* April 26, 2015. http://blogs.plos.org/neuroanthropology/2015/04/25/scott-atran-on-youth-violent-extremism-and-promoting-peace/.

"Shared Values." Source Watch (blog). Accessed February 11, 2018. https://www.sourcewatch.org/index.php/Shared_Values.

"Softly Does It." *The Economist,* July 18, 2015. https://www.economist.com/news/britain/21657655-oxbridge-one-direction-and-premier-league-bolster-britains-power-persuade-softly-does-it.

"Sorry, Politicians, but Fighting Poverty Isn't Going to Defeat Terrorism," Zócalo, August 1, 2016. www.zocalopublicsquare.org/2016/08/01/sorry-politicians-but-fighting-poverty-isnt-going-to-defeat-terrorism/ideas/nexus/.

"Students Wish to Spread Kindness with a Hashtag and a Pledge." *Panther Press Online.* http://www.pantherpressonline.org/students-wish-to-spread-kindness-with-a-hashtag-and-a-pledge/.

"Submit Documents to WikiLeaks." Cable: 08LAHORE302_a. https://www.wikileaks.org/plusd/cables/08LAHORE302_a.html.

"Subscribe to the FT to Read: Financial Times Battling Isis: A Long Campaign Ahead." *Financial Times.* http://www.ft.com/intl/cms/s/0/33a0e52c-0ac9-11e5-a8e8-00144feabdc0.html#axzz3eC78ScSv.

"Taco Bell Invests in Potential." Taco Bell press release, August 12, 2015. https://www.tacobell.com/news/taco-bell-invests-in-potential.

"Terrorism Challenges for the Trump Administration," *CTC Sentinel* 9, no. 11 (November/December 2016). https://www.ctc.usma.edu/v2/wp-content/uploads/2016/11/CTC-Sentinel_Vol9Iss1113.pdf.

"2017 Annual Meeting of Stockholders of Facebook, Inc." United States Securities and Exchange Commission. Accessed February 25, 2018. https://www.sec.gov/Archives/edgar/data/1326801/000132680117000016/facebook2017definitive prox.htm.

"2017 Edelman Trust Barometer." Edelman, January 15, 2017. https://www.edelman.com/trust2017/.

"United States Committee on Armed Services." December 9, 2015. https://www.armed-services.senate.gov/hearings/15-12-09-us-strategy-to-counter-the-islamic-state-of-iraq-and-the-levant-and-us-policy-toward-iraq-and-syria.

"UPDATE: List of Charities and Steps to Donate as Harvey Relief Grows." Houston Public Media, August 30, 2017. https://www.houstonpublicmedia.org/articles/news/2017/08/30/234047/update-list-of-charities-and-steps-to-donate-as-harvey-relief-grows/.

"US and Saudi Arabia Block Funds of Al-Haramain Islamic Foundation." https://fas.org/irp/news/2002/03/dot031102fact.html.

"US Embassy Cables: Afghan Taliban and Haqqani Network Using United Arab Emirates as Funding Base." *Guardian,* December 5, 2010. https://www.theguardian.com/world/us-embassy-cables-documents/242756.

"US Embassy Cables: Lashkar-e-Taiba Terrorists Raise Funds in Saudi Arabia." *Guardian,* December 5, 2010. https://www.theguardian.com/world/us-embassy-cables-documents/220186.

"U.S. Government Efforts to Counter Violent Extremism: Hearing before the Subcommittee on Emerging Threats and Capabilities of the Committee on Armed Services, United States Senate, One Hundred Eleventh Congress, Second Session, March 10, 2010." Library of Congress. https://www.loc.gov/item/2011506933/.

"U.S. Public Diplomacy: State Department Efforts to Engage Muslim Audiences Lack Certain Communication Elements and Face Significant Challenges." U.S. Government Accountability Office, n.d. https://www.gao.gov/assets/260/250038.html.

"U.S. Public Diplomacy: State Department Expands Efforts but Faces Significant Challenges." Report to the Committee on International Relations, House of Representatives. U.S. General Accounting Office, September 2003. https://www.gao.gov/new.items/d03951.pdf.

"Video: Muslim/American—Can Faith Be Fashionable?" Greenespace. http://www.thegreenespace.org/story/-demand-video-can-faith-be-fashionable/.

"The Virtual 'Caliphate': Understanding the Islamic State's Propaganda Strategy." Quilliam Foundation, n.d.

"We Are Losing the War against ISIS on Social Media." Muftah. http://muftah.org/we-are-losing-the-war-against-is-on-social-media/#.VY2y1flVhBd.

"Web Analysis for Browngrassbook—Browngrassbook.com." CuteStat.com. https://webcache.googleusercontent.com/search?q=cache:bwCkGKgIg1EJ:https://browngrassbook.com.cutestat.com/+&cd=3&hl=en&ct=clnk&gl=us.

"The Webby Awards Consumer Survey." White paper. Harris Poll on behalf of the Webby Awards, October 2015.

"What I Believe." Tariq Ramadan official website. https://tariqramadan.com/english/what-i-believe-2/.

"What Is PD?" USC Center on Public Diplomacy, uscpublicdiplomacy.org/page/what-pd.

"What Is Saudi Arabia Going to Do?" *Al-Hayat,* May 19, 2003.

"What to Do with Islamic State's Child Soldiers." *The Economist,* June 17, 2017. https://www.economist.com/news/middle-east-and-africa/21723416-cubs-caliphate-are-growing-up-what-do-islamic-states-child.

"Why 'Lost Einsteins' Are Hurting Our Economy." Marketplace, December 5, 2017. https://www.marketplace.org/2017/12/05/tech/why-lost-einsteins-are-hurting-our-economy.

"Working Meeting on Youth-Oriented Online Hate Speech." Berkman Center for Internet & Society at Harvard University and Institute for Strategic Dialogue, Spring 2015.

"Younger Users Spend More Daily Time on Social Networks." EMarketer, November 18, 2014. https://www.emarketer.com/Article/Younger-Users-Spend-More-Daily-Time-on-Social-Networks/1011592.

Abkowitz, Alyssa. "In China, Videogames Will Now Start Limiting Screen Time for You." *Wall Street Journal,* July 4, 2017. https://www.wsj.com/articles/gaming-company-tencent-questioned-over-honor-cuts-kids-play-time-1499173348.

Abrams, Elliott. Interview with the author, April 11, 2016.

Ackerman, Xanthe. "Innovation and Action in Funding Girls' Education." Working Paper. Brookings Institution, March 2015. https://www.brookings.edu/wp-content/uploads/2016/07/Ackerman-Girls-Education-v2.pdf.

Al Qa'idy, Abu Amru. "A Course in the Art of Recruiting: A Graded, Practical Program for Recruiting via Individual Da'wa." https://www.onemagazine.es/pdf/al-qaeda-manual.pdf. Accessed January 31, 2018.

Al Raffie, Dina. "Whose Hearts and Minds? Narratives and Counter-Narratives of Salafi Jihadism." *Journal of Terrorism Research* 3, no. 2 (September 22, 2012). https://jtr.st-andrews.ac.uk/article/10.15664/jtr.304/.

Ali, Luqman. "There Can Be No 'Shared Society' Without Investment in Arts and Culture." Huffington Post UK, March 21, 2017. http://www.huffingtonpost.co.uk/luqman-ali/shared-society_b_15513474.html.

———. "Why Is ISIL Able to Find Recruits in the West?" *National,* January 30, 2016. https://www.thenational.ae/opinion/why-is-isil-able-to-find-recruits-in-the-west-1.186514.

Amanullah, Shahed. Interview with the author, July 5, 2016.

Amanullah, Zahed. Interview with the author, November 3, 2016.

Amis, Jacob, and Alexander Meleagrou-Hitchens. "The Making of the Christmas Day Bomber." Hudson Institute, July 23, 2010. https://www.hudson.org/research/9878-the-making-of-the-christmas-day-bomber.

Anderson, David. "The Terrorism Acts in 2014: Report of the Independent Reviewer on the Operation of the Terrorism Act 2000 and Part 1 of the Terrorism Act 2006." Presented to Parliament, London, September 2015.

Ansar, Bashir Ahmad. "Islamic Scholars Go Head-to-Head with ISIS Propaganda Machine." Cipher Brief, October 26, 2017. https://www.thecipherbrief.com/column_article/islamic-scholars-go-head-head-isis-propaganda-machine.

Anthony, Andrew. "Losing Their Religion: The Hidden Crisis of Faith among Britain's Young Muslims." *Observer*. May 17, 2015, https://www.theguardian.com/global/2015/may/17/losing-their-religion-british-ex-muslims-non-believers-hidden-crisis-faith.

Ap, Tiffany. "Al-Shabaab Recruit Video with Trump Excerpt: U.S. Is Racist, Anti-Muslim." CNN, January 3, 2016. http://www.cnn.com/2016/01/02/middleeast/al-shabaab-video-trump/.

ASDA'A Burson-Marsteller Dubai PR Agency, Dubai. http://www.asdaabm.com/detail_news.php?_id=74.

Atran, Scott. "Don't Just Denounce Radicalized Youth, Engage with Them." https://www.washingtonpost.com/opinions/dont-denounce-radicalized-youth-engage-with-them/2017/08/15/2e514cfa-81d8-11e7-902a-2a9f2d808496_story.html?utm_term=.ebe3f576910e.

Bacchus, Arif. "Internal Email Reveals Microsoft CEO Satya Nadella's Thoughts on Charlottesville Protests." OnMSFT, n.d. https://www.onmsft.com/news/internal-email-reveals-microsoft-ceo-satya-nadellas-thoughts-on-charlottesville-protests.

Ball, Charing. "'Covered Is the New Couture': How the Islamic Community Is

Changing the Modesty Fashion Game." MadameNoire, September 2, 2015. http://madamenoire.com/584464/islam-modesty-fashion/.

Baran, Z. *Citizen Islam: The Future of Muslim Integration in the West.* New York: Continuum, 2011.

Beall, George. "8 Key Differences between Gen Z and Millennials." Huffington Post, November 5, 2016. https://www.huffingtonpost.com/george-beall/8-key-differences-between_b_12814200.html.

Beer, Jeff. "Why Taco Bell Created a $1 Million Scholarship for Dreamers, Innovators, and Outsiders." *Fast Company,* January 18, 2016. https://www.fastcompany.com/3055567/why-taco-bell-created-a-1-million-scholarship-for-dreamers-innovators-and-outsiders.

Behr, Ines von, Anaïs Reding, Charlie Edwards, and Luke Gribbon. "Radicalisation in the Digital Era: The Use of the Internet in 15 Cases of Terrorism and Extremism." RAND Corporation, 2013.

Berg, Lora. Interview with the author, September 19, 2016.

Bergeaud-Blackler, Florence, Johan Fischer, and John Lever. *Halal Matters: Islam, Politics and Markets in Global Perspective.* New York: Routledge, 2016.

Berger, J. M. "How Terrorists Recruit Online (and How to Stop It)." Markaz, Brookings Institution, November 9, 2015. https://www.brookings.edu/blog/markaz/2015/11/09/how-terrorists-recruit-online-and-how-to-stop-it/.

———. "The Myth of Anwar Al-Awlaki." *Foreign Policy,* August 10, 2011. http://foreignpolicy.com/2011/08/10/the-myth-of-anwar-al-awlaki/.

Berger, J. M., and Jonathan Morgan. "The ISIS Twitter Census: Defining and Describing the Population of ISIS Supporters on Twitter." Analysis Paper, Brookings Institution, March 2015.

Berger, J. M., and Heather Perez. "The Islamic State's Diminishing Returns on Twitter: How Suspensions Are Limiting the Social Networks of English-Speaking ISIS Supporters." Occasional Paper, GW Program on Extremism, February 2016. https://cchs.gwu.edu/sites/cchs.gwu.edu/files/downloads/Berger_Occasional%20Paper.pdf.

Bernal, Martha E., and George P. Knight. *Ethnic Identity: Formation and Transmission Among Hispanics and Other Minorities.* Albany: State University of New York Press, 1993.

Bhattacharya, Ananya. "Fake News Will Be a Topic at Facebook's Annual Shareholder Meeting." *Quartz,* April 15, 2017. https://qz.com/960360/facebook-shareholder-proxy-proposal-about-fake-news/.

Bickert, Monika. "Hard Questions: How We Counter Extremism." Facebook Newsroom, June 15, 2017. https://newsroom.fb.com/news/2017/06/how-we-counter-terrorism/.

Bishop, Todd. "Exclusive: Satya Nadella Reveals Microsoft's New Mission Statement, Sees 'Tough Choices' Ahead." GeekWire, June 25, 2015. https://www.geekwire.com/2015/exclusive-satya-nadella-reveals-microsofts-new-mission-statement-sees-more-tough-choices-ahead/.

Blanford, Nicholas. "Decades Needed to Defeat ISIS: U.S. General." *Daily Star* (Lebanon), June 4, 2015. http://www.dailystar.com.lb/News/Middle-East/2015/Jun-04/300490-decades-needed-to-defeat-isis-us-general.ashx.

Blattberg, Eric, Mark Weiss, Yuyu Chen, and Jill Manoff. "2014: The Year in Millennial Media Consumption." Digiday, December 15, 2014. https://digiday.com/marketing/2014-year-millennial-media-consumption/.

Boult, Adam. "#YouAintNoMuslimBruv: A 'Very London' Response to Leytonstone Tube Terror Attack." *Telegraph,* December 6, 2015. http://www.telegraph.co.uk/news/uknews/12035744/YouAintNoMuslimBruv-A-very-London-response-to-Leytonstone-Tube-terror-attack.html.

Bowman, Tom. "Ike's Warning of Military Expansion, 50 Years Later." Interview by Renee Montagne, *Morning Edition,* NPR, January 17, 2011, audio, 6:53. https://www.npr.org/2011/01/17/132942244/ikes-warning-of-military-expansion-50-years-later.

Brinkley, Alan. "The Legacy of John F. Kennedy." *The Atlantic,* August 2013. https://www.theatlantic.com/magazine/archive/2013/08/the-legacy-of-john-f-kennedy/309499/.

Brizendine, Louann, and Dava H. Shoffner. "The Female Brain." *Issues in Mental Health Nursing* 29, no. 7 (2008): 789–90. https://www.tandfonline.com/doi/full/10.1080/01612840802129343.

Brooking, Emerson. Interview with the author, November 28, 2015.

Brown, Emma, and Moriah Balingit. "Transgender Students' Access to Bathrooms Is at Front of LGBT Rights Battle." *Washington Post,* February 29, 2016. https://www.washingtonpost.com/local/education/transgender-students-access-to-school-bathrooms-is-new-front-in-war-over-lgbt-rights/2016/02/29/ba66d676-da61-11e5-925f-1d10062cc82d_story.html?utm_term=.c9bea0b8ff25.

Brown, Katherine, Chris Hensman, and Palak Bhandari. "2015 Comprehensive Annual Report on Public Diplomacy & International Broadcasting: Focus on FY 2014 Budget Data." U.S. Advisory Commission on Public Diplomacy, September 22, 2015. https://www.state.gov/documents/organization/247329.pdf.

Browne, Pamela K., and Catherine Herridge. "Accused Fort Hood Shooter Releases Statement to Fox News." Fox News, July 26, 2013. http://www.foxnews.com/politics/2013/07/26/accused-fort-hood-shooter-claims-us-military-at-war-with-his-religion.html?utm_source=feedburner&utm_medium=feed&utm_campaign=Feed%253A+foxnews%252Fpolitics+%2528Internal+-+Politics+-+Text%2529.

Brynjolfsson, Erik. Interview with the author, June 2016.

Bryza, Matthew. Interview with the author, February 3, 2016.

Busch, Nathan E., and Austen D. Givens. "Public-Private Partnerships in Homeland Security: Opportunities and Challenges." *Homeland Security Affairs* 8 (October 2012). https://www.hsaj.org/articles/233.

Butt, Yousaf. "How Saudi Wahhabism Is the Fountainhead of Islamist Terrorism." Huffington Post, March 22, 2015. https://www.huffingtonpost.com/entry/saudi-wahhabism-islam-terrorism_b_6501916.

Byard, Eliza. Interview with the author, November 11, 2017.

Byman, Daniel. "Should We Treat Domestic Terrorists the Way We Treat ISIS?" *Foreign Affairs,* October 11, 2017. https://www.foreignaffairs.com/articles/united-states/2017-10-03/should-we-treat-domestic-terrorists-way-we-treat-isis.

Callahan, David. "A Few Things to Know About My New Book on Philanthropy, The Givers." Inside Philanthropy, April 17, 2017. https://www.insidephilanthropy.com/home/2017/4/17/a-few-things-to-know-about-my-new-book-on-philanthropy-the-givers.

Captain, Sean. "This Chatbot Is Trying Hard to Look and Feel Like Us." *Fast Company,* November 15, 2017. https://www.fastcompany.com/40495681/this-chatbot-is-trying-hard-to-look-and-feel-like-us.

Carone, Christa. "Want to Inspire Innovation? Reward Risk Takers." *Forbes,* September 12, 2013. https://www.forbes.com/sites/christacarone/2013/09/12/reward risktakers/#7812b27e46ca.

Catching Up with Gen Y and Understanding Gen V. Prepared for HBO by Trendera. January 2016.

Cellucci, Thomas A. "Innovative Public-Private Partnerships: Pathway to Effectively Solving Problems." Department of Homeland Security, July 2010. https://www.dhs.gov/xlibrary/assets/st_innovative_public_private_partnerships_0710_version_2.pdf.

Chang, Jeff. "It's a Hip-Hop World." *Foreign Policy,* November 1, 2007. http://www.jstor.org/stable/25462232?seq=1#page_scan_tab_contents.

Chang, Lulu. "ISIS Has a 24/7 'Jihadi Help Desk' to Aid Would-Be Terrorists." Digital Trends, November 24, 2015. https://www.digitaltrends.com/web/isis-jihadi-help-desk/.

Charlton, Corey. "Britain Should Consider Putting Boots on the Ground Because It Will Take a 'Generation' for Iraqi Army to Be Able to Defeat ISIS, British General Warns." *Daily Mail Online,* May 25, 2015. http://www.dailymail.co.uk/news/article-3095963/Britain-consider-putting-boots-ground-generation-Iraqi-army-able-defeat-ISIS.html#ixzz3e6hyMnX8.

Chee, Nyuk Yan. "Gender Equality in Malaysia: Islamic Feminism and Sisters in Islam." Lund University, 2007. http://lup.lub.lu.se/luur/download?func=downloadFile&recordOId=1320691&fileOId=1320692.

Cheshire, Tom. "Twitter Boss Jack Dorsey: There Is a 'Middle Ground' in Encryption Row." Sky News, March 28, 2017. https://news.sky.com/story/twitter-boss-jack-dorsey-there-is-a-middle-ground-in-encryption-row-10816229.

Choksy, Carol E. and Jamsheed K. Choksy. "The Saudi Connection: Wahhabism and Global Jihad." *World Affairs,* May/June 2015. //www.worldaffairsjournal.org/article/saudi-connection-wahhabism-and-global-jihad.

Chu, Ben. "What Is 'Nudge Theory' and Why Should We Care? Explaining Richard Thaler's Nobel Economics Prize-Winning." *Independent,* October 9, 2017. http://www.independent.co.uk/news/business/analysis-and-features/nudge-theory-richard-thaler-meaning-explanation-what-is-it-nobel-economics-prize-winner-2017-a7990461.html.

Chulov, Martin. "Saudi Society Is Rigid, Its Youth Restless. The Prince's Reforms Need to Succeed." *Observer,* September 2, 2017. https://www.theguardian.com/world/2017/sep/02/saudi-prince-reforms-society-rigid-youth-restless.

Clark, Joe. "Extremist YouTube Videos Could Cost Google $750m." *Computer Business Review,* March 2017. http://www.cbronline.com/news/mobility/extremist-youtube-videos-cost-google-750m/.

Clay, A. H. *America's Attempt at Public Diplomacy in the Arab World.* American University, 2009.

Clemetson, Lynette. "F.B.I Tries to Dispel Surveillance Concerns." *New York Times,* January 12, 2006. http://query.nytimes.com/gst/fullpage.html?res=990DE6D8163FF931A25752C0A9609C8B63.

Clifford, Catherine. "Millennials Check Their Phones 43 Times a Day. This Is What They're Looking For. (Infographic)." *Entrepreneur,* June 4, 2014. https://www.entrepreneur.com/article/234531.

Complete List of Unicorn Companies. https://www.cbinsights.com/research-unicorn-companies.

Confino, Jo. "Best Practices in Sustainability: Ford, Starbucks and More." *Guardian,* April 30, 2014. https://www.theguardian.com/sustainable-business/blog/best-practices-sustainability-us-corporations-ceres.

Coy, Charles. "Reward Failures to Crush Employees' Fear of Innovation." Rework (blog), June 27, 2014. https://www.cornerstoneondemand.com/rework/reward-failures-crush-employees-fear-innovation.

Cozens, Claire. "US Scraps Muslim Ad Campaign." *Guardian,* January 17, 2003. https://www.theguardian.com/media/2003/jan/17/advertising.

Crampton, William, and Dennis Patten. "Social Responsiveness, Profitability and Catastrophic Events: Evidence on the Corporate Philanthropic Response to 9/11." *Journal of Business Ethics* 81, no. 4 (September 2008).

Crumpton, Henry A. "The Role of Public and Private Partnerships in the Global War on Terrorism." Remarks, 5th Annual International Counterterrorism Conference: Public and Private Partnerships, April 20, 2006. https://2001-2009.state.gov/s/ct/rls/rm/2006/64977.htm.

Davis, Susan. "Trump Attacks Obama as 'the Founder of ISIS.'" NPR, August 11, 2016. https://www.npr.org/2016/08/11/489607788/trump-attacks-obama-as-the-founder-of-isis.

Deibel, Terry L., and Walter R. Roberts. *Culture and Information: Two Foreign Policy Functions.* Beverly Hills, CA: Sage, 1976.

Dhakshinamoorthy, Dash. Interview with the author, January 24, 2017.

Dunlap, Charles J., Jr. "The Military-Industrial Complex." *Daedalus* 140, no. 3 (Summer 2011): 135–47. https://scholarship.law.duke.edu/faculty_scholarship/3382/.

Dutton, Kevin, and Dominic Abrams. "What Research Says About Defeating Terrorism." *Scientific American,* March 25, 2016. https://www.scientificamerican.com/article/what-research-says-about-defeating-terrorism/.

Eisenhower, Dwight D. "Special Message to the Congress on the Situation in the Middle East." Speech, Washington, D.C., January 5, 1957. American Presidency Project. http://www.presidency.ucsb.edu/ws/?pid=11007.

Engel, Pamela. "Here's the Manual That Al Qaeda and Now ISIS Use to Brainwash People Online." *Guardian,* July 2, 2015. https://www.businessinsider.in/Heres-the-manual-that-al-Qaeda-and-now-ISIS-use-to-brainwash-people-online/articleshow/47915154.cms.

Erikson, Erik H. *Identity, Youth, and Crisis.* New York: Norton, 1968.

Fadl, Khaled Abou El, Joshua Cohen, and Ian Lague. *The Place of Tolerance in Islam.* Boston: Beacon, 2002.

Farwell, James P. "The Media Strategy of ISIS." *Survival: Global Politics and Strategy* 56, no. 6 (2014): 49–55.

Fauzi Abdul Hamid, Ahmad. "ISIS in Southeast Asia: Internalized Wahhabism Is a Major Factor." Middle East Institute, May 18, 2016. http://www.mei.edu/content/map/isis-southeast-asia-internalized-wahhabism-major-factor.

Ferla, Ruth La. "For Ramadan, Courting the Muslim Shopper." *New York Times,* June 24, 2015. https://www.nytimes.com/2015/06/25/fashion/for-ramadan-courting-the-muslim-shopper.html.

Ferziger, Jonathan. "Evangelical Christians Head to Jerusalem to Rally Behind Israel." Bloomberg, September 19, 2017. https://www.bloomberg.com/news/articles/2017-09-19/zionist-evangelicals-trail-trump-to-holy-land-with-cash-in-hand.

Fetherston, Julia, Allison Bailey, Stephanie Mingardon, and Jennifer Tankersley. "The Persuasive Power of the Digital Nudge." BCG, May 17, 2017. https://www.bcg.com/publications/2017/people-organization-operations-persuasive-power-digital-nudge.aspx.

Filucci, Sierra. "How to Spot Fake News (and Teach Kids to Be Media-Savvy)." Common Sense Media (blog), March 20, 2017. https://www.commonsensemedia.org/blog/how-to-spot-fake-news-and-teach-kids-to-be-media-savvy.

Fioretti, Julia. "Social Media Giants Step up Joint Fight Against Extremist Content." Reuters, June 26, 2017. https://www.reuters.com/article/us-internet-extremism/social-media-giants-step-up-joint-fight-against-extremist-content-idUSKBN19H20A.

First-Time Students, by year of student first visa/permit decision. Information Reporting & Analysis, Ministry of Business, Innovation & Employment (Immigration), New Zealand. July 5, 2016.

Fischer, Johan. *The Halal Frontier: Muslim Consumers in a Globalized Market.* New York: Palgrave Macmillan, 2011.

———. "Muslim Consumption and Anti-consumption in Malaysia." *Tidsskrift for Islamforskning* 9, no. 2 (2017): 68. doi:10.7146/tifo.v9i2.25353.

———. *Proper Islamic Consumption: Shopping among the Malays in Modern Malaysia.* Copenhagen: NIAS Press, 2008.

Fitzpatrick, Jen. "Sorry for Our Google Maps Search Mess Up." Official Blog for

Google Maps, May 21, 2015. https://maps.googleblog.com/2015/05/sorry-for-our-google-maps-search-mess-up.html.

Fox, Justin. "Why Twitter's Mission Statement Matters." *Harvard Business Review,* November 13, 2014. https://hbr.org/2014/11/why-twitters-mission-statement-matters.

Friend, Tad. "Hollywood and Vine." *The New Yorker,* June 19, 2017. https://www.newyorker.com/magazine/2014/12/15/hollywood-vine.

Gallup Inc. "How Millennials Want to Work and Live." Gallup.com. http://news.gallup.com/reports/189830/millennials-work-live.aspx.

GAO-06-535, U.S. Public Diplomacy: State Department Efforts to Engage Muslim Audiences Lack Certain Communication Elements and Face Significant Challenges. May 3, 2006. https://www.gao.gov/assets/260/250038.html.

Garcia, Antero. "How Remix Culture Informs Student Writing & Creativity." *School Library Journal,* May 26, 2016. https://www.slj.com/2016/05/students/how-remix-culture-informs-student-writing-creativity/#_.

Garcia, Patricia. "Introducing the Founders: The Post-millennial Generation." *Vogue,* February 1, 2017. https://www.vogue.com/article/founders-post-millennial-generation.

Gartenstein-Ross, Daveed, Nathaniel Barr, and Bridget Moreng. "The Islamic State's Global Propaganda Strategy." International Centre for Counter-Terrorism. The Hague, May 2016. https://www.icct.nl/wp-content/uploads/2016/03/ICCT-Gartenstein-Ross-IS-Global-Propaganda-Strategy-March2016.pdf.

Gasser, Urs. Interview with the author, May 14, 2017.

Gause, F. Gregory, III. "The Future of U.S.-Saudi Relations." *Foreign Affairs,* July 28, 2016. https://www.foreignaffairs.com/articles/united-states/2016-06-13/future-us-saudi-relations.

Ghoshal, Baladas. "Arabization." *India Quarterly* 66, no. 1 (2010): 69–89. doi:10.1177/097492841006600105.

Gibson, Caitlin. "Who Are These Kids?" *Washington Post,* March 25, 2016. http://www.washingtonpost.com/sf/style/2016/05/25/inside-the-race-to-decipher-todays-teens-who-will-transform-society-as-we-know-it/?utm_term=.b3fa3edc8f1f.

Gilliat-Ray, Sophie. *Muslims in Britain: An Introduction.* Cambridge: Cambridge University Press, 2011.

Goodell, Roger. "A Letter from the Commissioner." National Football League, June 15, 2011. http://www.nfl.com/news/story/09000d5d82054f96/article/a-letter-from-the-commissioner.

Graves, Chris. Interview with the author, May 14, 2017.

Green, Shannon N., and Keith Proctor. "Turning Point: A New Comprehensive Strategy for Countering Violent Extremism." Center for Strategic and International Studies, November 2016. https://csis-ilab.github.io/cve/report/Turning_Point.pdf.

Greenberg, Andy. "Google's Clever Plan to Stop Aspiring ISIS Recruits." *Wired,*

September 7, 2016. https://www.wired.com/2016/09/googles-clever-plan-stop-aspiring-isis-recruits/.

Grim, Ryan, and Sam Stein. "CIA Privately Skeptical About New Syria Strategy, Sources Say." Huffington Post, September 17, 2014. http://www.huffingtonpost.com/2014/09/17/cia-syria_n_5834850.html.

Gross, Daniel. "Coke Applies Supply-Chain Expertise to Deliver AIDS Drugs in Africa." Daily Beast, September 25, 2012. https://www.thedailybeast.com/coke-applies-supply-chain-expertise-to-deliver-aids-drugs-in-africa.

Guerrini, Federico. "Facebook Launches New Initiative Against Online Extremism and Hate Speech." *Forbes,* January 19, 2016. https://www.forbes.com/sites/federicoguerrini/2016/01/19/facebook-launches-new-initiative-against-online-hate-speech-in-europe-and-beyond/#48067dff2952.

Handlin, Oscar. "Comments on Mass and Popular Culture." *Daedalus* 89, no. 2 (1960): 325–32. http://www.jstor.org/stable/20026574.

Hansen, Pelle Guldborg. "What Is Nudging?" Behavioral Science & Policy Association. Accessed February 28, 2018. https://behavioralpolicy.org/what-is-nudging/.

Hargittai, Eszter, and Amanda Hinnant. "Digital Inequality: Differences in Young Adults' Use of the Internet." *Communication Research* 35, no. 5 (October 2008): 602–21.

———. "Digital Na(t)Ives? Variation in Internet Skills and Uses Among Members of the 'Net Generation.'" *Sociological Inquiry* 80, no. 1 (February 2010): 92–113.

Haring, Bruce. "21st Century Fox CEO James Murdoch Donates $1M to ADL: 'Standing Up to Nazis Is Essential.'" *Deadline,* August 17, 2017. http://deadline.com/2017/08/20th-century-fox-ceo-james-murdoch-calls-for-standing-up-to-nazis-donates-1-million-to-adl-1202151582/.

Harris, Tristan. "How Technology Hijacks People's Minds—from a Magician and Google's Design Ethicist." Tristan Harris (blog), May 19, 2016. http://www.tristanharris.com/2016/05/how-technology-hijacks-peoples-minds%e2%80%8a-%e2%80%8afrom-a-magician-and-googles-design-ethicist/.

Hasan, Mehdi. "What the Jihadists Who Bought 'Islam for Dummies' on Amazon Tell Us About Radicalisation." Huffington Post UK, October 20, 2014. https://www.huffingtonpost.co.uk/mehdi-hasan/jihadist-radicalisation-islam-for-dummies_b_5697160.html.

Havlicek, Sasha. "Fw: Technology for 'Duplicating' Individuals for Question and Answering Messaging." E-mail, November 15, 2017.

Heimlich, Russell. "The View Before 9/11: America's Place in the World." Pew Research Center for the People and the Press, October 18, 2001. www.people-press.org/2001/10/18/the-view-before-911-americas-place-in-the-world/.

Henderson, M. Todd, and Anup Malani. "Corporate Philanthropy and the Market for Altruism." *Columbia Law Review* 109, no. 571 (2009). https://chicagounbound.uchicago.edu/cgi/viewcontent.cgi?referer=&httpsredir=1&article=8004&context=journal_articles.

Henig, Robin Marantz. "What Is It About 20-Somethings?" *The New York Times*

Magazine, August 10, 2010. https://www.nytimes.com/2010/08/22/magazine/22Adulthood-t.html?pagewanted=all.

Hochman, Charlotte. Interview with the author, January 16, 2017.

Hoffman, Bruce. "A First Draft of the History of America's Ongoing Wars on Terrorism." *Studies in Conflict & Terrorism* 38, no. 1 (11, 2014): 75–83. http://dx.doi.org/10.1080/1057610X.2014.974405.

———. "A Growing Terrorist Threat on Another 9/11." *Wall Street Journal,* September 8, 2017. https://www.wsj.com/articles/a-growing-terrorist-threat-on-another-9-11-1504888986.

———. Interview with the author, October, 1, 2017.

Hogan, Susan. "Apple CEO Tim Cook Blasts Trump's Response to Charlottesville, Pledges $2 Million to Anti-Hate Organizations." *Washington Post,* August 17, 2017. https://www.washingtonpost.com/news/morning-mix/wp/2017/08/17/apple-ceo-tim-cook-blasts-trumps-response-to-charlottesville-donates-2-million-to-anti-hate-organizations/?utm_term=.10d8aed24b49.

Holtmann, Philipp. "Countering Al-Qaeda's Single Narrative." *Perspectives on Terrorism* 7, no. 2 (2013). http://www.terrorismanalysts.com/pt/index.php/pot/article/view/262/html.

Howe, Neil. "Introducing the Homeland Generation (Part 1 of 2)." *Forbes,* October 27, 2014. https://www.forbes.com/sites/neilhowe/2014/10/27/introducing-the-homeland-generation-part-1-of-2/#6194f0792bd6.

Hubler, Shawn. "Redondo Beach Schools Ban Gang-Related Clothing." *Los Angeles Times,* September 6, 1990. http://articles.latimes.com/1990-09-06/local/me-806_1_redondo-beach-city-school.

Ilyas, Sara. "Is Muslim Fashion Finally 'on Trend'?" *Guardian,* April 26, 2012. https://www.theguardian.com/fashion/fashion-blog/2012/apr/26/muslim-fashion-on-trend.

Ingram, Haroro J. "An Analysis of Islamic State's Dabiq Magazine." *Australian Journal of Political Science* 51, no. 3 (2016): 458–77.

Institute for Government. "Jonathan McClory." July 6, 2017. https://www.instituteforgovernment.org.uk/person/jonathan-mcclory.

Interview: Anwar al-Awlaki, February 7, 2010. http://www.aljazeera.com/focus/2010/02/2010271074776870.html.

Janmohamed, Shelina. Interview with the author, June 12, 2016.

Jiddawi, Narriman. "Pearl Farming in Zanzibar." SPC Pearl Oyster Information Bulletin, November 2008. https://spccfpstore1.blob.core.windows.net/digitallibrary-docs/files/b4/b4deb33fbf5ece8fac66f62506d505ed.pdf?sv=2015-12-11&sr=b&sig=BZTKg3QSywPXrUlUg31%2BiUdbFV4Hg1seJqj9rjRXOSc%3D&se=2018-08-19T16%3A11%3A32Z&sp=r&rscc=public%2C%20max-age%3D864000%2C%20max-stale%3D86400&rsct=application%2Fpdf&rscd=inline%3B%20filename%3D%22POIB18_18_Jiddawy.pdf%22.

John F. Kennedy Presidential Library and Museum. "John F. Kennedy Quotations."

Overview. https://www.jfklibrary.org/Research/Research-Aids/Ready-Reference/JFK-Quotations.aspx.

Kahane, Gabriel. "How the Amtrak Dining Car Could Heal the Nation." *New York Times,* November 28, 2017. https://www.nytimes.com/2017/11/28/arts/gabriel-kahane-amtrak-8980-brooklyn-academy-of-music.html.

Kamisar, Ben. "Former Pentagon Chief: Obama's Goal of Defeating ISIS Unrealistic." *Hill,* February 1, 2015. Accessed March 18, 2018. http://thehill.com/blogs/blog-briefing-room/231391-former-defense-secretary-long-way-from-defeating-isis.

Kaplan, David E. "Of Jihad Networks and the War of Ideas." *U.S. News & World Report,* June 22, 2006.

Kenny, Charles. "Saudi Arabia Is Underwriting Terrorism. Let's Start Making It Pay." *Politico,* December 7, 2015. http://www.politico.com/magazine/story/2015/12/san-bernardino-isil-saudi-arabia-213421.

Kentish, Benjamin. "Arnold Schwarzenegger Donates $100,000 to Anti-Hate Charity after Charlottesville Violence." *Independent,* August 16, 2017. http://www.independent.co.uk/news/world/americas/arnold-schwarzenegger-charlottesville-donation-anti-hate-charity-simon-wiesenthal-center-a7897251.html.

Kepel, Gilles, and Lawrence Freedman. *Jihad: The Trail of Political Islam.* Cambridge, MA: Belknap Press, 2002.

Khan, Humera. "The Viral Peace Workshop Series: Youth Engagement Using Social Media." Viral Peace, May 2013.

Khan, Sadiq. "London Shares Manchester's Sorrow. Together We Will Root Out Extremism." Op-ed, *Guardian,* May 24, 2017. https://www.theguardian.com/commentisfree/2017/may/24/londoners-share-manchester-heartbreak-crush-home-grown-extremism.

Khan, Shehab. "Paris: #MuslimsAreNotTerrorist Starts Trending on Twitter After Attacks." *Independent,* November 14, 2015. http://www.independent.co.uk/news/world/europe/paris-terror-muslimsarenotterrorist-starts-trending-on-twitter-after-paris-attack-a6734571.html.

Kifayat, Adnan. Interview with the author, June 21, 2016.

Kilpatrick, Ryan. "Hiring Refugees Is Hurting Starbucks' Brand, Analysts Say." *Fortune,* March 9, 2017. http://fortune.com/2017/03/09/starbucks-refugee-hiring-backlash/.

King, Sarah. "Assorted Notes." Selected notes and comments. September 2009–December 2012.

Kliegman, Julie. "The New Era of Suicide Prevention." Ringer (blog), April 24, 2017. https://www.theringer.com/2017/4/24/16038130/social-media-suicide-prevention-policies-5490c2c224e0.

Koehn, Nancy. Interview with the author, February 20, 2017.

Kolmer, Christian, and Roland Schatz. "Annual Dialogue Report on Religion and Values." Media Tenor International, 2015.

Konnikova, Maria. "The New Normal." *The New Yorker,* October 12, 2017. https://www.newyorker.com/science/maria-konnikova/how-norms-change.

Kott, Lidia Jean. "For These Millennials, Gender Norms Have Gone Out of Style." NPR, November 30, 2014. https://www.npr.org/2014/11/30/363345372/for-these-millennials-gender-norms-have-gone-out-of-style.

Larouz, Ahmed. Interview with the author, December 2016.

Larson, Selena. "Twitter Suspends 377,000 Accounts for Pro-Terrorism Content." CNN, March 21, 2017. http://money.cnn.com/2017/03/21/technology/twitter-bans-terrorism-accounts/index.html.

Leftly, Mark. "Exclusive: London Mayor Sadiq Khan on Religious Extremism, Brexit and Donald Trump." *Time,* May 9, 2016. http://time.com/4322562/london-mayor-sadiq-khan-donald-trump/.

Liang, Christina Schori. "Cyber Jihad: Understanding and Countering Islamic State Propaganda." Policy paper, Geneva Center for Security Policy, February 2015.

Lister, Tim. "ISIS: What It Will Take to Beat Terror Group." CNN, August 22, 2014. http://www.cnn.com/2014/08/21/world/meast/isis-iraq-syria-beat-lister/.

LJ Web Management Inc. Muslimconsumergroup.com. http://www.muslimconsumergroup.com/personal_care_products.html.

Lomas, Natasha. "Google to Ramp Up AI Efforts to ID Extremism on YouTube." *Tech Crunch,* June 19, 2017. https://techcrunch.com/2017/06/19/google-to-ramp-up-ai-efforts-to-id-extremism-on-youtube/.

Maheshwari, Sapna. "Bowing to the Inevitable, Advertisers Embrace Advocate Role." *New York Times,* October 1, 2017. https://www.nytimes.com/2017/10/01/business/media/advertising-week-politics.html?smid=tw-nytimes&smtyp=cur.

Mansfield, Peter. *The Arabs.* Harmondsworth, England: Penguin Books, 1978.

Marcus, Leonard, and Eric McNulty. Interview with the author, March 2016.

Martin. "The Google Way of Motivating Employees." Cleverism (blog), September 25, 2014. https://www.cleverism.com/google-way-motivating-employees/.

McCann, Kate. "Facebook Using Artificial Intelligence to Combat Terrorist Propaganda." *Telegraph,* June 16, 2017. http://www.telegraph.co.uk/news/2017/06/16/facebook-using-artificial-intelligence-combat-terrorist-propaganda/.

McClory, John. *The New Persuaders: An International Ranking on Soft Power 2010.* http://www.instituteforgovernment.org.uk/sites/default/files/publications/The%20new%20persuaders_0.pdf.

McNamee, Roger, and Scott Simon. How Dangerous Is Misinformation on Facebook?" NPR, January 20, 2018. https://www.npr.org/2018/01/20/579330287/how-dangerous-is-misinformation-on-facebook.

Medina, Xaviera. "What Do Muslim Women Want? Finding Women's Rights in Islam." Open Global Rights, October 2, 2014. https://www.openglobalrights.org/what-do-muslim-women-want-finding-womens-rights-in-islam/.

Mele, Nicco. *The End of Big: How the Internet Makes David the New Goliath.* New York: St. Martin's Press, 2013.

Mernissi, Fatima. *Islam and Democracy: Fear of the Modern World*. Reading, MA: Addison-Wesley, 1992.

———. *The Veil and the Male Elite: A Feminist Interpretation of Women's Rights in Islam*. Reading, MA: Addison-Wesley, 1991.

———. *Women's Rebellion & Islamic Memory*. Atlantic Highlands, NJ: Zed Books, 1996.

Mesko, Bertalan. "The Future of Extremism: Artificial Intelligence and Synthetic Biology Will Transform Terrorism." Futurism, November 14, 2016. https://futurism.com/the-future-of-extremism-artificial-intelligence-and-synthetic-biology-will-transform-terrorism/.

Meyer, Henry, and Heidi Couch. "Harrods Sees Profit from Islamic Fashion as Qatar Takes Control." Bloomberg, July 12, 2010. https://www.bloomberg.com/news/articles/2010-07-12/harrods-sees-profits-in-islamic-fashion-as-qatari-owners-showcase-abayas.

Miller, Greg. "Panel Casts Doubt on U.S. Propaganda Efforts Against ISIS." *Washington Post,* December 2, 2015. https://www.washingtonpost.com/world/national-security/panel-casts-doubt-on-us-propaganda-efforts-against-isis/2015/12/02/ab7f9a14-9851-11e5-94f0-9eeaff906ef3_story.html?utm_term=.6e841e29af6e.

Miller, Greg, and Scott Higham. "In a Propaganda War Against ISIS, the U.S. Tried to Play by the Enemy's Rules." *Washington Post,* May 8, 2015. https://www.washingtonpost.com/world/national-security/in-a-propaganda-war-us-tried-to-play-by-the-enemys-rules/2015/05/08/6eb6b732-e52f-11e4-81ea-0649268f729e_story.html?utm_term=.77483cb8dfe4.

Mmochi, Aviti, and Narriman Jiddawi. "WIOMSA Annual Report 2008." Tanzania: Western Indian Ocean Marine Science Association, 2008.

Mohamed, Besheer. "A New Estimate of the U.S. Muslim Population." Pew Research Center, January 6, 2016. http://www.pewresearch.org/fact-tank/2016/01/06/a-new-estimate-of-the-u-s-muslim-population/#content.

Mohammed, Riyadh. "Hot Trend to Watch in 2017: Rise of Islamic Banks on Main St. USA." CNBC, December 5, 2016. https://www.cnbc.com/2016/12/02/under-the-radar-islamic-banks-rise-in-th.html.

Mol, Joeri M., and Nachoem M. Wijnberg. "Competition, Selection and Rock and Roll: The Economics of Payola and Authenticity." *Journal of Economic Issues* 41, no. 3 (2007): 701–14. doi:10.1080/00213624.2007.1150.

Molteni, Megan. "Artificial Intelligence Is Learning to Predict and Prevent Suicide." *Wired,* March 17, 2017. https://www.wired.com/2017/03/artificial-intelligence-learning-predict-prevent-suicide/.

Murphy, Dean E. "Mrs. Clinton Says She Will Return Money Raised by a Muslim Group." *New York Times,* October 26, 2000. http://www.nytimes.com/2000/10/26/nyregion/mrs-clinton-says-she-will-return-money-raised-by-a-muslim-group.html?pagewanted=all.

Nacos, Brigitte L., and Oscar Torres-Reyna. *Fueling Our Fears: Stereotyping, Media Coverage, and Public Opinion of Muslim Americans*. Lanham, MD: Rowman & Littlefield, 2007.

Neal, Meghan. "IGen? Homelanders? The Next Generation Needs a Name." Motherboard, March 14, 2014. https://motherboard.vice.com/en_us/article/ypwvgy/igen-homelanders-the-next-generation-needs-a-name.

Neustadt, Richard E. *Presidential Power and the Modern Presidents: The Politics of Leadership from Roosevelt to Reagan.* New York: Free Press, 1990.

Newton, Paul. "Purported Al-Awlaki Message Calls for Jihad Against U.S." CNN, March 17, 2010. http://www.cnn.com/2010/WORLD/europe/03/17/al.awlaki.message/index.html.

Noorani, Daniyal. Interview with the author, January 29, 2017.

Nyce, Caroline Mimbs. "Can School Dress Codes Help Curb Gang Violence?" *The Atlantic,* May 24, 2016. https://www.theatlantic.com/notes/2016/05/can-dress-codes-rules-help-curb-gang-violence/482976/.

Nye, Joseph S. *The Future of Power.* New York: PublicAffairs, 2011.

———. "JFK50 Insight Interview—Joseph Nye on JFK's Legacy and Foreign Policy." Interview by Molly Lanzarotta, Kennedy School of Government, February 28, 2011. https://www.youtube.com/watch?v=x1CNboaLeoY.

———. *Soft Power: The Means to Success in World Politics.* New York: PublicAffairs, 2004.

O'Brien, Cally. "Eriksonian Identity Theory in Counterterrorism." *Journal of Strategic Security* 3, no. 3 (2010).

Ortutay, Barbara. "Tech Companies Continue Efforts to Banish Extremist Accounts." AP News, August 19, 2017. https://www.apnews.com/735276c42a36494e8d3e02f2ef114869.

———. "What Major Tech Companies Are Doing on Hate Groups." *U.S. News & World Report,* August 17, 2017. https://www.usnews.com/news/best-states/virginia/articles/2017-08-17/what-major-tech-companies-are-doing-on-hate-groups.

Otani, Akane. "Millennials Are More Scared of the Internet Than Anyone Else." Bloomberg, March 12, 2015. https://www.bloomberg.com/news/articles/2015-03-12/millennials-are-more-scared-of-the-internet-than-anyone-else.

Pach, Chester J., Jr. "Dwight D. Eisenhower: Foreign Affairs." University of Virginia, Miller Center. https://millercenter.org/president/eisenhower/foreign-affairs.

Palfrey, John, and Urs Gasser. *Born Digital: Understanding the First Generation of Digital Natives.* New York: Basic Books, 2008.

Pandith, Farah. "Muslim Engagement in the 21st Century." Speech, Fletcher School of Law and Diplomacy, February 2, 2010. https://www.facebook.com/note.php?note_id=326573004045.

Perliger, Arie. "Comparative Framework for Understanding Jewish and Christian Violent Fundamentalism." *Religions* 6, no. 3 (08, 2015): 1033–47. doi:10.3390/rel6031033.

Perliger, Arie, and Ami Pedahzur. "Counter Cultures, Group Dynamics and Religious Terrorism." *Political Studies* 64, no. 2 (12, 2014): 297–314. doi:10.1111/1467-9248.12182.

Peterson, Mike. "Young: Strategy, Leadership Needed Against ISIS." KMAland.com, June 10, 2015. http://www.kmaland.com/news/young-strategy-leadership-needed-against-isis/article_1d3a3c2a-0f79-11e5-8134-33746f0e3147.html.

Pink, Joanna. "Muslim Societies in the Age of Mass Consumption: Politics, Culture and Identity between the Local and the Global." *Journal of Marketing Management* 30, nos. 13–14 (2014): 1513–17. doi:10.1080/0267257x.2014.9477.

Porter, Tom. "Isis: General Tells US Senate 'Send 20,000 Troops to Fight IS or Risk Losing the War.'" *International Business Times,* May 24, 2015. http://www.ibtimes.co.uk/isis-news-general-tells-us-senate-send-20000-troops-fight-risk-losing-war-1502548.

Powell, Colin L. President's International Affairs Budget for 2004. U.S. Department of State, February 12, 2003. https://2001-2009.state.gov/secretary/former/powell/remarks/2003/17644.htm.

Qutb, Sayyid. *Milestones: Ma'alim fi'l-Tareeq*. Birmingham: Maktabah Booksellers and Publishers, 2006.

Raffie, Dina Al. "Social Identity Theory for Investigating Islamic Extremism in the Diaspora." *Journal of Strategic Security* 6, no. 4 (12 2013): 67–91. doi:10.5038/1944-0472.6.4.4.

Ramadan, Tarek. BBC Interview. https://www.youtube.com/watch?v=xCqrwrzefAc.

Rehman-Malik, Abdul. "Report to the Open Society Foundations." Institute for Strategic Dialogue, January 2011.

Renz, Loren, and Leslie Marino. "Giving in the Aftermath of 9/11: 2003 Update on the Foundation and Corporate Response." Foundation Center, December 2003.

Riedel, Bruce. "The Grave New World: Terrorism in the 21st Century." Brookings Institution, July 28, 2016. https://www.brookings.edu/articles/the-grave-new-world-terrorism-in-the-21st-century/.

Rogin, Josh, and Eli Lake. "FBI Rounding Up Islamic State Suspects." Bloomberg, June 25, 2015. http://www.bloombergview.com/articles/2015-06-25/fbi-rounding-up-islamic-state-suspects?utm_campaign=trueAnthem%3A+Trending+Content&utm_content=558ca6e504d3010676000001&utm_medium=trueAnthem&utm_source=twitter.

Rosand, Eric, and Alistair Millar. "How the Private Sector Can Be Harnessed to Stop Violent Extremism." Brookings Institution, January 31, 2017. https://www.brookings.edu/blog/order-from-chaos/2017/01/31/how-the-private-sector-can-be-harnessed-to-stop-violent-extremism/.

Rose, Randall L., and Stacy L. Wood. "Paradox and the Consumption of Authenticity Through Reality Television." *Journal of Consumer Research* 32, no. 2 (09 2005): 284–96. doi:10.1086/432238.

Sahgal, Neha. "Aming Muslims, Internet Use Goes Hand-in-Hand with More Open Views Toward Western Culture." Pew Research Center, May 31, 2013. http://www.pewforum.org/2013/05/31/among-muslims-internet-use-goes-hand-in-hand-with-more-open-views-toward-western-culture/.

Said, Edward W. *Covering Islam: How the Media and the Experts Determine How We See the Rest of the World.* New York: Vintage, 1981.

Sarsour, Linda. "Muslims Do Not Need to Justify Themselves in the Face of Extremism." *New York Times,* October 9, 2014. https://www.nytimes.com/roomfordebate/2014/10/09/do-muslims-need-to-defend-their-faith-against-extremists/muslims-do-not-need-to-justify-themselves-in-face-of-extremism.

Saudi Arabia Beyond Oil: The Investment and Productivity Transformation. https://www.mckinsey.com/~/media/McKinsey/Global%20Themes/Employment%20and%20Growth/Moving%20Saudi%20Arabias%20economy%20beyond%20oil/MGI%20Saudi%20Arabia_Full%20report_December%202015.ashx

Saul, Heather. "Isis Leader Abu Bakr Al-Baghdadi Resurfaces in Audio Urging Supporters to Join Terror Group." *Independent,* May 15, 2015. http://www.independent.co.uk/news/world/middle-east/isis-leader-abu-bakr-al-baghdadi-resurfaces-in-audio-urging-supporters-to-join-terror-group-10251955.html.

Schlesinger, Arthur M., Jr. *A Thousand Days: John F. Kennedy in the White House.* Boston: Houghton Mifflin, 1965.

Schmid, Alex P. "Al-Qaeda's 'Single Narrative' and Attempts to Develop Counter-Narratives: The State of Knowledge." The Hague: International Centre for Counter-Terrorism, 2014. https://www.icct.nl/download/file/Schmid-Al-Qaeda%27s-Single-Narrative-and-Attempts-to-Develop-Counter-Narratives-January-2014.pdf.

Schmitt, Eric. "U.S. Intensifies Effort to Blunt ISIS' Message." *New York Times,* February 16, 2015. https://www.nytimes.com/2015/02/17/world/middleeast/us-intensifies-effort-to-blunt-isis-message.html?_r=1.

Schwab, Katharine. "Can a Chatbot Be a Good Therapist? This Scientist-Founded Startup Says Yes." *Fast Company,* June 6, 2017. https://www.fastcodesign.com/90128341/can-a-chatbot-be-a-good-therapist-this-scientist-founded-startup-says-yes.

Schwartz, Seth J., et al. "Terrorism: An Identity Theory Perspective." *Studies in Conflict & Terrorism* 32, no. 6 (2009): 537–559. doi:10.1080/10576100902888453.

Scott, Mark, and Janosch Delcker. "Free Speech vs. Censorship in Germany." *Politico,* January 6, 2018. https://www.politico.eu/article/germany-hate-speech-netzdg-facebook-youtube-google-twitter-free-speech/.

Seetharaman, Deepa. "Facebook Acknowledges Some Social-Media Use Is Harmful." *Wall Street Journal,* December 15, 2017. https://www.wsj.com/articles/facebook-acknowledges-some-social-media-use-is-harmful-1513379765.

Shane, Scott. "The Lessons of Anwar Al-Awlaki." *New York Times,* August 27, 2015. https://www.nytimes.com/2015/08/30/magazine/the-lessons-of-anwar-al-awlaki.html?mcubz=0.

———. "Saudis and Extremism: 'Both the Arsonists and the Firefighters.'" *New York Times,* August 25, 2016. https://www.nytimes.com/2016/08/26/world/middleeast/saudi-arabia-islam.html?_r=0.

Slackman, Michael. "Bin Laden Says West Is Waging War Against Islam." *New York*

Times, April 24, 2006. http://www.nytimes.com/2006/04/24/world/middle east/bin-laden-says-west-is-waging-war-against-islam.html.

Sloan, J. Alexander. Interview with the author, March 17, 2017.

Smart, Christopher. "The Clash of the Data Titans." Project Syndicate, August 18, 2017. https://www.project-syndicate.org/onpoint/the-clash-of-the-data-titans-by-christopher-smart-2017-08?barrier=accesspaylog.

———. "Why We Need a Transatlantic Charter for Data Security and Mobility." Chatham House, June 28, 2017. https://www.chathamhouse.org/expert/comment/why-we-need-transatlantic-charter-data-security-and-mobility.

Smith, Chris. "Mark Zuckerberg Says Facebook Will Fight Online Extremism." BGR, August 17, 2017. http://bgr.com/2017/08/17/facebook-online-extremism-not-tolerated/.

Soft Power 30. http://softpower30.portland-communications.com/ranking.

Solon, Olivia. "Counter-Terrorism Was Never Meant to Be Silicon Valley's Job. Is That Why It's Failing?" *Guardian,* June 29, 2017. https://www.theguardian.com/technology/2017/jun/29/silicon-valley-counter-terrorism-facebook-twitter-youtube-google.

Soufan, Ali. "Re: Hi and a Question!" E-mail, June 14, 2017.

Starbucks & Youthbuild USA. Institute for Business in the Global Context. http://fletcher.tufts.edu/~/media/Fletcher/Microsites/IBGC/Inclusion%20Inc/Case%20Studies/Starbucks_IncIncCase.pdf.

Starr, Barbara. "Carter: Iraqis Showed 'No Will to Fight' in Ramadi—CNNPolitics." CNN, May 24, 2015. http://www.cnn.com/2015/05/24/politics/ashton-carter-isis-ramadi/.

Statt, Nick. "Mark Zuckerberg Just Unveiled Facebook's New Mission Statement." The Verge, June 22, 2017. https://www.theverge.com/2017/6/22/15855202/facebook-ceo-mark-zuckerberg-new-mission-statement-groups.

Stiffman, Eden. "Dozens of 'Hate Groups' Have Charity Status, Chronicle Study Finds." *Chronicle of Philanthropy,* December 22, 2016. https://www.philanthropy.com/article/Dozens-of-Hate-Groups-/238748.

Su, Alice. "Harmony and Martyrdom Among China's Hui Muslims." *The New Yorker,* June 19, 2017. https://www.newyorker.com/news/news-desk/harmony-and-martyrdom-among-chinas-hui-muslims.

Telvick, Marlena. "Identity Crisis: Old Europe Meets New Islam 7." http://www.pbs.org/wgbh//pages/frontline/shows/front/special/roots.html.

Thompson, Mark. "Borders Could Cost Europe $20 Billion a Year." CNNMoney, March 4, 2016. money.cnn.com/2016/03/04/news/economy/europe-borders-schengen-cost-of-collapse/index.html.

Thompson, Steven R. "Countering the Narrative: Combating the Ideology of Radical Islam."*/luce.nt/: A Journal of National Security Studies, United States Naval War College* (2012): 17–22.

Thornton, Richard. "White House Summit Combating Terrorism International Law Enforcement Leaders." C-span. https://www.c-span.org/video/?324398-2

/white-house-summit-combating-terrorism-international-law-enforcement-leaders&start=519.

Toor, Amar. "Facebook Launches Program to Combat Hate Speech and Terrorist Propaganda in the UK." The Verge, June 23, 2017. https://www.theverge.com/2017/6/23/15860868/facebook-hate-speech-terrorism-uk-online-civil-courage-initiative.

Torok, Robyn. "ISIS and the Institution of Online Terrorist Recruitment." Middle East Institute, January 29, 2015. http://www.mei.edu/content/map/isis-and-institution-online-terrorist-recruitment.

Trudon, Taylor. "Teens Aren't Part of the Lazy, Apathetic Generation You Think They Are. Just Ask Them." MTV News, December 3, 2015. http://www.mtv.com/news/2680317/generation-z-the-founders/.

Tsang, Amie. "Amazon 'Reviewing' Its Website After It Suggested Bomb-Making Items." *New York Times,* September 20, 2017. https://www.nytimes.com/2017/09/20/technology/uk-amazon-bomb.html?mcubz=0.

Tsavaris, Heather. "Re: Follow up Call." E-mail, October 10, 2017.

U.S. Department of State, Office of the Historian. "The Eisenhower Doctrine, 1957." Milestones: 1953–1960. https://history.state.gov/milestones/1953-1960/eisenhower-doctrine.

———. "Public Diplomacy After September 11." December 18, 2002. https://2001-2009.state.gov/r/us/16269.htm.

———. "2015 Comprehensive Annual Report on Public Diplomacy and International Broadcasting." https://www.state.gov/pdcommission/reports/c68558.htm.

Urwin, Rosamund. "YouTube CEO Susan Wojcicki on Tackling Online Extremism and Silicon Valley Sexism." *Evening Standard,* August 1, 2017. https://www.standard.co.uk/lifestyle/london-life/youtube-ceo-susan-wojcicki-on-tackling-online-extremism-and-silicon-valley-sexism-a3601391.html.

Volker, Kurt. Interview with the author, March 7, 2016.

Wakabayashi, Daisuke. "YouTube Sets New Policies to Curb Extremist Videos." *New York Times,* June 18, 2017. https://www.nytimes.com/2017/06/18/business/youtube-terrorism.html.

Waldman, Peter, and Hugh Pope. "'Crusade' Reference Reinforces Fears War on Terrorism Is Against Muslims." *Wall Street Journal,* September 21, 2001. https://www.wsj.com/articles/SB1001020294332922160.

Walker, Kent. "Four Steps We're Taking Today to Fight Terrorism Online." Google in Europe (blog), June 18, 2017. https://blog.google/topics/google-europe/four-steps-were-taking-today-fight-online-terror/.

Wallace, Kelly. "Is 'Fake News' Fooling Kids? New Report Says Yes." CNN, April 3, 2017. http://www.cnn.com/2017/03/10/health/fake-news-kids-common-sense-media/index.html.

Walsh, Declan. "WikiLeaks Cables Portray Saudi Arabia as a Cash Machine for Terrorists." *Guardian,* December 5, 2010. https://www.theguardian.com/world/2010/dec/05/wikileaks-cables-saudi-terrorist-funding.

Walt, Stephen M. "Five Ways Donald Trump Is Wrong About Islam." *Foreign Policy,* February 17, 2017. http://foreignpolicy.com/2017/02/17/five-ways-donald-trump-is-wrong-about-islam/.

Wamsley, Laurel. "Here's How You Can Help People Affected by Harvey." NPR, August 28, 2017. https://www.npr.org/sections/thetwo-way/2017/08/28/546745827/looking-to-help-those-affected-by-harvey-here-s-a-list.

Wang, Christine. "Trump: If Elected, I'll Ban Immigration from Areas with Terrorism Ties." CNBC, June 13, 2016. https://www.cnbc.com/2016/06/13/trump-if-elected-ill-ban-immigration-from-areas-with-terrorism-ties.html.

Watson, Ben. "This Is How Little the US-Led Air War Against ISIS Has Achieved." Defense One, June 3, 2015. http://www.defenseone.com/threats/2015/06/how-little-us-led-air-war-against-isis-has-achieved-so-far/114319/.

Waytz, Adam. "The Psychology Behind Fake News." *Kellogg Insight,* March 6, 2017. https://insight.kellogg.northwestern.edu/article/the-psychology-behind-fake-news.

———. "A Web Comedy Series Is 'Walking the Line Between Hipsters and Hijabis.'" Interview, *Fresh Air,* NPR, April 12, 2016, audio, 35:34. https://www.npr.org/2016/04/12/473924951/a-web-comedy-series-is-walking-the-line-between-hipsters-and-hijabis.

Weinberg, David. Interview with the author, June 28, 2016.

Weinberger, Matt. "Google CEO Sundar Pichai on Charlottesville and Barcelona: 'Terrorism Is Terrorism, and It Takes Many Forms.'" *Business Insider,* August 17, 2017. http://www.businessinsider.com/google-ceo-sundar-pichai-on-barcelona-and-charlottesville-terror-attacks-2017-8.

Whaley, Floyd. "Is Corporate Social Responsibility Profitable for Companies?" Devex.com, February 20, 2013. https://www.devex.com/news/is-corporate-social-responsibility-profitable-for-companies-80354.

White, Mark. "Tech Firms 'Invest £100m' in Fight Against Terror Propaganda." Sky News, October 11, 2017. https://news.sky.com/story/tech-firms-invest-100m-in-fight-against-terror-propaganda-11076597.

Wiktorowicz, Quintan. "Anatomy of the Salafi Movement." *Studies in Conflict & Terrorism* 29, no. 3 (2006): 207–39. doi:10.1080/10576100500497004.

———. "A Genealogy of Radical Islam." *Studies in Conflict & Terrorism* 28, no. 2 (2005): 75–97. doi:10.1080/10576100590905057.

Williams, Alex. "Move Over, Millennials, Here Comes Generation Z." *New York Times,* September 18, 2015. https://www.nytimes.com/2015/09/20/fashion/move-over-millennials-here-comes-generation-z.html?_r=0.

Winograd, Michael and Morley Hais. "A New Generation Debuts: Plurals." Huffington Post, May 7, 2012. https://www.huffingtonpost.com/michael-hais-and-morley-winograd/plurals-generation_b_1492384.html.

Wollan, Malia. "Fresno State Loves Its Bulldogs, but So Does a Gang." *New York Times,* November 7, 2013. http://www.nytimes.com/2013/11/10/sports/ncaafootball/fresno-adopts-its-college-team-but-so-does-a-gang.html.

Wong, Jacky. "Tencent Slips in Beijing's Game of Thrones." *Wall Street Journal,* July 4, 2017. https://www.wsj.com/articles/tencent-slips-in-beijings-game-of-thrones-1499171065.

Youseftuqan. "'Arabs Be Like'—The Modern Middle East." YouTube. December 22, 2016. https://www.youtube.com/watch?v=nAUIQOY3Y0M.

Zarate, Juan. Interview with the author, January 22, 2016.

Zohdy, Nada. "The Recent Destruction of Islamic Heritage Sites." Assignment by Nada Zohdy to Farah Pandith, Senior Fellow, Kennedy School of Government, Harvard University. Prepared April 2016.

INDEX